CORPORATE SOCIAL RESPONSIBILITY ACROSS THE GLOBE

This book demonstrates many ways that CSR can be applied by law to overcome regulation and governance challenges around the world. Using interdisciplinary and comparative models and perspectives, *Corporate Social Responsibility Across the Globe* challenges dominant understandings of CSR, such as neo-liberal voluntarism, and demonstrates the regulatory and governance implications of an interdependent relationship between CSR and law. The book identifies substantive and procedural barriers for CSR in national, public and private international law. By analysing, deconstructing and reframing CSR in these contexts, the book underlines opportunities for more effective application of CSR as a governance mechanism. Chapters investigate relevant regulation concepts, paradigms and approaches for CSR; methods for infusing CSR in corporate governance; and ways to facilitate private regulation of CSR in more developed, emerging and developing jurisdictions.

Onyeka K. Osuji is Professor of Law and Dean of Essex Law School, University of Essex, UK. He is a member of the Editorial Advisory Board of the *Social Responsibility Journal*, Editorial Committee of the Law and Business Research Network, and the Advisers' Colleges of Global Principles for Sustainable Securities Lending and Sustainable Finance, the Law and Stakeholders Network.

Franklin N. Ngwu is Associate Professor of Strategy, Corporate Governance and Risk Management, and Director of Lagos Business School (LBS) Sustainability Centre, Pan-Atlantic University. He also co-ordinates the LBS Public Sector Initiative aimed at promoting more public–private partnerships for Nigeria's sustainable and inclusive growth and development. He is a member of several bodies including the Nigerian Private Sector Advisory Group (PSAG) on the UN Sustainable Development Goals and the Expert Network, World Economic Forum.

Corporate Social Responsibility Across the Globe

INNOVATIVE RESOLUTION OF REGULATORY AND GOVERNANCE CHALLENGES

ONYEKA K. OSUJI
Essex Law School, University of Essex

FRANKLIN N. NGWU
Pan-Atlantic University Lagos Business School

WITH CONTRIBUTIONS FROM
GARY LYNCH-WOOD
University of Manchester Law Department

CAMBRIDGE
UNIVERSITY PRESS

CAMBRIDGE
UNIVERSITY PRESS

University Printing House, Cambridge CB2 8BS, United Kingdom

One Liberty Plaza, 20th Floor, New York, NY 10006, USA

477 Williamstown Road, Port Melbourne, VIC 3207, Australia

314–321, 3rd Floor, Plot 3, Splendor Forum, Jasola District Centre, New Delhi – 110025, India

103 Penang Road, #05–06/07, Visioncrest Commercial, Singapore 238467

Cambridge University Press is part of the University of Cambridge.

It furthers the University's mission by disseminating knowledge in the pursuit of education, learning, and research at the highest international levels of excellence.

www.cambridge.org
Information on this title: www.cambridge.org/9781108470025
DOI: 10.1017/9781108558006

First published 2023

A catalogue record for this publication is available from the British Library.

A cataloguing-in-publication data record for this book is available from the Library of Congress.

ISBN 978-1-108-47002-5 Hardback

To Nkiruka, Onyeka and Olaedo, my family, for the love we share
Onyeka K. Osuji

To my parents, Ozor Jacob I Ngwu and Lolo Anthonia C. Ngwu, and my family – Chisom, Chinelo and Oluebubechukwu
Franklin N. Ngwu

Contents

Figures

Table of Cases

Caparo Industries Plc *v.* Dickman [1990] 2 AC 605, [1990] 1 All ER 568
Chandler *v.* Cape plc [2012] EWCA Civ 525
Cohen *v.* Beneficial Industrial Corp 337 US 541 (1949)
Commonwealth of Massachusetts *v.* McKinsey & Company, Inc. United States (Complaint), 4 February 2021. Available at www.mass.gov/doc/massachusetts-mckinsey-complaint/download
Commonwealth *v.* McKinsey & Company, Inc. United States (Suffolk Superior Court)
Dafen Tinplate Co. *v.* Llanelly Steel Co. Ltd [1920] 2 Ch 124
Das *v.* George Weston Limited [2017] ONSC 4129
DC Accountancy Services Ltd *v.* Education Development International Plc [2013] EWHC 3378 (QB)
Doe d Murray *v.* Bridges (1831) 1 B & Ad 847
Dorchester Finance *v.* Stebbing [1989] BCLC 498
Dovey *v.* Cory [1901] AC 477
DSG Retail Ltd *v.* Oxfordshire County Council [2001] 1 WLR 1765, (2001) 165 JP 409
Durham *v.* BAI (Run Off) Ltd [2012] UKSC 14
Edwards *v.* Halliwell [1950] 2 All ER 1064
Electra Private Equity Partners *v.* KPMG Peat Marwick [2001] 1 BCLC 589
Equitable Life Assurance Society *v.* Bowley [2004] 1 BCLC 180
Estmaco Ltd *v.* GLC [1982] 1 WLR 2
Ethiopian Orthodox Tewahedo Church of Canada St. Mary Cathedral *v.* Aga, 2021 SCC 22
Fish & Fish Ltd *v.* Sea Shepherd UK [2015] UKSC 10
Flaherty *v.* National Greyhound Racing Club [2005] EWCA Civ 1117
Foss *v.* Harbottle (1843) 2 Hare 461, [1843] 67 ER 189
Gallagher *v.* Jones (Inspector of Taxes), Threfall *v.* Jones [1993] STC 537, [1994] Ch 107
Gibson *v.* Barton [1875] LR 10 QB 329
Gorringe *v.* Calderdale Metropolitan Borough Council [2004] 1 WLR 1057
Gramophone and Typewriter Ltd *v.* Stanley [1908] 2 KB 89
Greenhalgh *v.* Ardene Cinemas [1951] Ch 286
Gundel *v.* Fed. Equestre Int'l, CAS 92/63, Award of 1993, Digest of CAS Awards I 1986–98
Halsall *v.* Champion Consulting Ltd [2017] EWHC 1079 (QB)
Hamilton *v.* Allied Domecq Plc [2007] UKHL 33
Harold Holdsworth & Co. *v.* Caddies [1955] 1 WLR 352
Harris *v.* Evans [1998] 1 WLR 1285
Heather *v.* PE Consulting Group [1973] 1 All ER 843
Henderson *v.* Merrett Syndicates Ltd (No. 1) [1995] 2 AC 145, [1994] 3 WLR 761, [1994] 3 All ER 506
Herbert Smith *v.* Honour [1999] STC 173

HL Bolton (Engineering) Co. *v.* TJ Graham & Sons [1957] 1 QB 159
Hovenden *v.* Millhoff [1900] 83 LT 4
Howard Smith Ltd *v.* Ampol Petroleum Ltd [1974] AC 821
In re Abbott Laboratories Derivative Shareholders Litigation 325 F.3d 795 (7th Cir. 2003)
International Energy Group Ltd *v.* Zurich Insurance Plc UK [2015] UKSC 33
Jackson *v.* Murray [2015] UKSC 5
Jesner *v.* Arab Bank, Plc 138 S.Ct 1386 (2018)
John Shaw & Sons (Salford) Ltd *v.* Shaw [1935] 2 KB 113, 134
Johnson *v.* Gore Wood & Co. [2002] 2 AC 1, [2001] 1 BCLC 313
Johnston *v.* Britannia Airways Ltd [1994] STC 763
Jyri Lehtonen and others *v.* Fédération Royale Belge des Sociétés de basket-ball ASBL [2000] Case C-176/96
Kasky *v.* Nike 27 Cal. 4th 939, 946, 45 P.3d 243, 247, 119 Cal. Rptr 2d 296 (Cal. 2002)
Kennedy *v.* Cordia (Services) LLP [2016] UKSC 6
Kern *v.* Dynalectron Corp., 577 F Supp 1196 (ND Tex 1983)
Kidd *v.* Thomas A. Edison, Inc., 239 F. 405, 408 (SDNY 1917)
Kiobel *v.* Royal Dutch Petroleum Co. 569 US 108 (2013)
Lee *v.* Ashers Baking Company Ltd [2018] UKSC 49
Lennard's Carrying Co. *v.* Asiatic Petroleum Co. [1915] AC 705
Lidl lawsuit (re working conditions in Bangladesh) (2010). Available at www.business-humanrights.org/en/lidl-lawsuit-re-working-conditions-in-bangladesh.
Lloyd Cheyham *v.* Littlejohn [1987] BCLC 303
Lonrho Ltd *v.* Shell Petroleum Co. Ltd (No. 2) [1982] AC 173
Macaura *v.* Northern Assurance Co. [1925] AC 619
Macdougall *v.* Gardiner [1875] 1 Ch D 13
Marino *v.* FM Capital Partners Ltd [2020] EWCA Civ 245
Marks and Spencer plc *v.* BNP Paribas Securities Services Trust Company (Jersey) Ltd [2015] UKSC 72
MCA Records Inc. *v.* Charly Records Ltd [2003] 1 BCLC 93
McCall *v.* Scott (6th Cir. 2001) 239 F.3d 808
McDonald *v.* National Grid Electricity Transmission Plc [2014] 53
McGuire *v.* Sittingbourne Cooperative Society (1976) 120 SJ 197, [1976] Crim. LR 268
Menier *v.* Hooper's Telegraph Works (1874) LR 9 Ch 250
Metal Manufacturer Ltd *v.* Lewis (1988) 13 NSWLR 315
Montgomery *v.* Lanarkshire Health Board [2015] UKSC 11, [2015] AC 1430
Morley *v.* Statewide Tobacco Services Ltd [1993] VR 423
Morris *v.* Kanssen [1946] AC 459
National Rivers Authority (Southern Region) *v.* Alfred McAlpine Homes East Ltd [1994] 4 All ER 286, [1994] Env. LR 198
Nestlé USA, Inc. *v.* Doe et al., Cargill, Inc. *v.* Doe et al. 593 US (2021)

Table of Legislation

AUSTRALIA

Corporations Act 2001 (Commonwealth)
Public Offers of Securities Regulations 1995, SI 1995/1537 as amended by Amendment Regulations of 1999 (SI/1999/734) and of 2001 (SI2000/3649)

EUROPEAN UNION

Directive 2013/34/EU of the European Parliament and of the Council of 26 June 2013 on the annual financial statements, consolidated financial statements and related reports of certain types of undertakings, amending Directive 2006/43/EC of the European Parliament and of the Council and repealing Council Directives 78/660/EEC and 83/349/EEC, *OJ L* 182, 29.6.2013, 19
Directive 2014/95/EU of the European Parliament and of the Council of 22 October 2014 amending Directive 2013/34/EU as regards disclosure of non-financial and diversity information by certain large undertakings and groups, *Official Journal of the European Union* L/330/1, 15.11.2014
European Convention on Human Rights 1950

INDIA

Companies Act 2013
Companies (Corporate Social Responsibility) Rules 2014

NIGERIA

Companies and Allied Matters Act 2020

UK

Companies Act 2006
Consumer Rights Act 2015
Employers' Liability (Compulsory Insurance) Act 1969
Equality Act (Sexual Orientation) Regulations (Northern Ireland) 2006
Fair Employment and Treatment (Northern Ireland) Order 1998
Financial Services and Markets Act 2000
Modern Slavery Act 2015
Public Interest Disclosure Act 1998
Trade Descriptions Act 1968

US

Sarbanes-Oxley Act 2002

1

Introduction: The Centrality of Regulation in Corporate Responsibility

Onyeka K. Osuji and Franklin N. Ngwu

What is the argument on the other side? Only this, that no case has been found in which it has been done before. That argument does not appeal to me in the least. If we never do anything which has not been done before, we shall never get anywhere. The law will stand still while the rest of the world goes on, and that will be bad for both.

(*Parker* v. *Parker* (1953) 2 All ER 127, 129 (Lord Denning))

[O]ne of the statutory draftsman's major problems is to look into existent behaviour beforehand, to make sure that his formula, when it becomes an official rule, will not merely bask in the sun upon the books. He must so shape it as to induce its application . . . or else . . . his blow is spent in air.

(Llewellyn, 1930, p. 431)

1.1 OVERVIEW AND MISSION

This book provides an account of creative ways in which corporate social responsibility (CSR) can be applied to overcome or address regulation and governance challenges in different national and supranational contexts. Drawing inspiration from Lord Denning's statement in *Parker* v. *Parker* (1953), cited above, we show that the elucidation of an arguably interdependent relationship among CSR, law, regulation and governance, including challenging conventional understandings, will offer opportunities for more effective application of CSR in national and transnational contexts. In addition to the neo-liberal voluntarism orthodoxy in some disciplines, there are substantive and procedural barriers to CSR in public international law, private international law and national law.

A key aim of the book is to avoid being circumscribed by the existing orthodoxy of voluntary-type disclosure regulation (e.g., UK) and codes of conduct (e.g., UN Global Compact) as well as legal compliance approaches (e.g., the UN Guiding Principles on Business and Human Rights) and complete prescriptive regulation models (e.g., Indonesia) and to identify different methods of corporate governance and different areas of law that can be used to promote CSR and to encourage and enforce its private regulation. In doing this, however, we are cognisant of the need for 'application', as

Llewellyn (1930, p. 431) stressed in the quotation at the start of the chapter. The book therefore articulates a range of innovative theoretic models, regulatory reforms and pragmatic solutions for improving the effectiveness of CSR in developing, emerging and developed economies and for tackling issues of a global or transnational concern. It demonstrates how barriers to the effectiveness of regulatory CSR can be identified and tackled and how positive factors for effectiveness can be recognised and improved on.

This mission is against the backdrop that the popular notion of CSR is now so ubiquitous in the economic, political and legal circles globally that one could possibly be tempted to assume that its pathways are all clear. Nonetheless, existing parallels to the growing popularity of CSR and the reporting of related policies and activities are varying debates on the framing and scope of CSR, the design and implementation of tools for evaluating CSR policies and performance, the role of government and other public and private sector actors, the utility of CSR as a method of addressing governance and other challenges, and the overall effectiveness of CSR as a mechanism for highlighting the role of business in society. It has not helped that CSR exists in different guises in scholarship, practice and policy, including as corporate sustainability, corporate social performance, corporate citizenship, corporate social accountability, corporate moral responsibility, corporate community involvement, corporate social responsiveness, corporate social leadership, stakeholder management, stakeholder engagement, business and society, responsible business, responsible investment and, more recently, environment, social and governance (ESG) criteria. No wonder CSR has been described as an 'umbrella' term for various normative, instrumental and descriptive approaches (Garriga and Melé, 2004; Dahlsrud, 2008; Okoye, 2009).

1.2 LAW, REGULATION AND CSR

The law is one area of contestation for CSR. In one informal conversation, a law and management expert insisted: 'Once you start talking of law, then you are excluding CSR. Legal obligations are not CSR although one of the components of CSR is compliance with the law.' This voluntarist approach to CSR is rather simplistic, as Figure 1.1 illustrates.

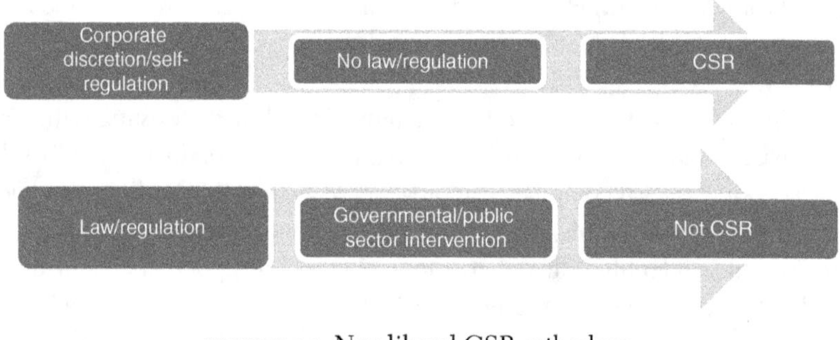

FIGURE 1.1 Neo-liberal CSR orthodoxy

The reality of varying regulatory developments in a number of jurisdictions arguably confronts the neo-liberal orthodoxy of voluntarist CSR and corporate self-regulation that leaves no room for external regulation. Moreover, insights from regulation studies and the application of regulation theories to CSR can demonstrate a range of possibilities for public and private persons beyond the simplistic prescriptive regulation and self-regulation divide assumed by the voluntarist approach. While it has received modest attention in scholarship and its boundaries are largely not fully charted, the regulatory perspective of CSR (Osuji, 2015) suggests the potential utilisation of regulatory methodologies and tools along the CSR journey. Figure 1.2 shows the possibility of legal or regulatory intermediation in fifteen ingredients of CSR.

Notwithstanding the potential for regulation, conceptual and practical obstacles to CSR do exist in the law. Traditional company law, particularly of certain more advanced countries, does not allow the coexistence of private and public goals and private enforcement of public goals. More broadly, gaps in the substance and enforcement of international law and national laws have demonstrated the law's weaknesses as a minimum standard-setting tool and have heightened concerns about relying on a 'voluntary' perspective to CSR as a complement to the law. Particularly illustrative of this are multinational enterprises operating through subsidiaries, affiliates and supply and purchasing chains in developing and emerging countries where regulatory and institutional standards may be comparably weaker.

Another subject of debate in CSR is the appropriateness of ideas, tools and practices in certain temporal, geographical, institutional and other contexts. On the one hand, scholars, policymakers and non-governmental organisations (NGOs), social movements, civil society groups and business interest associations are continually seeking ways to promote 'universal' principles and international best standards in corporate practices globally. On the other hand, no binding code of corporate responsibility at the global level exists, while there is a growing realisation that contextualism is a relevant consideration in CSR that, among others, allows local priorities to be set and context-sensitive solutions to local needs to be adopted. For example, owing to differences in institutional factors, CSR agendas can differ between developing and emerging countries and developed countries even if certain standards are assumed to be universal. While there is an emergent recognition that CSR and public governance can share common goals and aspirations with roles for private entities such as enterprises, it is equally acknowledged that different countries may be at different developmental stages. There may be disparities in the regulatory capacities of public and private institutions that have a significant impact on the ability to regulate businesses and enforce good standards.

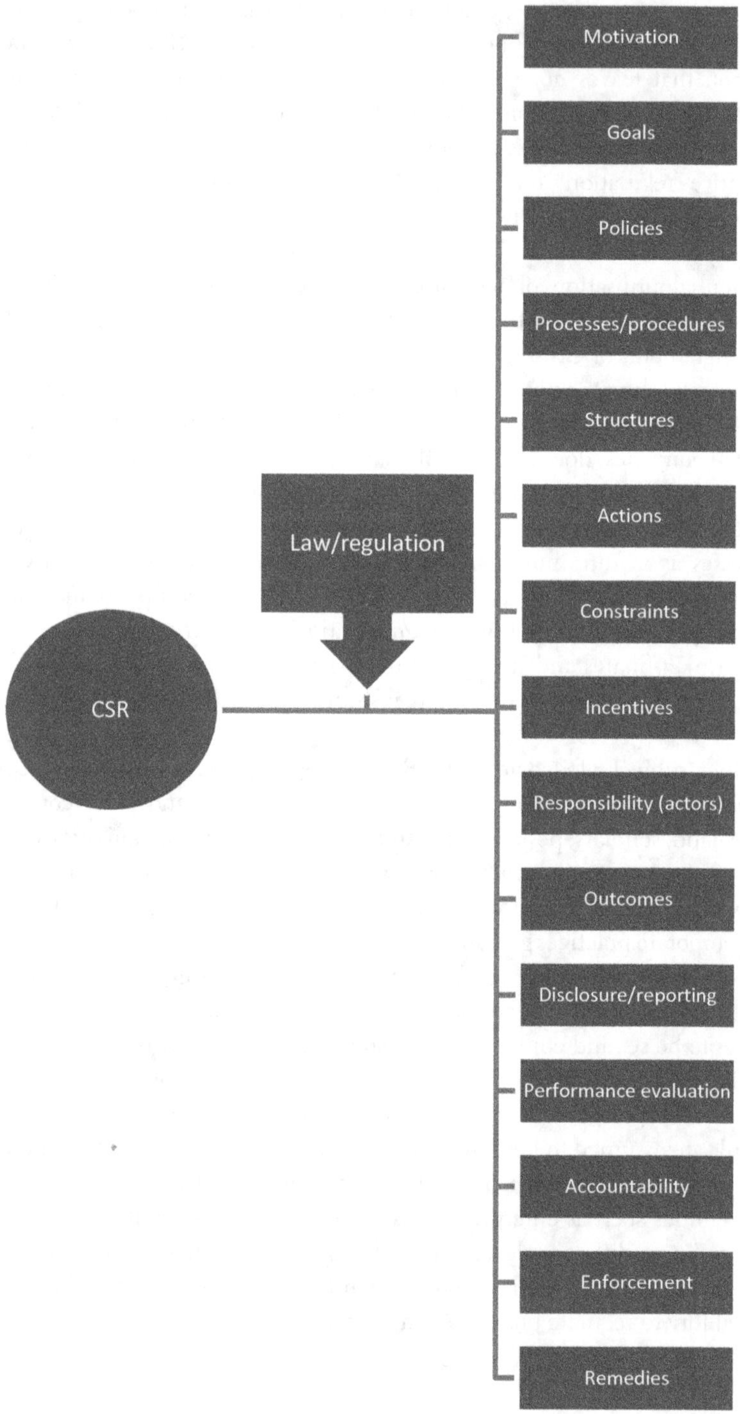

FIGURE 1.2 Spectrum of legal/regulatory intermediation for CSR

1.3 SETTING THE FRAMEWORK

The spectrum of responses to CSR ranges from one extreme of a vigorous governance tool at national and transnational levels to the other of an ineffectual puppet for public relations, 'whitewash' or 'bluewash' owing to a growing case of corporate irresponsibility in different countries, especially the developing and emerging markets, that can be traced to regulatory and institutional factors. The parallel views of CSR as a veritable 'solution' and an insurmountable 'problem' have arguably combined to stall its development. The book therefore investigates these overarching questions:

1. How can the policies and practices of political, regulatory and institutional factors/actors exert regulatory influences on CSR and enable it to undertake or disable it from undertaking governance functions?
2. In what ways can a reconstructed and innovative concept of CSR enable the promotion of an effective, flexible, context-sensitive, inclusive and sustainable regulatory environment for CSR?

Different aspects of the questions are addressed in the following ten chapters, which include discussions of the merits, disadvantages, potential and possible measures to overcome weaknesses in regulating CSR in defined topics or for specific actors. The chapters are organised in three parts.

Part I (*Regulation Concepts, Paradigms and Approaches for Corporate Social Responsibility*) consists of Chapters 2, 3 and 4, which provide conceptual and theoretical insights into better understanding the interrelated roles of regulation and CSR.

Taking on the theme of regulatory diversity in Chapter 2 (*The Values System Paradigm As a Regulatory Alternative to Stakeholder Needs CSR*), Onyeka Osuji argues that 'stakeholder needs' and a 'value system paradigm' are alternative approaches to regulating CSR. Drawing on Pound's Theory of Social Interests and the institutional and stakeholder theories, the chapter highlights the importance of contextualism in CSR and demonstrates that a values system paradigm may be a more suitable regulatory strategy, particularly in developing and emerging markets. It is suggested that the stakeholder needs approach should be coupled with a values system paradigm for more effectiveness when stakeholder responsiveness is desired.

In Chapter 3 (*Incentives, Public Procurement and Market Mechanisms*), Franklin Ngwu examines the concept of regulation and a range of regulatory and non-regulatory options, including market and non-market mechanisms, that governments have used and can use to advance CSR. A six-step model for developing a CSR policy framework is recommended for governments of developing and emerging countries. The chapter therefore reiterates the more nuanced approach to regulation of CSR than the voluntarism orthodoxy acknowledges.

Using global poverty as a case study subset of human rights, Onyeka Osuji (with contributions from Gary Lynch-Wood) in Chapter 4 (*Governance of Firms, Poverty and Shared Responsibilities for Human Rights in UNGPs: Smart-Mix Regulation and CSR within Coalitions of the (Un)Willing*) expands the smart-mix regulation discourse to the field of human rights where there is little legal affirmation of the methods for tackling challenges such as poverty. The chapter shows how the UN Guiding Principles on Business and Human Rights (UNGPs) exemplify governance reluctance and uncertainties in international human rights law. It argues that, if properly designed, CSR can potentially address governance gaps for human rights beyond the scope of the UNGPs. Thus, CSR can be utilised by willing actors for safeguarding rights and overcoming the unwillingness of powerful political and economic entities to accept the legalisation of business responsibility for human rights.

Chapters 5, 6 and 7 constitute Part II (*Infusing Corporate Social Responsibility in Corporate Governance*) and proceed on the basis that an appropriate corporate governance framework is essential for CSR to be effective as a governance tool. In Chapter 5 (*CSR, Directors and Top Management Officers: Responsibility and Accountability Pathways*), Onyeka Osuji draws on the organic theory of the corporation, tone-at-the-top organisational theory and resource dependency, agency and stewardship theories to demonstrate an anthropocentric approach to corporate governance. This approach identifies critical corporate insiders for CSR-related responsibilisation and accountability.

In Chapter 6 (*Structural Limits and Structural Opportunities for Shareholder Regulation*), David Williamson and Gary Lynch-Wood examine the underlying assumptions behind using increased regulatory oversight to control shareholder behaviour. They argue that variations in shareholder capacity to comply with conditions of regulation are likely to render regulatory oversight less effective. They therefore propose a *minmax* approach to shareholder regulation as an effective method of accommodating shareholder differences.

Contextualism is highlighted in Chapter 7 (*SMEs: An Untapped Platform for Sustainable CSR Penetration and Practice in Developing and Emerging Markets*), where Franklin Ngwu shows that small and medium-sized enterprises (SMEs) are more suited than multinational enterprises for wider CSR activities and impacts in developing and emerging markets. While highlighting institutional conditions for enabling socially responsible practices by firms, the chapter argues that an appropriate regulatory environment is necessary to enhance the potential of SMEs.

The central aim of Chapters 8, 9, 10 and 11, which form Part III (*Stimulating Private Regulation of Corporate Social Responsibility*), is to demonstrate different ways the law can facilitate private regulation of CSR. In Chapter 8 (*Shareholders, Institutional Investors and Socially Responsible Investment*), Franklin Ngwu argues that socially responsible investment (SRI) can be linked to long-term financial success and therefore should be part of investors' CSR strategy. The chapter traces the origins of SRI and investigates the range of powers and responsibilities, procedures and opportunities that can be applied to stimulate a greater degree of participation of different kinds of investor, particularly institutional investors, in SRI.

Onyeka Osuji focusses on the critical role of professional advisory services in promoting CSR-sensitive corporate governance in Chapter 9 (*Professional Advisory Services and CSR Responsibilisation, Accountability and Transparency*). The chapter draws on insights from responsive regulation and institutional theories to make the case for including professional advisory services in the CSR legal infrastructure. Proposing an inclusive and limited stakeholder approach, the chapter outlines creative ways for enabling the CSR responsibility, accountability and transparency of professional advisory services.

In Chapter 10 (*Inventive Interventionist Regulation of Transnational Business, Sport, Cultural and Entertainment Organisations*), Onyeka Osuji examines the potential and the limitations of CSR as an inventive interventionist tool for indirect regulation of transnational business, sport, cultural and entertainment organisations. The chapter shows that CSR can be used to plug regulatory and governance gaps in international law and overcome obstructive solidarity and relational signals. This will facilitate national regulation of transnational NGOs.

Finally, in Chapter 11 (*Postscript: Rendezvous of Regulation and Corporate Social Responsibility*), the authors summarise the contributions of the book to scholarship, policy and practice. The chapter identifies appropriate theoretical directions for CSR regulation and proffers suggestions on how to design and implement more effective regulatory CSR strategies and models for different institutional contexts.

The ideas, frameworks and innovative solutions to CSR and questions relating to its regulation articulated in the book are centred on the objective of resolving impediments to effective regulation of CSR. The book therefore offers unique and important contributions for legal, regulation, business ethics, corporate governance, economics, management and political economy studies. Businesses, policymakers, scholars and practitioners in jurisdictions at different stages of development will therefore benefit from the inter-exchange of theoretical concepts, practical methodologies and public and private regulatory frameworks that the book has undertaken. We hope that the subject matter approach to CSR adopted in the book will facilitate comparative lessons for law reform, public regulation, co-regulation and enforced self-regulation in a variety of national and transnational contexts.

REFERENCES

Dahlsrud, A. (2008). How corporate social responsibility is defined: an analysis of 37 definitions. *Corporate Social Responsibility and Environmental Management*, **15**(1), 1–13.

Garriga, E. and Melé, D. (2004). Corporate social responsibility theories: mapping the territory. *Journal of Business Ethics*, **53**, 51–71.

Llewellyn, K. (1930). A realistic jurisprudence – the next step. *Columbia Law Review*, 30(4), 431–65.
Okoye, A. (2009). Theorising corporate social responsibility as an essentially contested concept: Is a definition necessary? *Journal of Business Ethics*, 89(4):613–627.
Osuji, O.K. (2015). Corporate social responsibility, juridification and globalization: 'inventive interventionism' for a 'paradox'. *International Journal of Law in Context*, 11, 265–98.

PART I

Regulation Concepts, Paradigms and Approaches for Corporate Social Responsibility

2

The Values System Paradigm As a Regulatory Alternative to Stakeholder Needs CSR

Onyeka K. Osuji

Nearly all legislation involves a weighing of public needs as against private desires; and likewise a weighing of relative social values.

(Justice Louis D. Brandeis in *Truax* v. *Corrigan* (1921))[1]

It is not our affluence, or our plumbing, or our clogged freeways that grip the imagination of others. Rather, it is the values upon which our system is built. These values imply our adherence not only to liberty and individual freedom, but also to international peace, law and order, and constructive social purpose. When we depart from these values, we do so at our peril.

(Senator J. W. Fulbright, *Congressional Record* (United States Government, 1961, p. 11703))

The task of the modern educator is not to cut down jungles but to irrigate deserts. The right defence against false sentiments is to inculcate just sentiments. By starving the sensibility of our pupils we only make them easier prey to the propagandist when he comes.

(C. S. Lewis, *The Abolition of Man* (1944), ch. 1)

2.1 INTRODUCTION

This chapter aims to investigate the use of 'stakeholder needs' and the 'value system paradigm' as alternative approaches to regulating corporate social responsibility (CSR). It considers the extent to which a value system approach can improve or complement the stakeholder needs model in a regulatory framework for CSR. Owing to the need to address institutional (contextual and behavioural) challenges to CSR, the chapter therefore examines the normative role of law and its implications for a regulated CSR framework. In addition to descriptive approaches to definitions of the concept of CSR, an underlying normativity is also evident, especially in the philosophical sense of right or wrong (Garriga and Melé, 2004; Dahlsrud, 2008; Okoye, 2009) and even within pure voluntary approaches to CSR.

Businesses are often encouraged or pressured to undertake certain actions owing to perceptions of their desirability or to refrain from activities considered undesirable.

Nevertheless, questions may arise regarding the standard for determining whether an activity is good or bad and as to the legitimacy of any persons putting such standards forward. If these questions are not clarified, the CSR arena can be open to different interpretations of what it constitutes. Lack of clarity of an evaluative standard, which is further complicated by cultural diversities and local priorities coexisting with global standards and expectations, can arguably make corporations 'distantiated' (Herlin and Solitander, 2017, p. 10) from the social responsibilities expected by critical stakeholders. When a corporation, for example, proclaims its undertaking of activity A or refraining from activity B as CSR, stakeholders may not easily challenge such assertions unless assisted by some independent overarching evaluative standards. As Marique and Marique (2019, p. 280) argued in another context, there may be difficulties when self-regulation is promoted or applied through 'discretion which is very minimally constrained by either procedures or substantive principles'. With regard to CSR, stakeholders may not be able to challenge corporate decisions even when there is demonstrably unwillingness to appreciate, or lack of awareness of, the appropriateness and consequences of CSR-themed activities.

Moreover, while responding to/engaging with stakeholders is considered one of the attributes of CSR (Osuji, 2011, 2012), the reality is that corporations operate within a network of stakeholders that may and often do have conflicting interests. Owing to the fact that CSR 'is often a difficult balancing act' (Waterman Jr, 1994, p. 26) for corporations amid competing stakeholder demands and expectations, lack of clarity of evaluative standards for CSR aggravates the situation. Whichever way a corporation acts, then, it may leave some unhappy stakeholders behind and suffer the consequences in addition to posing an obstacle to collaborative partnerships among multiple stakeholders for the success of CSR.

This is further compounded by the apparent necessity of contextualism, as underlined by the institutional theory, in applying CSR to account specifically for differences such as geographical locations, sectors and cultural backgrounds. Thus, CSR practice can understandably differ from jurisdiction to jurisdiction, which means that consideration of corporations as socially responsible may depend equally on jurisdictional perceptions of the meaning and components of CSR. This suggests that, even when corporations express CSR commitments, lack of an evaluative standard within a jurisdiction can prevent co-ordination between public and private sectors as well as lead to inconsistencies in corporate practices and stakeholder expectations.

These are real issues for CSR practice and for designing an effective regulatory framework as they can derail the CSR agenda at corporate, national and even global levels, particularly when voluntary or regulated CSR proceeds on the basis of stakeholder needs. Adopting a stakeholder needs approach for regulating CSR conceivably may reflect the necessity of responding to stakeholder interests and ensuring suitability for specific jurisdictional contexts. The stakeholder needs approach is evidently reflected in India's Companies Act 2013, plausibly in consideration of the needs of the country and its population. Nonetheless, using stakeholder needs as the basis for promoting CSR may entail some adverse consequences.

Examples from jurisdictional contexts such as Nigeria show that the stakeholder needs approach can involve untrammelled corporate discretion that opens up possibilities for advancing goals that have nothing to do with CSR or are even capable of impeding it. The impact can be felt in the regulatory infrastructure and by corporations. On the one hand, a stakeholder needs approach can result in insufficient clarity of goals, disguised motivations and covert corruption, all of which can affect the achievement of regulatory objectives. On the other hand, corporations, even when they are motivated to do good for the sake of doing good, can attract legal responsibilities they may not have intended while undertaking stakeholder needs CSR.

This chapter therefore argues in favour of a 'values system' approach to CSR, particularly when CSR is applied as a regulatory tool. The chapter draws on Pound's Theory of Social Interests and the institutional and stakeholder theoretic models to make the original argument that a stakeholder needs approach may be inadequate for promoting CSR, particularly in a developing or emerging country context. It uniquely shows the need to acknowledge that, for a regulated CSR to be effective, a values approach should be attached to contextualism in CSR understanding and application.

The chapter is structured as follows. With the stakeholder theoretic model as a starting point, the chapter examines the stakeholder needs approach to CSR with India's Companies Act 2013 as an illustration. The alternative values paradigm approach is then considered with references to Pound's (1943, 1968) Theory of Social Interests. Following a comparison of the two approaches and, with references to the institutional theoretic model (including Scott, 2001, 2008), the chapter considers their contextual implications for CSR. Using corruption and CSR as a case study, the contextual analysis includes the impact of either approach on the behaviour of social actors such as corporations, public officials and other stakeholders to demonstrate the relative merits of the values system paradigm in addressing institutional challenges. The advantages include ease of contextualism, clarification of the normativity–business case conflict, provision of objective assessment criteria, influence on the behaviour of social actors, impact on motivation, attitude and corporate governance, resolution of competing interests, controlling discretion in self-regulation, delimitation of legal responsibilities and adaptation for gatekeeper responsibility and glocalisation. Before concluding, the chapter considers different ways in which the values system paradigm can be reflected in a CSR regulatory infrastructure, including by clear statements of overarching values and provisions for statutory duties, implied terms and whistle-blowing.

2.2 STAKEHOLDER NEEDS APPROACH TO CSR

The stakeholder model largely provides a theoretical underpinning for CSR (Garriga and Melé, 2004; Dahlsrud, 2008; Okoye, 2009) and Freeman's (1984, p. 46) definition of 'stakeholder' as 'any group or individual who can affect or is affected by the achievement of the organisation's objectives' is often cited to underscore stakeholders' role in signposting obligations required for CSR and the need to respond to obligations indicated by stakeholder expectations.

In other words, the stakeholder model, first, assists in demonstrating the importance of the corporation–stakeholder relationship in CSR. Waterman Jr's (1994, p. 26) reference to 'social and economic relations' illustrates the need to positively manage relationships with stakeholders for the mutual benefit of corporations and stakeholders. In undertaking CSR, a corporation ensures that it maintains good relationships with stakeholders whose support it needs for survival in the longer term, as decisions of stakeholders such as consumers, creditors and host communities can affect corporations' economic prospects. Barnett's (2007, p. 807) definition of CSR as 'a discretionary allocation of corporate resources toward improving social welfare that serves as a means of enhancing relationships with key stakeholders' is another emphasis on the mutuality of benefits.

The second implication of the stakeholder model is the need for corporations to identify suitable stakeholders and their interests, and to address stakeholder expectations and demands. This is implicit from the European Commission's 2001 initial definition of CSR as 'a concept whereby companies integrate social and environmental concerns in their business operations and in their interaction with their stakeholders on a voluntary basis' (Commission of the European Communities (CEC), 2001). It then follows that the third implication of the stakeholder model is the need for corporations to consider the impact of corporate activities on stakeholders and to ensure that stakeholders are not adversely affected. This is, for example, suggested by the European Commission's revised definition of CSR as 'the responsibility of enterprises for their impacts on society' (CEC, 2011), although society appears to have been used here to represent all stakeholders.

Once 'society' is understood as a stakeholder by itself and as a representative term for all stakeholders, it follows that another implication of the stakeholder model is providing justification for the social contribution perspective of CSR. Here, corporations are potentially 'active partners' that can contribute to society's 'economic growth and opportunity [which should be] equitable and sustainable' (Jamali and Mirshak, 2007, p. 244). Similarly, Carroll (2016, p. 4) argued that '[b]usiness is expected to be a good corporate citizen, that is, to give back and to contribute financial, physical, and human resources to the communities of which it is a part'. The World Business Council for Sustainable Development (2001) likewise suggested that CSR is 'the commitment of business to contribute to sustainable economic development, working with employees, their families and the local communities', a description that explicitly links corporate social contributions to stakeholder welfare. The social contribution perspective therefore suggests that, being part of society, corporations should contribute to the resolution of public interest or social issues affecting stakeholders who are equally part of society and should refrain from focussing on profit maximisation to the detriment of society or any of its segments.

If its activities negatively affect stakeholders in any of these four aspects of stakeholder needs highlighted by the stakeholder model (see Figure 2.1), a corporation may be considered socially irresponsible. This shows that the stakeholder model promotes public and collective interest issues as against exclusive pursuit of corporate self-interest. The argument goes that the stakeholder model is 'the most viable alternative to the competitive individualism which has left many casualties in society, and arguably damaged the quality of life for everyone' (Hamilton and Clarke, 1996, p. 39). The stakeholder model assists in conveying a different perception of business responsibility and providing justifications for addressing stakeholder concerns contrary to suggestions that '[t]he purpose of a business is to make a profit so that the business can do something more or better [and that] "something" becomes the real justification for the business' (Handy, 2002, n.p.).

Expressions such as 'voluntary basis' (CEC, 2001) and 'discretionary' (Barnett, 2007, p. 807) used in describing CSR are indicative that stakeholder needs can be the basis of voluntary CSR practice while reflecting any of the four justifications from the stakeholder model. India's Companies Act 2013 shows that a regulated CSR framework can equally – implicitly or explicitly – embody the stakeholder needs approach.

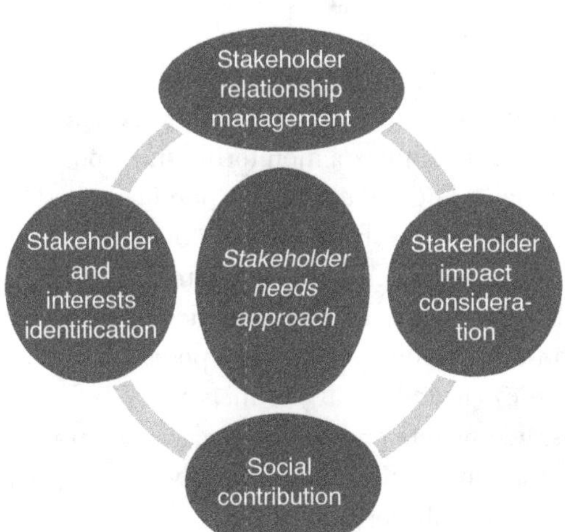

FIGURE 2.1 Justifications and components of the stakeholder needs approach

Section 135 of the Act requires corporations of a certain net-worth, turnover or profit to spend at least 2 per cent of their average net profits over three financial years on CSR activities specified in Schedule VII, although Rule 2(d) of the subsidiary legislation, the Companies (Corporate Social Responsibility) Rules 2014 as amended by the Companies (Corporate Social Responsibility Policy) Amendment Rules 2021, confirms that the statutory list is not exclusive. According to Schedule VII, CSR activities include 'eradicating extreme hunger and poverty, promotion of education, reducing child mortality and improving maternal health, combating human immunodeficiency virus, acquired immune deficiency syndrome and other diseases, employment enhancing vocational skills, social business projects [and] contributing to the Prime Minister's National Relief Fund or any other fund set up by the Central Government or the State Government for socioeconomic development and relief'. In undertaking CSR activities, corporations are required to give preference to local areas of their operations. Although determined by the government and not corporations, the statutory statement of CSR activities arguably indicates pertinent public interest issues and, in other words, suggests the identification of stakeholder interests as the stakeholder model encourages. It also reflects the social contribution perspective justified by the stakeholder model. India's traditionally dominant perception of CSR as corporate responsiveness and contributions to social and development initiatives (Mitra, 2009; Gouda et al., 2016) explains the statutory direction.

The comply-or-explain method of section 135 of India's Companies Act 2013 encourages stakeholder engagement and relationship management. This is also implicit in the requirement to have a 'CSR Committee' of the board of directors for recommending and monitoring CSR policies and expenditure, all of which has to be disclosed in directors' reports and on corporate websites. These disclosure requirements, which suggest the need for managing relationships with stakeholders who can access corporate statements, are also reflected in the Companies (Corporate Social Responsibility Policy) Rules 2014 as amended by the Companies (Corporate Social Responsibility Policy) Amendment Rules 2021, with Rule 5(2)(d) going further to require 'a monitoring and reporting mechanism for the projects or programmes'. The appeal to the public interest elements is further strengthened by the Rules in clarifying the statutory references to 'CSR activities'. The exclusion of activities 'undertaken in pursuance of [the] normal course of business' (Rule 2(d)(i)), activities that are beneficial to the company's employees (Rule 2(d)(iv)), sponsorships for marketing purposes (Rule 2(d)(v)) and contributions to political parties (Rule 2(d)(iii)) is meant to reinforce the public interest element of CSR justified by references to the stakeholder model.

While India's legislation signifies the possibility of using stakeholder needs for regulating CSR, the approach poses some difficulties that may distort the public interest element of CSR and derail the achievement of regulatory objectives owing to lack of evaluative standards. Before considering the difficulties associated with the stakeholder needs perspective, it is useful to explain the values paradigm, which is arguably an alternative approach.

2.3 VALUE SYSTEM PARADIGM APPROACH TO CSR

As mentioned already, evaluative standards are critical for signalling society expectations and for assessing CSR-related policies and activities. The value system paradigm, which designates overarching ethical evaluative standards, is not simply about identifying and addressing stakeholder needs; it provides criteria for determining or influencing beliefs of truth or falsity, judgements of decisions and actions as right or wrong, and conceptions of good and bad culture or practice. In the values system paradigm, 'values' is applied in the sociological sense of broad guidelines for behaviour. As Rokeach (1973, p. 5) suggested, '[v]alues are generalized, enduring beliefs about the personal and social desirability of certain modes of conduct or end-states of existence'.

Owing to the essential role of ethical content (Barrett, 2006; Painter-Morland, 2008; Painter et al., 2019), 'values' also reflects the philosophical sense of being intrinsically good rather than for the economic or instrumental benefit of the actor. In this regard, 'values-driven' for a 'business is generally understood to refer to enterprises that espouse visions, missions and behaviours grounded in ethical values, rather than simply financial considerations or fear of litigation or other sanctions' (Painter et al., 2019, p. 965). While some see CSR as 'values-driven' (Painter et al., 2019), it is not necessarily so and can be motivated by instrumental reasons linked to profit maximisation, especially in the longer term. While managerial and institutional factors can motivate CSR engagement (Jain et al., 2017, p. 702), either case may focus on the instrumental objective of identifying and managing stakeholder needs to ensure positive stakeholder relationships in the corporation's interest. Ethical values may not be considered at all and, at best, may merely coincide with an overriding instrumental objective in corporate decisions.

Nonetheless, it is possible for CSR to be propelled by a values system assimilated voluntarily or driven by stakeholder pressure or external regulation. This is suggested by the sociological observation that '[t]alents, needs, knowledge, values, norms, laws and culture regulate hopes and expectations, determine access to resources and constrain behavioural possibilities[, while] our physical, psychological and social infrastructures temper our ability to exercise freedom' (Braithwaite, 2009, p. 33). If CSR is, for example, regarded as the 'voluntary corporate commitment to exceed the explicit and implicit obligations imposed on a company by society's expectations of conventional corporate behaviour' (Falck and Heblich, 2007, p. 247), it facilitates the voluntary integration and prioritisation of values as part of CSR. This is owing to the fact that 'conventional' rules of society would normally expect its human members to conform to shared ethical values and to refrain from being driven exclusively by self-interest and, when transposed to CSR, it would mean a high priority to ethical, shared and collective interests of all segments of society in contrast to self-centred profit-maximisation.

The significant role of law in securing the assimilation of values, particularly when conflicting values exist or ethical values clash with instrumental goals of segments of society, needs to be emphasised. Pound (1968), for example, emphasised law's unparalleled position in determining and advancing values and enabling the assessment of demands and desires. As Pound (1943, p. 9) noted, the fulfilment of 'human claims and demands and desires is constant, not the exact machinery of satisfying them'. Pound's (1943) theory of social interests consequently identifies individual, public and social interests as categories of 'demands and desires' or values. While individual and public interests can be grouped under the social interest category of 'a whole social group' (Pound, 1943, p. 2), the social interests theory suggests that these are all distinct categories and that demands and desires within each category should be assessed 'on the same plane' (Pound, 1943, p. 2) and not with other categories. Owing to the possibility of conflicting interests, a tool is needed to balance the interests of different categories and to determine their relative priority. While, regarding 'some new aspect or new situation, it is important to subsume the individual interests under social interests and to weigh them as such' (Pound, 1943, p. 3), there is no determinative mechanism for doing this.

In any event, the social interests theory stresses the importance of fulfilling the 'demands or desires which humans, either individually or in groups or associations or relations, seek to satisfy' (Pound, 1943, p. 1). The theory therefore assists in demonstrating that the law can adopt a values system approach in providing a regulatory framework for CSR. In underlining the need for considering social interests within 'a whole social group' (Pound, 1943, p. 2), the theory spotlights contextualism with the implicit suggestion that a jurisdiction can constitute a social group for determining a values system. Since the values system paradigm differs from the stakeholder needs approach, Section 2.4 considers their implications, especially when institutional challenges confront CSR.

2.4 CSR APPROACHES AND INSTITUTIONAL CHALLENGES

As discussed in Chapter 9 of this book, the institutional theoretic model denotes the need for situating a regulated CSR scheme within its institutional environment. If a regulatory scheme is disconnected from the realities of its institutional environment, it is unlikely to effectively align the social actors' activities to the regulatory objectives. The assertion that the institutional theory 'offers a powerful explanation of both individual and organisational actions and processes' (Li et al., 2008, p. 328) therefore underscores the need for using the theory to assess and predict the effectiveness level of regulatory approaches. While a regulated CSR framework can be based on, or reference, 'stakeholder needs' or a 'values system', the relative implications can be assessed by applying factors accentuated by the institutional theory.

2.4.1 *Ease of Contextualism*

First, it is useful to investigate the acknowledgement of contextualism in the stakeholder needs and values system approaches. Contextualism enables the adaptation of CSR to different national or jurisdictional environments for more effectiveness. While the institutional theory calls attention to dissimilarities between countries and regions (Kang and Moon, 2012), it is also increasingly accepted that country development strategies can reflect culturally adapted practices (Robertson, 2009).

A stakeholder needs approach can enable contextual needs to be identified and prioritised within the umbrella of CSR. The regulated CSR scheme in India's Companies Act 2013, for example, is perhaps against the backdrop of the country's socio-economic circumstances (Mitra, 2009; Osuji, 2015; Gouda et al., 2016). The pursuit of contextualism via the stakeholder needs approach to CSR can therefore facilitate the identification and resolution of 'institutional necessities' (Jamali and Mirshak, 2007), as the institutional theory emphasises. Nonetheless, CSR equally needs to be 'systematic, focused and institutionalised' (Jamali and Mirshak, 2007, p. 243), which is particularly pertinent to the question of whether regulatory schemes are sufficiently determinative of the quality and suitability of decisions and activities undertaken by corporations and other social actors in furtherance of CSR or its regulatory goals.

The values system paradigm arguably provides relatively greater room for clearer and more effective contextual adaptation of CSR. Reference needs to be made to the notion of 'institutional logics' (Jamali et al., 2017) denoting that CSR can be adaptable to different contexts owing to such differences as religious beliefs and cultural norms. Implicit in the recognition of institutional logics within the institutional theoretic scholarship is the importance of context-specific values within regulatory frameworks. Using the values system approach will therefore enable the law to determine and influence relevant institutional logics and facilitate their effective application to CSR.

2.4.2 *Clarifying Normativity and Business Case*

Against the backdrop that the notion of institutions includes rules as well as 'norms' (Hoffman, 1999, p. 351), the values system paradigm accentuates the role of evaluative standards in a regulatory environment, although the source of such standards need not be law. This is arguably clearer in the three-class categorisation of regulatory, normative and cognitive institutions (Scott, 2001, 2008; MacCormick and Weinberger, 2013; Pillay and Kluvers, 2014). First, normative institutions refer to norms, values and beliefs consciously shared by members of society and which are applied to determine and interpret social actors' behaviour. Second, unlike cognitive institutions, normative institutions are explicitly imposed and social actors act with full awareness of them, even if the actors choose to ignore them.

The normative element of institutions is intrinsic to the values system approach owing to the inclusion of evaluative criteria, which also suggests that the approach is more suited to promoting ethical values regarded by some as fundamental to the concept of CSR. Baden and Harwood (2013, p. 617), for example, insisted that 'once CSR loses its foundation in ethics it becomes not only irrelevant, but counter-productive as it distracts attention from more effective solutions to social and environmental impacts'. In contrast, the stakeholder needs approach will at best provide rules for identifying and addressing stakeholder interests and expectations without indicating evaluative standards.

When emphasis is placed on corporate responsiveness to 'stakeholder needs', it may embody business case and morally neutral justifications. Owing to the absence of ethical justifications when a morally neutral position is adopted, corporate actors may be affected by internalisation difficulties and may be solely driven by instrumental factors that are, for instance, unconnected to CSR or its regulatory objectives. Consequently, corporations and corporate managers may refrain from genuine CSR activities if they cannot attach any business case in the foreseeable future to their involvement (Osuji, 2011). The business case also has a potentially negative effect on CSR-related disclosures. As Bradshaw (2013) argued, '[t]here is also the added danger that the business case provides scope for corporations to attach misleading or exaggerated CSR claims to what may be relatively shallow environmental efforts; the business case may permit or encourage "greenwash" activities'.

2.4.3 *Objective Assessment Criteria*

A corollary to the normative element of the values system approach is a focus on prescribing ethical criteria for objectively assessing the appropriateness and suitability of CSR-related policies and activities. The existence of objective criteria for making judgements will assist in spotting, preventing and challenging undesirable activities and also enables the prioritisation of certain interests or activities, especially if there are competing demands and expectations.

As India's Companies Act 2013 shows, a stakeholder needs approach to CSR can facilitate decisions that align with regulatory goals or promote the common good in addition to highlighting areas of priority. Nonetheless, the subjectivity element of the approach may allow both desirable and undesirable activities to be cloaked with CSR. As Justice Louis D. Brandeis once observed, '[w]hat, at any particular time, is the paramount public need, is necessarily, largely a matter of judgement'.[2] The discussions that follow on camouflaging corruption as CSR reveal the problematic nature of a subjective stakeholder needs judgement without coupling it with a values system. It will be difficult in that type of situation to assert that CSR consists 'empirically . . . of clearly articulated and communicated policies and practices of corporations that reflect business responsibility for some of the wider societal good' (Matten and Moon, 2008, p. 405).

2.4.4 *Social Actors' Behavioural Impact*

Impact on the behaviour of corporations, stakeholders and other social actors is another possible basis for comparing the stakeholder needs approach and the values system approach to CSR. This is important because, as Young (1994, p. 30) observed, '[a] governance system that has little behavioural impact, by contrast, is ineffective'. The institutional theory consequently underlines the existence of linkages between the behaviour of social actors and the 'institutional setting in which actors find themselves' (Ohnesorge, 2007, p. 268).

The stakeholder needs approach is less likely than a values system to be structured and determinative in providing objective criteria for assessing activities and interpreting their alignment with regulatory objectives. The institutional significance is in providing 'a structure in their organisations, institutions, and relationships which makes events clearly interpretable and predictable' (Hofsted, 1994, p. 116). While a stakeholder needs approach can plausibly influence behaviour by identifying activities that may be in line with regulatory objectives, it may not provide evaluative criteria for judging good or bad behaviour. There are no such indications, for instance, in the stakeholder needs–based scheme for CSR in India's Companies Act 2013. The values system approach, in contrast, may provide greater clarity for social actors on how to behave in different circumstances and enable them to apply defined criteria in making assessments. The approach is therefore more likely to have greater positive behavioural impact by indicating evaluative standards for appropriateness of social actors' decisions and activities.

2.4.5 *Motivational Impact*

A specific aspect of analysing the impact of institutions on behaviour is the motivation of social actors in acting one way or another. Braithwaite (2009, p. 20) explained that motivational postures arise from 'sets of beliefs and attitudes that sum up how individuals feel about and wish to position themselves in relation to another social entity'. This suggests that, while motivational postures are subjective (Braithwaite, 2009, p. 20), they can be informed by external factors. Being that motivational postures 'have coherence for the self and are socially acceptable to significant others' and 'provide the narrative within which the authority's message is given meaning' (Braithwaite, 2009, p. 20), a values system plays a signposting role to social actors and others they interact with. It is more likely than a stakeholder needs approach to facilitate the adoption of motivations that are aligned with regulatory goals through the provision of overarching values to be actively considered in the thinking and decision-making processes.

In contrast, the stakeholder needs approach can create room for the actual motivations for CSR-themed decisions and actions to be disguised, even to defeat regulatory objectives, as the church building case study in Section 2.5 shows. By merely using CSR to address identified stakeholder needs without references to certain fundamental values, the approach can open up opportunities for corporations, with or without the collaboration of the stakeholders concerned, to pursue goals that are undesirable or unrelated to the regulatory scheme, although the relevant decisions and actions may be labelled as such. It can be problematic when a regulatory scheme allows the motivation for CSR-themed decisions and actions not to be genuinely connected to CSR or the regulatory goals. Rather than providing solutions, CSR in this instance can be damaging, including by providing a cover for corrupt activities.

2.4.6 *Attitudinal Impact*

Like motivation, the impact of either approach on social actors' attitude is important. While motivational postures 'bind together the cognitive, emotional and behavioural components of attitude' (Braithwaite, 2009, p. 20), attitudes are manifested in response to specific rules and the overall working of regulatory systems. In this regard, attitude can be described as 'a relatively enduring organisation of beliefs, feelings, and behavioural tendencies towards socially significant objects, groups, events or symbols' (Braithwaite, 2009, p. 150). When social actors have the 'right' or 'correct' attitude towards a regulatory scheme, they are more likely to genuinely promote, and not deflect, the achievement of the regulatory goals. Absent this positive attitude, the tendency is for 'organisations [to] create symbolic structures as visible efforts to comply with law, but their normative value does not depend on effectiveness so they do not guarantee substantive change' (Edelman, 1991, p. 75).

Therefore, a key challenge to regulatory schemes is the need for their institutionalisation in 'the regulations, norms and mindsets' (Bansal, 2002). Arguably, it is easier to demonstrate 'symbolic compliance' with regulations when the emphasis is on identifying and addressing stakeholder needs without indicating some overarching values. These values may accompany the thinking and decision-making processes and enable self- and independent evaluation of decisions and activities undertaken in the name of CSR.

2.4.7 *Corporate Governance Impact*

Further to the discussions on behaviour, motivation and attitude, it is useful to consider the impact of the stakeholder needs and values system approaches on corporate governance, a specific determinant of corporate behaviour. It is pertinent to ensure the existence and sustenance of strategies that are supposed to direct corporate actors towards appropriate decisions and behaviour, including CSR-related governance.

The stakeholder needs approach is aptly captured in Prentice's (1993, p. 25) observation that corporate governance 'at its broadest level involves the issue of the relationship between the stakeholders in a company and those who manage its affairs'. Explicit references to stakeholder needs can be seen in the definition of corporate governance as '[t]he process by which corporations are made responsive to the rights and wishes of stakeholders' (Demb and Neubauer, 1992, p. 9); 'the design of institutions that induce or force management to internalise the welfare of stakeholders. The provision of managerial incentives and the design of a control structure must account for their impact on the utilities of all stakeholders in order to induce or force internalization' (Tirole, 2001, p. 4); 'the determination of the broad uses to which organisational resources will be deployed and the resolution of conflicts among the myriad participants in organisations' (Daily et al., 2003, p. 371); or 'the system of checks and balances, both internal and external to companies, which ensures that companies discharge their accountability to all their stakeholders and act in a socially responsible way in all areas of their business activity' (Solomon, 2007, p. 14).

In contrast, a role for the values system paradigm is implicitly acknowledged when corporate governance is expounded as 'the whole set of legal, cultural, and institutional arrangements that determine what public corporations can do, who controls them, how that control is exercised, and how the risks and return from the activities they undertake are allocated' (Blair, 1995, p. 3); 'all the influences affecting the institutional processes, including the appointing of the controllers and/or regulators involved in organising the production and sale of goods and services' (Turnbull, 1997, p. 181); or as being 'concerned with holding the balance between economic and social goals and between individual and communal goals. The governance framework is there to encourage the efficient use of resources and equally to require accountability for the stewardship of those resources. The aim is to align as nearly as possible the interests of individuals, corporations, and society' (Iskander and Chamlou, 2000, p. vi).

While a popular definition by the UK Cadbury Committee of corporate governance as 'a system by which companies are directed and controlled' (Cadbury, 1992, p.15) makes no reference to stakeholder needs and values system, these are both, in fact, reflected in prevailing conceptions of corporate governance. Nonetheless, as already indicated, relative advantages of the values system approach include the provision of objective evaluative criteria for corporate decisions and activities and enabling ethical values to instrumental or business case goals, especially when both are in conflict. Additionally, as detailed in Section 2.4.8, the approach can provide greater clarity regarding balancing and prioritisation of competing stakeholder interests.

2.4.8 *Resolving Competing Interests*

Another comparative analytical lens for the stakeholder needs and values system approaches is their potential for balancing and resolving competing interests, including stakeholder expectations, in society. As discussed in Section 2.3, Pound's (1943) theory of social interests is premised on competing demands and interests while advocating for the law to resolve differences within and between different categories (Pound, 1968).

A recent illustration of the reality of competing interests in society and the need for clarifying the priority criteria is *Lee* v. *Ashers Baking Company Ltd*.[3] In that case, the appellant bakery declined to bake a cake containing a pro-gay marriage message. Relying on the Equality Act (Sexual Orientation) Regulations (Northern Ireland) 2006 (SORs) and the Fair Employment and Treatment (Northern Ireland) Order 1998 (FETO), both the district court and the Court of Appeal found the bakery to have directly and indirectly discriminated against the respondent on grounds of sexual orientation and/or religious belief or political opinion. In contrast, the Supreme Court held that there was no discrimination and pointed out the appellants' rights to freedom of thought, conscience and religion and to the freedom of expression respectively guaranteed by Articles 10 and 9 of the European Convention on Human Rights 1950 (ECHR). In other words, the Supreme Court accepted that the values expressed in the ECHR as rights superseded any provisions of, or rights granted by, the SORs and FETO.

While a values system approach enabled the Supreme Court to resolve a complicated and controversial dispute in *Lee* v. *Ashers Baking Company Ltd*, recourse to a stakeholder needs approach would have been problematic. It is true that the stakeholder needs approach may acknowledge the existence of competing stakeholder interests in *Lee*'s case since the stakeholder model stresses that corporations 'have to operate within a complex of social and economic relationships' (Waterman Jr, 1994, p. 26). The indication of 'CSR activities' in India's Companies Act 2013 discussed in Section 2.2 also suggests that it is possible to prioritise some stakeholder needs within a regulated CSR framework. Nonetheless, owing to lack of statement of values and their hierarchy, it may simply be a case of selecting one of the stakeholder interests one prefers to advance or prioritise even when the regulatory scheme has identified some stakeholder needs.

2.4.9 *Discretion within Enforced Self-Regulation*

As noted in Sections 2.4.3 and 2.4.4, if the intended targets of regulation are allowed unbounded discretion (Marique and Marique, 2019, p. 280) this may encourage problematic self-regulatory arrangements. The question then arises as to the discretionary effect of either the stakeholder needs or the values system approach. On the one hand, if corporations can simply focus on identifying and addressing stakeholder needs without having some overarching values for guidance, there is a greater degree of flexibility for pursuing activities within the CSR umbrella that may be undesirable and contrary to regulatory objectives. In such instances, it is possible for CSR-themed activities to be determined by 'personal discretion, hindsight and initiative'

(Jamali and Mirshak, 2007) that may be unrelated to CSR and regulatory goals and in fact designed to advance some ulterior agenda such as corruption, as evident from the church building case study discussed in Section 2.5. Problematic discretion is still possible even when a regulatory scheme such as India's Companies Act 2013 defines 'CSR activities' since corporate actors can simply label their actions as being, for instance, for health care or education provision.

This suggests that the stakeholder needs approach is more likely than a values system to encourage the orthodox voluntariness conception of CSR referenced in the statement that 'responsible business activities are discretionary and reach beyond the rule of law' (Dentchev et al., 2015). An English High Court supported this position in *R (on the application of People & Planet)* v. *HM Treasury*[4] by declining an application for judicial review of a company's climate change and human rights policies and decisions. The court insisted that 'to seek to impose [the court's] own policy in relation to combating climate change and promoting human rights on the board of the Royal Bank of Scotland, contrary to the decision of the board' of directors, would amount to an undue interference with the discretion exercisable by the board on the company's behalf. The lack of core values for evaluating corporate decisions and activities meant that the stakeholders' challenge and judicial review were not legally possible.

On the other hand, the importance of CSR and the matters it advances, such as environment protection, suggests the need for tempering unbounded discretion with some evaluative standards under the values system approach. The Economic Community of West African States (ECOWAS) Court of Justice in *SERAP* v. *Attorney General of Nigeria* similarly acknowledged that 'a vital resource of such importance to all mankind, such as the environment, cannot be left to the mere discretion of oil companies and possible agreements on compensation they may establish with the people affected by the devastating effects of this polluting industry'.[5]

2.4.10 *Gatekeeper Responsibility Adaptation*

A potential comparative lens for the stakeholder needs and values system approaches is their adaptation for gatekeeper responsibility for CSR. The gatekeeper responsibility concept promotes the idea that 'private parties ... are able to disrupt misconduct by withholding their cooperation from wrongdoers' (Kraakman, 1986, p. 53). Responsibility is not based on wrongdoing by the duty-holders but rather reflects their power and influence over the primary actors.

Evidence suggests that stakeholders expect some sort of gatekeeper responsibility that requires businesses to exercise due diligence in dealings with legally separate entities, prompting the assertion that CSR can be used for holding 'firms responsible for actions far beyond their boundaries, including the actions of suppliers, distributors, alliance partners, and even sovereign nations' (Davis et al., 2008, p. 32). Stakeholder pressures on Nike and Levis-Strauss to monitor the labour standards in their supply chains and to disclose the identities and locations of their suppliers' factories for the purpose of independent verification (Doorey, 2011) are examples of gatekeeper responsibility outside a formal regulatory framework.

Extended responsibility via gatekeeper responsibility is arguably easier to impose when a specific values system guides it. It can assist in promoting individual responsibility, corporate responsibility and corporate group responsibility by providing overarching guidelines for assessing the motivations, attitudes and behaviours of corporate actors and stakeholders. This will facilitate the application of CSR for private regulation of behaviour in different contexts, especially when corporations are in a position of power and influence, including over their operations, supply, purchasing and consumption chains. Values can also assist in clarifying the nature and limits of the relationships that corporations may have with public and private stakeholders, including government agencies and officials.

Furthermore, a values system, unlike the stakeholder needs approach, can be the bedrock of disclosure-based regulation. In this regard, home and host governments of corporations can institute extraterritorial regulation using the values system paradigm to impose some responsibility for tackling governance failures and institutional voids. This form of gatekeeper responsibility is reflected to an extent in the emergent disclosure obligations within the anti-modern slavery legislations of jurisdictions such as the UK, Australia and California, USA.

2.4.11 *Ease of Glocalisation*

Stakeholder needs and values system CSR approaches can be compared in relation to the extent to which they facilitate glocalisation, a term that refers to a combined employment of universal and local standards and is particularly relevant to multinational enterprises (MNEs) operating across countries and jurisdictions. While universalisation of standards may help to 'create a template which can be applied only if we infuse them with the factual circumstances of a given society, of its own patterns of disadvantage' (Sadurski, 2004, p. 154), the reality is that 'the idea of "think global, act local" recognises that most CSR issues manifest as dilemmas, rather than easy choices' (Visser, 2010, p. 17).

Unlike a stakeholder needs approach, the values system paradigm promotes a balanced duality required for glocalisation. If jurisdictional value systems are clearly stipulated by law, for example, it will be easier for MNEs and other corporations to create global standards from commonalities in values systems while addressing local priorities. In other words, the values paradigm can facilitate the benefits of both universalisation and local adaptation.

2.4.12 *Delimitation of Legal Responsibilities*

A possible method of comparing the stakeholder needs and values system approaches is their relationship to legal responsibilities towards stakeholders.

Despite the orthodoxy of voluntariness in CSR scholarship (see Falck and Heblich, 2007, p. 247; Berliner and Prakash, 2012, p. 219; Dam and Scholtens, 2012; Fransen, 2013, p. 213) as highlighted in Chapter 1 of this book, the cases examined here show that some legal responsibilities may be associated with even voluntarily adopted CSR practices.

A values system seems more effective in clarifying the boundaries of legal responsibilities that corporations may owe to stakeholders. This is via its role of providing overarching objective assessment criteria for decisions and activities. *Kern* v. *Dynalectron Corp*,[6] for example, suggests that a values system required by a legal system can determine rights and obligations under an employment contract even if there are no explicit references therein. In that case, an overriding religion-based set of values affected a contract sought to be enforced in a jurisdiction where the values were legally stipulated. A values system prohibiting secret payments has similarly been applied to transactions between commercial parties even when the underlying contracts were silent on such payments.[7]

In contrast, the stakeholders needs approach may allow CSR policies and activities to be used as evidence of assumption of legal responsibility towards certain stakeholders. This is possible even when corporations see CSR as voluntary social contributions. The potential exposure to unintended assumption of legal responsibility can be buttressed, firstly, by reference to consumer protection law. A consumer and a consumer protection body in the US case of *Kasky* v. *Nike*[8] and the German case of *Lidl lawsuit*[9] respectively sued corporations for unfair trading through false and misleading CSR statements. Actually, the defendants were not legally required to make the CSR statements at issue and did not intend in the subjective sense to owe any legal obligations towards the consumers that got acquainted with the statements. The applicable unfair trading laws of California, USA and Germany, however, allowed legal challenges to be brought even though neither case was ultimately decided on their substantive merits.

The tortious law of negligence is another possible avenue for corporate exposure to legal responsibilities arising from CSR activities. In the English case of *Chandler* v. *Cape plc*,[10] the Court of Appeal held that a parent company voluntarily assumed a duty of care within the tort of negligence to its subsidiary's employees by imposing its health and safety policies on them. The parent company, which would ordinarily not be legally liable to those employees owing to the twin concepts of corporate personality and limited liability,[11] was found to have breached that duty of care. Following a UK Supreme Court's[12] decision on judicial jurisdiction over negligence claims against parent companies of foreign subsidiary companies, the claimants' solicitors commented: 'I hope this judgment [*Vedanta* v. *Lungowe*, 10 April 2019] will send a strong message to other large multinationals that their CSR policies should not just be seen as a polish for their reputation but as important commitments that they must put into action' (Leigh Day, 2019, n.p.).

In the first place, potential unintended assumption of legal responsibility, conceivably, creates a dilemma for corporations as to whether to take up CSR beyond the confines of strict legal obligations. Secondly, a stakeholder needs approach does not enable corporations to articulate any underlying values for decisions and activities like the defendant employer was able to do in *Kern* v. *Dynalectron Corp*. References to legally stipulated values may therefore be helpful to corporations keen to demonstrate the extent of their commitments.

Moreover, the absence of a values system can trigger questions regarding possible abuse of CSR as a conduit for corruption with the legal consequences that entails. The stakeholder needs approach may make it easier for corrupt activities to be disguised as CSR since corporate actors can identify certain stakeholders as having some needs even when there are direct or indirect benefits to them or third parties, such as public officers, they have dealings with. Since corruption 'distorts economic and social development' (Stapenhurst and Langseth, 1997, p. 311), cloaking it as CSR presents significant obstacles to a regulatory scheme. A case study of the reality of differences between the stakeholder needs and values system approaches now follows against the backdrop of corruption, a persistent public governance issue in some developing and emerging markets.

2.5 COMPARATIVE CASE STUDY: CORRUPTION AND CSR

Corruption has been defined as 'the misuse of public office, public resources or public responsibility for private – personal or group – gain' (Szeftel, 2000, p. 407). This definition suggests the existence of corruption when public offices, resources and responsibilities are misused or abused for private benefits. It also underlines different dimensions of private benefit as being individual (benefit to the decision-maker or action-taker) or group (to which the decision-maker or action-taker belongs). Anti-corruption rules are therefore needed to prevent or address conflicts of interest. A conflict of interest can arise in a variety of ways, including through a principal–agent relationship, between a principal represented by an agent and a third party, or by an agent representing a principal and a third party. The conflict of interest analysis makes it easier to appreciate the potential of disguising corruption as CSR-labelled decisions and activities. This is illustrated by a controversial 'CSR project' undertaken by a multinational company in Nigeria.

In 2012, an Italian construction company, Gitto Costruzioni Generali Nigeria Ltd (GCG), built and donated a church to the hometown of Nigeria's president, Goodluck Jonathan. According to GCG, the church-building was a CSR project (ThisDay, 2012) presented to the president's community, which needed it. The company claimed that CSR 'is an established practice in our Mother country (Italy) and Italian firms in Nigeria have engaged in this practice[,] rendering free construction, medical and advisory services as well as providing scholarships to various communities within Nigeria'. In other words, the company relied on the stakeholder needs approach.

A presidential spokesperson corroborated GCG's view of the stakeholder needs approach, claiming:

> Yes, a contractor who has worked and continues to work in Bayelsa State and other parts of Nigeria thought it fit, in fulfilment of its corporate social responsibility, to facilitate the renovation of the small church in the President's home town of Otuoke ... It is indeed ironic that the groups and individuals now castigating the President because a company freely chose to fulfil its corporate social responsibility by helping to renovate a communal place of worship are also amongst those who constantly berate companies doing business in the Niger Delta for not doing enough to support the development of their host communities. (Ogbu, 2012, n.p.)

Independent commentators, however, criticised the company's gesture and doubted its motivations, despite its claim that the church project was solely CSR in a stakeholder community's interest. An online commentator ('Lekan'), for instance, stated: 'New dictionary meaning of BRIBE is corporate social responsibility. Abati has now introduced another definition of BRIBE. He has introduced new dimension to propagation of corruption and bribery by defining as corporate social responsibility. It is dangerous dimension to incorporate this bribe to president as social responsibility of "corrupt contractor". SHAME ON Rueben Abati for legimatizing bribe' (PMNews, Nigeria, 2012).

An editorial in a leading Nigerian newspaper, *ThisDay*, similarly opined:

> Of course there is the argument that it is only a church building but Gitto is not known to be a missionary outfit; it is a construction firm that bids for and wins contracts in Nigeria. Against the backdrop that the record of the company with regards to performance has left much to be desired, it becomes more obvious that the president goofed in accepting the questionable gift and worse still, that he would seek to justify it ... We note particularly that corruption thrives in Nigeria today because public officials do not know how and where to draw the line. It is therefore no surprise that some of these foreign construction companies do things they dare not try in their home countries. Gitto is surely no Santa Claus; it is a profit-seeking company accountable to its shareholders. When the company therefore spends millions of dollars on a 'gift', its management would expect returns so it is easy to understand why the costs of contracts in Nigeria are the highest in the world. (ThisDay, 2012, n.p.)

These comments suggest that justifications for CSR based exclusively on stakeholder needs could be problematic, particularly in terms of a conflict of interests analysis of corruption. The indications were that the president benefited indirectly from the church-building at least by being in the good books of his community, who were additionally potential voters in elections he or his associates would participate in. Further, GCG would benefit in demonstrating its 'friendship' to, and with, the president, who was directly, or through those answerable to him, in control of the government's construction budget. Overall, the case study shows that when CSR is not underpinned by a values system, it can cause or be a manifestation of corruption, especially in its covert form, which goes against what CSR should stand for. The chapter therefore continues by considering ways in which the values system paradigm can be integrated into a CSR regulatory scheme.

2.6 PROMOTING THE VALUES SYSTEM PARADIGM IN REGULATED CSR

Since the distinction between the stakeholder needs and values system approaches to CSR is both real and significant, the question is how a regulatory scheme can integrate a values system paradigm and ensure its greater effectiveness in influencing corporate actors and stakeholders. Against the backdrop that institutional theory assists 'in capturing institutional complexity, processes of institutional diffusion, and reciprocal influences between the organisation and its context' (Jamali and Neville, 2011, p. 600), Figure 2.2 has suggestions for subsuming the values system paradigm in regulated CSR schemes.

2.6.1 *Statement and Hierarchy of Overarching Values*

Following institutional theory's propositions regarding the contextual and behavioural impact of institutions, explicit statutory statements of values are essential for incorporation of the values system paradigm in regulated CSR. Law occupies a unique position within the institutional environment that can be enhanced with clear statutory statements of values system. As Latour (2015, p. 332) observed in another context, 'everyone seems to agree that law has its own way of defining true and false, although everyone also agrees that such a way does not resemble what is needed for extending the scope of referential statements'.

In stating the applicable values system, the law therefore needs to act as both a regulatory and a normative institution within the tripartite categorisations of institutions that scholars (Scott, 2001, 2008; MacCormick and Weinberger, 2013; Pillay and Kluvers, 2014) have identified. Acting as a regulatory institution without the normative flavour may not facilitate an effectively regulated CSR. In a combined regulatory and normative institutional role, however, the law may actively seek to deviate from the positions of other institutions and encourage them to adopt its own. Over time, this conscious approach may help the law to influence the unconsciously occurring cognitive institutions to be aligned with its regulatory objectives.

Furthermore, it may be necessary to stipulate a hierarchy of values. As cases such as *Lee* v. *Ashers Baking Company Ltd* and *Kern* v. *Dynalectron Corp*, examined in Sections 2.4.8 and 2.4.12 respectively, show, resolution mechanisms are necessary for different interests existing and competing in society. In *Lee*, for example, resolution came from the ECHR 1950 held by the UK Supreme Court to contain the relevant ultimate set of values.

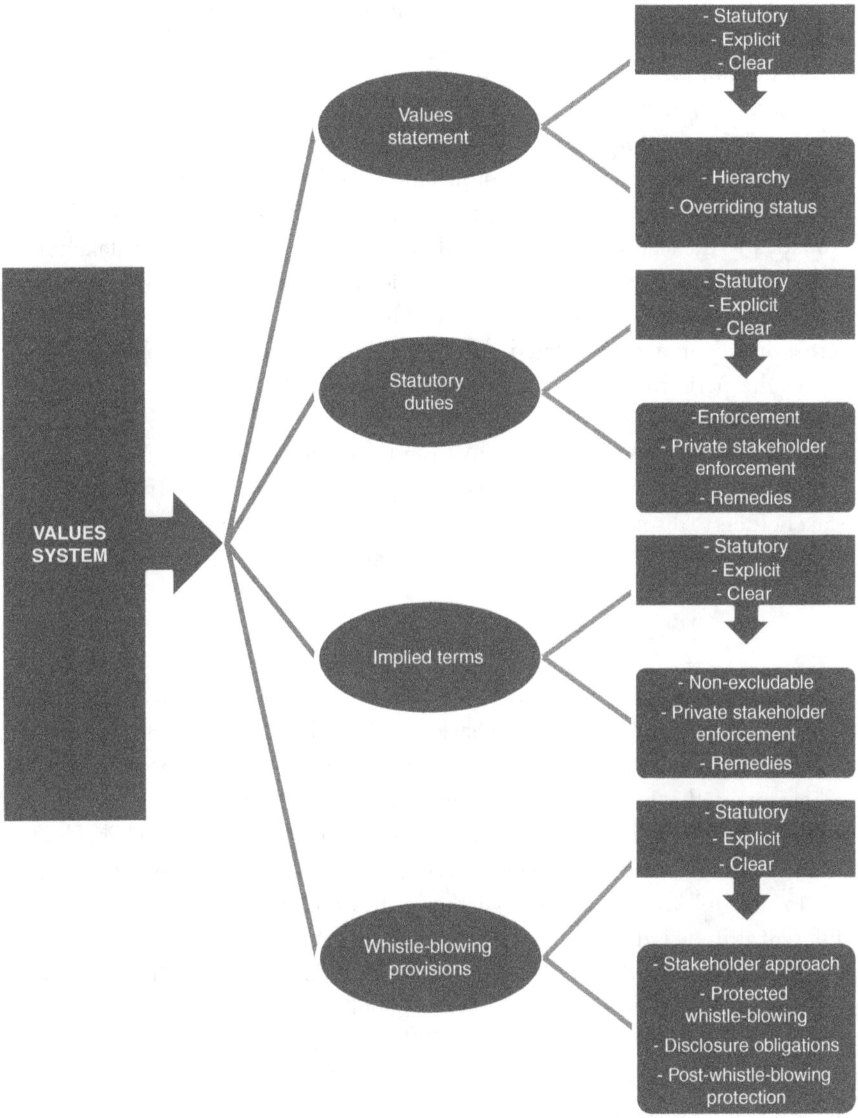

FIGURE 2.2 Strengthening the values system paradigm

2.6.2 *Statutory Duties and Liability*

The effectiveness of a values system paradigm can be enhanced when there are explicit provisions creating statutory duties aligned with the desired values. If such provisions exist, corporate actors are incentivised to evaluate proposed decisions and activities to ensure that they are in conformity with the values of the regulatory scheme. The provisions will also encourage corporations to undertake due diligence and risk assessments in dealings with independent entities to avoid flouting the values system imposed by the regulatory scheme. In *Kennedy* v. *Cordia (Services) LLP*,[13] for example, the UK Supreme Court confirmed that employers' common-law duty of care to employees includes the conducting of proper risk assessments.

Provisions for statutory duties can be further strengthened by expressly indicating the availability of private-law rights for stakeholders. A long-standing reasoning of the courts in England, for example, confirms that a breach of statutory duties does not automatically translate to a right of action and remedies for private stakeholders unless the enabling statute clearly states otherwise and prescribes the manner of private enforcement. The rule can be traced to the case of *Doe d. Murray* v. *Bridges* where Lord Tenterden CJ stated that 'where an Act creates an obligation, and enforces the performance in a specified manner … that performance cannot be enforced in any other manner'.[14] This has been confirmed by the courts in a number of cases[15] and applies even when a statute is intended to protect the public interest or a section of society.[16] It is therefore necessary to specify statutory duties and liability to stakeholders to displace the judicial presumption against enforcement and enable stakeholders to use the values system for evaluating decisions and activities.

2.6.3 *Implied Terms*

Another method of integrating a values system paradigm is by statutory implication of terms in contracts between certain persons. While the English courts, for instance, can imply terms to reflect the contractual parties' objective intention through the mechanism of the business efficacy and officious bystander test,[17] the judicial implication of CSR-related terms may be far-fetched. The common law is reluctant to imply contractual terms and would normally insist that it is 'inappropriate for the court to step in'[18] and rule on what the parties ought to decide for themselves. A different attitude is discernible with respect to legislated implied terms. The courts are more open towards implying terms in accordance with statutory rights or regulatory obligations applicable to a type of contract.[19] The imposition of contractual terms will ensure that the version of CSR promoted in the regulatory scheme is reflected in private contracts between, for example, businesses and their supply, purchasing and consumption chains. Clear statutory statements to that effect are important to give directions to stakeholders and to informal and formal institutions such as the courts.

A values-based approach to statutory implication of terms is exemplified by the fairness provisions for business-to-consumer contracts in the UK Consumer Rights Act 2015. Extending such an approach to CSR may enhance the effectiveness of its regulatory framework. Legislated implied terms in aid of CSR can include statements to the effect that contractual rights and obligations are subject to specified values and parties may be disallowed from excluding or opting out of statutory implied terms in order to strengthen the values system paradigm. The Consumer

Rights Act 2015 is also an example of this regulatory strategy, which can aim at protecting parties who may not be in a strong position to insist on CSR-related terms.

2.6.4 *Whistle-Blowing Provisions*

A values system approach to regulating CSR may need to be propped up by legal provisions to encourage whistle-blowing. Taking a stakeholder approach to whistle-blowing by including provisions for the 'voice' (Schneper et al., 2013) of specific stakeholders is important. A necessary step in that direction is to specify the applicable values system as a ground for protected whistle-blowing. Another is to impose disclosure obligations on certain persons when a values system is being eroded. This may be useful since 'a failure . . . to speak might be regarded as morally questionable [but] that is different from . . . a legal duty to speak'.[20]

In other words, such explicit whistle-blowing statements will assist stakeholders in resolving ethical dilemmas. As Lindblom (2007, p. 415) observed, '[t]he debate on morality whistleblowing centres on the conflict between the duty of loyalty to the firm or organisation in which one works and the liberty to speak out against wrongdoing'. A corollary to the statements of protected whistle-blowing is the need to ensure that whistle-blowers acting in furtherance of the values system are adequately protected by legal provisions, including against victimisation and reprisal.

2.7 CONCLUSION

This chapter has investigated the relative use and effectiveness of the stakeholder needs and values system paradigm approaches to regulating CSR and makes original arguments in favour of the latter as a more effective alternative, or complement, to the former. Proceeding on the basis that normativity is a feature that both law and CSR can advance, the chapter uniquely highlights the difficulties associated with the underlying justification of CSR by the stakeholder theoretic model, including competing stakeholder interests and lack of clarity of evaluative standards, which can affect the effectiveness of a stakeholder needs approach. These problems, which are aggravated by considerations of contextualism and behavioural impact, can result in conflicting corporate practices and stakeholder expectations in addition to inconsistencies with regulatory objectives.

With theoretical insights from institutional theory and Pound's social interests theory, and drawing examples from jurisdictions such as India, Nigeria and the UK, the chapter compares the stakeholder needs and values system approaches in a novel manner. Using a corruption and CSR case study, it demonstrates that the stakeholder needs approach presents practical and significant challenges, including creating opportunities for undesirable activities and covert corruption to be disguised as CSR, especially in a developing or emerging market context. In contrast, the values system approach provides some benefits, including facilitating contextualism and resolution of competing interests and the normativity–business case conflict, and provision of objective criteria for assessing CSR-themed decisions and activities. It can have a more effective influence on social actors' behaviour and on motivation, attitude and corporate governance, assist in reducing the opportunities to act corruptly under the guise of exercising discretion arising from self-regulation, and enable clearer delimitation of legal responsibilities and easier adaptation of standards for gatekeeper responsibility and glocalisation.

While the stakeholder needs approach can be used to identify and respond to stakeholder needs as required by CSR, there are real issues that determine the effectiveness of the regulatory system if CSR is not underpinned by certain values containing objective criteria for assessing decisions and activities undertaken within the CSR umbrella. The chapter further provides innovative suggestions on how to strengthen a values system-based regulatory infrastructure for CSR, including provisions for clear statements of values and their hierarchy to enable objective evaluation of decisions and activities, statutory duties, implication of contractual terms and whistle-blowing encouragement and protection. The proposals encourage effective co-regulation of CSR using the values system paradigm, which provides a suitable method for ensuring that social actors' behaviours are appropriately aligned with regulatory objectives designed to promote CSR in a specific context.

NOTES

1. *Truax* v. *Corrigan* 257 US 312 (1921), 357 (Justice Louis D. Brandeis).
2. *Truax* v. *Corrigan* 257 US 312 (1921), 357 (Justice Louis D. Brandeis).
3. [2018] UKSC 49.
4. (2009) EWHC (Admin).
5. *Social and Economic Rights Advocacy Project (SERAP)* v. *Federal Republic of Nigeria and the Attorney-General of Nigeria and another*, ECOWAS Court of Justice General List No. ECW/CCJ/APP/08/09 [2012], 44.
6. 577 F. Supp 1196 (ND Tex. 1983).
7. See *Hovenden* v. *Millhoff* [1900] 83 LT 4; *Anangel Atlas Compania Naviera SA* v. *Ishikawajima-Harima Heavy Industries Co.* [1990] 1 Lloyd's Rep 167; *Marino* v. *FM Capital Partners Ltd* [2020] EWCA Civ 245.
8. 27 Cal. 4th 939, 946, 45 P.3d 243, 247, 119 Cal. Rptr.2d 296 (Cal. 2002).
9. *Lidl lawsuit (re working conditions in Bangladesh)* (2010). www.business-humanrights.org/en/lidl-lawsuit-re-working-conditions-in-bangladesh.
10. [2012] EWCA Civ 525.
11. *Salomon* v. *Salomon & Co.* [1897] AC 22; *The Albazero* [1977] AC 744; *Re Union Carbide Gas Plant Disaster at Bhopal India* 634 F. Supp. 842 (SYDY 1986), 25

ILM 771 (1986), affirmed as modified 809 F. 2nd 195 (2nd Cir. 1987), 26 ILM 1008 (1987), cert. den. 108 S.Ct 199 (1987); *Adams* v. *Cape Industries Plc* [1990] 2 WLR 786; *Re Polly Peck International Plc (No. 3)* [1996] BCLC 428; *Prest* v. *Petrodel Resources Ltd* [2013] UKSC 34.

12. *Vedanta* v. *Lungowe* [2019] UKSC 20.
13. [2016] UKSC 6.
14. *Doe d Murray* v. *Bridges* (1831) 1 B & Ad 847, 859.
15. See *Benjamin* v. *Storr* (1874) LR 9 CP 400, 407; *Badham* v. *Lambs Ltd* [1946] KB 45; *Lonrho Ltd* v. *Shell Petroleum Co. Ltd (No. 2)* [1982] AC 173, 185 (Lord Diplock); *Harris* v. *Evans* [1998] 1 WLR 1285; *Gorringe* v. *Calderdale Metropolitan Borough Council* [2004] 1 WLR 1057; *Poole Borough Council* v. *GN & Anor* [2019] UKSC 25.
16. *R* v. *Deputy Governor of Parkhurst Prison Ex p. Hague* [1992] 1 AC 58, 170; *DC Accountancy Services Ltd* v. *Education Development International Plc* [2013] EWHC 3378 (QB).
17. *Marks and Spencer plc* v. *BNP Paribas Securities Services Trust Company (Jersey) Ltd* [2015] UKSC 72, [23] [40] (Lord Neuberger).
18. *Marks and Spencer plc* v. *BNP Paribas Securities Services Trust Company (Jersey) Ltd* [2015] UKSC 72, [40] (Lord Neuberger).
19. *Timeload* v. *British Telecommunications* [1995] EMLR 459.
20. *Hamilton* v. *Allied Domecq Plc* [2007] UKHL 33 [20].

REFERENCES

Baden, D. and Harwood, I. A. (2013). Terminology matters: a critical exploration of corporate social responsibility terms. *Journal of Business Ethics*, **116**, 615–27.

Bansal, P. (2002). The corporate challenges of sustainable development. *Academy of Management Perspectives*, **16**(2), 122–31.

Barnett, M. (2007). Stakeholder influence capacity and the variability of financial returns to corporate social responsibility. *Academy of Management Review*, **32**(3), 794–816.

Barrett, R. (2006). Achieving value-added corporate performance management. *Credit Control*, **27**(7/8), 34–8.

Berliner, D. and Prakash, A. (2012). From norms to programs: the United Nations global compact and global governance. *Regulation and Governance*, **6**, 149–66.

Blair, M. (1995). *Ownership and Control: Rethinking Corporate Governance for the Twenty First Century*. Washington, DC: The Brookings Institution.

Bradshaw, C. J. (2013). The environmental business case and unenlightened shareholder value. *Legal Studies*, **33**(1), 141–61.

Braithwaite, V. (2009). *Defiance in Taxation and Governance: Resisting and Dismissing Authority in a Democracy*. Cheltenham, UK: Edward Elgar.

Cadbury, A. (1992). *Report of the Committee on the Financial Aspects of Corporate Governance*. London: Gee.

Carroll, A. B. (2016). Carroll's pyramid of CSR: taking another look. *International Journal of Corporate Social Responsibility*, **1**(3), 1–8.

Commission of the European Communities (CEC). (2001). *Promoting a European Framework for Corporate Social Responsibility*. EU Doc. COM(2001) 366 final. www.europarl.europa.eu/meetdocs/committees/deve/20020122/com(2001)366_en.pdf.

Commission of the European Communities (CEC). (2011). *A Renewed EU Strategy 2011–14 for Corporate Social Responsibility*. EU Doc. COM(2011) 681 final. www.europarl.europa.eu/meetdocs/2009_2014/documents/com/com_com(2011)0681_/com_com(2011)0681_en.pdf.

Dahlsrud, A. (2008). How corporate social responsibility is defined: an analysis of 37 definitions. *Corporate Social Responsibility and Environmental Management*, **15**(1), 1–13.

Daily, C., Dalton, D. and Cannella Jr, A. (2003). Corporate governance: decades of dialogue and data. *Academy of Management Review*, **28**(3), 371–82.

Dam, L. and Scholtens, B. (2012). Does ownership type matter for corporate social responsibility? *Corporate Governance: An International Review*, **20**(3), 233–51.

Davis, G. F., Whitman, M. V. N. and Zald, M. N. (2008). The responsibility paradox. *Stanford Social Innovation Review*, Winter, 31–7.

Demb, A. and Neubauer, F. F. (1992). The corporate board: confronting the paradoxes. *Long-Range Planning*, **25**(3), 9–20.

Dentchev, N. A., van Balen, M. and Haezendonck, E. (2015). On voluntarism and the role of governments in CSR: towards a contingency approach. *Business Ethics: A European Review*, **24**(4), 378–97.

Doorey, D. J. (2011). The transparent supply chain: from resistance to implementation at Nike and Levi-Strauss. *Journal of Business Ethics*, **103**(4), 587–603.

Edelman, L., Petterson, S., Chambliss, E. and Erlanger, H. (1991). Legal ambiguity and the politics of compliance: affirmative action officers' dilemma. *Law & Policy*, **13**(1), 73–97.

Falck, O. and Heblich, S. (2007). Corporate social responsibility: doing well by doing good. *Business Horizons*, **50**, 247–54.

Fransen, L. (2013). The embeddedness of responsible business practice: exploring the interaction between national-institutional environments and corporate social responsibility. *Journal of Business Ethics*, **115**, 213–27.

Freeman, R. E. (1984). *Strategic Management: A Stakeholder Approach*. Boston, MA: Pitman.

Garriga, E. and Melé, D. (2004). Corporate social responsibility theories: mapping the territory. *Journal of Business Ethics*, **53**, 51–71.

Gouda, S., Khan, A. G. and Hiremath, S. L. (2016). *Corporate Social Responsibility in India: Trends, Issues and Strategies*. Hamburg: Anchor Academic.

Hamilton, L. and Clarke, T. (1996). The stakeholder approach to the firm: a practical way forward or a rhetorical flourish? *Career Development International*, **1**(2), 39–41.

Handy, C. (2002). What's a business for? *Harvard Business Review*, December. https://hbr.org/2002/12/whats-a-business-for.

Herlin, H. and Solitander, N. (2017). Corporate social responsibility as relief from responsibility: NPO legitimizations for corporate partnerships in contested terrains. *Critical Perspectives on International Business*, **13**(1), 2–22.

Hoffman, A. J. (1999). Institutional evolution and change: environmentalism and the U.S. chemical industry. *Academy of Management Journal*, **42**(4), 351–71.

Hofsted, G. (1994). *Cultures and Organizations*. London: HarperCollins.

Iskander, M. R. and Chamlou, N. (2000). *Corporate Governance: A Framework for Implementation Overview*. Washington, DC: International Bank for Reconstruction and Development/World Bank.

Jain, T., Aguilera, V. and Jamali, D. (2017). Corporate stakeholder orientation in an emerging country context: a longitudinal cross industry analysis. *Journal of Business Ethics*, **143**, 701–19.

Jamali, D. and Mirshak, R. (2007). Corporate social responsibility (CSR): theory and practice in a developing country context. *Journal of Business Ethics*, **72**(3), 243–62.

Jamali, D. and Neville, B. (2011). Convergence versus divergence of CSR in developing countries: an embedded multi-layered institutional lens. *Journal of Business Ethics*, **102**, 599–621.

Jamali, D., Karam, C. M., Soundararajan, V. and Yin, J. (2017). CSR logics in developing countries: translation, adaptation and stalled development. *Journal of World Business*, **52** (3), 343–59.

Kang, N. and Moon, J. (2012). Institutional complementarity between corporate governance and corporate social responsibility: a comparative institutional analysis of three capitalisms. *Socio-economic Review*, **10**(1), 85–108.

Kraakman, R. H. (1986). Gatekeepers: the anatomy of a third-party enforcement strategy. *Journal of Law, Economics, and Organization*, **2**(1), 53–104.

Latour, B. (2015). The strange entanglement of jurimorphs. In K. McGee, ed., *Latour and the Passage of Law*. Edinburgh: Edinburgh University Press, pp. 331–53.

Leigh Day. (2019). *Legal Briefing: Lungowe and Others v Vedanta and KCM: Parent Company Liability Clarified*. April. www.leighday.co.uk/media/w5rjukxp/legal-briefing-zambia-april2019.pdf.

Lewis, C. S. (1944). *The Abolition of Man or Reflections on Education with Special Reference to the Teaching of English in the Upper Forms of Schools*. San Francisco, CA: HarperOne.

Li, J., Moy, J., Lam, K. and Chu, W. (2008). Institutional pillars and corruption at the societal level. *Journal of Business Ethics*, **83**(2), 327–39.

Lindblom, L. (2007). Dissolving the moral dilemma of whistleblowing. *Journal of Business Ethics*, **76**, 413–26.

MacCormick, N. and Weinberger, O. (2013). *An Institutional Theory of Law: New Approaches to Legal Positivism*. Dordrecht: Springer.

Marique, E. and Marique, Y. (2019). Sanctions on digital platforms: beyond the public–private divide. *Cambridge International Law Journal*, 8(2), 258–81.

Matten, D. and Moon, J. (2008). Implicit and explicit CSR: a conceptual framework for a comparative understanding of corporate social responsibility. *Academy of Management Review*, **33**(2), 404–24.

Mitra, M. (2009). *It's Only Business! India's Corporate Social Responsiveness in a Globalized World*. New Delhi: Oxford University Press India.

Ogbu, A. (2012). Jonathan: I don't own any church. *ThisDay*, 5 April. www.thisdaylive.com /articles/jonathan-i-don-t-own-any-church/113030/.

Ohnesorge, J. K. (2007). Developing development theory: law and development orthodoxies and the Northeast Asian experience. *University of Pennsylvania Journal of International Economic Law*, **28**, 219–308.

Okoye, A. (2009). Theorising corporate social responsibility as an essentially contested concept: is a definition necessary? *Journal of Business Ethics*, 89(4), 613–27.

Osuji, O. (2011). Fluidity of regulation–CSR nexus: the multinational corporate corruption example. *Journal of Business Ethics*, **103**, 31–57.

Osuji, O. (2012). Corporate social responsibility – fairness and promise as the fundaments for juridification of social disclosures. *Contemporary Issues in Law*, **12**(1), 46–76.

Osuji, O. (2015). Corporate social responsibility, juridification and globalization: 'inventive interventionism' for a 'paradox'. *International Journal of Law in Context*, **11**(3), 1–34.

Painter, M., Pouryousefi, S., Hibbert, S. and Russon, J. (2019). Sharing vocabularies: towards horizontal alignment of values-driven business functions. *Journal of Business Ethics*, **155**, 965–79.

Painter-Morland, M. (2008). *Business Ethics as Practice*. Cambridge: Cambridge University Press.
Pillay, S. and Kluvers, R. (2014). An institutional theory perspective on corruption: the case of a developing democracy. *Financial Accountability & Management*, 30(1), 95–119.
PMNews, Nigeria. (2012). Otuoke church: Jonathan committed no crime. 4 April. http://saharareporters.com/2012/04/04/%E2%80%98otuoke-church-%E2%80%98jonathan-committed-no-crime%E2%80%99.
Pound, R. (1943). A survey of social interests. *Harvard Law Review*, 57(1), 1–39.
Pound, R. (1968). *Social Control through Law*. Hamden, CT: Archon Books.
Prentice, D. D. (1993). Some aspects of the corporate governance debate. In D. D. Prentice and P. R. J. Holland, eds., *Contemporary Issues in Corporate Governance*. Oxford: Oxford University Press, pp. 25–44.
Robertson, D. (2009). Corporate social responsibility and different stages of economic development: Singapore, Turkey, and Ethiopia. *Journal of Business Ethics*, 88(4), 617–33.
Rokeach, M. (1973). *The Nature of Human Values*. New York: Free Press.
Sadurski, W. (2004).Universalism, localism and paternalism in human rights discourse. In A. Sajó, ed., *Human Rights with Modesty: The Problem of Universalism*. Leiden: Martinus Njihoff, pp. 141–60.
Schneper, W. D., Wernick, D. A. and Von Glinow, M. A. (2013). Stakeholder voice, corporate dysfunction and change: an organization learning perspective. In R. J. Burke and C. L Cooper, eds., *Voice and Whistleblowing in Organizations: Overcoming Fear, Fostering Courage and Unleashing Candour*. Cheltenham, UK: Edward Elgar, pp. 113–36.
Scott, W. (2001). *Institutions and Organizations*. Thousand Oaks, CA: Sage.
Scott, W. (2008). Approaching adulthood: the maturing of institutional theory. *Theory and Society*, 37(5), 427–42.
Solomon, J. (2007). *Corporate Governance and Accountability*. Hoboken, NJ: John Wiley.
Stapenhurst, F. and Langseth, P. (1997). The role of the public administration in fighting corruption. *Journal of Public Sector Management*, 10(5), 311–30.
Szeftel, M. (2000). Clientalism, corruption and catastrophe. *Review of African Political Economy*, 27(85), 427–41.
ThisDay. (2012). A most questionable gift: the Italian construction company Gitto's church gift to Jonathan. Editorial, 1 April. http://saharareporters.com/2012/04/01/most-questionable-gift-italian-construction-company-gittos-church-gift-jonathan-thisday.
Tirole, J. (2001). Corporate governance. *Econometrica*, 69(1), 1–35.
Turnbull, S. (1997). Corporate governance: its scope, concerns and theories. *Corporate Governance: An International Review*, 5(4), 180–205.
United States Government. (1961). *Congressional Record. Proceedings and Debates of the 87th Congress First Session*. Vol. 107, Pt 9. 26 June to 14 July. Washington, DC: United States Government Printing Office. www.govinfo.gov/app/details/GPO-CRECB-1961-pt9/context.
Visser, W. (2010). The age of responsibility: CSR 2.0 and the new DNA of business. *Journal of Business Systems, Governance and Ethics*, 5(3), 7–22.
Waterman Jr, R. (1994). *The Frontiers of Excellence: Learning from Companies That Put People First*. London: Brealey.
World Business Council for Sustainable Development (WBCSD). (2001). *Corporate Social Responsibility*. Geneva: WBCSD.
Young, O. R. (1994). *International Governance: Protecting the Environment in a Stateless Society*. Ithaca, NY: Cornell University Press.

3

Incentives, Public Procurement and Market Mechanisms

Franklin N. Ngwu

3.1 INTRODUCTION

In economic discourse, while situations of government failure are sometimes corrected through the invitation of the market (private sector) to provide the needed efficiency and capital to revitalise the economy, situations of market failure are normally modified or corrected mainly through government interventions using policies and regulations. In between these two extremes, there are conditions that might not be described as strictly government failure or market failure. In such conditions, what should be done in terms of who should be responsible, the government or the market? Another option might be a joint responsibility such as a public–private partnership. As the promotion of corporate social responsibility (CSR), particularly in developing and emerging markets (DEMs), is arguably one of such conditions, the question is how it should be pursued. From Milton Friedman's perspective, the primary responsibility of firms is shareholder satisfaction through profit growth and payment of dividends. Issues such as CSR should not concern the firm as it is the responsibility of the government to whom the firms pay taxes. However, from a stakeholder's understanding, the task of a firm is beyond shareholder interests. There are other stakeholders outside the shareholders whose interests should also be considered. Moreover, pursuing the wider interests of other stakeholders might even enhance those of the shareholders.

Even if we tentatively agree that CSR should be approached from a stakeholder perspective, the question is how governments should get involved. Being one of the critical stakeholders and known to use mainly rules and regulations to advance its interests, the further question is whether the government should be adopting its traditional approach (rules and regulations) in the pursuit of CSR engagement and practice. Recalling that firms can maintain that they pay their taxes and comply with extant rules and regulations, will coercing them to also pursue CSR achieve the desired result, namely, sustainable CSR growth and impact in DEMs? If it is ascertained that using regulation might achieve the desired outcomes, a follow-up question is what kind of regulation? Will it be coercive and punitive regulation or will it be pursued using a softer approach such as incentive, responsive and performance-based regulation.

Moreover, with regulatory costs and limited regulatory outcomes common across DEMs (see Kaufmann and Kray 2020), another question is whether there are alternatives to regulations that can be used. Are there other ways that the government can engage with the market and the private sector, particularly in DEMs, to achieve a more sustainable and impactful CSR? Suggestions include that the roles of government in promoting CSR can be classified into four of mandating, facilitating, partnering and endorsing. In addition to these roles, the government can also enhance CSR in DEMs through engagement in activities such as responsible investment, corporate governance, inclusive stakeholder engagement, formulation and monitoring of compliance to minimum standards and promotion of pro-CSR production and consumption, among other factors.

The aim of this chapter, therefore, is to examine the different options that governments have used or can use in their engagement and pursuit of CSR in DEMs. It will critically identify and analyse both regulatory and non-regulatory options including market and non-market mechanisms such as fiscal, reputational and other incentives, public procurement, as well as contract, certification and labelling that can be applied in advancing CSR awareness and practice in DEMs. The remaining sections of the chapter will proceed as follows: Section 3.2 will examine the concept of regulation, which is the traditional way government has intervened in the market, especially in correcting market failure. While Section 3.3 will analyse why governments are interested in CSR and the factors influencing government CSR policies, Section 3.4 will identify CSR policy instruments and the top five action areas. Based on these, Section 3.5 will examine a possible model that could be adopted by DEMs and then the six steps to developing a CSR policy framework. Section 3.6 concludes.

3.2 CONCEPT AND TYPES OF REGULATION

Regulation as a concept attracts varied contributions and definitions that motivated Ogus (2004) to observe that it may be understood as any process of behavioural control, irrespective of the origin. Regulation is a form of protection or control of certain valued societal activities through the consistent and intentional operations of public agencies (Selznick, 1985). Relatedly, Majone (1994) is of the view that regulation as a concept should be understood from its socio-economic and political undertone, which is that appreciation of the varied economic organisations and legal structures that sustain regulation will enhance its comprehension. Regulation can also be understood as a procedure that aims to achieve certain social-economic policy intentions through the application of legal mechanisms. The use of legal mechanisms ensures compliance by the participants through the application of appropriate sanctions against non-compliance, which enhances the realisation of the desired benefits of regulation (Den Hertog, 2000; Koop and Lodge, 2015). However, Ogus (2004) notes that even though the emphasis is on a centralised and public agency form of regulation, some forms of regulation are also carried out through self-regulatory agencies and the use of other regulatory instruments such as tax and denial of societal privileges.

There are two major theories of regulation – public interest and private interest. The public interest theory generally maintains that regulation is a product of the desire to pursue public interests in socio-economic endeavours. Politicians and policymakers are therefore guided by the motive to achieve and protect the collective goals and interests in the design and implementation of the regulation (Den Hertog, 2000). However, there are wide-ranging criticisms of the public interest theory. For instance, Ogus (2004) argues that a consensus on what can be regarded as collective interest is difficult to achieve. This is in the sense that legislation is normally the product of conflicting expressions of the original intent of the legislation. Even if the contradictions are resolved, the underlying reason for its formulation and passage might have some private interest permutations.

The private interest theory of regulation maintains that regulation is the process through which the vested interests of a certain group of individuals in society are protected. Politicians and policymakers, therefore, enact legislations with the principal aim of realising their private interests or those of their vested groups (Peltzman, 1989; Ogus, 2004). There have been attempts to modify the theory in line with emergent factors such as issues of deregulation and the application of self-regulation (Jarrell, 1984) or, in social regulation, issues with efforts to achieve a balance among the vested interests (Weingast, 1981). In line with the concept and meaning of CSR, it can be argued that the two theories are applicable to the regulatory developments of CSR. While earlier understanding and practice of CSR, which focussed mainly on altruistic or firm-specific interests and decisions, can be linked to private interest theory, the current interest of both governments and other stakeholders in having more involvement and regulation of CSR can be explained with public interest theory.

The application of regulation can be identified mainly under economic and social regulation. While economic regulation aims to ensure reasonable competition in the market, social regulation relates to other issues such as market failures, consumer protection and asymmetric information factors (Viscusi et al., 2001; Ogus, 2004). In CSR, both economic and social regulations are applicable but somewhat dependent on the stakeholders involved. For instance, while the demand from institutional investors for environmental, social and governance (ESG) issues to be included in investment decisions can be examined under economic and social regulation, the advocacy from non-governmental organisations (NGOs) and other socially oriented organisations can be analysed under social regulation. Economic justifications of the need for regulation are normally explained using the positive sub-theory while identification of the appropriate type of regulation in terms of efficiency and cost is carried out using the normative sub-theory (Hennipman, 1992; Blaug, 1993; Den Hertog, 2000).

Den Hertog (2000) maintains that a cost–benefit analysis of the regulatory instrument is normally carried out to identify the most efficient type of regulation to apply. The cost–benefit analysis focusses on:

> i. Costs of formulating and implementing regulation, ii. The costs of maintaining regulation, iii. The costs of compliance with the rules for the industry and the deadweight costs resulting from distortive changes in connection with [i–iii]. The benefits consist of improvements in the static and dynamic efficiency in the application of scarce resources. While the static efficiency comprises productive and allocative efficiency, dynamic efficiency refers to future improvements in the application of scarce resources. (Den Hertog, 2000, p. 225)

In line with the above, Ogus (2004) is of the view that the mere existence of a market failure might not justify regulation as the failure might be corrected by the application of appropriate market transactions or private law solutions without state involvement. Regulation can be justified if its costs are lower than the non-regulation approaches. Even when regulation is considered important, further relevant issues that will enhance the effectiveness of the regulation include the selection of regulatory instruments, levels of intervention and institutional decisions (Bishop, 1990; Rose-Ackerman, 1992; Ogus, 2004).

In line with economic analysis of institutional arrangements using the principal–agent theory (Bishop, 1990), the fundamental focus is on how to achieve targeted outcomes through the effective selection of relevant institutions and rules. This will provide the required incentives that will sustain enforcement and compliance. It also relates to issues of the level of enforcement and the consequent costs in line with the targeted compliance and penalties for non-compliance (Polinsky and Shavell, 1979). This relates to Posner's (1974) view that 'pure' economic theorising of regulation sometimes ignores certain variables such as monitoring and enforcement costs that enhance regulatory effectiveness. It is on this basis that Ogus (2004) argues that the concept of regulatory failure might be better understood by appreciation of the inadequacies of the earlier 'economic' contributions and that this has triggered a better economic input in regulatory discourse.

Appreciating the many factors and actors in contemporary governance and with a high inclination towards regulation of CSR, Steurer (2013) uses the concept of actor constellations to identify seven types of regulation, which will be explained in Section 3.3. While four of the types can be attributed and allocated to public policies with different levels of government involvement, three can be said to be determined by three groups or factors – civil societies (civil regulations), businesses (industry or business self-regulation) or both (civil co-regulation). But the questions are why should the government be interested in CSR and what kinds of regulation or non-regulation should be used to promote CSR?

3.3 GOVERNMENT INTEREST IN CSR

With CSR described as activities or actions of a firm to go beyond legal or regulatory demands and integrate social and environmental concerns in their business decisions and operations, what then is the interest of the government in CSR? This can be attributed to four factors. First is that with the acceptance of the importance of sustainable development goals (SDGs) and their pursuit through policies and regulations, CSR presents a good opportunity through which governments can shape, coerce or persuade the private sector to join in the national SDG agenda. Moreover, the SDG initiative is clearly in line with the CSR concept with the emphasis on inclusion of social, environmental and economic elements in both firm and government plans through a stakeholders' approach (European Council, 2006; Steurer, 2013).

Second, as governments normally use both hard and soft regulations in pursuit of social goals, their interest in CSR can be linked more with the soft regulatory approach through which CSR is mainly pursued and which is in line with the increasing reform and acceptance of the concept of 'new governance' or 'network governance' (see Steurer, 2013). With globalisation and the emergence of multinational firms with immense resources as well as social and environmental cross-border impacts, it is increasingly being accepted that pursuit of public policy goals cannot be done only by governments; also needed are the collaboration and shared responsibility of the relevant stakeholders (network governance), particularly the private sector and the civil society (Knill and Lehmkuhl, 2002; Bartle and Vass, 2007; Esmark, 2009; Steurer, 2013). This emerging new form of inclusive or shared governance can be observed in the increasing use of concepts such as public–private partnerships where societal goals or problems are now tackled through a shared responsibility approach.

As private sector firms are seemingly happy and willing to accept their expanding responsibility in the new shared governance environment, which they pursue through CSR, among other ways, the interest of the government in the CSR policies and activities of private sector firms is better understood. It can be attributed to wanting to ensure, through either hard or soft regulation, that the private sector and other stakeholders perform their agreed responsibility in the shared governance framework. Even in the absence of hard regulation, the interest of the government in CSR can still be justified as the CSR activities of private sector firms will complement and support government efforts in providing social goals and good governance. Therefore, supporting the CSR activities of private sector firms and other stakeholders through a variety of approaches including hard or soft regulation and policies is in the government's interest as it helps to lessen its governance burden with private sector CSR contributions and activities (Stoker, 1998; Howlett, 2009; Steurer, 2013).

Third, following on from the previous point, some governments such as Norway and Sweden promote the CSR activities of private sector firms owing to their understanding of CSR from an ethical inclination and belief that it is the appropriate thing to do. Arguably, this thinking is even more convincing in situations where voluntary interventions are perceived as the most appropriate method of resolving global challenges or in developing countries with weak institutional and governance outcomes (see Gjølberg, 2010; Steurer, 2013).

The fourth factor relates to emerging issues such as increasing globalisation of markets and supply chains, technological advances, significant corporate governance failures such as Enron, Parmalat and the 2008 global financial crisis (GFC), and heightened interest and engagement of civil society organisations in the management and governance of private sector firms, especially multinational ones. With civil society organisations making demands for better governance and management of private sector firms, their interest in CSR is in line with the government's interest to include and share its governance burdens with private sector firms (Steurer, 2013).

3.4 FACTORS INFLUENCING GOVERNMENT CSR POLICIES

In its efforts towards a better society, the government is developing its thinking along the lines of three major related factors – politics, polity and policies. The first factor, politics, is in terms of political contention about what is right, the objectives and goals, and the needed actions (policies). Even though public CSR policies are generally approached and perceived as soft regulations, they are nevertheless understood and interpreted from varied political inclinations and as such pursued from the political stance of the government in question. A key area of contention is how CSR policies should be applied. Should regulation be hard or soft, demanding or flexible, compulsory or voluntary? For instance, while civil society organisations normally push for compulsory policies such as CSR reporting, business leaders, to a large extent, prefer a voluntary CSR policy. In the same vein, while politicians, policymakers and business leaders with neo-liberal inclinations perceive CSR policies as efforts to divert businesses from their profit-making focus, civil society organisations with a social inclination perceive CSR and related policies as mechanisms for weakening hard regulation (Banerjee, 2008; Steurer, 2013). This is also the case with labour unions that perceive CSR with caution sometimes, thinking that it might weaken social regulations, particularly their position as a social partner.

The second factor, polity, relates to the structural issues in terms of allocation of responsibilities. Of the many agencies of government that get involved in formulation and implementation, the ones responsible for labour and social affairs are perceived as central, particularly in co-ordinating CSR action plans. In some countries such as France, Belgium and Cyprus, CSR policies are pursued through inter-ministerial CSR committees given the perception of CSR as requiring cross-sectional perspectives and approach. For others such as Denmark and Poland, CSR policies and activities are pursued through specially created centres or agencies that manage and co-ordinate other CSR stakeholders (Knopf et al., 2011; Steurer, 2013).

Related to polity is the third factor, policies. These are the actions or inactions that can be used to effect behavioural changes in both individuals and organisations. With CSR generally accepted as important and needed, the politics of CSR are perceived as being dictated by the policies (Steurer, 2013). However, it can also be argued that the subsequent policies will be determined by the consequent politics of the initial policies. It is therefore a kind of cyclical process. Even though CSR policies are generally pursued more from a soft regulatory approach, they are perceived from varied political inclinations, which results in differences in the way the policies are formulated and implemented by different governments. A good example is a question on the nature of policies in terms of the requirements and expectations of the CSR policy or regulation. For instance, while businesses will prefer soft policies such as voluntary participation and compliance, civil society organisations expectedly advocate and push for binding regulations such as CSR reporting (Banerjee, 2008; Steurer, 2013). In line with the concept of power constellations, the different stakeholders of a business understand and pursue CSR policies from their varied and respective inclinations.

CSR policies are therefore varied in terms of issues demanding attention, policy instruments used and stakeholders involved. Numerous typologies therefore emerge with each attempt to segment CSR policies based on factors such as the issues to be tackled (Lepoutre et al., 2007), the stakeholders involved (governments, businesses and civil society) and the platforms of interaction used or needed (Riess and Welzel, 2006; Lorzano et al., 2008). With the different typologies, there seems to be an absence of a coherent and convincing understanding of the natures and types of policy instrument required for effective government intervention and regulation of CSR. There is therefore a lack of detailed strategy on how governments should intervene in CSR (Steurer, 2013).

Even with the variations, CSR public policies can be argued to exhibit some coherence, with similarities across them. First is that all policies seem to advocate features of voluntariness and partnership. Second, there is an inherent inclination towards a soft approach in regulation and policies. Third, all policies seem to agree to the synergy of CSR and sustainable development and then the application of the policies as complements to hard regulations. Leveraging Fox et al. (2002) to rethink CSR typologies, Steurer (2010) offers an alternative typology that identifies five policy instruments under four themes that can be used to better understand CSR public policies.

3.5 CSR POLICY INSTRUMENTS

In line with Howlett and Ramesh (1993), there are tools, means and methods generally referred to as instruments through which governments implement policies. In CSR discourse, five such instruments can be identified: informational instruments, fiscal-economic instruments, legal instruments, partnering instruments and hybrid instruments (Steurer, 2013).

3.5.1 *Informational Instruments*

With campaigns, training sessions and information websites as examples, informational instruments are mainly pursued through persuasions and advocacy of the consequences of policies in terms of costs and benefits. With no binding requirements, the selling point is normally the perceived wealth of knowledge of the government or the promoter, for instance, to convince different stakeholders, particularly business organisations, and sometimes implore them to take note, of the need for action or inaction with regard to the issue under consideration. Given the central role of governments in moderating social goals and the infancy of CSR, government efforts in raising awareness and building capacity for CSR are pertinent ways through which the importance of CSR, particularly the need for proper consideration of ESG factors in organisational and societal decisions, can be pursued. In addition to training, campaigns and information websites, further examples through which governments can raise CSR awareness and practice include award schemes, disclosure of payments to public institutions, labelling and disclosure of performing and non-performing firms (UN Global Compact and Bertelsmann Stiftung [hereafter UN Global Compact], 2010). With the increasing importance attached to transparency and disclosure of the ESG activities of organisations by almost all stakeholders, particularly investors, it is an area that governments can effectively use in promoting CSR. By advocating, emphasising, demanding and disseminating such reports, governments will, directly and indirectly, advance CSR awareness and practice.

3.5.2 *Fiscal-Economic Instruments*

As the name suggests, these are tools such as grants, taxes, tax refunds and abatements, subsidies and exemptions used by the government to shape or influence organisational or individual behaviours towards a targeted goal or outcome. Their use can be described as an incentive-driven approach or regulation through which businesses are encouraged or incentivised to be more inclined towards CSR in their business decisions and activities. Even though it is generally voluntary, providing incentives such as tax breaks and subsidies expectedly can enhance compliance. That compliance, which can be described as incentivised, can be attributed to the cost-reduction benefits achievable, which, directly or indirectly, will enhance the profitability and performance of the complying firms as compared to firms that are not complying. Moreover, to be perceived or rated as a firm with a good compliance record also comes with additional benefits such as high investor interest.

3.5.3 *Legal Instruments (Mandating and Soft Laws)*

These are legislative instruments that the government normally uses such as laws, regulations and directives, that is, executive and judicial powers, to shape the choices and actions of the different actors in an economy or society through use or application of hierarchy and authority. Using such instruments, the government can set and enforce minimum standards for businesses on CSR-related issues such as environmental protection, anti-competition and labour laws. While observance of, or compliance with, CSR demands is widely voluntary, the government can also pursue it through mandatory laws. In this case, compliance is enforced through laws and regulations with non-compliance punished through sanctions such as fines. A good example is a regulatory requirement for firms to annually report their CSR initiated and compliance activities (see UN Global Compact, 2010; Steurer, 2013).

In line with the concept and meaning of CSR, an interesting aspect of both fiscal-economic and legislative instruments in advancing CSR is the soft law approach. In most cases, the soft laws are normally different from the statutory ones, in not being binding, and in having limited or no enforcement. They are normally non-regulatory interventions. Examples include advocacy for principles such as the UN Global Compact and the *OECD Guidelines for Multinational Enterprises*, the demand for corporate responsibility requirements in the administration of public procurements and the creation of a national CSR action plan (UN Global Compact, 2010). Even though governments are not expected to enforce soft laws, they still have important advocacy and mandating roles. Through advocacy and promotion of the compliance benefits of such soft laws, governments can increase firms' CSR awareness and practice. Moreover, the soft laws can also be combined with other instruments such as the fiscal-economic instruments to enhance compliance with the soft laws.

3.5.4 *Partnering and Hybrid Instruments*

Expanding on the above three, Steurer (2013) adds the partnering and hybrid instruments. In line with the shared responsibility feature of CSR, partnering instruments refer to tools such as stakeholders' fora, negotiated agreements and public–private partnerships that can be used to foster joint or shared involvement in promoting CSR awareness and practice. For hybrid instruments, these are tools, means or methods that combine the other instruments in advancing CSR policies. Good examples include CSR platforms, centres and other strategies for promoting awareness and practice of CSR. A good aspect of both the partnering and the hybrid approaches is that the expertise, competencies and resources of both the public and the private sectors can be combined to achieve a higher CSR impact. For instance, the government can act as the initiator, moderator or facilitator and, with such a collaborative approach, important issues such as poverty reduction, access to health and safety, and social and educational empowerment can be pursued (UN Global Compact, 2010; Steurer, 2013).

A very good example of a government facilitating role is the promotion of socially responsible investment (SRI). While the importance of protecting the interests of shareholders in a firm is not disputed, it is also becoming increasingly clear that these interests can be pursued and enhanced through consideration and pursuit of the interests of other stakeholders. This is what SRI does. In considering the economic, social, environmental and/or other ethical issues in organisational decisions (including investments), it is maintained that SRI creates a mutual synergy between the interests of shareholders and those of other stakeholders (Scholtens et al., 2008, Steurer, 2010, 2013).

In acting as an initiator, the government can also lead by example (walk the talk). This relates to the need for the government to lead from the front and not just dish out policies and regulations. With effective identification of CSR expectations and requirements, the government can advance CSR awareness and practice through its own way of performing certain activities. For example, it can: 1) attach a level of ESG performance as a criterion to qualify for participation in public procurement; 2) ensure that SRI principles are applied in the governance and management of government funds such as pension funds; 3) use CSR management systems (such as Eco-Management and Audit Scheme (EMAS)) in government ministries and agencies; and 4) lead proactively through timely and transparent disclosure and reporting of its ESG performance, just as private sector firms are encouraged and sometimes required to report on their ESG performance.

With the above instruments and approaches, governments' CSR agenda has focussed on several areas such as education, human rights, poverty, environment, health and safety, involvement in society and social inequality challenges (UN Global Compact, 2010). While most of these issues are common social problems across societies and economies, the specific areas to be intervened in are normally dictated by context-specific issues or peculiarities. However, to achieve maximum impact across the issues identified requires action in three cross-cutting areas.

3.6 TOP THREE CSR ACTION AREAS

The top three areas in which CSR intervention can achieve positive results across societies and economies are discussed in this subsection.

3.6.1 *Corporate Governance*

With cases such as the Enron failure and the 2008 GFC having significantly attributed to failures in corporate governance, there is an increasing demand for more effort on the part of the government to ensure a higher level of governance (transparency and accountability) across firms. Through such interventions, the diminishing trust and confidence in businesses might be redeemed. With corporate governance generally defined as a set of rules and principles used in ensuring that firms are managed and governed in line with agreed levels of authority, accountability, stewardship, leadership, direction and control, it means that interventions and reforms aimed at improving or enthroning effective corporate governance of firms will be in line with the aim of higher CSR practices.

An interesting definition of corporate governance by Sir Adrian Cadbury further affirms this: 'Corporate governance is concerned with holding the balance between individual and communal goals … The aim is to align as nearly as possible the interests of individuals, corporations and society' (Cadbury, 1999). This means that, with improved corporate governance, the interests of all stakeholders will be better aligned for the sustainable growth of businesses and the economy. Moreover, the pressure for improved corporate governance can also be attributed to the increasing growth of SRI and its investors' insistence on compliance with certain ethical guidelines. For instance, while SRI accounted for 46 per cent of the global USD 30.7 trillion total managed assets in 2018, in Europe SRI accounted for 41.6 per cent of the total assets under management in 2020 (Norrestad, 2021). What is therefore required of governments is to proactively join or lead the reforms for improved corporate governance, for instance through promotion of responsible investment (PRI). Through collaboration with the private sector and other stakeholders, governments can initiate reforms for improved corporate governance frameworks. In South Africa, for instance, the Black Economic Empowerment Initiative (BEEI) is a reform for social sustainability with a binding requirement on firms for equity and fairness in employment and other aspects of business governance (UN Global Compact, 2010; Mthanti and Ojah, 2017).

3.6.2 *Reporting and Disclosure*

With increasing demand for and scrutiny of business activities by different stakeholders, governments can advance CSR awareness and activities through the promotion of reforms and advocacies for more transparency in both internal and external communication of firms. Expectedly, such increased communication and scrutiny will induce more involved discussions of both financial and non-financial issues relating to the firm's vision, corporate values, activities, successes, challenges and strategic plans. Also contributing to the demand for more transparent communication is the increased awareness and advocacy of ESG issues, SDGs and other factors such as human rights violations, labour laws and corruption. As a response to these demands, governments are promoting both mandatory and voluntary reporting and disclosures. In Sweden, for instance, the Globalt Ansvar initiative demands the reports of member firms on their activities and implementation of the principles of the UN Global Compact and/or the *OECD Guidelines for Multinational Enterprises*. This is also the case with the South African Black Economic

Empowerment programme, the impacts and challenges of which can be said to have been influenced through more reporting and disclosures, particularly by the media (see UN Global Compact, 2010; Thomas, 2014; Mthanti and Ojah, 2017).

3.6.3 *Community Involvement and Development*

While businesses normally perform CSR activities particularly around their host communities, there is a need for more concerted and impactful involvement in societal development and provision of public goods such as infrastructure (for instance transport and road), natural resources (water, air, energy, etc.) and qualified and healthy employees. Even though these public goods will benefit the host communities, they can also be beneficial to businesses; for instance, having healthy and skilled employees can bring the possibility of securing more market share and customers through the production and offering of products and services suitable to the different segments of society; it is like the 'bottom of the pyramid'. There is therefore a good economic incentive for businesses to get involved in the development needs of not only their host communities but also the broader society. Moreover, given the peculiarities of some societies and economies such as weak enforcement mechanisms, scarce resources including human capital skills, absence of political will and lack of knowledge of the importance of some public goods, the need for more interest and participation of businesses in the provision of public goods becomes more pertinent. As such, partnership might be the trigger for more meaningful and sustainable development of societies; thus, governments should proactively engage with the private sector to create the required public–private partnerships for the collective provision of public goods and sustainable development of economies (see UN Global Compact, 2010; Osuji et al., 2019).

3.7 IS THERE A MODEL TO BE ADOPTED BY DEMS?

While public sector interest and engagement in CSR can still be described as new and emerging, there are encouraging examples across the globe that provide good lessons for governments in DEMs interested in promoting CSR. As will be clearer from the three examples discussed in this section, a key factor in their successes is the effective partnering and facilitating role of the government, which significantly helps in creating the appropriate framework and environment for CSR and responsible business activities. Another important lesson is that CSR acceptance and practice may be better achieved when pursued or promoted from a voluntary approach and embedded into the national context by the government. This enhances the practice of CSR as a good complement to legal demands and even beyond compliance.

At a regional level, the European example is instructive. With a mandate from the European Council (2000), CSR was advocated and crafted from a sustainable development inclination in a green paper published in 2001. To strengthen the CSR agenda, the European Commission issued a communique in 2002 that contained detailed policy options for more transparency and a harmonised CSR approach across Europe. While influenced by the political and philosophical leanings of European leaders, the European CSR approach has moved from a proactive co-regulatory style to an inclination that advocates for more business self-regulation (European Commission, 2006; Steurer, 2013). In addition to the efforts of the European Commission, many European countries, especially those in the Western, Central and Northern parts, are very active in pushing for more CSR both in their countries and across Europe. As these efforts in European countries and at the European Commission level have contributed to a good perception of Europe in CSR policy development, it is important to appreciate that the leadership can be described as young, with the UK the only country in Europe with a longer history of CSR and CSR policies that dates back to the 1970s (see Pedersen, 2015; Steurer, 2015).

Bringing it down to countries, Denmark, Botswana and China appear to be good models of effective public sector–driven CSR.

3.7.1 *Denmark*

In Denmark, the National Action Plan for Corporate Social Responsibility launched in 2008 can be described as a major turning point in the promotion of CSR. Co-ordinated by the Ministry of Economic and Business Affairs in collaboration with the Confederation of Danish Industries, the Danish Commerce and Companies Agency (DCCA), the Danish Institute for Human Rights and others, the main objective of the plan is promotion of CSR across small, medium and large Danish firms, through which those firms' competitiveness and responsible growth can be better achieved. The plan has about thirty initiatives pursued across four key areas. The first is encouraging firms to report on their CSR activities while using internationally recognised principles and standards to provide training and guidance. The second is government efforts to integrate CSR demands into government procedures and activities, such as public procurement. The third key area is direct and indirect government promotion of responsible ESG practices across business sectors, which is mainly pursued through efforts to convince businesses to increase energy efficiency, reduce greenhouse gas emissions and come up with innovative global climate solutions. The fourth approach is promotion of Denmark's reputation as a front-line advocate and leader in practising responsible growth, which expectedly will benefit Danish firms (see Fox et al., 2002; UN Global Compact, 2010; Steurer, 2015).

In pursuing these objectives, the government is combining mandating, soft law, partnering and awareness-raising. Through such an approach, a mandatory law requiring more than 1,100 of the largest Danish companies to report their CSR activities was adopted. Using soft laws, the government endorsed universal principles such as the UN Global Compact, while partnership is promoted through regular consultation with the private sector, NGOs, academia and the public. Arguably, the combination and usage of a hybrid approach can be said to have contributed to the encouraging and many successes achieved. While there are many achievements, it is important to note a few. In 2008, the Danish parliament adopted an amendment to the Danish Financial Statements Act (the Report on Social Responsibility for Large Businesses). While voluntary, the law required more than 1,100 of the largest Danish businesses (both private and public sector firms) to prepare and annually submit their CSR activity and performance reports, including on SRI. What is more encouraging is not the requirement to report or the compliance by firms but the content of the reports, which instils a sense of responsibility and ownership in the firms. Firms report not only on their policies but also on the execution of those policies in terms of moving from plans to actions/activities and then a review of activities to ascertain the extent or level of achievements vis-à-vis the plans and targets. For firms yet to adopt CSR or SRI policies, it is also required that their annual report contains an explanation of their reasons for non-adoption and the state of their CSR or SRI practice (Fox et al., 2002; UN Global Compact, 2010; Steurer, 2015).

Another interesting achievement is the creation of the Social Responsibility Council in 2009. Functioning as an advisory body to the government on CSR-related issues, it draws its membership from the business sector, the investment community, trade unions, NGOs, consumer groups and academia. This ensures robust engagement and an inclusive CSR/SRI approach through the involvement and contributions of different stakeholders. In addition to this inclusive approach, another step that can be described as a good achievement is the development of several online tools by the government to support CSR/SRI understanding and practice. Some of the tools include the 'Ideas Compass', which supports SMEs in applying more creativity and innovation in CSR activities; the 'CSR Compass', which provides real-world direction and support on issues relating to responsible supply chain management; the 'Climate Compass', for companies to learn and use in their efforts to reduce carbon emissions; and the 'Global Compact Self-Assessment Tool', which supports firms in understanding and practising the ten principles of the UN Global Compact. These tools, among other factors, have resulted in a rapid increase in the number of Danish firms participating in the UN Global Compact, currently at more than 490 firms (see Fox et al., 2002; UN Global Compact, 2010; Steurer, 2015; UN Global Compact, 2021).

3.7.2 *Botswana*

In Botswana, the African Comprehensive HIV/AIDs Partnership (ACHAP) can be described as a good example of public sector involvement and promotion of social responsibility. With the key stakeholders – local communities, NGOs, academia, the private sector, development institutions and government agencies – involved, a stable and reliable structure was created through ACHAP that enabled the government to achieve positive and sustainable results. Given the success achieved, ACHAP has been emulated by other countries such as China, which created a similar public–private partnership in 2005 (see Fox et al., 2002; UN Global Compact, 2010).

The success of ACHAP can also be attributed to the main partners and the partnership roles played by the government of Botswana. With Merck & Co and the Bill & Melinda Gates Foundation as the main partners, the government of Botswana acted as a critical partner on several fronts – from moderator to facilitator – in harnessing and synergising the expertise, competencies and resources of the Botswana public service with those of both Merck & Co and the Bill & Melinda Gates Foundation. Established in 2000 as a five-year partnership, Merck effectively utilised both its experience as a pharmaceutical company and its involvement in other philanthropic projects, particularly those relating to access to medicines, to help develop a detailed and convincing framework that touched on all aspects of HIV/AIDS. This was followed by a contribution of USD 50 million each from Merck and the Gates Foundation to jump-start ACHAP. With a focus on helping reduce the spread of HIV/AIDS and also mitigating the impact of infections in Botswana, ACHAP in 2003 helped in the development of a National Strategic Framework for HIV/AIDS in Botswana for 2003–9 and then in 2009, the plan for the second phase covering 2009–12 was developed. To achieve the focus of the plan, six main objectives were pursued: 1) scaling up HIV prevention; 2) increasing HIV/AIDS treatment services; 3) expanding HIV counselling and testing capacities, including post-test services; 4) advocating and empowering communities and people living with HIV/AIDS; 5) improving ACHAP's institutional capacity; and 6) strengthening partnership and capacity-building aimed at combating HIV/AIDs in Botswana (see Fox et al., 2002; UN Global Compact, 2010; African Comprehensive HIV/AIDs Partnership (ACHAP), 2018).

Having developed several strategies to combat the spread of HIV/AIDs including the National Condom Management Strategy, the Blood Safety and Youth HIV Prevention Programs, the Behaviour Change Communication Campaign and the targeting of the co-infection of tuberculosis and HIV with the knowledge of the link of the two diseases, ACHAP can be said to have recorded many achievements and is presently perceived as a continental agency focussed on addressing health challenges and issues (ACHAP, 2018):

1. Focussing on the demand to implement the TB in the Mining Sector in Southern Africa project (TIMS), ACHAP was able, through prudent and effective use of grants in collaboration with the East African National Networks of AIDS Service Organizations (EANNASO), to deliver one module

of the grant, Community System Strengthening (CSS), in ten South African developing countries (SADCs) – Botswana, Lesotho, Malawi, Mozambique, Namibia, South Africa, Swaziland, Tanzania, Zambia and Zimbabwe. They also identified two Civil Society Organizations (CSOs) in each of the SADCs to implement the project in their respective countries (ACHAP, 2018).

2. In addition to the advancements in HIV/AIDS treatment, the partnership has also led to a significant increase in the number of HIV-infected people who receive antiretroviral therapy (ART) from about 5 per cent in 2000 to about 84 per cent in 2016. Both the infection rate and the number of deaths are also declining, with infection falling to below 10,000 in 2016 from about 30,000 in 2000. This is also the case with the number of deaths, which declined from about 15,000 in 2000 to fewer than 5,000 in 2016 (World Health Organization (WHO), 2017). Currently, with free treatment being provided for all, it is believed that, in comparison with other Sub-Saharan African countries, Botswana has achieved the highest rate of access to ART treatment (WHO, 2017; ACHAP, 2018).
3. With about 90 per cent ART compliance as of 2009, Botswana is presently believed to be among the highest in the world. Not only has the mortality rate among HIV/AIDS-positive adults significantly declined but mother to child infection has also highly reduced, resulting in an about 80 per cent decline in new infections among children (see WHO, 2017; ACHAP, 2018).
4. With good experience in the Voluntary Medical Male Circumcision (VMMC) program since 2009, Botswana is presently ranked as having one of the lowest levels of reluctance towards VMMC in Africa, with an increasing number of men receiving VMMC. Consequently, the 2017 target of 10,370 circumcisions was surpassed by 6 per cent, with total achieved circumcisions of 11,044 (ACHAP, 2018).
5. To enhance a sense of responsibility and ownership for the sustainability of the project, ACHAP has since 2004 significantly incorporated important cultural factors of Botswana through the involvement, employment and use of local experts to manage both medical and non-medical elements of the projects (UN Global Compact, 2010, ACHAP, 2018).

3.7.3 *China*

China's CSR Guidelines for State-Owned Enterprises, co-ordinated by the State-owned Assets Supervision and Administration Commission of the State Council (SASAC), which rely more on its advocacy for voluntary compliance and are focussed on achieving sustainable development in China, can be said to have succeeded as an effective complement of formal state regulation. With good advocacy of the link between economic profit and sustainable development and its branding as enhancing a firm's reputation and competitiveness, voluntary participation and acceptance are high, with the additional belief that a firm's social and environmental footprints can be advanced through the process (see UN Global Compact, 2010; Tang, 2012; Song and Wen, 2020). Since China joined the World Trade Organization in 2001 and President Hu Jintao launched the 'go global' strategy for Chinese companies in 2002, there has been an increasing acceptance and perception of CSR as an important factor in business decisions and operations (see UN Global Compact, 2010; Tang, 2012). Moreover, with the influence of SASAC such as its ownership of most state-owned enterprises (SOEs), the CSR guidelines can be described as a fundamental shift in CSR development and support in China. In addition to the perception of the guidelines as recommendations, there is an embedded projection of the guidelines as helping in building a 'harmonious society' with the demand for firms to balance economic profit with sustainability and development in their business decisions and actions. Not only are firms encouraged and required to integrate corporate sustainability in their strategies and operations but SOEs are also required to submit reports on their current CSR activities and plans (see UN Global Compact, 2010; Tang, 2012). To further embed CSR, SASAC also recommends that firms should have specially created internal CSR units, collaborate with international organisations for knowledge exchange and sustain stakeholders' dialogues (UN Global Compact 2010).

While SASAC's CSR guidelines can be said to be enjoying wide acceptance, there are other CSR-related laws in China, such as the 2006 Corporate Law and the 2008 Labour Contract Law. There is also the Code of Corporate Governance for Listed Companies in China, issued by the China Securities Regulatory Commission, the State Economic and Trade Commission, the Taida Environmental Index of the Shenzen Stock Exchange and the Green Banking Award (see UN Global Compact 2010; Tang, 2012; Garnaut et al., 2018). However, even with the above laws, the success and achievement of SASAC's guidelines can be attributed to the central involvement of SASAC and the clear objectives of the guidelines. These include advocacy of a 'harmonious society' as the fulcrum of Chinese sustainability; high levels of compliance with the rules and requirements; achievement of energy security; and pursuit of sustainable economic development. Other important objectives also include continuous innovation for better products and services; elimination of corruption; environmental protection; pursuit of employee rights; increasingly efficient extraction of natural resources; and pursuit of a positive international image for China and Chinese SOEs as a way of advancing their global competitiveness and acceptance (see UN Global Compact, 2010; Tang, 2012; Garnaut et al., 2018).

With SASAC's commitment to the guidelines and their influence on SOEs, it can be argued that remarkable progress has been made starting with its 2008 report, the first high-ranking agency of the State Council to publicly issue a social responsibility report. As early as 2009, about thirty-five high-level SOEs had published sustainability reports on their activities in Africa. This was followed by reports from China National Petroleum Corporation (CNPC) on its sustainability activities in Kazakhstan and Sudan and the listing of China Mobile on the Dow Jones Sustainability Index. Other remarkable achievements include the increasing creation of CSR committees and special units in firms, starting with about fifty firms in 2009; incorporation of CSR into management systems, with about fifty firms in 2009; and increasing awareness and practice of better risk management systems through the setting up of such systems and units in big firms such as China Ocean Shipping Company (COSCO), State Grid and China Mobile (see UN Global Compact, 2010).

While there is no doubt that the CSR efforts and achievements in Botswana, Denmark and China are very encouraging and possibly can be expanded and replicated in other countries, there are obvious differences in the needs and approaches used. This suggests that it might be difficult to identify a 'one size fits all' that can be applied across all societies and economies. With differences in culture, governance styles and regulations, needs and other peculiarities across nations in line with institutional theory (see North, 1990), the question is what model can be used to achieve the required outcomes in different societies? As there might not be a 'one size fits all' approach, insights from the experiences and approaches used in different countries can help in providing a guideline of key steps that countries can utilise in developing and implementing a coherent and impactful CSR framework (see UN Global Impact, 2010).

3.8 DEVELOPING A CSR POLICY FRAMEWORK: SIX KEY STEPS

With embedding and increasing awareness and practice of CSR across businesses for long-term societal benefits including improvements in ESG arguably the key aim of government involvement in CSR, there are six critical steps that can help every government or economy in creating a meaningful CSR policy framework.

3.8.1 *Step 1: What Is the Context and What Are the Peculiarities?*

With every society having a set of specific peculiarities, a key step to start formulating a CSR framework is a deep understanding of the context – the cultural systems including norms and values, formal and informal political structures and leadership dynamics, formal and informal economic systems, religious groups and activities, government and society relationships. On the socio-cultural systems, it is important to understand the social embeddedness (peculiar norms and values) and its interaction with the formal institutional systems and how their interaction determines the governance system and then the allocation of resources within the society (see Williamson, 2000). Also important is the make-up of the society in terms of tribal homogeneity or heterogeneity (plural society) and how the make-up influences intratribal integration, intertribal synergy, state–society relations and governance competence and coherence (see Woolcock, 1998). Examination of the above factors will help in understanding issues such as the level of social cohesion and related problems such as gender/class relations and management, openness to negotiation and conflict management, group and individual participation in groups such as NGOs and other public-oriented engagements. In addition to these, it might also be important to consider issues relating to corporate governance, reporting and disclosure, responsible production and consumption, community involvement and development (see North, 1990; Ngwu et al., 2016).

On the economic factors, it is important to understand economic structures and divisions into formal and informal sub-economies and how their interactions influence and determine economic activities (see North, 1990; Williamson, 2000). Also important is the level of development of the economy and its integration into the global economy. This relates to issues of export/import balances, levels of both foreign direct and foreign portfolio investments (FDI and FPI), types of economic policy and disposition to issues of liberalisation, privatisation and nationalisation, diversification of the economy in terms of economic sectors, levels of development and performance (see UN Global Compact, 2010; Dicken, 2015).

For political factors, it is important to understand the levels of government capacity and competence in discharging governance responsibilities. These can be ascertained from the performance of the country in key governance indicators such as the rule of law, regulatory quality and government effectiveness, voice and accountability, and level of corruption (see Kaufman and Kray, 2020). Related to the above factors is the need to understand other factors such as the perception and level of connectedness and integration of the country/government with the global political and economic power circles (see UN Global Compact, 2010; Dicken, 2015).

3.8.2 *Step 2: Contextual Understanding and Definition of CSR*

While the general definition of CSR is not in doubt, the understanding and meaning vary across societies owing to differences in specific institutional peculiarities (UN Global Compact, 2010; Jamali and Karam, 2018). It therefore suggests that a good appreciation of local peculiarities is important in crafting a CSR definition that will be meaningful, accepted and owned by the key stakeholders of the society in question (see Amaeshi et al., 2016; Jamali and Karam, 2018). Moreover, as the increasing demand on businesses to take more interest in contributing to solving societal problems can be described as new and emerging, a robust understanding of CSR issues on the part of government is critical to support effective integration of CSR in government policies and actions (Fox et al., 2002; UN Global Compact, 2010; Steurer, 2015). With such an approach, governments will be in a more informed position in formulating CSR policies, engaging the private sector and other stakeholders and guiding the relationships for sustainable positive impacts. To achieve such outcomes, it might be helpful to consider the following:

1. While some governments are trying to make CSR mandatory, it is important to understand that it is inclined more to voluntary business actions.
2. CSR policies should be formulated and communicated as something good for businesses, government and society; as CSR is good for all, it should be perceived and practised as something beyond regulations and compliance. To buttress this, the three-dimensional aspects of CSR should always be noted. First is that CSR is good for business as it focusses on addressing key issues that are central to a firm's sustainable growth such as labour and human rights, ESG factors and their links to and impacts on management, profitability, risks and other performance issues. Second is that CSR helps in transforming firms into responsible corporate citizens through the actions and inactions of businesses, particularly as they relate to fundamental social demands. Third, CSR helps in the wider progressive development of society through mechanisms such as public–private partnerships and self-regulatory frameworks (see Fox et al., 2002; UN Global Compact, 2010; Steurer, 2015).
3. It is also important to note, with the focus of CSR on ESG issues, that not only are the negative impacts (externalities) that might emanate from the activities and inactions of businesses reduced but higher standards of behaviour that will moderate subsequent activities and behaviours are inadvertently established.
4. With the increasing awareness and practice of the benefits of CSR and its focus on things such as ESG, it suggests that CSR, while still in search of new frameworks for better public–private partnerships, can also help in better allocation of responsibilities for social problems principally between the public and the private sectors (Fox and Howard, 2002; UN Global Compact, 2010; Steurer, 2015).
5. CSR should not be perceived as a replacement or substitute for state intervention; rather, it should be considered and pursued as a complement.

3.8.3 *Step 3: Locating or Integrating CSR within a Government Structure or Agency*

To ensure good ownership, monitoring and leadership in the formulation and execution of CSR policies, it is recommended that a specific government agency is made responsible and that critical internal and external stakeholders are strategically involved in the design and execution process. Two important steps might be helpful to achieve this:

1. First, there is a need to establish and sustain CSR competency. As CSR awareness and practice are still emerging, particularly in developing and

emerging economies, the need for competency, consistency, co-ordination and commitment to the formulation and execution of CSR policies cannot be overemphasised. Achieving that will require identification or creation of a government agency that will co-ordinate the definition and vision of CSR policies, as well as the formulation, communication, implementation, monitoring and impact assessment of those CSR policies. In certain circumstances, there might be an existing government agency that already has the required competency such that it can be allocated the CSR co-ordination task. A good example is Germany where the responsibility is allocated to the Ministry of Employment and Social Affairs. In other situations where there is no pre-existing agency with the needed competency, a new one can be created, as is the case in Costa Rica. Irrespective of the situation, what is evident is that the effective formulation and execution of CSR policies might be better handled through a specific government agency that co-ordinates with a good understanding of the interdisciplinary and interconnected nature of CSR (see Fox and Howard, 2002; UN Global Compact, 2010; Steurer, 2015).

2. With such orientation of the interdisciplinary nature of CSR, it means that all CSR activities such as formulation, communication, execution, impact monitoring and reporting should be pursued in a somewhat collegial manner, drawing on and utilising the rich and diverse knowledge and expertise of the different stakeholders such as NGOs, trade unions, scientific and academic communities, host communities and other government agencies. Through this approach, a sense of ownership of and responsibility for all the CSR activities will be embedded across the different stakeholders and expectedly may result in better and wider involvement and outcomes. Moreover, with such a rich reservoir of knowledge, the government is better endowed to initiate policies that will gain wide interest, participation and impact. Engagement of stakeholders can be in different forms, such as consultation meetings during policy formulation stages, and then advance to continuous engagement and involvement in the implementation and monitoring stages (see Fox and Howard, 2002; UN Global Compact, 2010; Steurer, 2015).

3.8.4 *Step 4: Contextualised Definition of the CSR Public Policy Rationale*

With good appreciation of the contextual peculiarities of CSR's comprehensive scope and meaning, and awareness of the existing or potential government structures and agencies that can be used to support CSR, the government will be in a better position to craft rationales behind any CSR policy framework. Expectedly, the rationales will be dictated or influenced by peculiar social problems to be tackled and the sectors they fall into, the attitudes and dispositions of both local private and civil society stakeholders, the extent of integration with both formal national and global economies, and the state of development of the society's economic system and structures. While the rationales for DEMs normally include efforts to integrate their economies into the global markets and to address key development challenges such as poverty, child labour and unemployment, rationales that can be said to apply to both developed and developing economies include:

1. to achieve growth and development that can be described as equitable and sustainable;
2. to improve both national and international competitiveness, starting with creating a supportive local business environment;
3. to provide deliberate support to local businesses to encourage them to engage in export-oriented activities, including activities and operations outside the country;
4. to proactively understand and manage the pressures and influences of external actors;
5. to identify and resolve major social and environmental problems, particularly those that impede sustainable socio-economic growth and development;
6. to improve the capacity and capability of the government and its pursuit of cross-sectoral partnerships to achieve objectives and goals (see Fox and Howard, 2002; UN Global Compact, 2010; Steurer, 2015).

3.8.5 *Step 5: Identifying Appropriate Types of Policy Intervention for CSR*

With the wide differences in societal peculiarities, selecting the policy interventions suitable for a particular society or economy is crucial in formulating and executing impactful CSR policies. It is therefore imperative for the government to ensure that the policy options are unambiguous and in line with the contextual realities and rationales for CSR intervention. To enhance both the formulation and the execution of policies, already existing local policies and external ones from other countries can be leveraged by the government to achieve better outcomes. Interestingly, the above can be pursued through the awareness-raising, partnering, soft law and mandating roles and instruments of government (see UN Global Compact, 2010).

3.8.6 *Step 6: Monitoring and Impact Assessment*

As noted in Section 3.7, the sustainable positive impact being achieved by the governments of Denmark, Botswana and China in their efforts to promote CSR awareness and practice can be attributed to specific factors, including an embedded and effective monitoring and evaluation system. While few governments have a properly established monitoring and evaluation process, it is perceived as crucial and the last step of the CSR public policy framework. It helps to ascertain the continued commitment of all the relevant stakeholders and then the gaps in the different steps, processes, policies and activities towards achieving the set goals and objectives. The inherent feedback in the monitoring and evaluation process also provides an opportunity for the review and strengthening of the CSR plans and strategy. Key areas to focus on in a monitoring and evaluation process include:

1. the nature and scale of activities;
2. the intended impact of the activities such as the targeted number and type of beneficiaries of the activities;
3. the level of impact and inclusiveness achieved with the activities, such as the diversity of businesses impacted;
4. how the micro, local and regional activities are co-ordinated, harmonised and integrated into the national strategic plan; and
5. the possibility of replicating the impactful activities in other local or national contexts.

With a focus on the above areas and others as might be required based on the contextual peculiarities, the government can better understand the interests and challenges of the business community relative to the CSR agenda and, through such interaction and feedback, better engagement, policies and governance can be achieved. This can be attributed to the extent of performance or preparedness on key governance issues such as rule of law, regulatory quality and government effectiveness (see Kaufman and Kray, 2020).

3.9 CONCLUSION

While CSR started as a task and concern of the private sector, it is gradually also becoming a major public sector concern and discourse. In a traditional market economy, government intervention through policies and regulations is normally used to correct market failures, while government failures are normally corrected by the invitation of market forces through the private sector for better productivity, efficiency and profitability. In the case of CSR, it is neither a market failure nor a government failure. It is more of a shared responsibility that mutually benefits both the private and the public sectors.

For the government, CSR helps in reducing the governance burden through the CSR activities of the private sector, which complement government development efforts. In the same vein, CSR provides both short- and long-term benefits to firms, with evidence of the better performance of CSR-inclined firms in the long term as compared to non-CSR-inclined firms. The role of the government is therefore in combining both regulatory and non-regulatory strategies to enhance awareness and practice of CSR. CSR policy instruments include informational instruments, fiscal-economic instruments, legal instruments (mandatory and soft laws) and partnering and hybrid instruments. With these instruments and based on the context and peculiarities of the environment in question, the government can formulate and implement a coherent CSR framework using the six-step approach outlined in Section 3.8 as a guide.

REFERENCES

African Comprehensive HIV/AIDS Partnership (ACHAP). (2018). *2017 Annual Report*. Gaborone, Botswana: ACHAP Head Office. www.achap.org/resources/2017_ACHAP_Annual_Report.pdf.

Amaeshi, K., Adegbite, E., Ogbechie, C., Idemudia, U., Seny Kan, K. A., Isa, M. and Anakwue, O. (2016). Corporate social responsibilities in SME: a shift from philanthropy to institutional works? *Journal of Business Ethics*, **138**, 385–400. doi10.1007/s10551-015-2633-1.

Banerjee, S. B. (2008). Corporate social responsibility: the good, the bad and the ugly. *Critical Sociology*, **34**(1), 51–79.

Bartle, I. and Vass, P. (2007). Self-regulation within the regulatory state: towards a new regulatory paradigm? *Public Administration*, **85**(4), 885–905.

Bishop, A. J. (1990). Western mathematics: the secret weapon of cultural imperialism. *Race & Class*, **32**(2), 51–65.

Blaug, M. (1993). Pieter Hennipman on Paretian welfare economics: a comment. *De Economist*, **141**(1), 127–9.

Cadbury, A. (1999). Foreword to *Corporate Governance: A Framework for Implementation: Overview*. World Bank Report. Washington, DC: World Bank.rtog, P. (2000). Knowledge-intensive business services as co-producers of innovation. *International Journal of Innovation Management*, **4**(4), 491–528.

Dicken, P. (2015). *Global Shift-Mapping the Changing Contours of the World Economy*, 7th ed. Guildford, UK: Guildford Publications.

Esmark, A. (2009). The functional differentiation of governance: public governance beyond hierarchy, market and networks. *Public Administration*, **87**(2), 351–70.

European Commission. (2006). *Implementing the Partnership for Growth and Jobs: Making Europe a Pole of Excellence on Corporate Social Responsibility*. COM (2006) 136 final. http://eur-lex.europa.eu/LexUriServ/site/en/com/2006/com2006_0136en01.pdf.

European Council. (2000). Presidency conclusions. *Lisbon European Council*, 23 and 24 March, DOC/00/8. http://ue.eu.int/en/Info/eurocouncil/index.htm.

European Council. (2006). *Renewed EU Sustainable Development Strategy*. 10917/06. http://ec.europa.eu/sustainable/docs/renewed_eu_sds_en.pdf.

Fox, T., Ward, H. and Howard, B. (2002). *Public Sector Roles in Strengthening Corporate Social Responsibility: A Baseline Study*. Washington, DC: World Bank. http://pubs.iied.org/pdfs/16017IIED.pdf.

Garnaut, R., Song, L. and Fang, C., eds. (2018). *China's 40 Years of Reform and Development 1978–2018*. Melbourne: Australian University Press.

Gjølberg, M. (2010). Varieties of corporate social responsibility (CSR): CSR meets the 'Nordic Model'. *Regulation & Governance*, **4**(2), 203–29.

Hennipman, P. (1992). The reasoning of a great methodologist: Mark Blaug on the nature of Paretian welfare economics. *De Economist*, **140**(4), 413–45.

Howlett, M. (2009). Governance modes, policy regimes and operational plans: a multi-level nested model of policy instrument choice and policy design. *Policy Sciences*, **42**(1), 73–89.

Howlett, M. and Ramesh, M. (1993). Patterns of policy choice. *Policy Studies Review*, **12**, 3–24.

Jamali, D. and Karam, C. (2018). Corporate social responsibility in developing countries as an emerging field of study. *International Journal of Management Reviews*, **20**(1), 32–61.

Jarrell, G. A. (1984). Change at the exchange: the causes and effects of deregulation. *Journal of Law and Economics*, **27**(2), 273–312.

Kaufmann, D. and Kray, A. (2020). *Worldwide Governance Indicators*. Washington, DC: World Bank.

Knill, C. and Lehmkuhl, D. (2002). Private actors and the state: internationalization and changing patterns of governance. *Governance*, **15**(1), 41–63.

Knopf, J., Kahlenborn, W., Hajduk, T., Weiss, D., Feil, M., Fiedler, R. and Klein, J. (2011). *Corporate Social Responsibility: National Public Policies in the European Union*. Brussels: European Commission; Directorate-General for Employment, Social Affairs and Inclusion.

Koop, C. and Lodge, M. (2015). What is regulation? An interdisciplinary concept analysis. *Regulation and Governance*, **11**(1), 95–108.

Lepoutre, J., Dentchev, N. and Heene, A. (2007). Dealing with uncertainties when governing CSR policies. *Journal of Business Ethics*, **73**(4), 391–408.

Lorzano, J. M., Albareda, L. and Ysa, T. (2008). *Governments and Corporate Social Responsibility: Public Policies Beyond Regulation and Voluntary Compliance*. Basingstoke, UK: Palgrave Macmillan.

Majone, G. (1994). The rise of the regulatory state in Europe. *West European Politics*, **17**(3), 77–101.

Mthanti, T. and Ojah, K. (2017). Entrepreneurial orientation (EO): measurement and policy implications of entrepreneurship at the macroeconomic level. *Research Policy*, **46**, 724–39.

Ngwu, F. N., Osuji, O. K. and Stephen, F. H. (2016). *Corporate Governance in Developing and Emerging Markets*. Abingdon, UK: Routledge.

Norrestad F. (2021). Europe: socially responsible investments as share of total managed assets 2014–2018. Statista. www.statista.com/statistics/717805/socially-responsible-investments-as-share-of-total-managed-assets-europe/.

North, D. C. (1990). *Institutions, Institutional Change and Economic Performance*. Cambridge: Cambridge University Press.

Ogus, A. (2004). Corruption and regulatory structures. *Law & Policy, University of Denver*, **26** (3–4), 329–46.

Osuji, O. K., Ngwu, F. N. and Jamali, D., eds. (2019). *Corporate Social Responsibility in Developing and Emerging Markets: Institutions, Actors and Sustainable Development*. Cambridge: Cambridge University Press.

Pedersen, E. R. G., ed. (2015). *Corporate Social Responsibility*. London: Sage.

Peltzman, S. (1989). *The Economic Theory of Regulation after a Decade of Deregulation*. Brookings Papers on Economic Activity (Microeconomics). www.brookings.edu/wp-content/uploads/1989/01/1989_bpeamicro_peltzman.pdf.

Polinsky, A. M. and Shavell, S. (1979). The optimal trade-off between the probability and magnitude of fines. *American Economic Review*, **69**(5), 880–91.

Posner, R. A. (1974). Theories of economic regulation. *Bell Journal of Economics and Management Science*, **5**, 335–58.

Riess, B. and Welzel, C. (2006). *Partner Staat? CSR-Politik in Europa*. Gütersloh: Bertelsmann Stiftung. www.bertelsmann-stiftung.de/fileadmin/files/BSt/Presse/imported/downloads/xcms_bst_dms_17243_17244_2.pdf.

Rose-Ackerman, S. (1992). *Rethinking the Progressive Agenda: The Reform of the American Regulatory State*. New York: Free Press.

Scholtens, B., Cerin, P. and Hassel, L. (2008). Sustainable development and socially responsible finance and investing. *Sustainable Development*, **16**(3), 137–40.

Selznick, P. (1985). Focusing organisational research on regulation. In R. Noll, ed., *Regulatory Policy and the Social Sciences*. Berkeley: University of California Press, pp. 363–4.

Song, B. and Wen, J. (2020). Online corporate social responsibility communication strategies and stakeholder engagements: a comparison of controversial versus noncontroversial industries. *Corporate Social Responsibility and Environmental Management*, **27**(2), 881–96.

Steurer, R. (2010). The role of governments in corporate social responsibility: characterising public policies on CSR in Europe. *Policy Sciences*, **43**(1), 49–72.

Steurer, R. (2013). Disentangling governance: a synoptic view of regulation by government, business and civil society. *Policy Science*, **46**, 387–410.

Steurer, R. (2015). CSR and governments: public policies on CSR in Europe. In E. R. G. Pedersen, ed., *Corporate Social Responsibility*. London: Sage, pp. 240–66.

Stoker, G. (1998). Governance as theory: five propositions. *International Social Science Journal*, **50**(155), 17–28.

Tang, L. (2012). Media discourse of corporate social responsibility in China: a content analysis of newspapers. *Asian Journal of Communication*, **22**(3), 270–88.

Thomas, A. (2014). Media-reported corporate governance transgressions in broad-based black economic empowerment deals in the South African mining sector. *African Journal of Business Ethics*, 8(2), 89–107.

UN Global Compact and Bertelsmann Stiftung. (2010). *The Role of Governments in Promoting Corporate Responsibility and Private Sector Engagement in Development*. New York: UN Global Compact Office. www.bertelsmann-stiftung.de/en/publications/publication/did/the-role-of-governments-in-promoting-corporate-responsibility-and-private-sector-engagement-in-devel/.

United Nations Global Compact. (2021). *UN Global Compact Strategy, 2021–2023*. New York: United Nations.

Viscusi, W., Vernon, J. and Harrington, Jr, J.E. (2001). *Economics of Regulation and Antitrust*. Cambridge, MA: MIT Press.

Weingast, B. R. (1981). Regulation, deregulation, and deregulation: the political foundations of agency clientele relationships. *Law and Contemporary Problems*, **44**, 147–77. https://scholarship.law.duke.edu/lcp/vol44/iss1/6.

Williamson, O. (2000). The new institutional economics: taking stock, looking ahead. *Journal of Economic Literature*, **38**(3), 595–613.

Woolcock, M. (1998). Social capital and economic development: toward a theoretical synthesis and policy framework. *Theory and Society*, **27**(2), 151–208.

World Health Organization (WHO). (2017). *Botswana HIV Country Profile: 2016*. Geneva: WHO. www.who.int/hiv/data/Country_profile_Botswana.pdf?ua=1.

4

Governance of Firms, Poverty and Shared Responsibilities for Human Rights in UNGPs: Smart-Mix Regulation and CSR within Coalitions of the (Un)Willing

Onyeka K. Osuji (with contributions from Gary Lynch-Wood[*]*)*

[N]o social phenomenon is as comprehensive in its assault on human rights as poverty. Poverty erodes or nullifies economic and social rights such as the right to health, adequate housing, food and safe water, and the right to education. The same is true of civil and political rights, such as the right to a fair trial, political participation and security of the person. This fundamental recognition is reshaping the international community's approach to the next generation of poverty reduction initiatives.[1]

4.1 INTRODUCTION

Firms play a critical role in helping to tackle poverty, as reflected across policies on private sector development (Department for International Development (DFID), 2011; Davis, 2016; Organisation for Economic Co-operation and Development (OECD), 2016; United Nations Development Programme (UNDP), 2018). In developing countries, for example, it is said that the private sector accounts for around 60 per cent of gross domestic product (GDP), 90 per cent of jobs and 80 per cent of capital flows (UNDP, 2018). The productive activities of firms help to raise standards of living (Lodge and Wilson, 2006; Shepherd and Mariotti, 2015). Firms create employment opportunities that provide people with resources, while appropriate working conditions can increase self-confidence, facilitate social participation, and offer security and prospects for advancement. The taxes that are generated by business growth and employment can fund programmes (e.g., education, health care, social security) that further help to address poverty.

Yet, the news is not all encouraging. Firms may trade in sectors where the competitive pressures to deliver 'more for less' can be passed to workers in the form of low wages, job insecurity and denial of basic human rights (Shepherd and Mariotti, 2015). Firms have been known to use their power to suppress people's efforts to escape poverty by contributing to human rights violations (Clapham and Jerbi, 2000; Wettstein, 2010; Amao, 2011; Gatto, 2011; International Federation for

Human Rights, 2016; Amnesty International, 2017; Nolan and Bott, 2018; Human Rights Watch, 2020). They have been known to buy products produced using forced or undeclared labour, or to source from firms using underage labour. They have been known to restrict, or to be complicit in restricting, freedom of expression and association, or to have worked with state agencies to suppress opposition or demonstrations. They have been known to force workers – or generate the structural conditions wherein supply-chain workers are forced – to work long and poorly paid hours in substandard conditions. Firms can contaminate or seize land and resources vital to local communities or displace indigenous communities from land for profit. Thus, people may be kept in conditions of poverty by the actions of for-profit enterprises.

There are, across the globe, fundamental human rights problems. The conventional position, embedded in international law, is that responsibility for protecting rights resides with states. This is because of the traditional concept of sovereignty and the jurisdictional authority of states, which has enabled them to abuse rights (e.g., suppressing demonstration) and to safeguard rights (e.g., through laws or constitutional measures). There has, however, been an increasingly vociferous challenge to this view since experiences have revealed that rights cannot be guaranteed by governments alone (Cassel, 2001) and because it is unsuited to a global society where firms wield considerable economic, social and political power (Spar, 1998; MacLeod and Lewis, 2004; Wettstein, 2010; Gatto, 2011; Renouard and Ezvan, 2018). Questions have been raised over whether private entities – predominantly multinational enterprises (MNEs) – should take a greater role in helping to safeguard people's rights. The developing role of the firms, in the context of shared responsibilities of multiple national and international actors, is the focus of this chapter. Considering international policies on poverty and rights, and the roles of different actors, the chapter considers the development and ongoing governance challenges around one of the main solutions to the human rights problem: the United Nations Guiding Principles on Business and Human Rights (UNGPs) (United Nations, 2011). The UNGPs, which have attracted considerable attention, resulted from years of pressure for more effective international measures to address corporate abuses, pressure fuelled, for example, by claims of 'sweatshop' labour in the apparel and footwear industries in Asia, Shell's activities in Nigeria, Unocal's and Total's complicity in forced labour in Burma, and Coca-Cola's depriving local communities of water in India (Harrison, 2013). The UNGPs have been widely supported at policy level and have been incorporated in other international instruments (Bonnitcha and McCorquodale, 2017). Yet, despite their contribution to human rights discourse, and some important applied developments (e.g., National Action Plans (NAPs)), the framework's soft principles continue to leave potential governance gaps, which we explore in this chapter. In considering the UNGPs, we draw from the idea of the 'coalitions of the willing' (Tondini, 2017; Erskine, 2018; Rodiles, 2020), which is used to describe the workings of international law, and suggest that their soft-law governance frameworks are a reflection of the (un)willingness of key players to act. At the same time, the UNGPs signify the potential wider governance role of corporate social responsibility (CSR) in that context. We start by providing a short context for the relationship between poverty and human rights, and then look at the development of the UNGPs before considering some of the ongoing governance challenges.

4.2 POVERTY IN A HUMAN RIGHTS CONTEXT

Global poverty is a critical and ongoing problem, one compounded by the Covid-19 pandemic that is likely to push more people into extreme poverty (World Bank Group, 2021). The problem of poverty does not only affect the unemployed. It was reported in 2019 that more than 630 million workers worldwide, almost 1 in 5, did not earn enough to remove themselves or their families from extreme or moderate poverty (International Labour Organization (ILO), 2020). Problems of low income are often associated with poor working conditions (ILO, 2020). Moreover, many of the world's poorest people have limited access to food, water, shelter, education and appropriate health care, some of the essential requirements for lifting people from poverty.

Tackling poverty is at the heart of international policy. It is central to the UN Sustainable Development Goals (SDGs), which superseded the Millennium Development Goals. They contain 17 goals and 167 targets intended to serve as a framework to guide global and national development, which member states have agreed to work towards by 2030. Goal 1 is to 'end poverty in all its forms everywhere'. The Agenda for 2030, the Agenda for Sustainable Development, recognises that eradicating poverty is among the greatest global challenges. Moreover, the complex problem of poverty is inextricably linked to human rights issues (Sen, 1999; Pogge, 2005; Vizard, 2006; Ferraz, 2008; Andreassen and Banik, 2010; Sofo and Wicks, 2017). Denying or restricting rights, the essential conditions for people to live with liberty and dignity, reinforces poverty, while those living in poverty often have restricted means of securing rights, or have them supressed. Thus, where you find poverty you are likely to uncover fragile human rights frameworks, and vice versa. Reframing poverty as a human rights issue (instead of, for example, as an issue that is dependent on charity) may lead to more fundamental institutional responses.

The link between poverty and human rights is central to international law frameworks. This is clear from the SDGs, which embrace issues relating to human rights.[2] Also, the 1945 UN Charter sets out the rights and duties of member states, reaffirms faith in fundamental rights and refers to the promotion of the economic and social advancement of all peoples. The Universal Declaration of Human Rights (UDHR), adopted by the UN General Assembly in 1948, is considered the foundation of international human rights law. Described as a crucial reference point for cross-cultural discussions of human freedom and dignity (Glendon, 1997), it remains an authoritative moral standard for global society (Hilgert, 2019). The Declaration was formulated on the acknowledgement that the inherent dignity and the inalienable rights of people provide the foundation of freedom, justice and peace. The text, for example its reference to social and economic rights, confirms how poverty is contrary to the spirit and terms of the UDHR. It says that people are entitled to realisation, through national efforts and international co-operation, and in accordance with state resources, of the economic, social and cultural rights indispensable for dignity and the free development of personality. It sets out a series of rights related to work, choice of employment, just and favourable work conditions, protection against unemployment, equal pay, freedom from discrimination, and remuneration ensuring an existence worthy of human dignity.

In several international instruments is found a network of economic, political and social rights that underpins poverty reduction. The UDHR is codified through two relevant treaties. The International Covenant on Civil and Political Rights (1966) covers issues such as forced labour, freedom of expression and freedom of association, while the International Covenant on Economic, Social and Cultural Rights (1966) guarantees such rights as just and favourable work conditions, forming and joining unions, and education. These instruments are important components of the UN system for protecting rights. Other Conventions focus on particular issues (e.g., racial and gender discrimination, working conditions). The International Labour Organization (ILO) Conventions, international treaties that are legally binding for states that have ratified them, cover numerous issues including minimum wages, discrimination and industrial relations.

Since human rights entered the language of international law, it has been clear that the primary actors responsible for protecting rights are states (as duty bearers) and intergovernmental organisations such as the UN (Frey, 1997; Brownlie, 2019). International instruments establish wide-ranging obligations that governments and their agencies owe to citizens. Broadly, states should use international policy instruments as a framework for policy guidance and development. They should take appropriate actions to respect rights by not impeding citizens' enjoyment of them, and to protect rights by ensuring that other actors (e.g., firms) do not obstruct them. States should also fulfil their obligations through measures ensuring that rights are realised (e.g., provision of accessible information, resources, remedies).

Given the ongoing problem of poverty, and its connection to human rights, questions have been raised over whether existing approaches are sufficient and whether states have it in their domain of influence to effectively address the problem. Tackling poverty and human rights issues is intertwined with economic, political and institutional processes, and firms have become integral to these processes. It is acknowledged across policy domains that single-actor, single-layer strategies are often inadequate. Tackling global problems requires partnerships, multi-stakeholder initiatives and shared responsibilities. This idea has become an important aspect of poverty and sustainable development, with the appreciation that addressing poverty issues requires collaborative approaches that embrace the ideas and resources of citizens, communities, non-governmental bodies, multilateral institutions, local and national government, businesses, academia and private philanthropy (United Nations, 2013). Yet, the idea of shared responsibilities raises complex problems. Who should be involved? What roles should different actors have? How do you design effective policy interventions for meaningful shared responsibility? Given the importance of firms to global economic processes, our focus turns to whether and how firms should have more responsibilities for human rights (and poverty) issues.

4.3 SHOULD FIRMS BE MORE ACCOUNTABLE?

The path of international law has seen considerable change and expansion (Ratner, 2001), but it is generally accepted, and human rights discourse is dominated by the view, that firms do not have legal personality or accountability at the international level (Kinley and Tadaki, 2004; Zerk, 2006; Wouters and Chané, 2013; Muchlinski, 2014; Wettstein, 2015; Latorre, 2020). As Kinley and Tadaki (2004, p. 935) have suggested, firms have 'barely [been] recognised, still less directly bound, whether with respect to human rights or any other field. There is no transnational regime of human rights law governing the activities of corporations.' This is not to suggest that firms cannot be held responsible for human rights actions, since responsibilities can be incorporated into national legal frameworks. Domestic measures with human rights implications include laws on health and safety, environmental protection and employment protection (Kinley and Tadaki, 2004).

A question often raised is whether firms should assume greater responsibilities as part of their social functions or status as global citizens. There has been a thriving discussion on the responsibilities of firms, particularly MNEs, since the mid-1990s (Wettstein, 2012; Wettstein et al., 2019), with conflicting views often influenced by ideological viewpoints (Muchlinski, 2001).

The challenges to firms assuming greater responsibilities are often linked, particularly from a Western viewpoint, to dominant political and economic beliefs consisting of neoclassical economics and neo-liberal political philosophies (Friedman, 1970; Thompson, 1990; MacEwan, 1999; Griffiths, 2001). Typically, they start with Friedman (1970), particularly the view that a firm's only social responsibility is to (lawfully) increase profits for shareholders. While there are different interpretations of Friedman (Cosans, 2009), a common reading is that firms should adopt only policies that increase ownership returns. This is based on the agreement between shareholders and managers, which binds the latter to pursuing the interests of the former. As such, pursuing other ends to the detriment of shareholder returns is tantamount to taxing shareholders, which is the task of elected governments (Kolstad, 2007). Firms do not exist, and should not be asked, to make judgements on moral, welfare or human rights issues. Elected officials should modify laws to improve the citizens' social conditions. Firms should not decide on human rights standards as they have been given no authority, do not necessarily have the skills and would be using resources inappropriately.

Other problems derive from the nature of competitive markets and the challenges that might present themselves when firms attempt to secure, say, work-related rights. Consider, for example, the sourcing decisions of firms. The criticisms of firms, of the human rights issues resulting from such decisions, show a misunderstanding of competitive markets and the pressures that buyers can face (Lynch-Wood, 2014). Since firms often face pressures to reduce costs, they may select suppliers offering lower wages or poorer conditions or choose not to invest in wider issues (e.g., local education). If a firm chooses otherwise (e.g., opting not to source from the lowest-cost suppliers), a competitor possibly will. The compassionate firm might then be at a competitive disadvantage (Muchlinski, 2001). Using more expensive sources could cause a firm to lose trade, or close. Many could then lose out as it would harm the work-related interests not only of suppliers but also of the buying firm's employees, possibly through job losses. Balancing work rights may be difficult, particularly in environments where motivations exist for practices that are less desirable.

Thus, given that a firm cannot provide work opportunities for everyone, is it not possible to regard firms as infringing the work-related interests of others whenever they choose to use one supplier rather than another (Lynch-Wood, 2014)? A firm may affect people's rights or interests when it awards orders to suppliers who treat workers with dignity or provide safer working environments, for it will not be giving work opportunities to others. A firm may breach rights norms when its activities lead to people losing jobs or experiencing declining conditions. Thus, through regular and routine business, firms could be impacting on rights if their decisions result in existing suppliers losing work or making redundancies. Firms may analyse their own working practices, and collect information for selecting between in-house production and outsourced alternatives, which may harm the interests of fellow employees. It is, therefore, arguably impossible to avoid some form of work rights 'abuse' since that would require an end to negotiations and buying decisions altogether. Accordingly, firms are faced with challenging decisions involving ethical choices – an intractable ethical impasse. When firms make important selections about resources, someone is likely to lose. What is 'protecting human rights' if it is not properly codified in law and providing rules for all (see Lynch-Wood, 2014)?

Such arguments suggest that firms may lack proper control over human rights matters. Firms are neither conditioned nor able to solve obdurate and structural human rights dilemmas, and should not be asked to. The main thrust of these rationalisations, partially at least, is the existence of unwillingness on the part of firms.

There are several arguments in favour of firms taking greater responsibility for human rights. They often fall into three broad groups: business case, power and influence, and human rights inalienability. First is the 'business case' or market position argument. It suggests that firms should move beyond the shareholder primacy view towards a broader stakeholder view of the firm (Freeman, 1984) since firms benefit when resource decisions consider the full range of stakeholders (Lynch-Wood et al., 2009; Rhou and Singal, 2020). Firms should adopt high standards, and provide human rights protections, as it is in their interests. Treating people with dignity and respect, and adhering to appropriate standards, means that firms are opening themselves to new markets, protecting themselves from the risk of accusations of abuse, or making themselves more appealing to loyal and skilled employees. The modern economy, with the emphasis placed on the importance of CSR, and with informed and digitally savvy consumers and market players who can monitor and publicise poor performance, means that firms should invest in human rights because this is expected of them: it is part of being a socially responsible firm (Mayer, 2009; Ramasastry, 2015). Of course, whether the business case is sufficiently ubiquitous that it can provide adequate human rights protections is open to question and requires rigorous empirical analysis.

The main arguments for greater responsibility, and for tougher institutional responses, are linked to the increasing power and jurisdictional reach of corporations in the modern global economy. The transformations in the global political and economic landscape, and the release of market forces, have enabled corporate ascendency, which has generated power disparities, exposed institutional weaknesses and presented challenges to governability (Strange, 1991, 1996; Brinkman and Brinkman, 2002; Detomasi, 2007; Kinley, 2009; Simons and Macklin, 2014; Babic et al., 2017; Wettstein et al., 2019). Multiple factors have combined to challenge governability, such as the liberalisation of markets providing corporations with greater levels of freedom to move across borders; value chains spanning multiple jurisdictions; weak civil society and institutional structures (e.g., ineffective trade unions) across some states; home state governments (a home state is where an MNE is headquartered) not choosing or being equipped to regulate firms for their conduct abroad; or host state governments failing to implement effective governance mechanisms (e.g., Babic et al., 2017; Schrempf-Stirling, 2018; Schrage and Gilbert, 2019; Wettstein et al., 2019). Corporations have become essential arrangers of economic activity and critical marketplace decision-makers. They are key players across many issues, can have powerful influences over information flows and can influence the policies of governments and the agendas of bodies such as the World Trade Organization (e.g., MacLeod and Lewis, 2004; Amnesty International, 2009). Firms are integral to policy-making processes and often having a strong hand in shaping (or perhaps subduing) rights-related laws (Muchlinski, 2001). Developing states often try to attract investment, giving firms increasing leverage over decisions on social issues (Amnesty International, 2009). Furthermore, firms have taken on what have traditionally been government functions, leading to a lack of distinctiveness over public and private provision. The shifts in power are, of course, contestable. Yet, supporting the point, Yeganeh (2020; see also Serafeim, 2014) describes how in 1980 the world's largest 1,000 MNEs earned USD 2.64 trillion in revenue, employed 21 million people and had a total market capitalisation of USD 900 billion. A little more than 30 years later, in 2012, the largest 1,000 MNEs made USD 34 trillion in revenue, employed 73 million people and had a total market capitalisation of USD 28 trillion. It was reported in 2018 that 69 of the top 100 economic entities were corporations and that the top 10 corporations made more than USD 3 trillion, while of the top 200 entities, 157 were corporations.[3] Babic et al. (2017) suggest that it is 'remarkable' that a business like Walmart has higher revenues than Spain or Australia, while Apple has greater revenues than Belgium, Mexico and Switzerland. The increasing power of firms raises questions over how they affect people's enjoyment of human rights and what they should do to protect them.

Finally, it is arguable that because human rights are inalienable they cannot be removed except in specific situations and according to due process. Human rights are claims of essential and core justice, to which each person is entitled, grounded in fundamental moral principles and set apart from established institutions (Ashford 2007; Latorre, 2020). Since they are inalienable, firms cannot disregard them. Their embeddedness is such that they transcend the ability of individual institutions to safeguard them. Accordingly, firms cannot ignore human rights because states are unable or unwilling to protect them. Irrespective of the capacity and willingness of states, if firms are capable of safeguarding rights, they should.

This is a brief account of the ongoing discussions over firms and human rights. That firms should share responsibilities is evidenced, at least partly, by the emergence of several non-binding international instruments, and particularly the UNGPs whose normative underpinnings are the view that the root causes of business and human rights predicaments are governance gaps created by globalisation (United Nations, 2008; see Cragg, 2015). We now consider the UNGPs and how they embody the shared responsibilities of multiple actors.

4.4 UNGPS AND SHARED RESPONSIBILITIES FOR HUMAN RIGHTS

Several attempts have been made to tackle the human rights impacts of businesses,[4] although they have largely lacked effectiveness owing to lack of political will or to corporate resistance (McCorquodale, 2009). Our focus is the UNGPs. As indicated, their context was the growing concern, particularly in the 1990s, over the harmful impacts of firms. There was a bold attempt to address these concerns with the UN Norms on Transnational Corporations and Other Business Enterprises with Regard to Human Rights 2003 (Backer, 2006). Prepared by an independent expert committee of the (then) Commission on Human Rights, the Norms were seen as something of a 'new vigour' on the part of the UN in regulating corporate abuses (Deva, 2003). It is not difficult to see why. The Norms were significant in trying to establish more of a horizontal effect, declaring that while states had principal responsibility, firms also had responsibilities for promoting and securing rights. By introducing to states obligations seen as comparable, the Norms were the first non-voluntary international initiative with a suggested legal authority that derived mainly from treaties and customary law (Weissbrodt and Kruger, 2003). They were abandoned in 2005 owing to opposition from governments and industry. The Norms were considered flawed from a doctrinal perspective (Jägers, 2011) and regarded as contrary to the positivist foundations of international law, a departure from traditional international law roles and lacking compatibility with states' law-making functions (Miretski and Bachmann, 2012). Though abandoned, the Norms were a milestone in the development of human rights policy, indicating a shift in thinking about corporations and opening new discourse around power and regulation (Backer, 2006).

In 2005, Professor John Ruggie was appointed Special Representative of the Secretary-General on Human Rights and Transnational Corporations and Other Business Enterprises (SRSG). Previously, he served as Assistant Secretary-General and Senior Adviser for Strategic Planning (1997 to 2001) and was one of the architects of the Global Compact.[5] As SRSG, Ruggie had a comprehensive mandate, spreading eventually over three phases (Sanders, 2015), to identify standards of responsibility and accountability for firms. The first phase, from 2005, involved a comprehensive mapping exercise – a programme of research scoping patterns of abuses and emerging practices across states and firms. In the second phase, in 2008, the SRSG presented, and recommended that the Human Rights Council endorse, a 'Protect, Respect and Remedy' framework and agenda for protecting human rights (United Nations, 2008). The framework comprised a state 'duty' to protect against human rights abuses by third parties, a business responsibility to 'respect' rights, and greater access to judicial and non-judicial 'remedies'. It was endorsed by the Human Rights Council, which extended the SRSG's mandate for a third operational phase from 2008 to 2011, so that the framework could be developed (Sanders, 2015). The SRSG posted a draft of the framework's UNGPs for public comment from November 2010 and, following many responses, presented in 2011 the full report for implementation (United Nations, 2011).

The UNGPs elaborate on methods to operationalise the protect, respect and remedy pillars. They are designed to provide substance for states and firms, highlighting what states should do to protect rights and providing guidance on how firms can respect rights. There are three sections, one for each pillar, with each section divided into two further units (part A covering Foundational Principles and part B covering Operational Principles). There are thirty-one principles, with each principle receiving commentary. They are divided as follows:

State Duty to Protect
Foundational Principles: 1 and 2
Operational Principles: 3 to 10
Corporate Responsibility to Respect
Foundational Principles: 11 to 15
Operational Principles: 16 to 21

Remediation
Foundational Principles: 22 to 24
Operational Principles: 25 to 31.

Briefly, the UNGPs set down a series of actions around the pillars. On state duties, they declare that states must protect against human rights abuses within their jurisdiction. This requires taking 'appropriate' steps to prevent, investigate, punish and redress abuses through effective policies and so on. There is discretion over how states may set about safeguarding rights, but they should consider various options, including regulation. While it receives only one reference in the commentary, an important requirement is for states to consider a 'smart mix' of measures – national and international, mandatory and voluntary – to promote business respect for human rights. The UNGPs confirm that while states are not responsible for abuses by firms, they may breach international law obligations where abuses are attributable to their (in)actions. A principle is that states should set down the expectation that firms domiciled in their jurisdiction respect human rights throughout their operations. That said, the UNGPs declare that states are 'not generally' required under international law to regulate the extraterritorial activities of firms domiciled in their jurisdiction, although neither are they 'generally prohibited from doing so' provided a jurisdictional basis exists. The guidance says that there are policy reasons for states to set out clearly the 'expectation' that firms respect rights abroad, particularly where states are involved with those firms. Also, the UNGPs declare that states should enforce appropriate laws, ensure that laws relating to the creation and ongoing operation of firms (e.g., corporate law) enable respect for rights, and provide guidance on how firms should respect rights throughout their operations.

While states retain the exclusive responsibility, firms have the standard of respecting rights. It is not a legal standard in international law but a social expectation (that may find its way into mandatory frameworks: Martin-Ortega, 2014). Firms are responsible for respecting rights, avoiding rights infringements and addressing adverse impacts. Confirming the inalienability of rights, the UNGPs suggest that these responsibilities exist independently of the state's ability to fulfil its obligations and above legal compliance. The responsibility applies to all firms, regardless of size, sector and organisational context. The UNGPs are clear, stating that to meet their responsibilities firms should have in place policies and processes appropriate to size and circumstances. It is recognised that different scales and complexities mean that firms will vary in capacity to meet responsibilities. Additionally, firms should address the impacts resulting from their own activities and their wider business relationships. To operationalise responsibilities, firms should, for example, consider expressing commitment through a policy statement and should undertake due diligence processes (for assessing actual and potential impacts). The due diligence framework, which describes the steps that firms should take to become aware of, prevent and address adverse impacts (United Nations, 2008), promotes adoption of policies and systems that enable effective human rights management.

On remediation, the UNGPs suggest that states should take appropriate steps to ensure that when abuses occur within their jurisdiction, those affected can access appropriate remedies. These may include apologies, restitution, rehabilitation, financial or non-financial compensation and sanctions (e.g., criminal, administrative), as well as prevention of harm through, for example, injunctions or guarantees of non-repetition. Responsibility for remedies is not only with states, as industry and other collaborative initiatives should ensure that effective grievance mechanisms are available. It is recognised that unless states address abuses, the duty to protect is hollow.

From an administrative perspective, it is worth noting that a Working Group on Business and Human Rights was established by the Human Rights Council in 2011. The Working Group, comprising five independent experts, has had its work renewed through successive resolutions. Its remit is to promote the effective and comprehensive dissemination and implementation of the UNGPs, to identify, exchange and promote good practices, and to offer capacity-building support. An important development occurred in June 2014, when the Council called on member states to develop NAPs to implement the UNGPs (Working Group on Business and Human Rights, 2014). A NAP is a state policy strategy outlining the strategic positioning and activities that address a particular issue (Working Group on Business and Human Rights, 2016). As NAPs have been used for some time, the call for NAPs to be used as tools for realising the UNGPs follows their increasing use across other policy domains (O'Brien et al., 2016). The creation of NAPs for human rights is considered important for increasing state accountability (International Corporate Accountability Roundtable (ICAR), 2017) and for identifying governance gaps (Rivera, 2019). The Working Group has encouraged all states, as part of their responsibility for implementing the UNGPs, to develop and update a NAP and has produced implementation guidance (Working Group on Business and Human Rights, 2016). Also, in 2015, owing to ongoing demands for better information from stakeholders, the UNGPs Reporting Framework was developed as a joint initiative to reinforce transparency and accountability.

The UNGPs are an important addition to the business and human rights landscape. Yet, there remain concerns over their capacity for addressing the governance gaps underpinning their development.

4.5 GOVERNANCE CHALLENGES AND UNGPS

When proposed, the UNGPs were seen as having potentially significant consequences for public policy and strategic and daily management of firms (Cragg, 2015). They were an important development in international policy that derived from a comprehensive programme of research. They made a substantial contribution to discourse on business and human rights over the adjustments required to the global landscape, and to discussions of corporate responsibilities (McCorquodale, 2009). Reflecting on the UNGPs, ten years following publication, they are no doubt a well-planned and thought-provoking attempt to bring human rights protections closer to firms. They have become a key reference point for efforts to address abuses (Working Group on Business and Human Rights, 2016). With respect to states, the UNGPs reinforce the duty to protect rights as central to international law. States are answerable and should adopt measures to prevent abuses. Importantly, the UNPGs have reinforced the messaging around effective regulation. For firms, the principles have embedded the view that they have a responsibility to respect rights, irrespective of size or context. At least symbolically, they provide an important institutional and policy riposte to the conventional view that human rights are only a challenge for states and are beyond the authority of firms. The UNGPs outline a deeper level of organisational responsibility, emphasising beyond compliance and due diligence. Finally, they confirm that securing human rights requires effective remedies.

The principles form a comprehensive body of methods and measures required for developing appropriate protection frameworks, and they have been given additional strength through measures such as NAPs and reporting. There are, however, several policy and governance issues requiring further exploration.

4.5.1 *Another Non-legal Framework*

Early on, partly to ensure that relevant parties remained at the table, it was claimed that the UNGPs lacked the teeth needed to hold accountable states and firms that are unwilling to safeguard rights (Jägers, 2011). They did not go far enough, according to several leading non-governmental organisations who openly criticised the framework (Blitt, 2012). One concern was that the UNGPs were another non-legal mechanism lacking authority to mandate change. As with other international soft instruments, they were potentially a blueprint for institutional and organisational lethargy. The UNGPs reinforce state duty, but this is embedded in international law. So, it was asked, what has restating an established, but sometimes neglected, duty done? The UNGPs describe themselves as a platform for action and cumulative progress, and ways forward are suggested. But their principles-based and non-legal frameworks leave legitimate concerns that states may disregard their duties, as many have systematically done. Some states may lack interest or capability or be actively involved in suppressing rights. It is not unknown for affluent states to struggle in their duties to protect against abuses by private enterprises. Even with a developed legal framework, it can be difficult to control certain sectors, as outlined in the UK in reports on sectors such as food, construction, hospitality, agriculture and car washes (Scott et al., 2012; Davies, 2019; Metcalf, 2019). What of some of the least developed states that may lack the appropriate political, administrative and regulatory structures? What if a state is an abuser of rights or assists firms in committing abuses? These are governance gaps that principle-based and non-legal mechanisms may not necessarily have answers for.

4.5.2 NAP Process

An important component of the governance framework, for establishing and organising what is needed to safeguard rights, is the NAPs (Working Group on Business and Human Rights, 2014). Properly undertaken, NAPs can reinforce the principles around business and human rights and enable adaptation of the UNGPs to national settings (De Felice and Graf, 2015; see also O'Brien et al., 2016). Not only can a properly developed NAP provide essential information on potential disparities between state obligations and practices but it can empower local pro-human rights organisations and ensure that public bodies have knowledge and capacities for effective action (De Felice and Graf, 2015). Undoubtedly, the utility and effectiveness of the NAP framework is dependent on the implementing state – its commitment, priorities and resource allocation – and its dedication to ensuring effective application of international obligations (Rivera, 2019).

But the NAP framework is not a panacea. This is not only because NAPs are dependent on state commitment, and the inconsistencies this may generate, but because NAPs may constitute a diversion from what states and firms need to do to identify and prevent the negative impacts of business activities (Rivera, 2019). NAPs are policy tools and, while they can be an effective development stage in the process towards the better regulation and protection of rights, there is the danger that they will become 'collaborative mirages' that avoid engaging in a serious conversation on the type of changes required to ensure action (Rivera, 2019, p. 216): mirages that 'seem to indicate that states have done their homework' (Rivera, 2019, p. 37), or a 'convenient fig leaf' to cover up state reluctance to take effective action (O'Brien et al., 2016, p. 21). It is only through proper identification of governance gaps and development of effective measures that the NAP framework will be fully effective (O'Brien et al., 2016; Rivera, 2019). There is a danger, at present, that there is little more than guidance to ensure that NAPs are tools for proper change.

The information available suggests that there have been positive trends in the development of NAPs and that NAPs are improving and containing increasing levels of useful information (ICAR, 2017). But there are problems. For example, progress has been relatively slow, with twenty-five states having published NAPs as of November 2020 (Danish Institute for Human Rights, 2020). Substantive issues have been identified with individual NAPs themselves (De Felice and Graf, 2015; ICAR, 2017). The International Corporate Accountability Roundtable (ICAR) – alongside the European Coalition for Corporate Justice and the Centre for the Study of Law, Justice, and Society – assessed existing NAPs that had been developed in 2017, as a development of previous NAPs (ICAR, 2017). Concerns were raised over process and content. On process, there was an observed lack of transparency over the drafting procedures, and no states published information on the budgets allocated for drafting NAPs. A further weakness was a failure to conduct adequate national baseline assessments to properly inform NAP content and guide future action. This is important. Since governance gaps are an underlying cause of human rights problems, national baseline assessments are important for ensuring that gaps are identified and addressed and for reinforcing the legitimacy and credibility of the NAP framework (O'Brien et al., 2016). Generally, NAPs were seen as requiring improvement as they had not met the standards required for thorough baseline assessments (ICAR, 2017). On content, a weakness was a failure to explore appropriate regulatory options and access to remedies. There was an emphasis on soft measures, for example, awareness-raising and training, despite the fact that regulatory actions were considered more likely to be effective at addressing governance gaps. Most NAPs only briefly considered access to remedies, a key pillar of the UN framework. Lastly, few states had addressed the full scope or their territorial jurisdictions, with most NAPs focussing on corporate abuses either at home or abroad (ICAR, 2017). A recent snapshot of NAP developments revealed that, while there was some positive progress, there were still inconsistencies and weaknesses in NAP content (Danish Institute for Human Rights, 2020). As an important component of the governance framework, NAPs will need to be closely scrutinised for consistency and substance.

4.5.3 *Regulating Business Overseas*

An issue that has surrounded debates over controlling large and powerful corporations in particular is the failure to oblige states, principally wealthy states, to scrutinise and regulate the practices of firms that are headquartered locally but function overseas. The UNGPs adopt a cautious approach. States should set out the expectation that businesses in their jurisdiction respect rights throughout their operations. While the duty to protect is primarily on host states, however, the duty does not overtly extend to business enterprises abroad. The commentary provides that states are 'not generally' required to regulate extraterritorial activities, although neither are they prohibited from doing so if there exists a recognised jurisdictional basis (United Nations, 2011).

This reflects the traditional view of international law, where the jurisdiction of states is almost entirely territorial (De Jonge, 2011; Omoteso and Yusuf, 2017). Owing to the territorialisation of regulatory jurisdiction, and its exercise by national authorities, there are no robust provisions in international law for addressing regulatory disparities and for intervening in cases of lax regulatory standards arising from governance failures, especially in developing host countries of MNEs. Paragraph 2 of the Concepts and Principles chapter of the OECD Guidelines on Multinational Enterprises (OECD, 2011) implicitly references the territorialisation perspective:

> Obeying domestic laws is the first obligation of enterprises. The Guidelines are not a substitute for nor should they be considered to override domestic law and regulation. While the Guidelines extend beyond the law in many cases, they should not and are not intended to place an enterprise in situations where it faces conflicting requirements. However, in countries where domestic laws and regulations conflict with the principles and standards of the Guidelines, enterprises should seek ways to honour such principles and standards to the fullest extent which does not place them in violation of domestic law.

The UNGPs, however, recognise that there might be strong policy reasons for home states to set out the expectation that businesses respect human rights abroad, especially where the state itself is in some way involved with or supports those businesses. The overall approach to extraterritorial obligations has been described as conservative and, although in line with a diplomatic stance when developing the UNGPs, appears to be contrary to the developments that have been taking place in international law and policy, such as the views of the Committee on Economic, Social and Cultural Rights in relation to rights to water and rights to health (see Davitti, 2016). The UNGPs withdraw from a convincing mandate, thus contributing to an already frail state of affairs with respect to the protection of human rights.

Moreover, the UNGPs pay too little regard to the point mentioned already that states should contribute to an international order where rights can be respected and achieved. Such an order may involve more well-resourced states, where corporations are headquartered, exercising controls where and when possible. Some home states may be in a stronger position to regulate (at least some) activities of firms operating overseas. Consider, too, that the headquarters of many of the Fortune Global 500 firms reside in a small number of states (e.g., USA 121, China 119, Japan 52, France 31, Germany 29, UK 17).[6] A reasonable adjustment and commitment by some would not solve all problems, but it may make a significant difference in terms of practice and the message it sends (that firms, even when operating across borders, are not beyond scrutiny). A proper framework that, for example, informs consumers and business customers what firms are doing would enable a market to function effectively by enabling informed decisions, something that policymakers often promote.

4.5.4 *Respect Principle*

An issue of concern is linked to the earlier point that the UNGPs are essentially a system of non-legal directives. Firms have a responsibility – not a duty – to respect rights, so the UNGPs do not create binding international law or impose direct obligations on firms (Blitt, 2012). The UNGPs arguably adopt a traditional, reserved view of the role of international human rights instruments. The respect principle is seen as a global standard of expected conduct for all firms, acknowledged in almost every voluntary and soft-law instrument relating to corporate responsibility (United Nations, 2012). It exists independently of states' abilities or willingness to fulfil their obligations (and does not diminish those obligations) and exists beyond compliance with national laws protecting human rights (United Nations, 2011). The principle is founded on a view that firms have a social licence to operate that is based on prevailing social norms that can be as important to the success of a business as legal norms (United Nations, 2009). In fact according to Ruggie and Sherman (2017, pp. 923–4), the responsibility to respect is rooted in a transnational social norm rather than an international legal norm and serves to meet a company's social licence to operate: 'it exists "over and above" all applicable legal requirements; and it applies irrespective of what states do or do not do'. Business and state actors may prefer to be on the right side of what Ruggie (United Nations, 2008, [54]) described as 'the courts of public opinion'.

In our conceptualisation, then, the respect principle to some extent embeds a reference to the notion of CSR. As the guidance to ISO 26000:2010 ([2.18]) notes:

> social responsibility is the responsibility of an organisation for the impacts of its decisions and activities on society and the environment through transparent and ethical behaviour that is consistent with sustainable development and the welfare of society; takes into account the expectations of stakeholders; is in compliance with applicable law and consistent with international norms of behaviour; and is integrated throughout the organisation.

While some (see Hudon and Sandberg, 2013, p. 563) regard human rights and CSR as parallel approaches, both can actually complement each other, particularly in addressing poverty (Osuji and Obibuaku, 2016). One of the impacts of the UNGPs is therefore a renewed emphasis on CSR as a mechanism for advancing human rights. Notable examples are the 2011 strategy document of the European Commission that explicitly refers to the UNGPs (Commission of the European Communities (CEC), 2011, p. 14) and the OECD Guidelines for Multinational Enterprises (OECD, 2011). The origins of the OECD Guidelines can be traced to the response of the major developed countries to the 1970s demand by developing nations for legally binding obligations of MNEs (Muchlinski, 2011).

If a state properly fulfils its duties, then firms should do all they can to fully comply with relevant laws. But an important feature of the respect principle, even allowing for organisational context, is that firms may need to go beyond compliance, introduce additional standards, undertake other commitments or activities and adopt a due diligence approach. To observe the respect principle, firms should have polices in place, must undertake ongoing human rights due diligence to identify, prevent, mitigate and account for their human rights impacts and must have processes to enable remediation for any adverse impacts (United Nations, 2012). Due diligence thus appears to be a demanding standard going 'beyond the corporate governance standard of risk management to include a whole range of purposes' (Martin-Ortega, 2014, p. 56). Such beyond compliance activities may be particularly important if domestic standards, as they often do, fall short. Part of the rationale for this, as outlined, is that rights are inalienable, making the responsibilities of firms independent of the abilities of states to fulfil their obligations. That said, and in accordance with the non-legal nature of the UNGPs, there are no provisions imposing consequences in the case of failure to perform adequate due diligence or to remediate adverse impacts (Martin-Ortega, 2014).

There is at least some danger in placing too much emphasis and reliance on a respect principle that is founded on a social licence concept, in the belief that it is capable of influencing firms, which themselves display any number of complex behaviours (Williamson and Lynch-Wood, 2021), to uphold human rights standards by undertaking a range of potentially exacting activities such as due diligence and other beyond compliance actions. The factors that determine the strength of the social licence are likely to be weak for a significant number of firms (Lynch-Wood and Williamson, 2007). Some firms, for instance, are unlikely to bridge any gaps between inadequate laws and standards of human rights that are embedded in law instruments or go beyond compliance when laws are in place, but there are no social norms that encourage them to do more. Encouraging firms to assume the levels of responsibility that accord with the respect principle presents a major hurdle. As Addo (2020) says, if business and human rights standards are not represented as legally binding, they will be less of a priority for a number of firms.

4.5.5 *Access to Remedies*

Considering that access to justice requires that '[f]irst, the system must be equally accessible to all, and second, it must lead to results that are individually and socially just' (Cappelletti and Garth 1978, p. 182), another governance challenge from the UNGPs is the three-pronged approach to accessing remedies: state responsibility, co-responsibility of states and business, and business responsibility.

Focussing on the primacy of state responsibility and complemented by Principles 26–29, the 'foundational' Principle 25 notes that, '[a]s part of their duty to protect against business-related human rights abuse, States must take appropriate steps to ensure, through judicial, administrative, legislative or other appropriate means, that when such abuses occur within their territory and/or jurisdiction those affected have access to effective remedy'. While the commentary to Principle 25 confirms that '[a]ccess to effective remedy has both procedural and substantive aspects', home and host countries may be unwilling to establish accountability mechanisms for corporate human rights obligations (Osuji and Abba, 2020) with obstacles such as unenforceability in national constitutions and legislation and lack of provisions for application of best international standards and protection of stakeholder rights. The unwillingness of key states to institute coercive methods for remedies is manifested by the National Contact Points provision in the OECD Guidelines for Multinational Enterprises (OECD, 2011) for complaints against MNEs in their home countries (see Tyler and Chambers, 2012). The commentary to chapter IV

(Human Rights) of the OECD Guidelines for Multinational Enterprises (OECD, 2011, [36]) confirms that Ruggie (see United Nations Special Representative of the Secretary-General on the Issue of Human Rights and Transnational Corporations and Other Business Enterprises (UN SRSG), 2010, [91–102]) influenced the alignment of the provision with the UNGPs.

Principle 28 promotes co-responsibility of states and enterprises by providing that 'States should consider ways to facilitate access to effective non-State based grievance mechanisms dealing with business-related human rights harms'. The commentary underlines co-responsibility in explaining that '[o]ne category of non-State-based grievance mechanisms encompasses those administered by a business enterprise alone or with stakeholders, by an industry association or a multi-stakeholder group'. While the provision appears sufficiently flexible to facilitate opportunities for access to remedy, the extent of its utilisation by home and host states of enterprises remains to be seen.

Business responsibility is the focus of Principles 29–30, which expect businesses – individually and collectively – to establish grievance mechanisms for remediation of human rights claims which, according to Principle 31, should be legitimate, accessible, predictable, equitable, transparent, rights-compatible and a source of continuous learning. With regard to individual business responsibility, Principle 29 states: 'To make it possible for grievances to be addressed early and remediated directly, business enterprises should establish or participate in effective operational-level grievance mechanisms for individuals and communities who may be adversely impacted.' Principle 31(h) adds that operational-level grievance mechanisms should be 'based on [stakeholder] engagement and dialogue'. Collective business responsibility is promoted in Principle 30. This states that '[i]ndustry, multi-stakeholder and other collaborative initiatives that are based on respect for human rights-related standards should ensure that effective grievance mechanisms are available'. While these provisions are encouraging for business responsibility via CSR (see Tyler and Chambers, 2012), going by the persistence of 'bluewash' and 'greenwash' claims (e.g., Sethi and Schepers, 2014) and transnational human rights cases (Schrempf-Stirling and Wettstein, 2017), there is as yet little evidence of grievance mechanisms reflecting the ideals that have been articulated in Principle 31 at operational and collective levels of business.

4.5.6 *Adjudication of Rights and Remedies*

One cannot realistically discuss access to remedies without referencing judicial adjudication, since '[l]itigation has arguably never been a more important tool to push policymakers and market participants to develop and implement effective means' (Burger et al., 2017, p. 8). The central role of litigation (see Schrempf-Stirling and Wettstein, 2017) in, and the lack of judicial enforcement routes for, corporate human rights obligations explain Resolution No. 2/2012 of the 75th

Conference of the International Law Association held in Sofia, Bulgaria, in 2012, which adopted the Sofia Guidelines on Best Practices for International Civil Litigation for Human Rights Violations. While access to courts is considered an essential component of the right to a fair hearing, for example under Article 6 of the European Convention on Human Rights 1950,[7] the recognition of 'legitimate and proportionate restrictions'[8] in national legislations, administrative policies and judicial decisions can affect accountability for human rights. Accordingly, Principle 26 of the UNGPs provides that 'States should take appropriate steps to ensure the effectiveness of domestic judicial mechanisms when addressing business-related human rights abuses, including considering ways to reduce legal, practical and other relevant barriers that could lead to a denial of access to remedy'. Nonetheless, the Sofia Guidelines alongside similar provisions in Articles 7 to 11 of the 2020 second revised draft of the proposal for a Legally Binding Instrument to Regulate, in International Human Rights Law, the Activities of Transnational Corporations and Other Business Enterprises,[9] remain proposals that are unlikely to be adopted by unwilling regulatory and judicial authorities and even corporations themselves.

The apparent lack of remedies for corporate human rights obligations can be attributed to several factors. First, international law does not have provisions for horizontal adjudication between individuals and corporations. The focus of debates on the status of corporations in international law on the regulatory dimension is similarly reflected in varying efforts, such as the draft Norms on Transnational Corporations and Other Business Enterprises with Regard to Human Rights 2003 and the ongoing discussions of a business and human rights treaty, for establishing some sort of corporate legal responsibilities for human rights. No supranational adjudication forum, however, exists or is planned for human rights claims against corporations.

Second, international law does not provide opportunities for states to institute human rights proceedings against firms in an international tribunal. International investment law, for instance, is designed for investor claims (Osuji and Taiwo, 2021). While states can counterclaim against investors in arbitral tribunals, human rights considerations are normally excluded in investment agreements. The corporate human rights obligations in Article 24 of the draft Pan African Investment Code 2016 are an emergent outlier and, even then, are not legally enforceable.

Another limitation is the application of the twin concepts of corporate personality and limited liability in a corporate group. Thus, the UN Committee on the Rights of the Child observed that 'the way in which transnational corporations are structured in separate entities can make identification and attribution of legal responsibility to each unit challenging' (United Nations Committee on the Rights of the Child (CRC), 2013, [67]). *Okpabi* and *Vedanta*, for example, did not alter the English law's approach to corporate personality and limited liability but were rather based on the assumption of a duty of care by a parent company for its subsidiaries' activities.

The principle established in *Chandler* v. *Cape Plc*[10] 'depends on the extent to which, and the way in which, the parent company availed itself of the opportunity to take over, intervene in, control, supervise or advise the management of the relevant operations (including land use) of the subsidiary'.[11] Equally, the French Corporate Duty of Vigilance Law 2017[12] seems to have gone slightly further, but the lack of enforcement provisions confirmed by the French court in a non-compliance claim against Total can be traced to the unwillingness of powerful economic and political actors to be less competitive (Lapierre et al., 2020).

The fourth factor is the obstacles imposed by private international law rules on jurisdiction, applicable law and recognition and enforcement of foreign judgments (see Fawcett et al., 2016). While recent cases such as *Okpabi* v. *Royal Dutch Shell Plc*,[13] *Vedanta* v. *Lungowe*[14] and *Four Nigerian Farmers and Milieudefensie* v. *Shell*[15] may suggest the opening up of judicial forums of home states of MNEs to claims by individuals and communities in host developing countries, the reality is that no recognised principle of private international law explicitly allows such transnational human rights litigation, as the US Supreme Court made clear in *Kiobel* v. *Royal Dutch Petroleum Co*[16] and subsequent cases.[17] Impediments to corporate accountability for human rights imposed by judicial authorities in home and host states of corporations (Osuji and Abba, 2020) include locus standi requirements, *forum non conveniens* doctrine and private international law rules on jurisdiction, applicable law and recognition and enforcement of judgments. For example, the *forum non conveniens* doctrine played a central role in the US Supreme Court's rejection of jurisdiction over transnational human rights claims in *Kiobel*. As Chief Justice Roberts explained, *forum non conveniens* prevents judicial interference in foreign policy matters.

There seems, therefore, to be a degree of unwillingness by the courts of more developed jurisdictions to intervene in extraterritorial human rights matters with the implicit nod to the host states that may equally be unwilling to allow effective corporate accountability for human rights (see Osuji and Abba, 2020). While incapacity could be a factor in host developing countries, the related cases of *Motto* v. *Trafigura Ltd*[18] and *Agouman* v. *Leigh Day*,[19] where the judicial authorities of Cote D'Ivoire colluded with other powerful actors to divert a compensation fund for human rights victims, show that unwillingness may be a factor. Moreover, jurisdiction-based objections of corporations to human rights claims in their home states show that they remain unwilling to assume human rights obligations despite their acknowledgement of shared responsibility and proclamation of CSR.

4.6 HUMAN RIGHTS, REGULATORY MIX AND CSR

Following on from the account of the governance challenges in the framework of the UNGPs, an issue requiring further exploration is the development of effective regulation. As noted in the *G20/OECD Principles of Corporate Governance*

(OECD, 2015, p. 13), 'a sound legal, regulatory and institutional framework' for corporate governance should involve a mix of 'legislation, regulation, self-regulatory arrangements, voluntary commitments and business practices that are the result of a country's specific circumstances, history and tradition'. An important feature of the state duty, as mentioned, is the need to design a 'smart mix' of regulatory instruments. A state should consider a combination of measures (e.g., mandatory, voluntary) for promoting business respect for human rights. The smart-mix approach has been a feature of reform policies for several years (Williamson and Lynch-Wood, 2021), and its approval and accepted logic is such that it has become a recognised response to the question of what appropriate policy design should resemble. One of the most important statements of the smart mix is provided by Gunningham and Grabosky (1998), who present a compelling case for designing effective combinations of policy instruments tailored to particular circumstances. They posit that using combinations of policy instruments will address different aspects of organisational behaviour and lead to better outcomes.

Despite initiatives such as the UNGPs giving considerable momentum, there are concerns regarding the smart-mix approach to business and human rights. While on paper the smart mix sounds like a good idea, ultimately, as with NAPs, its realisation depends on political commitments (Wettstein, 2015). This creates a (possibly unavoidable) problem in that the Guiding Principles 'effectively hand the regulatory authority for any binding, enforced or even merely monitored measures back to the governments, which have proven in the past that they are hardly willing to go it alone' (Wettstein, 2015, p. 166) As such, the UNGPs, according to Wettstein (2015, p. 166), 'fall prey to the problem they were supposed to fix, that is, the problem of growing governance gaps between companies' increasing sphere of activity and governments' decreasing ability or willingness to regulate them'. The problem of the smart-mix approach goes beyond handing powers to potentially unwilling participants. A further issue is a lack of clarity or specificity over what it means in terms of properly applied regulatory interventions, and there is concern that designing a smart mix could manifest itself as a concession to the global business movement (Kinderman, 2016). While the term is often presented as the ultimate solution to social problems – as combining 'the best of both worlds: the flexibility, dynamism, innovativeness, reflexivity and adaptability of voluntary market-based solutions and the authoritativeness, scope, and binding force of legal regulation' (Kinderman, 2016, p. 9) – there is insufficient work on the complex issue of what a smart mix should look like in a range of jurisdictional, legal, social, economic, industrial or commercial settings. A challenge is to decide what combination of tools to use across a range of areas from safe standards or fair remuneration in the workplace through to natural resource use affecting local communities. What type of hard regulation or command-and-control rules? What types of disclosure mechanism or market-based incentive, and to whom should they be applied? What mechanisms can best incorporate and engage stakeholders in decision-making processes? Through accommodation of different measures, both soft and direct, smart mixes seek to both force and steer, seeing the measures as complementary rather than contradictory forces for behavioural change.

Designing a smart mix is a difficult undertaking and clearly more work is needed to establish, across multiple business and human rights issues, what a smart mix means and how mixes may be shaped by compliance responses and performance sensitivities (Van Gossum et al., 2010). Generating more insight into and knowledge of the external and internal factors and influences that determine how firms perform in different situations and respond to different types of regulatory tool will help to inform us about an effective smart combination of voluntary and mandatory measures (Wettstein et al., 2019). The task of formulating such a range of measures, and implementing them, is not insignificant and will require constant analysis with evolving circumstances. In the area of human rights, this issue of efficacious adaptability of regulation is against the backdrop of the somewhat entrenched rival interests of critical state and non-state actors unwilling to shift ground, particularly in relation to legalisation. What would a smart-mix approach to regulation suggest in the circumstances?

In the first place, while maintaining human rights advocacy, it is crucial to explore alternative approaches to legalisation of responsibility in international law. Legalisation of corporate human rights obligations has proved controversial among state and non-state actors. States and corporations that failed to subscribe to the Draft Norms on the Responsibility of Transnational Corporations and Other Business Enterprises with Regard to Human Rights initiated by the UN Human Rights Commission (Wettstein, 2012, p. 744) are unlikely to agree to the ongoing proposal for a business and human rights treaty (see De Schutter, 2015; Bilchitz, 2016). A 'this or no other method is allowed' approach will lead to governance inertia if the strict rights-based approach of international human rights law is applied to exclude other methods that state and private actors may be willing to respond to. This is one of the lessons from the UNGPs that underline the potential of CSR – as a voluntary self-regulated or a state regulated scheme – and other regulatory arrangements in governance of human rights matters.

Then, CSR should be seen as capable of being utilised for human rights governance by public- and private-sector actors within national and transnational spheres (Osuji, 2015). As Osuji and Obibuaku (2016, p. 331) observed, 'human rights principles have normative dimensions to guide and help formulate policies, programmes and practices, which in turn allow for a creative use of and legal prop to CSR notwithstanding the concept's apparent "voluntary" character'. It is noteworthy that Ruggie confirmed the UNGPs as reference for 'a standard of expected conduct acknowledged in virtually every voluntary and soft-law instrument related to corporate responsibility' (UN SRSG, 2010, [55]). Ruggie stressed the role of CSR in subjecting 'companies to the courts of public opinion – comprising employees, communities, consumers, civil society, as well as investors – and occasionally to charges in actual courts. Whereas governments define the scope of legal compliance, the broader scope of the responsibility to respect is defined by social expectations – as part of what is sometimes called a company's social licence to operate' (UN, 2008, [54]). The UNGPs have not defined or limited the wider scope of CSR in formulating standards for business responsibilities for human rights in different contexts. Therefore, CSR can be underpinned by a variety of human rights instruments and jurisprudence beyond the UNGPs and can accommodate human rights matters, such as poverty alleviation, which are not explicitly discussed in the UNGPs.

Nonetheless, a major criticism is that corporations, at best, use CSR for 'green washing' defined as 'selective disclosure of positive information about a company's environmental or social performance without full disclosure of negative information on these dimensions so as to create an overly positive corporate image' (Lyon and Maxwell, 2011, p. 9). The UN Global Compact is a prominent example (see Sethi and Schepers, 2014). Therefore, CSR should be orientated towards achievement of human rights governance goals. Thus, the claimants' solicitors in *Vedanta* v. *Lungowe*[20] observed that the 'judgment will send a strong message to other large multinationals that their CSR policies should not just be seen as a polish for their reputation but as important commitments that they must put into action' (Leigh Day, 2019, n.p.).

4.7 CONCLUSION

This chapter has demonstrated that varied actors may need to align their interests and apply their powers and resources to human rights governance. Owing to their economic contribution, it is, however, important to foster an environment where firms can succeed and where people can benefit from the opportunities they produce. This environment requires safeguards to ensure that people's necessary and fundamental rights are respected. In recognising this, the UNGPs are an important development. Time was when the very suggestion that firms should have some responsibilities for human rights would have been considered something of a backwater. Now, the issue is on the policy stage. That said, as they stand, the UNGPs offer little solace to victims of human rights violations or those subject to conditions consigning them to poverty. There are some potentially significant governance gaps – the absence of a strong compliance mechanism, principles that can come across as vague and idealistic, the lack of proper consideration of how many firms respond to social and legal issues, and the minimalistic approach taken to the responsibilities that some (particularly powerful) states may have to help prevent extraterritorial abuses.

While the UNGPs are, of course, a platform for action, the continued agitation for legally binding treaty provisions for corporate human rights accountability suggests that some regard the governance gaps as so cavernous as to render the framework ineffective. The UNGPs clearly present real challenges, in terms of both understanding and managing different human rights impacts. While the focus of the UNGPs is predominantly states and firms, it is apparent that a range of stakeholders is needed to help properly understand what protecting human rights actually means in different organisational contexts and to foster a business environment and policy framework more responsive to human rights matters.

Governance inertia is not a solution, notwithstanding the challenges posed by unwilling political and economic actors in positions of power and influence. The governance of poverty and other human rights matters can be undertaken through CSR as an alternative to legalisation in international human rights law. While the UNGPs reflect some understandings of CSR, the latter's scope, application and jurisprudential underpinnings are wider. There is thus still the need for a more robust and flexible approach and utilisation of a smart mix of regulatory methods, including CSR, that should be aligned to the achievement of the governance goals.

NOTES

* Gary Lynch-Wood is a Senior Lecturer in Law and Regulation at the University of Manchester's Law Department. Gary's research has focussed on regulation problems and the challenges of designing effective forms of regulation, particularly in relation to how we can promote corporate social and environmental responsibility. He has published widely on this subject in leading journals (e.g., *Journal of Law and Society, Journal of Environmental Law, Journal of Business Ethics, Environmental Politics, Regulation & Governance*). His recent book *The Structure of Regulation* provides a general theory for understanding why regulation succeeds and fails. Gary is a member of MANREG, a research group that explores the functioning of regulation across a range of disciplines.

1. www.ohchr.org/EN/Issues/Poverty/DimensionOfPoverty/Pages/Index.aspx.
2. www.ohchr.org/en/issues/SDGS/pages/the2030agenda.aspx.
3. www.globaljustice.org.uk/news/2018/oct/17/69-richest-100-entities-planet-are-corporations-not-governments-figures-show.
4. The OECD Guidelines for Multinational Enterprises were originally adopted in 1976 as part of the Declaration on International Investment and Multinational Enterprises. The Guidelines provide non-binding principles and standards for responsible business conduct in a global context consistent with applicable laws and internationally recognised standards.
5. www.un.org/press/en/2005/sga934.doc.htm.
6. Data from 2019: see https://news.bloombergtax.com/daily-tax-report/insight-21.
7. *Golder* v. *United Kingdom* (1975) 1 EHRR 524; *Airey* v. *Ireland* (1979) 2 EHRR 305; *Osman* v. *United Kingdom* (2000) 29 EHRR 245.

8. *Ashingdane* v. *United Kingdom* (1985) 7 EHRR 528 [57]; *Steel and Morris* v. *United Kingdom*, Judgment of 15 February 2005 [62].
9. Following the resolution of the Human Rights Council (2014, [9]) to establish an intergovernmental working group 'to elaborate an international legally-binding instrument to regulate, in international human rights law, the activities of transnational corporations and other business enterprises', a second revised draft of a proposal for a Legally Binding Instrument to Regulate, in International Human Rights Law, the Activities of Transnational Corporations and Other Business Enterprises was adopted on 6 August 2020.
10. *Chandler* v. *Cape Plc* [2012] EWCA Civ 525.
11. *Okpabi* v. *Royal Dutch Shell Plc* [2021] UKSC 3 [25]; *Vedanta* v. *Lungowe* (2019) UKSC 20 [49].
12. LOI n° 2017-399 du 27 mars 2017 relative au devoir de vigilance des sociétés mères et des entreprises donneuses d'ordre (1) [LAW No. 2017-399 of 27 March 2017 relating to the duty of vigilance of parent companies and ordering companies (1)] NOR: ECFX1509096L. www.legifrance.gouv.fr/eli/loi/2017/3/27/ECFX1509096L/jo/texte.
13. *Okpabi* v. *Royal Dutch Shell Plc* [2021] UKSC 3.
14. *Vedanta* v. *Lungowe* (2019) UKSC 20.
15. *Four Nigerian Farmers and Milieudefensie* v. *Shell* ECLI:NL:GHDHA:2021:132 (Gerechtshof Den Haag).
16. *Kiobel* v. *Royal Dutch Petroleum Co.* 569 US 108 (2013).
17. See *RJR Nabisco, Inc.* v. *European Community* 136 S. Ct. 2090 (2016); *Jesner* v. *Arab Bank, Plc* 138 S. Ct.1386 (2018); *Nestlé USA, Inc.* v. *Doe et al, Cargill, Inc.* v. *Doe et al* 593 US__ (2021).
18. *Motto* v. *Trafigura Ltd* [2011] EWCA Civ 1150 (on costs).
19. *Agouman* v. *Leigh Day* [2016] EWHC 1324.
20. *Vedanta* v. *Lungowe* (2019) UKSC 20.

REFERENCES

Addo, M. K. (2020). Is Business and Human Rights Suitable for the Compliance Function? The University of Chicago Law Review Online. Available at: https://lawreviewblog.uchicago.edu/2020/01/07/is-business-and-human-rights-suitable-for-the-compliance-function-by-michael-k-addo/.

Amao, O. (2011). *Corporate Social Responsibility, Human Rights and the Law*. Abingdon, UK: Routledge.

Amnesty International. (2009). *Petroleum, Pollution and Poverty in the Niger Delta*. London: Amnesty International.

Amnesty International. (2017). *Amnesty International Report 2016/17: The State of the World's Human Rights*. London: Amnesty International.

Andreassen, B. and Banik, D. (2010). Editorial introduction: human rights and extreme poverty: African dimensions. *The International Journal of Human Rights*, 14(1), 4–12.

Ashford, E. (2007). The duties imposed by the human right to basic necessities. In T Pogge, ed., *Freedom from Poverty as a Human Right: Who Owes What to the Very Poor?* Oxford: Oxford University Press, pp. 183–218.

Babic, M., Fichtner, J. and Heemskerk, E. M. (2017). States versus corporations: rethinking the power of business in international politics. *The International Spectator*, **52**(4), 20–43.

Backer, L. (2006). Multinational corporations, transnational law: the United Nations norms on the responsibilities of transnational corporations as a harbinger of corporate social responsibility in international law. *Columbia Human Rights Law Review*, **37**(2), 287–389.

Bilchitz, D. (2016). The necessity for a business and human rights treaty. *Business and Human Rights Journal*, **1**, 203–27.

Blitt, R. (2012). Beyond Ruggie's Guiding Principles on Business and Human Rights: charting an embracive approach to corporate human rights compliance. *Texas International Law Journal*, 48(1), 33–62.

Bonnitcha, J. and McCorquodale, R. (2017). The concept of 'due diligence' in the UN Guiding Principles on Business and Human Rights. *European Journal of International Law*, **28**(3), 899–919.

Brinkman, R. and Brinkman, J. (2002). Corporate power and the globalization process. *International Journal of Social Economics*, **29**, 730–52.

Brownlie I. (2019). *Principles of Public International Law*, 9th ed. Oxford: Oxford University Press.

Burger, M., Gundlach, J., Kreilhuber, A., Ognibene, L., Kariukia, A. and Gachie, A. (2017). *The Status of Climate Change Litigation: A Global Review*. New York: UNEP/Sabin Centre for Climate Change Law, Columbia University.

Cappelletti, M. and Garth, B. G. (1978). Access to justice: the newest wave in the worldwide movement to make rights effective. *Buffalo Law Review*, **27**, 181–292.

Cassel, D. (2001). Human rights and business responsibilities in the global marketplace. *Business Ethics Quarterly*, **11**(2), 261–74.

Clapham, A. and Jerbi, S. (2000). Categories of corporate complicity in human rights abuses. *Hastings International and Comparative Law Review*, **24**, 339–49.

Commission of the European Communities (CEC). (2011). *Communication from the Commission to the European Parliament, the Council, the European Economic and Social Committee and the Committee of the Regions. A Renewed EU Strategy 2011–14 for Corporate Social Responsibility*, COM(2011) 881 final. Brussels: European Commission.

Cosans, C. (2009). Does Milton Friedman support a vigorous business ethics? *Journal of Business Ethics*, 87(3), 391–99.

Cragg, W. (2015). Ethics, enlightened self-interest, and the corporate responsibility to respect human rights: a critical look at the justificatory foundations of the UN Framework. *Business Ethics Quarterly*, **22**(1), 9–36.

Danish Institute for Human Rights (2020). Business and human rights national action plans – a snapshot in 2020. https://globalnaps.org/wp-content/uploads/2020/11/summary-of-bhr-naps-november-2020-dihr_final.pdf.

Davies, J. (2019). From severe to routine labour exploitation: the case of migrant workers in the UK food industry. *Criminology & Criminal Justice*, **19**(3), 294–310.

Davis, P. (February 2016). *Private Sector Development in Countries Progressing from Poverty*. Final Report, prepared for the Department for International Development. Rotterdam: ECORYS. https://assets.publishing.service.gov.uk/media/57a0895a40f0b6497400002e/61510_Private-Sector-Development-in-Countries-Progressing-from-Poverty_040416.pdf.

Davitti, D. (2016). Refining the protect, respect and remedy framework for business and human rights and its guiding principles. *Human Rights Law Review*, **16**(1), 55–75.

De Felice, D. and Graf, A. (2015). The potential of national action plans to implement human rights norms: an early assessment with respect to the UN Guiding Principles on Business and Human Rights. *Journal of Human Rights Practice*, **7**(1), 40–71.

De Jonge, A. (2011). Transnational corporations and international law: bringing TNCs out of the accountability vacuum. *Critical Perspectives on International Business*, **7**(1), 66–89.

Department for International Development (DFID). (2011). *The Engine of Development: The Private Sector and Prosperity for Poor People*. London: DFID.

De Schutter, O. (2015). Towards a new treaty on business and human rights. *Business and Human Rights Journal*, **1**, 41–67.

Detomasi, D. 2007. The multinational corporation and global governance: modelling global public policy networks. *Journal of Business Ethics*, **71**(3), 321–34.

Deva, S. (2003). UN's human rights norms for transnational corporations and other business enterprises: an imperfect step in the right direction. *ILSA Journal of International & Comparative Law*, **10**, 493–523.

Erskine, T. (2018). 'Coalitions of the willing' and the shared responsibility to protect. In A. Nollkaemper and D. Jacobs, eds., *Distribution of Responsibilities in International Law*, pp. 227–64. Cambridge: Cambridge University Press.

Fawcett, J. J., Ní Shúilleabháin, M. and Shah, S. (2016). *Human Rights and Private International Law*. Oxford: Oxford University Press.

Ferraz, O. (2008). Poverty and human rights. *Oxford Journal of Legal Studies*, **28**(3), 585–603.

Freeman, R. (1984). *Strategic Management: A Stakeholder Approach*. London: Pitman.

Frey, B. (1997). The legal and ethical responsibilities of transnational corporations in the protection of international human rights. *Minnesota Journal of Global Trade*, **6**, 153–88.

Friedman, M. (1970). The social responsibility of business is to increase its profits. *The New York Times Magazine*, **September**, 122–5.

Gatto, A. (2011). *Multinationals and Human Rights: Obligations under EU Law and International Law*. Cheltenham, UK: Edward Elgar.

Glendon, M. (1997). Knowing the universal declaration of human rights. *Notre Dame Law Review*, **73**(5), 1153–90.

Griffiths, B., (2001). The business corporation as a moral community. In B. Griffiths, R. Sirico, N. Barry and F. Field, eds., *Capitalism, Morality and Markets*. London: Institute of Economic Affairs, pp. 17–40.

Gunningham, N. and Grabosky, P. (1998). *Smart Regulation: Designing Environmental Policy*. New York: Oxford University Press.

Harrison, J. (2013). Establishing a meaningful human rights due diligence process for corporations: learning from experience of human rights impact assessment. *Impact Assessment and Project Appraisal*, **31**(2), 107–17.

Hilgert, J. (2019). Article 23(4) trade union rights and the United Nations policy of devolution on labour relations. *Labour History*, **60**(5), 503–19.

Hudon, M. and Sandberg, J. (2013). The ethical crisis in microfinance: issues, findings, and implications. *Business Ethics Quarterly*, **23**(4), 561–89.

Human Rights Council. (26 June 2014). *Elaboration of an International Legally Binding Instrument on Transnational Corporations and Other Business Enterprises with Respect to Human Rights*. A/HRC/RES/26/9. https://documents-dds-ny.un.org/doc/UNDOC/GEN/G14/082/52/PDF/G1408252.pdf?OpenElement.

Human Rights Watch. (2020). *World Report: 2020, Events of 2019*. New York: Human Rights Watch.

International Corporate Accountability Roundtable (ICAR) (2017). *Assessments of Existing National Action Plans (NAPS) on Business and Human Rights*. Washington, DC: ICAR.

International Federation for Human Rights. (2016). *Corporate Accountability for Human Rights Abuses A Guide for Victims and NGOs on Recourse Mechanisms*, 3rd ed. Paris: International Federation for Human Rights.

International Labour Organization (ILO). (2020). *World Employment and Social Outlook Trends 2020*. Geneva: International Labour Organization.

Jägers, N. (2011). UN Guiding Principles on Business and Human Rights: making headway towards real corporate accountability? *Netherlands Quarterly of Human Rights*, **29**(2), 159–63.

Kinderman, D. (2016). Time for a reality check: is business willing to support a smart mix of complementary regulation in private governance? *Policy and Society*, **35**(1), 29–42.

Kinley, D. (2009). *Civilising Globalisation: Human Rights and the Global Economy*. Cambridge: Cambridge University Press.

Kinley, D. and Tadaki, J. (2004). From walk to talk: the emergence of human rights responsibilities for corporations at international law. *Virginia Journal of International Law*, **44**(4), 931–1023.

Kolstad, I. (2007). Why firms should not always maximize profits. *Journal of Business Ethics*, **76**(2), 137–145.

Lapierre, T., Duverne, C. and Zorrilla, J. (2020). What if future EU mandatory human rights due diligence legislation comes to rescue of French Corporate Duty of Vigilance law? www.ibanet.org/Article/NewDetail.aspx?ArticleUid=0B9779EE-5105-4A43-B92E-EF4536E664F9#:~:text=The%202017%20French%20Corporate%20Duty,to%20prepare%2C%20publish%20and%20implement.

Latorre, A. (2020). In defence of direct obligations for businesses under international human rights law. *Business and Human Rights Journal*, **5**(1), 56–83.

Leigh Day (2019). Supreme Court rules Zambian villagers' case against Vedanta to be heard in English courts. www.leighday.co.uk/latest-updates/news/2019-news/supreme-court-rules-zambian-villagers-case-against-vedanta-to-be-heard-in-english-courts/.

Lodge, G. and Wilson, C. (2006). Multinational corporations and global poverty reduction. *Challenge*, **49**(3), 17–25.

Lynch-Wood, G. (2014). Poverty, human rights, and responsibilities. In M. Gudić, A. Rosenbloom and C. Parkes, eds., *Socially Responsible Organizations and the Challenge of Poverty*. Abingdon, UK: Routledge.

Lynch-Wood, G. and Williamson, D. (2007). The social licence as a form of regulation for small and medium enterprises. *Journal of Law and Society*, **34**(3), 321–41.

Lynch-Wood, G., Williamson, D. and Jenkins, W. (2009). The over-reliance on self-regulation in CSR policy. *Business Ethics: A European Review*, 18(1), 52–65.

Lyon, T. and Maxwell, J. (2011). Greenwash: corporate environmental disclosure under the threat of audit. *Journal of Economics and Management*, **20**(1), 3–41.

MacEwan, A. (1999). *Neo-liberalism or Democracy?* Oxford: Oxford University Press.

MacLeod, S. and Lewis, D. (2004). Transnational corporations: power, influence and responsibility. *Global Social Policy*, **4**(1), 77–98.

Martin-Ortega, O. (2014). Human rights due diligence for corporations: from voluntary standards to hard law at last? *Netherlands Quarterly of Human Rights*, **32**(1), 44–74.

Mayer, A. (2009). Human rights as a dimension of CSR: the blurred lines between legal and non-legal categories. *Journal of Business Ethics*, 88(4), 561–77.

McCorquodale, R. (2009). Corporate social responsibility and international human rights law. *Journal of Business Ethics*, 87(2), 385–400.

Metcalf, D. (2019). *United Kingdom Labour Market Enforcement Strategy 2019/20*. London: HM Government.

Miretski, P. and Bachmann, S. (2012). The UN 'norms on the responsibility of transnational corporations and other business enterprises with regard to human rights': a requiem. *Deakin Law Review*, 17(1), 5–41.

Muchlinksi, P. (2001). Human rights and multinationals: is there a problem? *International Affairs*, 77(1), 31–48.

Muchlinski, P. (2011). *The 2011 Revision of the OECD Guidelines for Multinational Enterprises: Human Rights, Supply Chains and the 'Due Diligence' Standard for Responsible Business*. A4ID Series on Responsible Business. London: Advocates for International Development (A4ID).

Muchlinski P. (2014). Corporations in international law. In R. Wolfrum, ed., *Max Planck Encyclopedia of Public International Law*. Oxford: Oxford University Press. https://opil.ouplaw.com/view/10.1093/law:epil/9780199231690/law-9780199231690-e1513.

Nolan, J. and Bott, G. (2018). Global supply chains and human rights: spotlight on forced labour and modern slavery practices. *Australian Journal of Human Rights*, **24**(1), 44–69.

O'Brien, C., Mehra, A., Blackwell, S. and Poulsen-Hansen, C. (2016). National action plans: current status and future prospects for a new business and human rights governance tool. *Business and Human Rights Journal*, 1(1), 117–26.

Omoteso, K. and Yusuf, H. (2017). Accountability of transnational corporations in the developing world: the case for an enforceable international mechanism. *Critical Perspectives on International Business*, **13**(1), 54–71.

Organisation for Economic Co-operation and Development (OECD). (2011). *OECD Guidelines for Multinational Enterprises: Recommendations for Responsible Business in A Global Context*. Paris: OECD.

Organisation for Economic Co-operation and Development (OECD). (2015). *G20/OECD Principles of Corporate Governance*. Paris: OECD.

Organisation for Economic Co-operation and Development (OECD). (2016). *Promoting Pro-poor Growth: Private Sector Development*. Paris: OECD.

Osuji, O. K. (2015). Corporate social responsibility, juridification and globalization: 'inventive interventionism' for a 'paradox'. *International Journal of Law in Context*, 11(3), 1–34.

Osuji, O. K. and Abba, P. (2020). Domestic adjudicative institutions, developing countries and sustainable development: Linkages and limitations. In O. K. Osuji, F. Ngwu and D. Jamali, eds., *Corporate Social Responsibility in Developing and Emerging Markets – Institutions, Actors and Sustainable Development*. Cambridge: Cambridge University Press, pp. 49–84.

Osuji, O. K. and Obibuaku, U. (2016). Right and corporate social responsibility – competing or complementary approaches to poverty reduction? *Journal of Business Ethics*, **136**(2), 329–47.

Osuji, O. K. and Taiwo, O. (2021). Contextual centrality of institutional arbitration framework for African Union legal order. In O. Amao, M. Olivier and K. Magliveras, eds., *The Emergent African Union Law: Conceptualization, Delimitation, and Application*. Oxford: Oxford University Press.

Pogge, T. (2005). World poverty and human rights. *Ethics & International Affairs*, 19(1), 1–7.

Ramasastry, A. (2015). Corporate social responsibility versus business and human rights: bridging the gap between responsibility and accountability. *Journal of Human Rights*, **14** (2), 237–59.

Ratner, S. (2001). Corporations and human rights: a theory of legal responsibility. *Yale Law Journal*, **111**(3), 443–545.

Renouard, C. and Ezvan, C. (2018). Corporate social responsibility towards human development: a capabilities framework. *Business Ethics: A European Review*, **27**(2), 144–55.

Rhou, Y. and Singal, M. (2020). A review of the business case for CSR in the hospitality industry. *International Journal of Hospitality Management*, **84**, 102330–4.

Rivera, H. (2019). National action plans on business and human rights: progress or mirage? *Business and Human Rights Journal*, **4**(2), 213–37.

Rodiles, A. (2020). *Coalitions of the Willing and International Law*. Cambridge: Cambridge University Press.

Ruggie, J. and Sherman III, J. (2017). The concept of 'due diligence' in the UN Guiding Principles on Business and Human Rights: a reply to Jonathan Bonnitcha and Robert McCorquodale. *European Journal of International Law*, **28**(3), 921–8.

Sanders, A. (2015). *The impact of the 'Ruggie Framework' and the United Nations Guiding Principles on Business and Human Rights on transnational human rights litigation*. LSE Law, Society and Economy Working Papers 18/2014, London School of Economics and Political Science Law Department. https://papers.ssrn.com/sol3/papers.cfm?abstract_id=2457983.

Schrage, S. and Gilbert, D. (2019). Addressing governance gaps in global value chains: introducing a systematic typology. *Journal of Business Ethics*, **170**, 657–72.

Schrempf-Stirling, J. (2018). State power: rethinking the role of the state in political corporate social responsibility. *Journal of Business Ethics*, **150**, 1–14.

Schrempf-Stirling, J. and Wettstein, F. (2017). Beyond guilty verdicts: human rights litigation and its impact on corporations' human rights policies. *Journal of Business Ethics*, **145**, 545–62.

Scott, S., Craig, G. and Geddes, A. (2012). *Experiences of Forced Labour in the UK Food Industry*. York: Joseph Rowntree Foundation.

Sen, A. (1999). *Development as Freedom*. Oxford: Oxford University Press.

Serafeim, G. (May 2014). *The role of the corporation in society: an alternative view and opportunities for future research*. Harvard Business School Working Paper No. 14–110.

Sethi, S. P. and Schepers, D. H. (2014). United Nations Global Compact: the promise–performance gap. *Journal of Business Ethics*, **122**, 193–208.

Shepherd, A. and Mariotti, C. (2015). *Getting to Zero: Tackling Extreme Poverty through Private Sector Development Policy Guide*. Washington, DC: Chronic Poverty Advisory Network.

Simons, P. and Macklin, A. (2014). *The Governance Gap: Extractive Industries, Human Rights, and the Home State Advantage*. London/New York: Routledge.

Sofo, F. and Wicks, A. (2017). An occupational perspective of poverty and poverty reduction. *Journal of Occupational Science*, **24**(2), 244–9.

Spar, D. (1998). The spotlight and the bottom line: how multinationals export human rights. *Foreign Affairs*, **77**(2), 7–12.

Strange, S. (1991). Big business and the state. *Millennium Journal of International Studies*, **20** (2), 245–50.

Strange, S. (1996). *The Retreat of the State*. Cambridge: Cambridge University Press.

Thompson, G. (1990). *The Political Economy of the New Right*. London: Pinter.

Tondini, M. (2017). Coalitions of the Willing. In A. Nollkaemper and I. Plakokefalos, eds., *The Practice of Shared Responsibility in International Law*, pp. 701–32. Cambridge: Cambridge University Press.

Tyler, K. and Chambers, R. (2012). *Rights, Regulation and Remedy: The Extractive Sector and Development*. London: Action for International Development (A4ID).

United Nations. (2008). *Protect, Respect and Remedy: A Framework for Business and Human Rights*. Report of the Special Representative of the Secretary-General on the Issue of Human Rights and Transnational Corporations and other Business Enterprises, John Ruggie, A/HRC/8/5. New York and Geneva: UN. https://documents-dds-ny.un.org/doc/UNDOC/GEN/G08/128/61/PDF/G0812861.pdf?OpenElement.

United Nations. (22 April 2009). *Promotion of All Human Rights, Civil, Political, Economic, Social and Cultural Rights, Including the Right to Development. Business and Human Rights: Towards Operationalising the "Protect, Respect and Remedy" Framework*. Report of the Special Representative of the Secretary-General on the issue of human rights and transnational corporations and other business enterprises. UN Doc A/HRC/11/13. www2.ohchr.org/english/bodies/hrcouncil/docs/11session/a.hrc.11.13.pdf.

United Nations. (2011). *Guiding Principles on Business and Human Rights: Implementing the United Nations 'Protect, Respect and Remedy' Framework*. Report of the Special Representative of the Secretary-General on Human Rights, John Ruggie, on the issue of human rights and transnational corporations and other business enterprises. UN Doc A/HRC/17/31. New York/Geneva: UN. https://documents-dds-ny.un.org/doc/UNDOC/GEN/G11/121/90/PDF/G1112190.pdf?OpenElement.

United Nations. (2012). *The Corporate Responsibility to Respect Human Rights: An Interpretive Guide*. UN Doc HR/PUB/12/02. New York/Geneva: UN. www.ohchr.org/en/publications/special-issue-publications/corporate-responsibility-respect-human-rights-interpretive.

United Nations. (May 2013). *A New Global Partnership: Eradicate Poverty and Transform Economies through Sustainable Development*. Report of the high-level panel of eminent persons on the post-2015 development agenda. https://sustainabledevelopment.un.org/index.php?page=view&type=400&nr=893&menu=1561.

United Nations Committee on the Rights of the Child (CRC). (2013). General comment No. 16 (2013) on State obligations regarding the impact of the business sector on children's rights. www2.ohchr.org/english/bodies/crc/docs/CRC.C.GC.16.pdf.

United Nations Development Programme (UNDP). (2018). *Making Markets Work for the SDGs: UNDP's Private Sector Development and Partnership Strategy (2018–2022)*. New York: UNDP. www.undp.org/publications/undp-private-sector-strategy-2018-2022.

United Nations Special Representative of the Secretary-General on the Issue of Human Rights and Transnational Corporations and Other Business Enterprises (UN SRSG). (9 April 2010). *Business and Human Rights: Further Steps Toward the Operationalization of the 'Protect, Respect and Remedy' Framework*. UN Doc A/HRC/14/27. www.reports-and-materials.org/Ruggie-report-2010.pdf.

Van Gossum, P., Arts, B. and Verheyen, K. (2010). From 'smart regulation' to 'regulatory arrangements'. *Policy Sciences*, **43**(3), 245–61.

Vizard, P. (2006). *Poverty and Human Rights: Sen's 'Capability Perspective' Explored*. Oxford: Oxford University Press.

Weissbrodt, D. and Kruger, M. (2003). Norms on the responsibilities of transnational corporations and other business enterprises with regard to human rights. *American Journal of International Law*, **97**(4), 901–22.

Wettstein, F. (2010). The duty to protect: corporate complicity, political responsibility and human rights advocacy. *Journal of Business Ethics*, **96**, 33–47.

Wettstein, F. (2012). CSR and the debate on business and human rights: bridging the great divide. *Business Ethics Quarterly*, **22**(4), 739–70.

Wettstein, F. (2015). Normativity, ethics, and the UN Guiding Principles on Business and Human Rights: a critical assessment. *Journal of Human Rights*, **14**(2), 162–82.

Wettstein, F., Giuliani, E., Santangelo, G. and Stahl, G. (2019). International business and human rights: a research agenda. *Journal of World Business*, **54**(1), 54–65.

Williamson, D. and Lynch-Wood, G. (2021). *The Structure of Regulation: Explaining Why Regulation Succeeds and Fails*. Elgar Studies in Law and Regulation. Cheltenham, UK: Edward Elgar.

Working Group on Business and Human Rights. (2014). *Open Consultation on the Strategic Elements of National Action Plans in the Implementation of the UN Guiding Principles on Business and Human Rights*. Geneva: UN. www.ohchr.org/sites/default/files/Documents/Issues/Business/Session7/CNOpenConsultation20Feb2014.pdf.

Working Group on Business and Human Rights. (2016). *Guidance on National Action Plans on Business and Human Rights*. Geneva: UN. https://globalnaps.org/wp-content/uploads/2018/01/guidance-on-national-action-plans-on-business-and-human-rights.pdf.

World Bank Group (2021). *The State of Economic Inclusion Report 2021*. Washington, DC: International Bank for Reconstruction and Development/The World Bank.

Wouters, J. and Chané, A. (December 2013). *Multinational corporations in international law*. Leuven Centre for Global Governance Studies Working Paper No. 129. https://papers.ssrn.com/sol3/papers.cfm?abstract_id=2371216.

Yeganeh, H. (2020). A critical examination of the social impacts of large multinational corporations in the age of globalization. *Critical Perspectives on International Business*, **16**(3), 93–208.

Zerk, J. (2006). *Multinationals and Corporate Social Responsibility*. Cambridge: Cambridge University Press.

PART II

Infusing Corporate Social Responsibility in Corporate Governance

5

CSR, Directors and Top Management Officers: Responsibility and Accountability Pathways

Onyeka K. Osuji

[E]thical enquiry must begin with human judgments and human experiences because human beings are the only type of creatures that we know of who can engage in such an enterprise.

(Cochrane, 2012, p. 49)

A company may in many ways be likened to a human body. It has a brain and nerve centre which controls what it does. It also has hands which hold the tools and act in accordance with directions from the centre. Some of the people in the company are mere servants and agents who are nothing more than hands to do the work and cannot be said to represent the mind or will. Others are directors and managers who represent the directing mind and will of the company and control what it does.

(Lord Denning in HL Bolton (Engineering) Co. v. TJ Graham & Sons)[1]

[A corporation is a]n ingenious device for obtaining individual profit without individual responsibility.

(Bierce, 2003 [1911], p. 19)

[Corporate personality] can act as a convenient shield for the key decision makers in the corporation. The corporation can effectively absorb the punishment, normally in the form of a fine, while its directors and senior managers are relatively rarely exposed to sanction.

(Tombs and Whyte, 2015, p. 98)

5.1 INTRODUCTION

The aim of this chapter is to examine how the effectiveness of a regulatory scheme for corporate social responsibility (CSR) can be enhanced through provisions for responsibility and accountability of key corporate insiders. Drawing on the organic theory of the corporation, tone-at-the-top organisational theory and resource dependency, agency and stewardship theories, the chapter adopts an anthropocentric approach to demonstrate that certain corporate insiders play crucial roles in corporate governance and, as such, are critical for the CSR orientations of companies they control. Corporate conduct and corporate culture are often linked to how the insiders view CSR and the legal responsibilities associated with it.

The chapter is contextualised against the backdrop of the importance of relationships in corporate governance and therefore the need for appropriate regulation. Although corporate governance broadly includes both internal and external operations of companies, the focal point is usually internal direction and control as epitomised by the *UK Corporate Governance Code* (Financial Reporting Council (FRC), 2018). When it focusses on the internal and external dimensions driven by certain insiders, corporate governance can be regarded as relating to 'a set of relationships between a company's management, its board, its shareholders and other stakeholders' (Organisation for Economic Co-operation and Development (OECD), 2015, p. 9).

Traditionally, agency theory underlines the need for resolution of conflict of interests between directors (and managers) and shareholders (Choudhry and Petrin, 2018) and between controlling and minority shareholders (Gutiérrez and Sáez, 2013). Beyond these two forms of conflict of private interests, the emergence of CSR has arguably created another form of agency problem between company management and society or the public interest. Corporate governance therefore needs to recognise the public interest element and promote a variety of regulatory mechanisms enabling accountability for social responsibilities expected from companies (Choudhry and Petrin, 2018).

Several classes of person take or can take decisions that affect the directions and operations of a company, including its attitude to, and compliance with, legal rules and ethical standards. These persons may be part of the company's internal governance structure or outside of it. The distinction is crucial since, for example, unlike communications between insiders, professional privilege may attach to documents produced by external advisers for their clients.[2] Even if the functions of insiders and outsiders coincide, the differentiation is maintained in corporate governance. For instance, external auditors are different from the audit committee recommended by the *UK Corporate Governance Code* (FRC, 2018, pp. 10–12), although the latter, alongside the senior management officers, usually determines the internal audit quality (Erasmus and Coetzee, 2018).

While Chapter 9 of this book investigates the CSR role of outsiders providing professional advisory services, this chapter considers individuals holding critical positions in internal corporate governance structures. The chapter addresses the pertinent issues of whether and how to allocate and determine corporate insiders' responsibility and accountability. These issues are critical to the effectiveness, efficiency and responsiveness of a CSR regulatory regime. If, for instance, key persons have no legal responsibility or sanctions are applied to wrong targets, this is likely to be detrimental to regulatory effectiveness. A crucial factor is identifying targets of responsibility and accountability provisions for the regulatory objectives.

Rules and sanctions can be of little use if they are incorrectly targeted at or enforced against persons whose behaviour and decisions are critical to the achievement of regulatory goals.

The chapter therefore proposes making responsible and accountable those individuals who hold decision-making positions or have significant influence on the corporate decision-making process (see Figure 5.1). The primary target of legal responsibilities under company law is often the directors, perhaps owing to the orthodoxy that the '[b]oards of directors are responsible for the governance of their companies' (Committee on the Financial Aspects of Corporate Governance (Cadbury Committee), 1992, [2.5]). The Anglo-American corporate governance model rarely provides for defined duties for occupiers of top corporate positions other than the directors possibly because the directors determine the company's policies and control the other actors it employs. The usual approach is to provide for directors' duties such as in sections 170 to 178 of the UK Companies Act 2006 (see Arden, 2010; Hood, 2013).

If corporate governance can, however, be defined as 'the system by which companies are directed and controlled' (Cadbury Committee, 1992, [2.5]), there are potentially other persons besides the directors to consider. The chapter therefore argues for a more expansive approach to accommodate individuals like de facto directors, shadow directors and other senior officers likely to take or be involved in taking critical CSR-related decisions. This broader conception of responsibility and accountability is required for an effective regulatory regime for CSR. Furthermore, some alignment of corporate governance with the stakeholder model (Lombard and Joubert, 2014) is necessary to encourage key corporate insiders to adopt an appropriate CSR attitude and assure their accountability. To this end, the chapter includes original propositions for inclusive definition of key corporate insiders, personal responsibility and protection of stakeholder interests as well as tracing different methods of accountability. These suggestions do not displace corporate responsibility but are cognisant of fraud studies (Cooper et al., 2013) showing individual, firm, organisational and society dimensions of corporate behaviour.

Following this introduction, the next part examines the organic theory of the corporation with references to agency and stewardship theories to underscore the need for corporate and personal responsibility in a CSR regulatory scheme. It demonstrates that both corporate and personal responsibility flow from an anthropocentric approach to responsibility signalled by the organic and tone-at-the-top theories. These theories assist in identifying directors, non-executive and independent directors, quasi directors, company secretary and other senior officers as possible candidates for CSR-related responsibilities. The chapter then draws on Keay and Loughrey's (2015) four-stage approach to the board of directors' accountability to outline innovative ways that accountability can be attached to the personal responsibility of key corporate insiders. Suggestions include reframing the duties of directors and senior officers in clear statements of responsibilities, explicit protection of

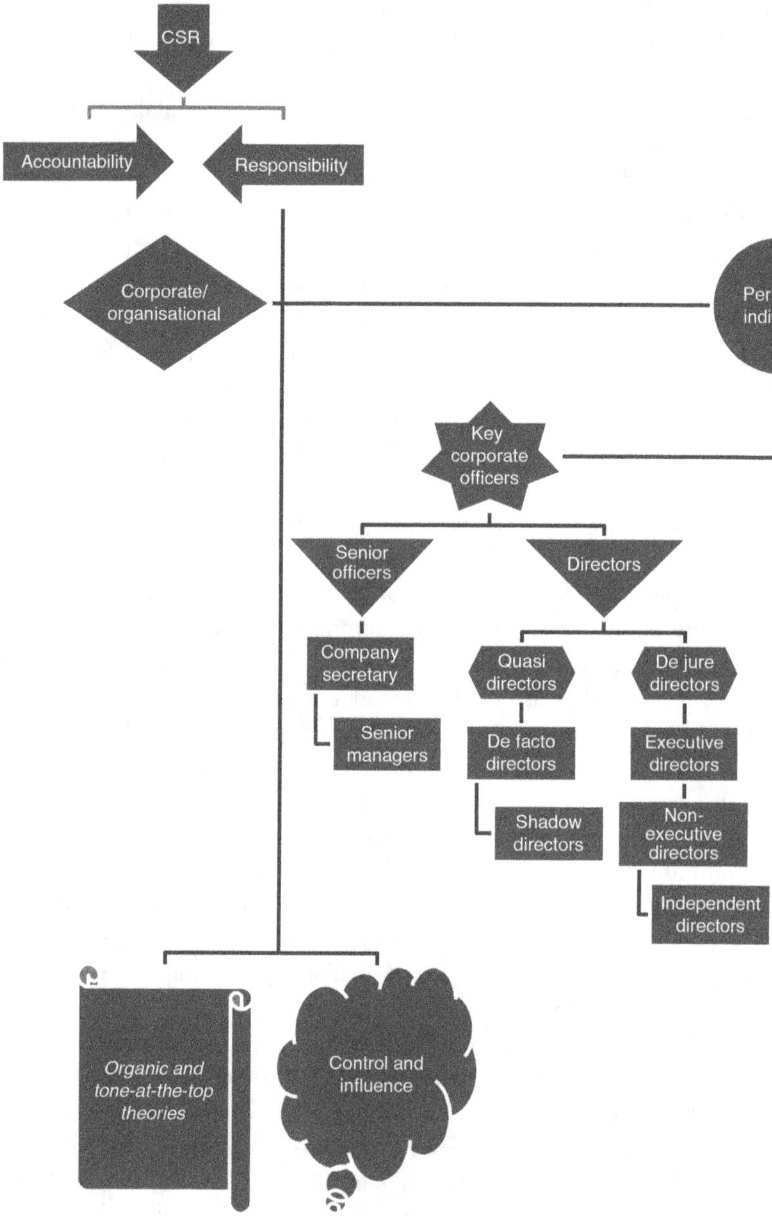

FIGURE 5.1 Tracing (corporate) responsibility

stakeholder interests, enhanced disclosure requirements, assurance provisions for CSR disclosures, whistle-blowing provisions, clarity of enforcement rights, disqualification provisions and collective responsibility, including through voluntary clubs (see Figure 5.2).

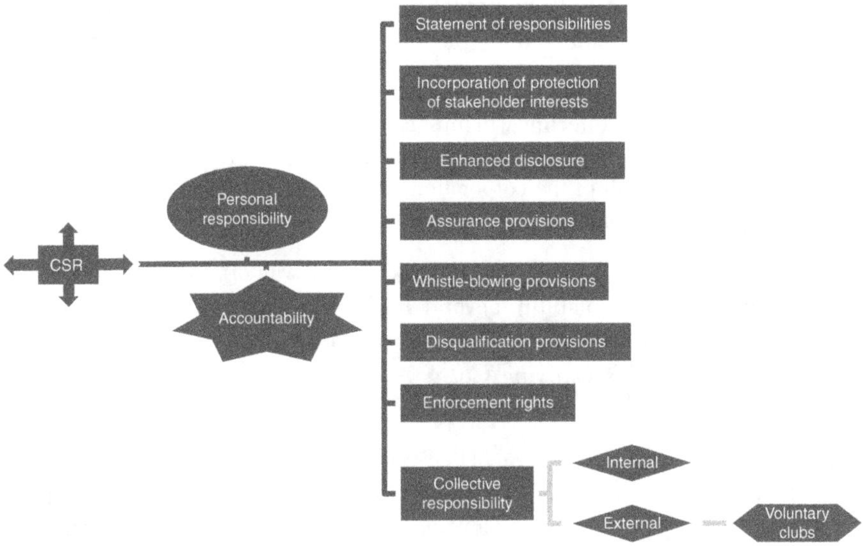

FIGURE 5.2 Accountability pathways for personal responsibility

5.2 ORGANIC THEORY AND (CORPORATE) RESPONSIBILITY

An arguably strong theoretical underpinning for responsibility questions in corporate affairs is the organic theory of the corporation. In contrast to the real theory that regards the corporation as a distinct entity separate from its members and management, the organic theory proceeds on the basis that a corporation is a legal abstraction lacking independent existence from the human actors behind it. As such, 'the corporation has no physical existence, neither body nor mind, [*sic*] it has always been understood that the corporation can only act through the agency of humans' (Stern, 1987, p. 667). In *Revenue and Customs Commissioners* v. *Holland*, Lord Hope of the UK Supreme Court equally pointed out that '[a] company is, of course, an artificial entity, a creature of statute [and s]o it can act only through human beings'.[3]

The organic theory is often cited with reference to the liability of corporations for the acts of the persons acting on their behalf (Capuano, 2010). The justification is that 'in the absence of human beings, corporations can do nothing; they can neither incur legal liabilities nor accrue legal rights' (Stern, 1987, p. 667) which suggests the need for finding out if a person 'is to be regarded as the company or merely as the company's servant or agent'.[4] This perhaps may explain why the organic theory is used to substantiate the imposition of tortious liability on corporations as principals without recourse to vicarious liability. In fact, the case of *Lennard's Carrying Co.* v. *Asiatic Petroleum Co.*[5] that pioneered the theory's recognition in the common law concerned tortious acts committed by a managing director. The court dismissed the company's argument that its liability could be founded only on the narrow grounds of vicarious liability and held that corporate liability as a principal tortfeasor is a legal possibility. The court explained that

> a corporation is an abstraction. It has no mind of its own any more than it has a body of its own; its active and directing will must consequently be sought in the person of somebody who for some purposes may be called an agent, but who is really the directing mind and will of the corporation, and [the] very ego and centre of the personality of the corporation.[6]

As Stern (1987, p. 669) noted, the organic theory was originally conceived 'to broaden corporate accountability beyond the confines of vicarious liability and permit personal liability to be applied to corporations'. The court implicitly confirmed this in *Lennard's Carrying Co.* v. *Asiatic Petroleum Co.*[7] by stating that corporate liability

> must be upon the true construction of that section in such a case as the present one that the fault or privity is the fault or privity of somebody who is not merely a servant or agent for whom the company is liable upon the footing respondeat superior, but somebody for whom the company is liable because his action is the very action of the company itself.

Lord Denning similarly observed that 'you will find in cases where the law requires personal fault as a condition of liability in tort, the fault of the manager will be the personal fault of the company'.[8] The intendment of the organic theory therefore lies in using potential liability to induce corporations to exercise due care in ensuring that they are represented by competent and proper persons.

The organic theory does not, however, displace the personal responsibility of the persons acting for the corporation to respect legal rules. As Stern (1987, p. 669) stated, the 'organic theory assumes that nothing in the nature or legal structure of corporations prevents the rules of personal liability from being applied just as they are applied to individuals'. The theory is meant to provide for a level of responsibility additional to that of the individual actors acting on the corporation's behalf.

Since '[i]nevitably it is human beings who must take decisions, and give effect to them by actions, if the company is to do anything at all',[9] the organic theory further throws up the question of whether legal responsibility should be attached to the corporation or to the human actors making decisions for it, or to both. As suggested by *Secretary of State* v. *Weston*[10] where directors were held personally responsible for their companies' non-compliance with statutory requirements, regulatory objectives may influence the choice of targets for responsibility and the extent to which they can be held accountable. Regulatory provisions may show that either corporate or individual responsibility, or both, is intended. If only corporate responsibility is intended, the individual corporate actor's culpability will not be an issue.[11] But situations may exist where corporate liability and individual liability can appropriately complement each other, be applied exclusively or be used in combination

(Clough and Mulhern, 2002, p. 8; Foster, 2008). It is 'undesirable' to treat either individuals or corporations as 'scapegoats' (Laufer, 2002) when either or both should be liable.

Individualism is not the default position in the Anglo-American corporate governance in which a collegiate principle applies to shareholders' general meetings and boards of directors in their roles as corporate organs.[12] The principle, which flows from the notion of companies as distinct entities with rights and obligations but acting only through their authorised organs, requires directors to act as the company's organ, and not as individuals, in managing its affairs in accordance with the corporate constitution. It is reflected in the provisions of the UK Companies Act 2006, including sections 394 and 414D. When the directors act as the corporate organ, the company that cloaked them with the capacity to represent it and that benefits from their decisions and actions on its behalf should ordinarily be responsible. After all, as stated in one old case, '[i]f a man select[s] another to act for him with some discretion, he has by that fact vouched to some extent for his reliability'.[13] Corporate responsibility therefore incentivises corporations to monitor and evaluate their processes and internal policing and implementation mechanisms to ensure compliance by their organs and agents (Clough and Mulhern, 2002, p. 6).

Nonetheless, projection of the principal–agent relationship does not fully capture the reality of corporate operations, particularly with regard to the possibility that certain individuals control the corporation and not the other way round. In some cases, 'there was nothing . . . that the principal could reasonably have been expected to do to prevent' (Hetherington, 1966, p. 115) those individuals' actions. Exclusive corporate responsibility may then unfairly target the company and undermine individual accountability where it may be needed. Judicial decisions indicate that, in some circumstances, responsibility is, at the least practically, on individual officers and not the company.[14] In *Tesco Supermarkets* v. *Nattrass*,[15] for example, the company proved that it had acted with due diligence although its manager's actions showed scant regard for the rules. The case suggests that in some situations it may be more appropriate to take action against individuals instead of, or as well as, the company (Cartwright, 2001, p. 119ff; see also Cartwright 1996).

If individual responsibility is not coupled with corporate responsibility, a divergence of interests may be created between the company and its human agents. Agency theory (Jensen and Meckling, 1976; Eisenhardt, 1989; Bendickson et al., 2016) has long called attention to the opportunities for conflicting interests in the principal–agency relationship between corporations and individuals acting on their behalf. Jensen and Meckling (1976, p. 318) postulated that '[i]f both parties to the relationship are utility maximisers[,] there is good reason to believe the agent will not always act in the best interest of the principal'. The agency problem arising from the conflict of interests is seen as a natural consequence of the separation of ownership and control of corporations (Fama and Jensen, 1983). As Berle and

Means (1932, p. 114) put it, corporate controllers 'can serve their own profits better by profiting at the expense of the company than by making profits for it'.

Agency theory labels the private arrangements to prevent abuses by corporate agents 'agency costs' (Jensen and Meckling, 1976; Fama, 1980; Maurović and Hasić, 2013). A difficulty with the theory's suggestion for resolving the agency problem is the reliance on shareholders, which is effectively a 'legal fiction' (Chandler Jr, 1977, p. 486) of their control of corporations. Since the middle of the twentieth century the critical 'decision-making control' (Berle, 1965, p. 81) has been with corporate managers rather than the 'owners'. In operation today is largely 'managerial capitalism', which has displaced previous dominations by financial institutions ('financial capitalism') and entrepreneurs or families ('family capitalism') (Chandler Jr, (1977, pp. 9–10; Dunlavy, 2004, p. 67).

Furthermore, conflicts of interests arise because circumstances may permit the human actors to detach themselves from the corporation's interest. As stewardship theory (Donaldson & Davis, 1991; Davis et al., 1997; Chrisman et al., 2007; Madison et al., 2016) suggests, corporate managers are more likely to advance the corporation's interests that are aligned with the managers' own interests. While it stresses the importance of governance mechanisms (Davis et al., 1997), stewardship theory asserts that managers are naturally inclined to act in the corporation's interest (Hernandez, 2008). The spate of corporate scandals across jurisdictions, however, gives credence to the agency theory's foundation on intrinsic opportunism in individual behaviour.

Another challenge is that both stewardship and agency theories advocate private ordering, principally by shareholders as the company 'owners', for moderating the managers' behaviour. But the reality of many modern corporations is 'the all-powerful board of directors' (Dunlavy, 2004, p. 86). Constitutionally, a majority of shareholders cannot interfere with the directors' exercise of management powers[16] and the directors' duty to promote the 'benefit of the company' is not equivalent to following the wishes of even a majority or substantial proportion of shareholders.[17] Shareholder control, through special resolutions, may be possible if the company's articles unusually allow it through provisions such as Article 4 in Schedule 1 of the UK Companies (Model Articles) Regulations 2008 prescribed under section 19 of the Companies Act 2006. In any event, section 283 of the Companies Act 2006 shows that special resolutions require a special majority of normally 75 per cent of shareholders following a stringent procedure.

The long-standing proper claimant rule established in *Foss* v. *Harbottle*[18] confirms that directors, and not shareholders, should normally authorise or undertake legal proceedings on the company's behalf.[19] As Jenkins LJ stressed in *Edwards* v. *Halliwell*,[20] derivative action is a key exception to the proper claimant rule (Wedderburn, 1957; Rider, 1978). Described as the 'chief regulator of corporate governance',[21] derivative action is designed to support shareholder oversight of managerial actions to check abuses and provide accountability (Reisberg, 2008;

Latella, 2009). Nonetheless, it has had modest impact on regulating directors' conduct through shareholder actions (Latella, 2010; Koutsias, 2017) as exemplified by the statutory derivative claim in the UK Companies Act 2006 several years after its introduction. A tiny proportion of the few cases of derivative claims lodged received the requisite court's permission to proceed (Keay, 2016). Equally, statutory derivative actions in Australia (Ramsay and Saunders, 2006), Hong Kong (Mezzanotte, 2017) and Singapore (Tang, 2020) have low numbers.

When the business judgement rule is activated, controlling managers can be problematic. Apart from the degree of discretionary power it confers on managers, the rule is founded on a presumption of 'external' authorities, including shareholders and the courts,[22] not interfering in the directors' commercial decisions while running the company's affairs. The rule, which applies on the basis of directors' subjective belief in acting in the company's best interests,[23] has been used to dismiss derivative suits in jurisdictions like the United States and can render private mechanisms of corporate accountability ineffective (Bowman, 1996, pp. 135–7).

The law can plausibly ensure the alignment of the interests of the corporation and its managers or controllers, including regarding legal compliance and its consequences and facilitating needful changes. But it is implicated (Bowman, 1996, p. 137) in creating the conditions for the emergence of 'managerial revolution' (Chandler Jr, 1977, pp. 484–500) by prioritising a private corporate decision-making process and structure. This has, in turn, made it difficult to rely on shareholders' private arrangements to provide for the human agents' responsibility and accountability. By counter analogy with the fundamental tort law principle that liability cannot be avoided by merely setting up the defence of acting as an agent,[24] the clash of interests can therefore be tackled in a regulatory scheme for CSR if individuals are legally responsible and accountable for the consequences of their decisions and actions, just like the corporations they represent or control.

When individual responsibility is lacking, regulatory goals may be defeated if corporations are not in a position to be accountable, including owing to insolvency, assets insufficiency, minimal capitalisation and even oversight or negligent actions of its human agents. In one case, for example, a company failed to provide a compulsory employee liability insurance contrary to the UK Employers' Liability (Compulsory Insurance) Act 1969.[25] The Supreme Court held that an injured employee could not claim against the insolvent company's directors despite the breach of statutory duty. Since, as underlined by the organic theory, the company's default was comparable to the directors' failure to act on its behalf, the directors might have been incentivised to undertake the required action on the company's behalf if the law had imposed personal responsibility and accountability on them.

On the other hand, exclusion of corporate responsibility in preference to individual responsibility may be problematic in some situations. Among other factors, complexities in the structure of corporations (Clough and Mulhern, 2002, p. 6) may hinder attempts at identifying the individuals that took decisions or actions. Multinational enterprises operating across jurisdictions, for instance, may maintain complex organisational and operational structures. For some reasons, including scarcity of enforcement resources, it may be difficult to prosecute individuals instead of corporations (Howells and Weatherill, 2005, p. 502). Situations involving the fault of more-junior officers, including the failure to carry out instructions, may not be enough for corporate liability.[26] Recourse may then be sought from vicarious liability, which normally requires proof that employees, notwithstanding their position in the company, acted in the course of employment.[27]

Moreover, the transient nature of individual roles may hamper efforts to effect lasting changes in corporate culture (Clough and Mulhern, 2002, p. 6) if individual responsibility is not coupled with corporate responsibility. For a field like CSR, which has attracted criticisms of symbolic compliance and generated terms such as 'greenwash' (Cherry and Sneirson, 2011; Parguel et al., 2011) and 'bluewash' (Berliner and Prakash, 2012, p. 151), the objectives of legal interventions should include the need to influence the corporate culture and to effect necessary and lasting changes. This may require a 'judicious' (Clough and Mulhern, 2002, p. 9) application of both corporate and individual responsibility techniques (United States Sentencing Commission, 2000, p. 403).

Combined corporate and individual responsibility is not unprecedented. For example, section 20 of the UK Trade Descriptions Act 1968 provides for joint corporate and individual responsibility for offences and specifically refers to liability of the company director, manager, secretary or other officer with evidence of the individual's consent, connivance or neglect. Likewise, sections 386 and 388 of the UK Companies Act 2006 require companies to keep accurate financial records while sections 387(1) and 389(1) of the Act provide for the criminal liability of 'every officer of the company who is in default'. Given the importance of individual responsibility, the chapter continues with analysis of critical individual roles in the CSR approaches of corporations.

5.3 CONSTRUCTING INDIVIDUAL RESPONSIBILITY

It is one thing to integrate individual responsibility into a regulatory CSR scheme, but it is equally crucial to identify key individual actors. After all, as Lord Denning aptly stated, individuals can be a company's 'brain and nerve centre which controls what it does' or its 'hands which hold the tools and act in accordance with directions from the centre'.[28] Tone-at-the-top theory (Lail et al., 2015; Patelli and Pedrini, 2015; Fischer and Friedman, 2019) likewise suggests that certain positions determine the corporation's direction in relation to legal rules and ethical standards. An important lesson from tone-at-the-top studies is to do with the role that individuals occupying 'top' positions play in establishing and sustaining corporate philosophies and culture and influencing other organisational actors. If the organic theory is placed side by side with tone-at-the-top theory, the implication is that corporate policies, attitudes and behaviour cannot be dissociated from how the occupiers of top positions in corporations are responsibilised and their perception of their responsibility for legal rules and ethical standards.

Signals from the top therefore have an impact on both organisational and individual behaviour. But narrow definitions of top positions are likely to affect regulatory effectiveness by excluding persons that can determine the tone-at-the-top and how it trickles down the organisational levels for the desired mindset and objectives to be achieved. It is important then to identify the top positions and their occupiers if initiatives, including regulations, are to have a real impact. This is arguably a question of the factual constitutive criteria of the management of corporations involving narrow and broader approaches to the interpretation of the role of 'manager'.

A narrow approach to the meaning of manager regards directors as the exclusive top positions and therefore the focus of legal and regulatory responsibilities. Particularly for criminal responsibility, it features the director as 'only a person who has the management of the whole affairs of the company, is in a position of real authority and has the power and responsibility to decide corporate policy and strategy'.[29] This will mean, for example, that directors are solely responsible for compliance with record-keeping requirements (Gale et al., 1999, p. 114 [6.4]). Accordingly, the UK Companies Act 2006 provides for directors' personal responsibility when companies fail to prepare strategic reports (section 414A(5)(6)) and if the reports are not backed by the board of directors' resolution (section 414D(2)(3)). Furthermore, the Act has mainly imposed CSR-related management responsibilities on directors as evident from provisions such as preparation of the yearly strategic reports (section 414A), the duty to promote the company's success through consideration of the long-term consequences of some stakeholder relationships and CSR matters (section 172) and the requirement of a 'section 172(1) statement' regarding how the directors have considered the matters specified in section 172(1)(a)–(f) (section 414CZA).

Nonetheless, there is no indication from organic and tone-at-the-top theories that the potential capability to act for the company or determine the organisational behaviour rests exclusively with directors. A spectrum of positions conceivably have such a capability, hence the theories may vindicate the 'Senior Managers and Certification Regime' of the UK Financial Conduct Authority, which requires its approval for the appointment of senior managers and imposes on senior managers responsibility for corporate activities. Corporations must also certify that their senior managers are fit and proper persons for their roles. This suggests that managing company affairs is a matter of degree and may involve a range of individuals in different critical positions.

Likewise, some cases[30] show that the notion of wrongdoers being in control for the purpose of derivative actions reflects both formal legal control and a factual test of the measure of influence exercised by those persons on others and in the corporate decision-making (Ahern, 2011). As Cheffins and Armour (2011, p. 59) noted, 'conceptually seeking influence and seeking control constitute points on a continuum rather than being fully distinct corporate governance phenomena'. This may explain why the courts, in practice, adopt a contextual approach in describing a 'manager' as being in 'a superior position'[31] or having 'real authority'[32] or representing 'the management of the whole affairs of the company [but not being an agent or a servant]'.[33]

Section 414C(9) of the UK Companies Act 2006 similarly defines a 'senior manager' as 'a person who (a) has responsibility for planning, directing or controlling the activities of the company, or a strategically significant part of the company, and (b) is an employee of the company'. This is a tacit acknowledgement of the broader conception which does not equate a manager with the managing director and other directors, or even a general manager, but covers 'any person who in the affairs of the company exercises a supervisory control which reflects the general policy of the company for the time being or which is related to the general administration of the company'.[34] In addition, individuals in 'the sphere of management' are not necessarily members of a company's board of directors or subject to specific instructions from the board.[35]

The broader understanding of management may be signalled using the expression 'officer'. In section 9 of the Corporations Act 2001 (Commonwealth) (Australia), for instance, apart from 'a director, or secretary of the corporation', 'officer' includes 'a person who makes, or participates in making, decisions that affect the whole, or a substantial part, of the business of the corporation; or who has the capacity to affect significantly the corporation's financial standing'. Likewise, section 1173 of the UK Companies Act 2006 defines 'officer' as including 'a director, manager or secretary'. While the provision goes further to give the meanings of 'director' and 'secretary', it gives no such indication regarding 'manager'. Drawing from the use of 'manager' in relation to section 221 of the UK Companies Act 1985 (now sections 386 and 388 of the Companies Act 2006), Gale et al. (1999, p. 114 [6.4]) suggested that it includes 'any employee of the company who has been entrusted by the directors to keep the accounting records in accordance with the statutory duty'. The broader conception of management in these statutory provisions reflects the practical description of a corporation as 'the modern form of artificial business entity owned by shareholders, overseen by a board of directors and operated day-to-day by officers' (Rost, 2004, p. 322).

In practice, directors may not be involved in the day-to-day management of company affairs (Klink, 2004, p. 198) and often delegate their management powers to other corporate officers (Cheffins, 1997, p. 44). It is legally acceptable for the directors to delegate powers,[36] notwithstanding their continuing individual and collective management roles, but only a few officers with delegated power sit on the board (Sheridan and Kendall, 1992, pp. 83–4; Cheffins, 1997, pp. 44, 603). The internal management rule equally seems to reflect an expansive approach to definition of company management. While the rule that 'persons contracting with a company and dealing in good faith may assume that acts within its constitution and powers have been properly and duly performed and are not bound to inquire whether acts of internal management have been regular'[37] is often used in reference to the authority of de facto directors, it implicitly acknowledges that the management of company affairs is not undertaken exclusively by directors.

It is noteworthy that in *Bolton Engineering*,[38] Lord Denning appeared to consider directors as a subclass of 'managers' – a term for persons occupying positions that enable them to provide directions for a company or manage its affairs. Millon (1990, p. 201) similarly applied 'management' or 'managers' interchangeably to 'refer collectively to the corporation's board of directors and senior officers'. The broader notion of management is therefore suggested for the CSR regulatory scheme to ensure that individuals in positions to initiate and implement CSR in corporations or influence organisational behaviour, including compliance with legal and ethical codes, are given responsibilities. As such, the components of CSR-related management are outlined in the rest of this section.

5.3.1 *Directors*

Being formally empowered to manage the affairs of companies,[39] such as through the power to bind companies in transactions with third parties in section 40 of the UK Companies Act 2006, directors are clearly within the contemplation of both the organic and the tone-at-the-top theories. Compared to other persons, including shareholders,[40] who legally have limited management roles, directors control corporations by being able to determine the scope and methods for carrying out long-term business objectives (Parkinson, 1993, p. 56; Cheffins, 1997, p. 44). While directors are expected to act 'with a proper sense of responsibility' and with regard to 'ordinary standards of commercial morality',[41] the law can signpost what these considerations might be, how they are assessed and what form of accountability they might require. As Menzies (1959, p. 164) observed, 'what is in general expected of directors will tend to become the measure of what is required of them'.

Directors' individual responsibility will allow room for their personal liability and reputational risk. This acknowledges the board of directors' resource and oversight roles (Bostrom, 2003) and can address directors' lack of interest in company affairs and assist in improving their performance (DeMott, 2004, pp. 27, 43). Personal liability is an appropriate response when directors have evidently shirked their duties or shown disregard for risks to the company.[42] It should apply even if directors have delegated management powers to other officers since such delegation does not discharge directors from the responsibility of undertaking appropriate supervision of tasks[43] and monitoring of delegated officers (Demb and Neubauer, 1992, p. 55; Clutterbuck and Waine, 1993, pp. 9–10; Cheffins, 1997, p. 605). To suggest otherwise[44] 'means unquestioning reliance [by directors] upon others to do their job'[45] and promoting 'conscious inaction'[46] to the detriment of the company's interests.[47] Consequently, in *Re Barings (No. 6)*,[48] the court disqualified a director for not maintaining competent supervision of other officers.

5.3.2 *Non-executive and Independent Directors*

Unlike executive directors who hold managerial positions in companies, non-executive directors are 'individuals that serve on the board [of directors] but do not work for the business enterprise on a fulltime basis' (Cheffins, 1997, p. 602). While there may be employment law significance for executive directorship, company law generally does distinguish between executive and non-executive directors. In the statement of directors' duties in part 10 of chapter 5 of the UK Companies Act 2006, for example, there are no distinctions between executive and non-executive directors who are equally expected to undertake those duties.

Nonetheless, there is the question of the effectiveness of a CSR regulatory framework if the distinction between executive and non-executive directors in corporate practice is maintained or discarded. On the one hand, expectations might be lower for non-executive directors than executive directors owing to the latter's involvement in the day-to-day company affairs. Non-executive directors, for instance, may exhibit 'heavy' (Cheffins, 1997, p. 611) dependence on executive directors and other members of the management for information and, as such, divergence in legal responsibilities may be necessary.

On the other hand, non-executive director status should not provide an escape route from legal responsibility.[49] The modern conception of directors' duty to protect the company's interests requires a 'more active and affirmative' (DeMott, 2004, p. 24) in its affairs (Johnson, 2003). All directors, irrespective of their title or status, are legally required to 'have a continuing duty to acquire and maintain a sufficient knowledge and understanding of the company's business to enable them properly to discharge their duties as directors'.[50] In this regard, duties such as promotion of the company's success and exercise of independent judgement and reasonable care, skill and diligence in sections 172, 173 and 174 of the UK Companies Act 2006 should apply equally to all directors. What is legally expected of non-executive directors is 'independence of judgment and supervision of the executive management'[51] and to not 'abdicate responsibility'.[52] Since the requirement includes awareness of, and compliance with, applicable rules,[53] a person can be disqualified from being a director for lacking relevant knowledge and understanding.[54] Otherwise, directors, who ought to display personal skills and judgement, may escape legal responsibilities simply by asserting their reliance on others. This will defeat the goals of a CSR regulatory scheme to the detriment of stakeholder interests sought to be protected.

Ideally, non-executive directors undertake a critical objective monitoring role over the management owing to their lack of managerial functions (Zalecki, 1993, pp. 848–55; Cheffins, 1997, p. 605; Higgs, 2003; European Commission, 2005). This oversight role includes both vigilance and advisory functions. The vigilance functions of acting as a watchdog for 'the interests of the company and its stakeholders' (DeMott, 2004, p. 29) may be more critical in enterprises with widely dispersed ownership than those of concentrated ownership (Coffee, 2005, p. 200). Therefore, legally framed CSR-related minimum standards of behaviour and performance should be applicable to anyone who accepts the office of director. Non-executive directors, just like other directors, should owe duties they cannot 'surrender' by 'washing their hands'.[55] Non-executive directors are a recognised part of company management in modern corporate governance and therefore should ordinarily be involved in the internal control and oversight processes (Moore, 2010), including the CSR-related ones.

Likewise, independent directors (Crespí-Cladera and Pascual-Fuster, 2014) who can potentially influence the attitude of the board of directors to legal rules and industry practices, such as accounting standards (Elshandidy and Hassanein, 2014), should be part of the framework of CSR-related legal responsibilities. Just like non-executive directors, independent directors should exercise personal skills and judgement and not be excused from legal responsibilities by demonstrating reliance on others or lack of involvement in the company's day-to-day affairs. In modern corporate governance discourse, independent directors who are not the controlling shareholders or their representatives are expected to monitor the latter. The monitoring role over other corporate insiders and in resolution of agency problems between the controlling and minority shareholders suggests that independent directors' accountability should be prominent in corporate governance (Gutiérrez and Sáez, 2013). The quality of independent directors' performance is therefore a critical ingredient for maintaining the balance of power between the board of directors and the shareholders (DeMott, 2004, p. 24). However, the lack of proprietary stake may not provide independent directors with an 'affirmative incentive' (DeMott, 2004, p. 25) to protect the interests of the company or its stakeholders unless their legal responsibilities are defined.

5.3.3 *Quasi Directors*

It is useful to consider the CSR-related responsibilities of 'quasi directors', used here to denote persons involved in company management without the formal title of director. Company law already recognises 'de facto' directors and 'shadow' directors[56] within this class and, in some instances, assigns them responsibilities. De facto directors, who assume, claim and purport to act as directors,[57] are responsible for their actions irrespective of the regularity or otherwise of their appointment. According to section 251 of the UK Companies Act 2006, a shadow director is one in accordance with whose directions the directors act or exercise any discretion conferred on them and, by section 170(5), directors' general duties in part 10 of chapter 5 of that Act apply to shadow directors 'where and to the extent that they are capable of so applying'. Shadow directorship is mainly based on 'a pattern of behaviour'[58] indicating the directors' receipt of instructions from the shadow director. A key factor is therefore proof of communication and the consequences of instructions or directions.[59]

Being that de facto and shadow directors factually occupy top positions that allow them to determine the company's decisions and actions, the organic and tone-at-the-top theories would suggest the need for their responsibilities in a CSR regulatory scheme. The basis of the de facto directors' responsibility is their performance of functions that could only be performed by directors.[60] If one assumes a role, one should also be ordinarily responsible for the consequences of actions taken under that role. Moreover, a de facto director can attract liability for the company since, as provided by section 161 of the UK Companies Act 2006, the validity of actions is unaffected by any defects in the appointment, qualification or status of a 'director'.

The shadow directors' pre-eminent position puts them squarely within the tone-at-the-top analysis since, factually, their relationship with the directors seems to be between a superior and subordinates. In that case, shadow directors as superiors should be responsible for the outcome of their directions or instructions to 'subordinates' and for the consequences of decisions and actions taken under their dominant influence. Likewise, company law provisions on shadow directors are designed to identify the persons with 'real influence in a company's affairs'.[61]

Arguably, it may be unnecessary to make specific references to de facto and shadow directors in CSR-related responsibilities since company law in the UK, for instance, captures them within the concept of director. Nonetheless, clarity is assured by providing the definitional scope for director and the CSR responsibilities attached to it, as some examples in UK law show. Notwithstanding the general definition of shadow director in section 251 of the Companies Act 2006, section 859 confirms that a shadow director is a director for the purposes of part 24 of the Act. Sections 4(2), 6(3)(c), 8(1), 9(2) and 22(4) of the Company Directors Disqualification Act 1986 declare that a director for the purposes of sections 6 and 7 includes a shadow director. As applied in cases such as *Secretary of State for Trade and Industry* v. *Deverell*,[62] section 22(5) of the 1986 Act defines a shadow director as 'a person in accordance with whose directions or instructions the directors of the company are accustomed to act'. These provisions are designed to ensure unequivocal application to shadow directors and to avoid controversies surrounding relevance of the general company law definition.

5.3.4 *Company Secretary*

A company secretary is normally a legal requirement, as seen in section 270 of the UK Companies Act 2006, although private companies can opt out under sections 271 to 279. While the combined effect of sections 273, 277 and 278 of the UK Companies Act 2006 suggests that individuals or firms can be a company secretary, this chapter focusses on corporate insiders and, as such, on the internal corporate governance post as against external advisory services covered under Chapter 9 of this book.

Once regarded as a purely administrative role,[63] the company secretary was at the lower end of the scale to attract application of the organic and tone-at-the-top theories. The company secretary was viewed as 'a mere servant; his position is that he is to do what he is told, and no person can assume that he has any authority to represent anything at all'.[64] Nowadays, the company secretary is a 'corporate governance officer' and 'corporate gatekeeper' (Lee, 2018) occupying a prime position under the organic and tone-at-the-top theories. Cases such as *Panorama Developments Ltd* v. *Fidelis Furnishing Fabrics Ltd*[65] have transformed the company secretary's status from 'a mere servant of the company to a statutory officer who takes on managerial functions such as chief of staff to the chairman or adviser to the board' (Lee, 2018, p. 110). Company secretaries can, for instance, act as a bridge between executive directors and independent and non-executive directors (McNulty and Stewart, 2015). Implicitly confirming these developments, the *UK Corporate Governance Code* (FRC, 2018, p. 7 [16]) recommends that 'directors should have access to the advice of the company secretary, who is responsible for advising the board on all governance matters'.

Company secretaries now play active roles in formulating and implementing companies' CSR agendas (Idowu, 2009) and in UK company law, for example, there is some emergent acknowledgement that they can undertake CSR-related functions. Section 414D(1) of the Companies Act 2006 is illustrative by requiring the board of directors' approval of strategic reports which the company secretary can sign in place of the directors. Therefore, as the company secretary holds a top corporate governance position, their responsibility is crucial for a CSR regulatory scheme.

5.3.5 *Other Corporate Officers*

Other corporate officers capable of being the 'directing mind and will of the company'[66] should have personal responsibility regulatory arrangements for CSR. Since some officers other than directors 'are put into a position of trust for the express purpose of attending to details of management',[67] they may be critical positions emphasised by the organic and tone-at-the-top theories. Corporate responsibility can be triggered by actions of corporate officers who are not directors but occupy significant positions. In *Meridian Global Finance* v. *Securities Commissioner*, for instance, a multinational company was found guilty of serious securities offences committed by middle-level managers. In contrast, *R* v. *Jukes*[68] demonstrates how corporate failings can be attributed to specific individuals. In that case, a transport and operations manager responsible for health and safety was convicted for failing in his duties.

Moreover, the duty to disclose corporate wrongdoing is not dependent on holding a particular office or exercising some supervisory functions.[69] Even when officers act as directors' agents, tort law suggests that this may not be an adequate defence[70] and criminal law generally shows that responsibility is not avoided merely by following superiors' directions. There are statutory precedents for the individual responsibility of officers who are not directors.

In the UK, sections 387 and 389 of the Companies Act 2006 provide for the liability of 'every officer in default'. This approach to personal responsibility is a departure from section 221(5) of the 1985 Companies Act and is also reflected in section 152 of the Financial Services and Markets Act 2000, which imposes liability on 'responsible persons' defined as the issuer, directors of the issuer, persons named with their authorisation as directors of the issuer, persons who accept and are so stated in the particulars as having accepted responsibility for all or any part of the particulars, and other persons who have authorised all or parts of the contents of the particulars. An identical set of provisions can be found in regulation 13 of Australia's Public Offers of Securities Regulations.[71] Regarded as imposing personal liability on 'all individuals who would in the normal course of business have the function to review and sign off financial statements and internal control reports' (Tanega, 2006, p. 171), section 302 of the US Sarbanes-Oxley Act 2002 specifies chief executive officers, chief financial officers 'or officers, or persons performing similar functions'. These provisions suggest that corporate officers' personal responsibility should be available if their roles are critical for achieving important regulatory goals, particularly those aimed at protecting the public interest.

5.4 TRACKING PERSONAL RESPONSIBILITY AND ATTACHING ACCOUNTABILITY

The preceding discussions have emphasised the need for personal responsibility of key corporate insiders. It has been shown that the law can, for good reasons, impose the personal responsibility and demand the accountability necessary for the achievement of regulatory goals. The case is made for attaching personal responsibility to individuals to whom corporate irresponsibility can be attributed in failing to undertake CSR-related responsibilities. Nonetheless, the personal liability of individuals acting on the company's behalf is normally considered contrary to the corporate personality and limited liability principles (Rajak, 2004, pp. 118–24; Ireland, 2010; Bainbridge and Henderson, 2016). Except when other persons relied on personal liability voluntarily assumed by individual corporate actors, a number of decisions[72] confirm that personal responsibility requires legislative framing.[73]

Being that corporate personality and its consequences continue to be essentially a matter of state concession, despite evolving understandings (Watson, 2019), it is equally necessary to provide for accountability pathways in a regulatory scheme for CSR. Coupling accountability to personal responsibility ensures that regulatory objectives are meaningful and not undermined by key individuals who decline to pursue organisational compliance. An example is the BHS group collapse (Ireland, 2018; Nelken and Levi, 2018), which triggered calls for employees and their representatives to be allowed to bring statutory derivative claims (Safari and Gelter, 2019). The United Kingdom House of Commons Work and Pensions and Business, Innovation and Skills Committees (2017, p. 54 [7]) found that '[m]any of those closest to the decisions that led to the collapse of BHS have walked away greatly enriched despite the company's failure'. The statement underscores the consequences of accountability gaps for actors 'closest to the decisions' and the need for recognising some form of stakeholder model to incentivise responsibility and accountability. In contrast, in *Office of Fair Trading* v. *Miller*,[74] the public enforcement authorities permitted by the fair trading law initially obtained an injunction against an unincorporated business selling kitchen units in breach of statutory terms on satisfactory quality and correspondence with description. Owing to the persistent unfair trading practices, action was taken against the business owner who was convicted of contempt of court even though he was not personally involved in selling defective products to consumers.

The law therefore ought to state the 'objective' and 'scope' (Zhao, 2019) of responsibilities it imposes and, as Australia's Corporations Act 2001 seems to provide in some instances (Cermak, 2018), legislation can provide for the accountability of persons identified following the application of the organic and tone-at-the-top theories. Nonetheless, accountability provisions need to reflect a framework that protects, and encourages legal compliance for, 'the common good' (Keay and Loughrey, 2015) that prompted regulatory intervention. In this regard, Keay and Loughrey's (2015) four-stage approach to the board of directors' accountability is helpful. With transparency as the driver, the first two disclosure-related stages require timely and credible information on relevant policies, responsibilities, judgements and actions accompanied by explanations and justifications. The third stage relates to scrutiny and assessment of the steps undertaken in the first two and the final stage is post-evaluation consequences, which can be adverse with sanctions or positive with rewards.

This accountability framework suggests that statements of CSR-related responsibilities are crucial. Since CSR is grounded in the stakeholder model (see Chapter 2 of this book), there is the need to specify what stakeholders and stakeholder interests, such as climate-related ones (Sjåfjell, 2018), are covered within the legal framework and to what extent. Clarity of these statements is essential. Apart from some recognition of creditors' interests[75] at the onset or imminence of insolvency (Keay, 2007, 2015; Milman, 2013), there is little room for public interest and stakeholder interest considerations in the Anglo-American approach to directors' duties. This is despite the notion of directors' duties having emerged in that legal tradition to counterbalance the corporate personality and limited liability doctrines and protect shareholders (Turner, 2020, pp. 246–9). Moreover, in the UK Companies Act 2006, the references to stakeholders in relation to the duty to promote company success in section 172 have generated a great deal of debates and uncertainties (Loughrey et al., 2008; Keay, 2019) in the more than fifteen since its enactment.

In furtherance of the stakeholder model, it is helpful to specify CSR-related duties and who can enforce them. In general, statutory duties can only be enforced as specified by the enabling instrument and enforcement rights should not be automatically assumed.[76] *Campbell* v. *Peter Gordon Joiners Ltd*,[77] discussed in Section 5.2 (see note 25), exemplifies the need for coupling enforcement rights to provisions aimed at protecting stakeholder interests. As the Canadian case of *Das* v. *George Weston Limited*[78] brought following the Rana Plaza collapse confirms, a company does not owe a duty of care to its stakeholders merely by acknowledging their existence and taking steps to protect them. As such, the defendant companies owed no duty of care to employees of their Bangladeshi suppliers despite ignoring their own CSR codes and social audits which revealed building deficiencies and labour malpractices. In contrast, a form of accountability is provided by section 1324 of Australia's Corporations Act 2001, which allows 'a person whose interests have been, are or would be affected by the conduct' of directors in contravention of its provisions to ask for a court injunction.

Specific references to CSR-related reputation in the statement of responsibilities may assist in providing clarity of regulatory intendment of accountability for the courts and other authorities. For example, while interpreting the directors' duty of care and diligence in managing company affairs in section 180(1) of Australia's Corporations Act 2001, Edelman J held in *Australian Securities and Investments Commission* v. *Cassimatis (No. 8)*[79] that the objective duty includes assessment of both financial and reputational risks.

Furthermore, Keay and Loughrey's (2015) accountability framework suggests that statements of responsibilities should include enhanced disclosure obligations. These obligations should be designed to ensure adequate and reliable disclosure to stakeholders, which is essential for them to undertake CSR-related civil regulation (Parkinson, 2003) and therefore an accountability mechanism. Different forms of qualitative and quantitative CSR-related narrative reporting are increasingly adopted (de Villiers et al., 2014; KPMG, 2015, 2017; Kiliç and Kuzey, 2018) and encouraged by initiatives such as the *G20/OECD Principles of Corporate Governance* (OECD, 2015, pp. 38–9). At face value, narrative reporting is normally cognisant of broader social contexts of business (Sinkovics et al., 2016) and can be used for evaluating management performance and extending rewards or sanctions just like in financial reporting (Siegel, 2006, p. 51).

Nonetheless, serious doubts about the credibility of CSR disclosures prompted Gray (2010, p. 48), for example, to observe that 'most business reporting on sustainability and much business representative activity around sustainability actually have little, if anything to do with sustainability'. Assurance services for CSR reports (Canning et al., 2019; Rinaldi, 2019) produced by key officers on the company's behalf can assist in improving their credibility and reliability for evaluation and comparison purposes, but some legal framework is useful. As discussed in Chapter 9 of this book, it is necessary to provide for the responsibility and accountability of auditors and other professional advisory services.

As Keay and Loughrey's (2015) framework shows that opportunities for questioning and assessing actors' decisions and actions are integral to accountability, clarity is also required regarding who can demand accountability from corporate actors assigned responsibilities. In contrast, the approach in the UK Companies Act 2006 arguably lacks such clarity. While largely orientated towards the shareholder primacy model, one of the limitations is that directors' duties are not really owed to shareholders but to the company as an entity separate from its shareholders and directors. As stated in the old case of *Foss* v. *Harbottle*,[80] '[i]n law[,] the corporation and the aggregate members of the corporation are not the same thing'. In *Macaura* v. *Northern Assurance Co.*,[81] the court stated that '[the shareholder,] even if he holds all the shares[,] is not the corporation'. Directors are normally given the power to undertake proceedings on the company's behalf[82] and, therefore, to enforce the directors' duties owed to the company. Even then, the reflective loss principle means that recoveries for any breach of the directors' duties are the company's alone,[83] which is little motivation for shareholders that may desire to undertake derivative actions on the company's behalf. As such, recourse to private shareholder actions for enforcing directors' duties is largely ineffective (Attenborough, 2020). Public enforcement of directors' duties (Keay, 2014a, 2014b) is an accountability mechanism that can assist in protecting and balancing the public interest and multi-stakeholder interests through a public agency acting independently of diverse stakeholders.

Whistle-blowing provisions are essential for accountability and for overcoming relational and solidarity signals that create conflicts of interest triggered by a sense of organisational loyalty. Effective whistle-blowing provisions need 'persons and organisations that may be able to effect action' (Near and Miceli, 1985, p. 4) as underlined by the organic and tone-at-the-top theories. Owing to 'the conflict between the duty of loyalty to the firm or organisation in which one works and the liberty to speak out against wrongdoing' (Lindblom, 2007, p. 415), a regulatory scheme for CSR may need to include corporate officers' legal responsibilities to disclose wrongdoing and to act on reports provided by others, including middle and lower management officers, employees, professional advisers and independent contractors. Adequate provisions are necessary for protecting whistle-blowers, including from corporations and key corporate actors.

A possible tool for promoting personal responsibility and accountability in corporate governance is disqualification of individuals from management of companies (Osuji and Moore, 2017). The European Commission (2003) similarly recognised disqualification as a tool for enhancing the effectiveness of directors' duties, although its proposals were not implemented (McCormack et al., 2017, pp. 25–6).

Properly framed, disqualification provisions aligned with legal responsibilities can serve as a method of demanding accountability, identifying deficiencies in the competence of individuals undertaking those responsibilities and acting as deterrence against irresponsibility. In the Australian case of *Australian Securities and Investments Commission* v. *Flugge (No. 2)*,[84] for example, the chairman-director of a company that made payments to a foreign government in contravention of a UN sanctions regime was disqualified. Nonetheless, *Secretary of State* v. *Weston*[85] suggests that the accountability provided by disqualification provisions may be far-fetched if they are not unequivocally worded, even if individuals have violated legal requirements. Clarity of legislative intention for linking CSR responsibilities to disqualification provisions is therefore necessary.

Another method for promoting accountability is through collective responsibility for CSR-related roles. The notion of collective responsibility is recognised in company law for corporate governance and operations, but this is normally in relation to general directors' duties. As such, in *Re Westmid*, Lord Woolf MR stressed that the directors' 'collegiate or collective responsibility must however be based on individual responsibility [and e]ach individual director owes duties to the company to inform himself about its affairs and to join with his co-directors in supervising and controlling them'.[86] Other than those general duties, linkages between collective responsibility and individual accountability need to be explicit, particularly when other corporate officers are also targeted in addition to directors.

Collective responsibility can be internal or external. In accordance with this chapter's suggestion of a more expansive approach to company management, internal collective responsibility may include directors and other individuals occupying top corporate positions in line with insights from the organic and tone-at-the-top theories. This collective responsibility may require key officers to report CSR-related wrongdoing by others to appropriate channels and to act as protected whistle-blowers when necessary, while failure to act can be a breach of duty. Externally, collective responsibility can be imposed through supportive legal provisions for stringent voluntary clubs that align them with regulatory objectives (see Chapter 9 of this book). As indicated in Chapter 9, the club approach can be grounded in the institutional (North, 1990) and resource dependency (Pfeffer and Salancik, 1978; Hillman et al., 2009; Miller et al., 2013) theories. Voluntary clubs can provide opportunities for learning and strategic alliances (Inkpen and Tsang, 2007), and establish forums for disseminating and implementing industry standards such as accounting (Elshandidy and Hassanein, 2014) that can inform corporate practices and platforms for receiving and acting on whistle-blowing. A club approach can assist in overcoming obstacles posed to accountability by company law's business judgement rule. The long-standing attitude encapsulated in the business judgement rule, which makes courts disinclined to challenge directors' management decisions, persists with low levels of director liability. More recent successful challenges of the business judgement rule in cases of insolvent private companies (Keay et al., 2020) remain an outlier.

5.5 CONCLUSION

This chapter has investigated the vital role of directors and top management officers in the achievement of CSR-related regulatory objectives. It draws on the organic theory of the corporation to demonstrate the need for both corporate and personal responsibility for an effective regulatory scheme. The dual responsibility approach provides an incentive for corporations and individuals acting on their behalf to align their decisions and behaviours with regulatory objectives. Otherwise, lack of responsibility may give credence to the proposition that 'individual profit without individual responsibility' (Bierce, 2003 [1911]:19) is irresistible to corporations and corporate law. If responsibility is fixed at the corporate level only, a divergence of interests may be created between the company and the individuals who effectively control or direct its affairs. With some references to agency theory and stewardship theory, the chapter therefore argues that both individual and collective responsibility are imperative for appropriate standards of behaviour and decision-making, including in relation to CSR and the public interest and stakeholder interests it involves.

Furthermore, the chapter draws on the organic theory and tone-at-the-top organisational theory to suggest that a CSR regulatory scheme needs to consider the capability of certain individuals to control and influence the decisions and behaviours of corporations and other corporate actors. Proposing a control and influence-based anthropocentric approach, the chapter argues that CSR responsibilities can extend the confines of the traditional focus on directors. It then identifies *de jure* directors, including executive, non-executive and independent directors, de facto directors and shadow directors as well as company secretaries and other senior management officers as possible candidates for CSR-related personal responsibility. A case is made for accountability provisions to bolster personal responsibility since lack of consequences for the decisions and actions of individuals acting on the company's behalf can derail regulatory objectives. Personal responsibility is not meaningful without accountability and if accountability provisions are lacking or placed exclusively on the corporation, this again signposts a bifurcation of the interests of corporations and individual actors in the regulatory scheme.

In making innovative suggestions for attaching accountability to personal responsibility, the chapter adapts Keay and Loughrey's (2015) four-stage approach to the board of directors' accountability. Essential for a CSR regulatory regime are clear statements of responsibilities of key corporate officers that may include provisions for identifying stakeholders and consideration of their interests, enhanced disclosure requirements and assurance services to improve their credibility and reliability. Whistle-blowing provisions are necessary to encourage corporate officers to act on wrongdoing or behaviour that is contrary to regulatory objectives. Post-event disqualification provisions can promote accountability through personal consequences for demonstrable lack of adherence to regulatory goals; they can also deter other corporate actors from personal irresponsibility. Collective responsibility can be stimulated within the company for corporate officers and externally through voluntary clubs. Enforcement provisions for the suggested accountability routes are crucial. Enforcement rights should be specified since statutory responsibilities are not automatically translated to rights of action on anyone.

Responsibility and accountability go to the root of effective regulatory schemes. Targets of legal responsibilities should be correctly identified as being in a position to determine decisions and actions necessary for achieving or capable of clogging regulatory goals. This chapter has demonstrated that directors and other top management officers are prime candidates for personal responsibility and accountability in regulating CSR.

NOTES

1. *HL Bolton (Engineering) Co.* v. *TJ Graham & Sons* [1957] 1 QB 159, 172 (Lord Denning).
2. *Three Rivers District Council* v. *Bank of England* [2004] UKHL 48; *Three Rivers District Council* v. *Bank of England* [2003] EWCA Civ 474.
3. *Revenue and Customs Commissioners* v. *Holland* [2010] UKSC 51, [20] (Lord Hope).
4. *Tesco Supermarkets Ltd* v. *Nattrass* [1972] AC 153, 170.
5. *Lennard's Carrying Co.* v. *Asiatic Petroleum Co.* [1915] AC 705.
6. *Lennard's Carrying Co.*, 713–14.
7. *Lennard's Carrying Co.*
8. *HL Bolton (Engineering) Co.*, 172 (Lord Denning).
9. *Revenue and Customs Commissioners*, [20] (Lord Hope).
10. *The Secretary of State for Business, Innovation and Skills* v. *Weston* [2014] EWHC 2933 (Ch).
11. *R* v. *Warwickshire County Council ex p. Johnson* [1993] AC 583, [1993] 2 WLR 1.
12. *Howard Smith Ltd* v. *Ampol Petroleum Ltd* [1974] AC 821.
13. *Kidd* v. *Thomas A. Edison, Inc.*, 239 F. 405, 408 (SDNY 1917).
14. E.g., *Tesco Supermarkets*; *McGuire* v. *Sittingbourne Cooperative Society* (1976) 120 SJ 197, [1976] Crim. LR 268; *Warwickshire County Council* v. *Johnson* (1992) 156 JP 577, 586 (Popplewell J).
15. *Tesco Supermarkets*.
16. *Automatic Self-Cleansing Filter Syndicate Co. Ltd* v. *Cuninghame* [1906] 2 Ch 34; *John Shaw & Sons (Salford) Ltd* v. *Shaw* [1935] 2 KB 113, 134 (Greer LJ); *Howard Smith Ltd*, 837 (Lord Wilberforce).
17. See *Menier* v. *Hooper's Telegraph Works* (1874) LR 9 Ch 250 (Mellish LJ); *Pender* v. *Lushington* (1877) 6 ChD 70, 75 (Jessell MR); *Alexander* v. *Automatic Telephone Co.* [1900] 2 Ch 56; *Allen* v. *Gold Reefs of West Africa* [1900] 1 Ch 671; *Dafen Tinplate Co.* v. *Llanelly Steel Co. Ltd* [1920] 2 Ch 124; *Prudential*

Assurance Co. Ltd v. *Newman Industries (No. 2)* [1981] Ch 257; *Estmaco Ltd* v. *GLC* [1982] 1 WLR 2; *Greenhalgh* v. *Ardene Cinemas* [1951] Ch 286; *Paramount Communications* v. *Time Inc.*, 571 A2d. 1140 (1989), 571 A2d. 1145 (Del. 1990).

18. *Foss* v. *Harbottle* [1843] 67 ER 189.
19. *Macdougall* v. *Gardiner* [1875] 1 Ch D 13.
20. *Edwards* v. *Halliwell* [1950] 2 All ER 1064.
21. *Cohen* v. *Beneficial Industrial Corp*, 337 US 541 (1949), 548.
22. *Re Macro (Ipswich) Ltd* [1994] 2 BCLC 354.
23. *Re Smith and Fawcett Ltd* [1942] 1 All ER 542.
24. *Vacher* v. *London Society of Compositors* [1913] AC 107, 131.
25. *Campbell* v. *Peter Gordon Joiners Ltd* [2016] UKSC 38.
26. *DSG Retail Ltd* v. *Oxfordshire County Council* [2001] 1 WLR 1765.
27. *National Rivers Authority (Southern Region)* v. *Alfred McAlpine Homes East Ltd* [1994] 4 All ER 286.
28. *HL Bolton (Engineering) Co.*, 172 (Lord Denning).
29. *R* v. *Boal* [1992] QB 59.
30. *Prudential Assurance Co. (No. 2)*, 219; *Smith* v. *Croft (No. 2)* [1988] Ch 114, 186.
31. *Re a Company* [1980] 1 All ER 284, 286–7 (Lord Denning).
32. *R* v. *Boal* (1992) 95 Cr. App. R. 272, 276 (Browne J).
33. *Gibson* v. *Barton* [1875] LR 10 QB 329, 356 (Blackburn J).
34. *Re a Company* [1980], 144 (Shaw LJ).
35. *Re a Company* [1980], 144 (Shaw LJ).
36. *Harold Holdsworth & Co.* v. *Caddies* [1955] 1 WLR 352.
37. *Morris* v. *Kanssen* [1946] AC 459, 474.
38. *HL Bolton (Engineering) Co.*, 172 (Lord Denning).
39. *Automatic Self-Cleansing Filter Syndicate*; *John Shaw & Sons (Salford) Ltd* v. *Shaw* [1935] 2 KB 113, 134 (Greer LJ); *Rose* v. *McGivern* [1998] 2 BCLC 604.
40. For e.g. *John Shaw & Sons (Salford) Ltd*.
41. *Re Swift 736 Ltd* [1993] BCC 312, 315 (Nicholls VC); *Re Grayan Building Services Ltd* [1995] BCC 554, 574 (Hoffmann LJ).
42. *McCall* v. *Scott* (6th Cir. 2001) 239 F.3d 808.
43. *Re Barings Plc (No. 5)* [2000] 1 BCLC 523, 535–6; *Re Barings Plc* [1998] BCC 583, 586 (Scott VC).
44. See *Re City Equitable Fire Insurance Co. Ltd* [1925] Ch 407, 429 (Romer J).
45. *Equitable Life Assurance Society* v. *Bowley* [2004] 1 BCLC 180, [41] (Langley J).
46. *In re Abbott Laboratories Derivative Shareholders Litigation*, 325 F.3d 795 (7th Cir. 2003), 809.
47. See also *Re Barings plc (No. 5)*, *Secretary for Trade and Industry* v. *Baker (No. 5)* [1999] 1 BCLC 433; *Norman* v. *Theodore Goddard* [1991] 1 BCLC 1028; *Dorchester Finance* v. *Stebbing* [1989] BCLC 498.

48. *Re Barings (No. 6), Secretary of State for Trade and Industry* v. *Baker* [2000] 1 BCLC 523.
49. *Dorchester Finance* v. *Stebbing* [1989] BCLC 498.
50. *Re Barings Plc (No. 5)* [2000] 1 BCLC 523, 536. See also *Re Kaytech International Plc* [1999] 2 BCLC 351; *Secretary of State* v. *Van Hengel* [1995] 1 BCLC 1; *Re City Investment Centres Ltd* [1992] BCLC 956; *Re Majestic Recording Studios Ltd* [1989] BCLC 1.
51. *Re Equitable Life Assurance Society* v. *Hyman* [2002] 1 AC 408, [41] (Langley J).
52. *Re Bradcrown Ltd* [2001] 1 BCLC 547, 561 (Collins J).
53. *Re Firedart* [1994] 2 BCLC 340; *Re New Generation Engineers Ltd* [1993] BCLC 435.
54. *Re Richborough Furniture Ltd* [1996] 1 BCLC 507.
55. *Metal Manufacturer Ltd* v. *Lewis* (1988) 13 NSWLR 315, 318 (Kirby J). See also *Morley* v. *Statewide Tobacco Services Ltd* [1993] VR 423, 442.
56. *Re Hydrodam (Corby) Ltd* [1994] 2 BCLC 180, 183 (Millett J).
57. *Re Hydrodan (Corby) Ltd* [1994] BCC 161, 163C-D (Millett J). See also *Secretary of State for Trade and Industry* v. *Jones* [1996] BCC 336.
58. *Re Hydrodan (Corby) Ltd* [1994] BCC 161, 163F (Millett J).
59. *Secretary of State for Trade and Industry* v. *Deverell* [2001] Ch 340, [2000] 2 WLR 907, [2000] 2 All ER 365.
60. *Re Hydrodan (Corby) Ltd* [1994] BCC 161, 163C-D (Millett J). Contrast *Secretary of State for Trade and Industry* v. *Hickling* [1996] BCC 678; *Re Richborough Furniture Ltd* also known as *Secretary of State for Trade and Industry* v. *Stokes* [1996] BCC 155, [1996] 1 BCLC 507.
61. *Secretary of State for Trade and Industry* v. *Deverell* [2001] Ch 340. See also *Re Kaytech International Plc* [1999] BCC 390; *Australian Securities Commission* v. *AS Nominees Ltd* (1995) 133 ALR 1.
62. *Secretary of State for Trade and Industry* v. *Deverell* [2001] 1 Ch 340.
63. *Re Maidstone Building Provisions Ltd* [1971] 1 WLR 1085.
64. *Barnnett, Hoares & Co.* v. *South London Tramways Co.* (1887) 18 QED 815 (Lord Esher, MR).
65. *Panorama Developments (Guildford) Ltd* v. *Fidelis Furnishing Fabrics Ltd* (1971) 2 QB 711.
66. *HL Bolton Engineering Co.*, 172.
67. *Dovey* v. *Cory* [1901] AC 477, 486 (the Earl of Halsbury LC).
68. *R (for and on behalf of the Health and Safety Executive)* v. *Paul Jukes* [2018] Lloyd's Rep FC 157.
69. *RBG Resources Plc* v. *Rastogi* also known as *RBG Resources Plc (in Liquidation)* v. *Rastogi* [2002] EWHC 2782 (Laddie J).
70. *Vacher* v. *London Society of Compositors* [1913] AC 107, 131.
71. Public Offers of Securities Regulations 1995, SI 1995/1537 as amended by Amendment Regulations of 1999 (SI/1999/734) and of 2001 (SI 2000/3649).

72. *C Evans and Sons Ltd* v. *Spritebrand Ltd* [1985] BCLC 105; *Williams* v. *Natural Life Health Foods Ltd* [1998] 1 WLR 830; *MCA Records Inc* v. *Charly Records Ltd* [2003] 1 BCLC 93; *Safeway Stores Ltd* v. *Twigger* [2010] EWCA Civ 1472.
73. *Williams* v. *Natural Life Health Foods Ltd* [1998] 1 WLR 830, 837 (Lord Steyn).
74. *Office of Fair Trading* v. *Miller* [2009] EWCA 34.
75. See *West Mercia Safetywear Ltd* v. *Dodd* (1988) 4 BCC 30; *Yukong Line Ltd* v. *Rendsburg Investments Corp* [1998] 1 WLR 294; *Re Pantone 485 Ltd* [2002] BCLC 260.
76. *Doe d. Murray* v. *Bridges* (1831) 1 B & Ad 847, 859 (Lord Tenterden CJ); *Lonrho Ltd* v. *Shell Petroleum Co. Ltd (No. 2)* [1982] AC 173, 185 (Lord Diplock); *Baker* v. *Quantum Clothing Group Ltd* [2011] UKSC 17; *McDonald* v. *National Grid Electricity Transmission Plc* [2014] 53; *Campbell* v. *Gordon* [2016] UKSC 38.
77. *Campbell* v. *Peter Gordon Joiners Ltd* [2016] UKSC 38.
78. *Das* v. *George Weston Limited* [2017] ONSC 4129.
79. *Australian Securities and Investments Commission* v. *Cassimatis (No. 8)* [2016] FCA 1023 [483].
80. *Foss* v. *Harbottle* (1843) 2 Hare 461 (Wigram VC).
81. *Macaura* v. *Northern Assurance Co.* [1925] AC 619, 633.
82. *John Shaw & Sons Ltd*, 134 (Greer LJ); *Howard Smith Ltd.*
83. *Prudential Assurance Co. Ltd (No. 2)*, 366–7; *Johnson* v. *Gore Wood & Co.* [2001] 1 BCLC 313; *Johnson* v. *Gore Wood & Co.* [2002] 2 AC 1.
84. *Australian Securities and Investments Commission* v. *Flugge (No. 2)* (2017) 342 ALR 478.
85. *The Secretary of State for Business, Innovation and Skills* v. *Weston* [2014] EWHC 2933 (Ch).
86. *Re Westmid Packing Services Ltd, Secretary of State for Trade and Industry* v. *Griffiths* [1998] 2 BCLC 646, 653 (Lord Woolf MR).

REFERENCES

Ahern, D. (2011). Directors' duties: broadening the focus beyond content to examine the accountability spectrum. *Dublin Law Journal*, **33**, 116–52.

Arden, DBE, M. (The Right Honourable Lady Justice) (2010). Regulating the conduct of directors. *Journal of Corporate Law Studies*, 10(1), 1–15.

Attenborough, D. (2020). Misreading the directors' fiduciary duty of good faith. *Journal of Corporate Law Studies*, **20**(1), 73–98.

Bainbridge, S. M. and Henderson, M. T. (2016). *Limited Liability: A Legal and Economic Analysis*. Cheltenham, UK: Edward Elgar.

Bendickson, J., Muldoon, J., Liguori, E. W. and Davis, P. E. (2016). Agency theory: background and epistemology. *Journal of Management History*, **22**(4), 437–49.

Berle, A. A. (1965). The impact of the corporation on classical economic theory. *Quarterly Journal of Economics*, **79**, 25–40.

Berle, A. A. and Means, G. C. (1932). *The Modern Corporation and Private Property*. New Brunswick, NJ: Transaction.

Berliner, D. and Prakash, A. (2012). From norms to programs: the United Nations Global Compact and global governance. *Regulation and Governance*, 6, 149–66.

Bierce, A. (2003 [1911]). *The Devil's Dictionary*. New York: Dover.

Bostrom, R. E. (2003). Corporate governance: developments and practices one year after Sarbanes-Oxley. *International Financial Law Review*, **22**(10), 189–204.

Bowman, S. R. (1996). *The Modern Corporation and American Political Thought. Law, Power, and Ideology*. University Park: Pennsylvania State University Press.

Canning, M., O'Dwyer, B. and Georgakopoulos, G. (2019). Processes of auditability in sustainability assurance: the case of materiality construction. *Accounting and Business Research*, **49**(1), 1–27.

Capuano, A. (2010). Catching the leprechaun: company liability and the case for a benefit test in organic attribution. *Australian Journal of Corporate Law*, **24**(2), 177–206.

Cartwright, P. (1996). Defendants in consumer protection statutes: a search for consistency. *Modern Law Review*, **59**(2), 225–40.

Cartwright, P. (2001). *Consumer Protection and Criminal Law*. Cambridge: Cambridge University Press.

Cermak, R. (2018). Directors' duties to respect human rights in offshore operations and supply chains: an emerging paradigm. *Company and Securities Law Journal*, **36**(2), 124–49.

Chandler Jr, A. D. (1977). *The Visible Hand: The Managerial Revolution in American Business*. Cambridge, MA: Harvard University Press.

Cheffins, B. R. (1997). *Company Law: Theory, Structure and Operation*. Oxford: Clarendon Press.

Cheffins, B. R. and Armour, J. (2011). The past, present and future of shareholder activism by hedge funds. *Journal of Corporation Law*, **37**(1), 51–103.

Cherry, M. A. and Sneirson, J. F. (2011). Beyond profit: rethinking corporate social responsibility and greenwashing after the BP oil disaster. *Tulane Law Review*, **85**(4), 983–1038.

Choudhry, B. and Petrin, M. (2018). Corporate governance that 'works for everyone': promoting public policies through corporate governance mechanisms. *Journal of Corporate Law Studies*, **18**(2), 381–415.

Chrisman, J. J., Chua, J. H., Kellermanns, F. W. and Chang, E. P. C. (2007). Are family managers agents or stewards? An exploratory study in privately held family firms. *Journal of Business Research*, **60**(10), 1030–8.

Clough, J. and Mulhern, C. (2002). *The Prosecution of Corporations*. Melbourne: Oxford University Press.

Clutterbuck, D. and Waine, P. (1993). *The Independent Board Director*. London: McGraw-Hill.

Cochrane, A. (2012). *Animals Rights without Liberation: Applied Ethics and Human Obligations*. New York: Columbia University Press.

Coffee, J. C. (2005). A theory of corporate scandals: why the United States and Europe differ. *Oxford Review of Economic Policy*, **21**(2), 198–211.

Committee on the Financial Aspects of Corporate Governance (Cadbury Committee). (1992). *Report of the Committee on the Financial Aspects of Corporate Governance*, London: Committee on the Financial Aspects of Corporate Governance and Gee and Co. Ltd.

Cooper, D. J., Dacin, T. and Palmer, D. (2013). Fraud in accounting, organizations and society: extending the boundaries of research. *Accounting, Organizations and Society*, **38**, 440–57.

Crespí-Cladera, R. and Pascual-Fuster, B. (2014). Does the independence of independent directors matter? *Journal of Corporate Finance*, **28**, 116–34.

Davis, J. H., Schoorman, F. D. and Donaldson, R. (1997). Toward a stewardship theory of management. *Academy of Management Review*, **22**(1), 20–47.

Demb, A. and Neubauer, F. F. (1992). *The Corporate Board: Confronting the Paradoxes*. New York: Oxford University Press.

DeMott, D. A. (2004). The texture of loyalty. *Studies in International Financial, Economic, and Technology Law*, **7**, 23–47.

de Villiers, C., Rinaldi, L. and Unerman, J. (2014). Integrated reporting: insights, gaps and agendas for future research. *Accounting, Auditing & Accountability Journal*, **27**(7), 1042–67.

Donaldson, L. and Davis, J. H. (1991). Stewardship theory or agency theory: CEO governance and shareholder returns. *Australian Journal of Management*, **16**(1), 49–64.

Dunlavy, C. A. (2004). From citizens to plutocrats: nineteenth-century shareholder voting rights and theories of the corporation. In K. Lipartito and D. B. Sicilia, eds., *Constructing Corporate America: History, Politics, and Culture*. Oxford: Oxford University Press, pp. 66–93.

Eisenhardt, K. M. (1989). Agency theory: an assessment and review. *Academy of Management Review*, **14**(1), 57–74.

Elshandidy, T. and Hassanein, A. (2014). Do IFRS and board of directors' independence affect accounting conservatism? *Applied Financial Economics*, **24**(16), 1091–102.

Erasmus, L. and Coetzee, P. (2018). The drivers of stakeholders' view of internal audit effectiveness: management versus audit committee. *Managerial Auditing Journal*, **33**(1), 90–114.

European Commission (2003). *Modernising Company Law and Enhancing Corporate Governance in the European Union – A Plan to Move Forward*. COM (2003) 284 final. https://eur-lex.europa.eu/legal-content/EN/TXT/PDF/?uri=CELEX:52003DC0284&from=EN.

European Commission (25 February 2005). *Commission Recommendation of 15 February 2005 on the Role of Non-executive or Supervisory Directors of Listed Companies and on the Committees of the (Supervisory) Board*, 2005/162/EC. *Official Journal of the European Union*, L/52/51. https://eur-lex.europa.eu/legal-content/EN/TXT/?uri=uriserv%3AOJ.L_.2005.052.01.0051.01.ENG&toc=OJ%3AL%3A2005%3A052%3AFULL.

Fama, E. F. (1980). Agency problems and the theory of the firm. *Journal of Political Economy*, **88**, 288–307.

Fama, E. F. and Jensen, M. C. (1983). Separation of ownership and control. *Journal of Law and Economics*, **26**, 301–25.

Financial Reporting Council (FRC). (July 2018). *The UK Corporate Governance Code*. London: FRC. www.frc.org.uk/getattachment/88bd8c45-50ea-4841-95b0-d2f4f48069a2/2018-UK-Corporate-Governance-Code-FINAL.PDF.

Fischer, D. and Friedman, H. H. (2019). Tone-at-the-top lessons from Abrahamic justice. *Journal of Business Ethics*, **156**, 209–25.

Foster, N. (2008). Personal civil liability of company officers for workplace torts. *Torts Law Journal*, **16**, 20–68.

Gale, M., Gale, S. and Scanlan, G. (1999). *Fraud and the Plc*. London: Butterworths.

Gray, R. (2010). Is accounting for sustainability actually accounting for sustainability . . . and how would we know? An exploration of narratives of organisations and the planet. *Accounting, Organizations and Society*, **35**(1), 47–62.

Gutiérrez, M. and Sáez, M. (2013). Deconstructing independent directors. *Journal of Corporate Law Studies*, **13**(1), 63–94.

Hernandez, M. (2008). Promoting stewardship behaviour in organizations: a leadership model. *Journal of Business Ethics*, 80, 121–8.
Hetherington, J. A. C. (1966). Trends in enterprise liability: law and the unauthorized agent. *Stanford Law Review*, 19(1), 76–128.
Higgs, D. (2003). *Review of the Role and Effectiveness of Non-executive Directors*. London: Department of Trade and Industry.
Hillman, A. J., Withers, M. C. and Collins, B. J. (2009). Resource dependence theory: a review. *Journal of Management*, 35(6), 1404–27.
Hood, P. (2013). Directors' duties under the Companies Act 2006: clarity or confusion. *Journal of Corporate Law Studies*, 13(1), 1–48.
Howells, G. and Weatherill, S. (2005). *Consumer Protection Law*, 2nd ed. Aldershot, UK: Ashgate.
Idowu, S. (2009). Corporate social responsibility from the perspective of corporate secretaries. In S. Idowu and W. L. Filho, eds., *Professionals' Perspectives of Corporate Social Responsibility*, Berlin Heidelberg: Springer-Verlag, pp. 49–70.
Inkpen, A. C. and Tsang, E. W. K. (2007). Learning and strategic alliances. *Academy of Management Annuals*, 1, 479–511.
Ireland, P. (2010). Limited liability, shareholder rights and the problem of corporate irresponsibility. *Cambridge Journal of Economics*, 34(5), 837–56.
Ireland, P. (2018). From Lonrho to BHS: the changing character of corporate governance in contemporary capitalism. *King's Law Journal*, 29(1), 3–35.
Jensen, M. C. and Meckling, W. H. (1976). Theory of the firm: managerial behaviour, agency costs and ownership structure. *Journal of Financial Economics*, 3(4), 305–60.
Johnson, L. (2003). After Enron: remembering loyalty discourse in corporate law. *Delaware Journal of Corporate Law*, 28, 27–73.
Keay, A. (2007). *Company Directors' Responsibilities to Creditors*. Abingdon, UK: Routledge.
Keay, A. (2014a). An assessment of private enforcement actions for directors' breaches of duty. *Civil Justice Quarterly*, 33(1), 76–92.
Keay, A. (2014b). The public enforcement of directors' duties: a normative inquiry. *Common Law World Review*, 43(2), 89–119.
Keay, A. (2015). The shifting of directors' duties in the vicinity of insolvency. *International Insolvency Review*, 24(2), 140–64.
Keay, A. (2016). Assessing and rethinking the statutory scheme for derivative actions under the Companies Act 2006. *Journal of Corporate Law Studies*, 8(1), 39–68.
Keay, A. (2019). Having regard for stakeholders in practising enlightened shareholder value. *Oxford University Commonwealth Law Journal*, 19(1), 118–38.
Keay, A. and Loughrey, J. (2015). The framework for board accountability in corporate governance. *Legal Studies*, 35(2), 252–79.
Keay, A., Loughrey, J., McNulty, T., Okanigbuan, F. and Stewart, A. (2020). Business judgment and director accountability: a study of case-law over time. *Journal of Corporate Law Studies*, 20(2), 359–87.
Kiliç, M. and Kuzey, C. (2018). Determinants of forward-looking disclosures in integrated reporting. *Managerial Auditing Journal*, 33(1), 115–44.
Klink, F. J. (2004). Director risk after Sarbanes-Oxley. In D. Campbell and S. Woodley, eds., *Trends and Developments in Corporate Governance*. The Hague: Kluwer Law, pp. 197–212.
Koutsias, M. (2017). The fallacy of property rights' rhetoric in the company law context: from shareholder exclusivity to the erosion of shareholders' rights. *International Company and Commercial Law Review*, 28(6), 217–33.

KPMG (2015). *Currents of Change: The KPMG Survey of Corporate Responsibility Reporting 2015*. Amsterdam: KPMG International.

KPMG (2017). *KPMG Survey of Corporate Responsibility Reporting 2017*. Amsterdam: KPMG International.

Lail, B., MacGregor, J., Stuebs, M. and Thomasson, T. (2015). The influence of regulatory approach on tone at the top. *Journal of Business Ethics*, **126**, 25–37.

Latella, D. (2009). Shareholder derivative suits: a comparative analysis and the implications of the European Shareholders' Rights Directive. *European Company and Commercial Law Review*, 6(2–3), 307–23.

Latella, D. (2010). The shareholder derivative suits: disfunction and remedies against a 'paradoxal' inactivity. *Corporate Ownership & Control*, 7(4–2), 297–302.

Laufer, W. S. (2002). Corporate prosecution, cooperation and the trading of favours. *Iowa Law Review*, 87(2), 643–67.

Lee, J. (2018). The corporate governance officer as a transformed role of the company secretary: an international comparison. *South Carolina Journal of International Law and Business*, **14**(2), 106–41.

Lindblom, L. (2007). Dissolving the moral dilemma of whistleblowing. *Journal of Business Ethics*, **76**, 413–26.

Lombard, S. and Joubert, T. (2014). The legislative response to the shareholders v stakeholders debate: a comparative overview. *Journal of Corporate Law Studies*, **14**(1), 211–40.

Loughrey, J., Keay, A. and Cerioni, L. (2008). Legal practitioners, enlightened shareholder value and the shaping of corporate governance. *Journal of Corporate Law Studies*, 8(1), 79–111.

Madison, K., Holt, D. T., Kellermanns, F. W. and Ranft, A. L. (2016). Viewing family firm behavior and governance through the lens of agency and stewardship theories. *Family Business Review*, **29**(1), 65–93.

Maurović, L. and Hasić, T. (2013). Reducing agency costs by selecting an appropriate system of corporate governance. *Economic Research-Ekonomska Istraživanja*, **26**(1), 225–42.

McCormack, G., Keay, A. and Brown, S. (2017). Directors' liability and disqualification. In G. McCormack, A. Keay and S. Brown, eds., *European Insolvency Law: Reform and Harmonization*. Cheltenham, UK: Edward Elgar, pp. 22–64.

McNulty, T. and Stewart, A. (2015). Developing the governance space: a study of the role and potential of the company secretary in and around the board of directors. *Organisational Studies*, **36**(4), 513–35.

Menzies, D. (1959). Company directors. *Australia Law Journal*, **33**, 156–79.

Mezzanotte, F. E. (2017). The unconvincing rise of the statutory derivative action in Hong Kong: evidence from its first 10 years of enforcement. *Journal of Corporate Law Studies*, **17**(2), 469–96.

Miller, C. C., Washburn, N. T. and Glick, W. H. (2013). The myth of firm performance. *Organization Science*, **24**(3), 948–64.

Millon, D. (1990). Theories of the corporation. *Duke Law Journal*, **39**(2), 201–62.

Milman, D. (2013). *The Governance of Distressed Firms*. Cheltenham, UK: Edward Elgar.

Moore, M. (2010). The evolving contours of the board's risk management function in UK corporate governance. *Journal of Corporate Law Studies*, **10**(2), 279–308.

Near, J. P. and Miceli, M. P. (1985). Organizational dissidence: the case of whistle-blowing. *Journal of Business Ethics*, **4**(1), 1–16.

Nelken, D. and Levi, M. (2018). Sir Philip Green and the unacceptable face of capitalism. *King's Law Journal*, **29**(1), 36–57.

North, D. C. (1990). *Institutions, Institutional Change and Economic Performance*. Cambridge: Cambridge University Press.

Organisation for Economic Co-operation and Development (OECD). (2015). *G20/OECD Principles of Corporate Governance*. Paris: OECD Publishing. www.oecd.org/daf/ca/Corporate-Governance-Principles-ENG.pdf.

Osuji, O. K. and Moore, I. (2017). Director disqualification as a corporate governance tool in developing and emerging markets. In F. N. Ngwu, O. K. Osuji and F. Stephen, eds., *Corporate Governance in Developing and Emerging Markets*. Abingdon, UK: Routledge, pp. 270–90.

Parguel, B., Benoît-Moreau, F. and Larceneux, F. (2011). How sustainability ratings might deter 'greenwashing': a closer look at ethical corporate communication. *Journal of Business Ethics*, **102**, 15–28.

Parkinson, J. (2003). Disclosure and corporate social and environmental performance: competitiveness and enterprise in a broader social frame. *Journal of Corporate Law Studies*, **3** (1), 3–39.

Parkinson, J. E. (1993). *Corporate Power and Responsibility: Issues in the Theory of Company Law*. Oxford: Clarendon Press.

Patelli, L. and Pedrini, M. (2015). Is tone at the top associated with financial reporting aggressiveness? *Journal of Business Ethics*, **126**, 3–19.

Pfeffer, J. and Salancik, G. R. (1978). *The External Control of Organizations: A Resource Dependence Perspective*. New York: Harper & Row.

Rajak, H. (2004). Company law, limited liability, and the small world of directors' negligence. *Studies in International Financial, Economic, and Technology Law*, **7**, 117–41.

Ramsay, I. M. and Saunders, B. B. (2006). Litigation by shareholders and directors: an empirical study of the Australian derivative action. *Journal of Corporate Law Studies*, **6**(2), 397–446.

Reisberg, A. (2008). *Derivative Actions and Corporate Governance: Theory and Operation*. Oxford: Oxford University Press.

Rider, B. A. K. (1978). Amiable lunatics and the rule in Foss v. Harbottle. *Cambridge Law Journal*, **37**(2), 270–87.

Rinaldi, L. (2019). Accounting for sustainability governance: the enabling role of social and environmental accountability research. *Social and Environmental Accountability Journal*, **39** (1), 1–22.

Rost, S. R. (2004). Control and liability questions for close private companies. In D. Campbell and S. Woodley, eds., *Trends and Developments in Corporate Governance*. The Hague: Kluwer Law, pp. 319–40.

Safari, N. and Gelter, M. (2019). British Home Stores collapse: the case for an employee derivative claim. *Journal of Corporate Law Studies*, **19**(1), 43–68.

Sheridan, T. and Kendall, N. (1992). *Corporate Governance: An Action for Profitability and Business Success*. London: Pitman.

Siegel, S. (2006). Global accounting dimensions of corporate governance. In J. J. Norton and J. Rickford, eds., *Corporate Governance Post-Enron: Comparative and International Perspectives*. London: BICL, pp. 49–66.

Sinkovics, N., Hoque, S. F. and Sinkovics, R. R. (2016). Rana Plaza collapse aftermath: are CSR compliance and auditing pressures effective? *Accounting, Auditing & Accountability Journal*, **29**(4), 617–49.

Sjåfjell, B. (2018). Beyond climate risk: integrating sustainability into the duties of the corporate board. *Deakin Law Review*, **23**, 41–62.

Stern, Y. Z. (1987). Corporate liability for unauthorized contracts – unification of the rules of corporate representation. *University of Pennsylvania Journal of International Business Law*, 9(4), 649–701.

Tanega, J. (2006). Sarbanes-Oxley financial crimes: on legal risk, potential liability and employee protection. In I. Bantekas and G. Keramidas, eds., *International and European Financial Criminal Law*. London: LexisNexis Butterworths, pp. 154–79.

Tang, S. S. (2020). The anatomy of Singapore's statutory derivative action: why do shareholders sue – or not? *Journal of Corporate Law Studies*, **20**(2), 327–57.

Tombs, S. and Whyte, D. (2015). *The Corporate Criminal: Why Corporations Must Be Abolished*. London: Routledge.

Turner, S. J. (2020). Corporate law, directors' duties and ESG interventions: analysing pathways towards positive corporate impacts relating to ESG issues. *Journal of Business Law*, **2020**(4), 245–64.

United Kingdom House of Commons Work and Pensions and Business, Innovation and Skills Committees. (2017). *BHS. First Report of the Work and Pensions Committee and Fourth Report of the Business, Innovation and Skills Committee of Session 2016–17* (HC 54). https://publications.parliament.uk/pa/cm201617/cmselect/cmworpen/54/54.pdf.

United States Sentencing Commission. (2000). *Federal Sentencing Guidelines Manual and Appendices*. www.ussc.gov/guidelines/archive/2000-federal-sentencing-guidelines-manual.

Watson, S. M. (2019). The corporate legal person. *Journal of Corporate Law Studies*, **19**(1), 137–66.

Wedderburn, K. W. (1957). Shareholders' rights and the rule in Foss v. Harbottle. *Cambridge Law Journal*, **15**(2), 194–215.

Zalecki, P. H. (1993). The corporate governance roles of the inside and outside directors. *University of Toledo Law Review*, **24**, 831–58.

Zhao, J. (2019). Extraterritorial attempts at addressing challenges to corporate sustainability. In B. Sjåfjell and C. M. Brunner, eds., *Cambridge Handbook of Corporate Law, Corporate Governance and Sustainability*. Cambridge: Cambridge University Press, pp. 29–42.

6

Structural Limits and Structural Opportunities for Shareholder Regulation

David Williamson and Gary Lynch-Wood*

6.1 INTRODUCTION

Increasing regulatory oversight to control shareholder behaviour will underperform because it rests on the invalid assumption that shareholders can be controlled and that they can be better steered if and when regulatory stringency is increased. This assumption runs counter to the conditions that a regulation must require of the entity it is regulating, since by requiring compliance with these conditions there is the necessary presumption that shareholders have the capacity to comply with those conditions. However, since shareholders vary in their requisite endowments of those conditions, we can anticipate that some shareholders will fail to respond to the increased regulatory oversight, some will comply with what is required and others will do more. When shortfalls in compliance do occur, they cannot be addressed by simply increasing the level of regulatory oversight, for this only results in a magnification of the conditions required by the regulation, which will likely increase non-compliance as a consequence of more shareholders being unable to meet that higher threshold. To address this, a *minmax* approach to shareholder regulation is proposed, as this can accommodate shareholder differences most effectively.

The role of shareholders in corporate governance remains an open question, with the issue resurfacing and gaining greater traction following the 2007–8 financial crises (Coffee, 2008; Hill, 2010; Fairfax, 2011; Monks, 2013; Subramanian, 2017; Alrayes, 2019). Indeed, the call for shareholder action has not gone away, with corporate greed, climate change, child labour and issues such as diversity continuing to drive the need for shareholders to be more active. There has also been a long-standing moral argument that posits the need for a connection between the firm and its constituencies for the good of all to prevail (Shaw and Post, 1993). This incorporates shareholders, directors and managers having responsibilities to stakeholders other than stockholders (Freeman and Reed, 1983; Goodpaster, 1991; Blair, 1995; Donaldson and Preston, 1995; Parkinson, 2003). We would add that shareholders have responsibilities to their stakeholders and that this results in differences in their own behaviour. An institutional investor, for instance, has responsibilities to its own constituent members, which can include individuals, universities and churches, and they will seek to accommodate the desires of those stakeholders. If the emphasis of the members of an institutional investor is on social issues, then it might be expected that the institutional investor would place greater emphasis on social issues in the companies it invests in than would an institutional investor whose members emphasise profit maximisation. In a similar manner, there is no reason to believe that asset management companies, investment holding companies, hedge funds and so forth would not have different views on how they should act as shareholders.

The pressure on shareholders to act, to be more active in how they interact with the companies they invest in, has materialised in different ways. Pressure has come from academics, with Bebchuk (2005, 2006, 2007), for instance, being an early advocate for shareholders approving major corporate decisions. Others have focussed more on adherence to codes of practice, where the responsibilities on shareholders are said to improve access to capital, to deter mismanagement and to improve accountability (Australian Securities Exchange, 2014; Organisation for Economic Co-operation and Development (OECD), 2015; Financial Reporting Council (FRC), 2016). In the UK, the legal tools to enable shareholders to be more active are mainly contained in the Companies Act 2006, as well as a suite of supporting statutory instruments relating to issues such as reporting. The legislation enables shareholders to call a general meeting if they have 5 per cent of voting rights (or, if they do not have voting rights, if they can get 5 per cent of those who do hold voting rights) and in doing so propose a specific resolution. There are additional powers, which include: the right of shareholders to inspect the company's register of members and register of beneficial interests, so that a shareholder can contact the members on the register to express their shareholder concern or garner member support; the right to attend and speak at a general meeting of the company and to vote at the annual general meeting (AGM) on issues such as the re-election of directors and the remuneration report; and the right to file a derivative claim against the company's directors or an unfair prejudice claim (Davies et al., 2019). Subject to the comply or explain approach, the UK Stewardship Code also requires that institutional investors have clear guidelines on how they will escalate their concerns in the companies in which they invest. Finally, if viable, shareholders can also increase their stake in the company to have a greater influence on the direction of the company (to the point that a 30 per cent or more shareholding would necessitate the making of an offer for the remaining shares).

The problem with these interventions, and indeed with any legal or regulatory interventions, is that they assume that shareholders will act as intended. That is, the regulation on shareholder intervention is predicated on shareholders equally applying the legal remedies available. Thus, shareholders will equally attend and vote at an AGM, comply with codes of practice and so forth. This, we will seek to show, is a misguided presumption. It is misguided because shareholders have different rule-following behaviours, such that they will respond differently to external events. Furthermore, these differences in shareholder behaviour are exacerbated by the regulations themselves, as the regulations require of shareholders a certain level of knowledge of the regulations, a certain level of acceptance of the need to comply with what is stipulated in the regulations and a certain level of resource to be able to meet the requirements of the regulations. Therefore, since the endowments of these 'conditions of regulation' differ between shareholders, as is reflected in their different rule-following behaviours, we can duly anticipate that shareholders will respond differently to shareholder regulations. To reduce the magnitude of the variation, we propose that shareholder regulation should be structured in a certain way so as to better accommodate shareholder differences. We call the approach behind the structure the minmax methodology (Williamson and Lynch-Wood, 2021). As will be shown, this will involve making certain trade-offs and, for those trade-offs decided upon, it provides the best structure for optimising compliance with shareholder regulation.

The chapter proceeds by providing a more detailed review of the regulation and governance frameworks that underpin the role of UK shareholders. This is followed by the first part of our argument on why shareholders will differ in how they behave, on why they have different rule-following orientations because of their situated positions. With that in hand, the analysis proceeds by considering the demands that shareholder regulation requires of shareholders. We will use the term regulation to include the wider features of governance from this point onwards. Moreover, we will refer to the demands of regulation as the 'conditions of regulation' and show that how they play out differently with different types of shareholder is pivotal to our overall argument. The *minmax* methodology is then introduced and explained, showing why it provides the most suitable structure for the regulation of shareholders. Finally, the conclusion summarises the overall argument and provides some suggestions for how shareholder regulation can be better structured.

6.2 POSITION OF (UK) SHAREHOLDERS

There are two particularly pertinent and interconnected precepts in capitalist economies. The first is that firms are the indispensable providers of goods, services and employment for societal well-being, and the second is that firms can best provide these goods and services when their owners (e.g., shareholders) and those who control them (i.e., directors) act in the best interests of the firm. Best interests can be interpreted to mean maximising profit-making potential within the politically and socially determined boundaries of law and ethics. From a UK perspective, this manifests as a shareholder value orientation, which places the interests of shareholders in front of other claimants (Ross, 1973; Jensen and Meckling, 1976; Fama and Jensen, 1983; Bainbridge, 1993; Roe, 2001; Keay, 2007). The Companies Act 2006 maintains shareholder primacy as a key principle of company law. Other stakeholder interests were accommodated through the requirement in s. 172(1) of the Act that directors should act in ways that they 'consider, in good faith, would be most likely to promote the success of the company' for the benefit of its members as a whole. As such, directors should have regard to other interests, such as those of employees, the community and the environment. This requirement is supported by other statutory instruments such as those on reporting requirements (e.g., Companies Act 2006 (Strategic Reports and Directors' Report) Regulations 2013; Companies, Partnerships and Groups (Accounts and Non-financial Reporting) Regulations 2016).

As shown in Section 6.1, there are several mechanisms for delivering shareholder primacy. Most obvious and immediate is to make the selling of shares as easy and trouble-free as possible. The Companies Act 2006, as amended, provides additional mechanisms, including the right for certain persons to receive notice of general meetings[1] and copies of annual accounts,[2] as well as the right to have an AGM.[3] In addition, depending on the shareholding held, there is the right to have an item placed on the agenda for discussion at a general meeting; to have annual accounts audited; to block a special resolution and, if the shareholding exceeds 50 per cent, to have control over the make-up of the board of directors and thus the direction and actions of the business. Typical reasons for intervening in the affairs of the company may include to block or force through a takeover, to penalise poor performance or to prevent excessive remuneration. Beside those mechanisms in the 2006 Act, legal action can be taken if a director believes that the fiduciary duty owed to the company has been compromised, such as when it is felt that the affairs of the company have been conducted in a manner that is 'unfairly prejudicial' to its interests.

Alongside the Companies Act 2006 and any additional judicial interpretation and reasoning, listed companies are required to comply with UK Listing Authority requirements, which are administered through the Financial Conduct Authority (FCA). This involves compliance with the FCA Disclosure and Transparency Rules, the Prospectus Rules and the Listing Rules (Financial Conduct Authority (FCA), 2020). A feature of the Disclosure and Transparency Rules is the linked corporate governance standards set out in the UK Corporate Governance Code. These standards, which cover issues such as the relationship between the chairman and the chief executive, the role of non-executive directors, nominations to the board, executive remuneration, risk and auditing, are principles that firms are expected to comply with. Known as comply or explain, since companies are required to explain if they decide or fail to comply with one or more standards, they are thought to provide a comprehensive framework for safeguarding the interests of shareholders.

Institutional investors are seen to be a particularly important group of shareholders and, accordingly, are required to adhere to additional requirements. One of these requirements is the 'prudent person' rule. This rule has its origins in the common law but has been incorporated into legislation,[4] and it posits that institutional investors should invest in ways that provide security, liquidity and profitability. Alongside this, the UK Stewardship Code (FRC, 2012), which operates on the same comply or explain basis as the UK Corporate Governance Code (FRC, 2016), sets out expected practices for institutional investors' engagement with investee companies. This pivots on seven principles, which are that institutional investors will: publicly disclose[5] how they will discharge their stewardship responsibilities; have a robust policy for managing conflicts of interest; monitor their investee companies; have clear guidelines on when and how they will escalate their stewardship activities; act collectively with other investors; operate under a clear policy on voting and disclosure of voting activity; and report periodically on their stewardship and voting activities. Importantly, the UK Stewardship Code is seen as being as important as the UK Corporate Governance Code, and is overseen by the FCA. Institutional support is also provided by the institutional investors' own Institutional Shareholders' Committee and through their industry associations.[6]

On face value, these various mechanisms appear to provide a comprehensive framework for shareholder practice. They can be said to be facilitative, in that company law is supported by delegated self-regulation in the form of listing rules or professional standards (Holland, 1999). Collectively, they have been said to constitute an amalgam of mechanisms to achieve policy success (Van Gossum et al., 2010). However, we will argue that there are fundamental forces at work that undermine these regulations and governance frameworks and, furthermore, that their amalgamation can by their very nature be inefficient and contradictory. To understand why, we need to firstly appreciate the situated position of shareholders and consider why this produces different rule-following behaviours.

6.3 THE SITUATED SHAREHOLDER

Shareholders come in different guises and with different entitlements. These include individuals, pension funds, insurance funds, mutual investment funds and foreign investors, alongside share entitlements that include ordinary shares, class A and B voting shares, non-voting shares, preference shares and redeemable shares. We can further subdivide this mix into minority and majority shareholders, activists and pressure groups pursuing different objectives, and methods of shareholder intervention that include public debate and briefings, submitting a shareholder proposal for an annual or extraordinary general meeting, and litigation (Filatchev and Dotsenko, 2015). If we look at minority shareholders in a little more detail, these are shareholders that have the capacity to have a high 'relative' stockholding.[7] For that reason, minority shareholders, such as pension funds, life insurers, mutual funds, hedge funds and sovereign wealth funds, are potentially an influential group of shareholders. They have a voice, mainly because they offer an important source of long-term capital. They are also becoming more globalised and are now considered pivotal to the provision of finance in developing and emerging markets (della Croce, 2014). Owing to their wealth, they are also considered to be, and are in fact expected to be, central to any discussions of shareholders. Indeed, shareholder activism presupposes that directors cannot be trusted (i.e., the agent–principal problem) and requires a willingness to engage in corporate governance matters; that shareholders have the resources to enable engagement in those matters; and that they have mechanisms that allow them to influence corporate governance strategic decision-making.

However, our ontology requires us to question the assumption that minority shareholders, or any shareholders, will act as expected. Specifically, we question whether regulation and governance frameworks can accommodate the differences among shareholder groups and whether shareholders will act according to a common set of frameworks. To justify this, we posit that the rule-following practices of shareholders are a learnt process, with those rule-following practices being a consequence of how they live their lives at both an individual and an institutional level. The premise and ontology are evident in the work of Pierre Bourdieu (1980, 1984), where it is shown that our knowledge of the world is seen to be a practical ability acquired as part of a taken-for-granted background to everyday life. This is why, for example, gang crime and religious devotion are best understood as regularities of behaviour that come about through learnt codes of masculinity and deliverance, respectively. As such, the learning is largely implicit, as it is a practical ability learnt through familiarisation or habituation. This leads Bourdieu to use the term 'habitus' to explain, among other things, judgements on taste and educational success. The acquisition of dispositions (i.e., behaviour) through practice suggests that habitus is generative and self-replicating, with the learning context sustaining behaviours and with those behaviours, in turn, sustaining the learning context. That is, the practice provides the structure for the practice and vice versa. Different learning contexts can accordingly be said to provide for the continuation of different behaviours.

Our dispositions, which accrue from our habitus, operate in domains of activity that Bourdieu refers to as 'fields'. There are many fields in which an individual can engage, including politics, journalism, education and corporate governance, as a constituent part of the economy. Corporate governance, then, is a field in which individuals interact with the rules of corporate governance, though not in any neutral way. It is not neutral because of the socialised tendencies that guide our behaviour and thinking (i.e., our habitus) and the way that our own social capital – that is, our social value as represented by the enhancing nature of our social, cultural, economic, etc. interactions – is played out in the field. This inevitably leads to disparities in how shareholders will perceive and respond to regulations on shareholder behaviour. And these disparities can be geographical and domain-specific, with, for example, hedge funds likely to respond differently to a regulation than would an environmental pressure group shareholder, or a small investment trust shareholder. In short, we can envisage that these shareholders would be relatively autonomous as they are likely to have quite distinct views on what constitutes a legitimate opinion and a legitimate action. Furthermore, we can anticipate that shareholders at an aggregate (i.e., collective of individuals) level, such as in the UK, may have a distinct view on what constitutes good shareholder practice and what the power relationship should be, say, between shareholders and companies. Indeed, we might expect the context to permeate the psychological experiences of those involved, so that those experiences affect their non-conscious reasoning and feelings. This would in turn reinforce those practices by shaping attitudes and group identities (Bargh et al., 1992; Greenwald and Banaji, 1995).

The view that practice is learnt, that practical consciousness is a tacit, habitual understanding of how to apply a rule in practice, requires that we take account of socio-economic structures because these provide the context within which practical consciousness is learnt. There are several reasons why this is relevant. One is that socio-economic structures, when they are similar, allow similar practices to exist across time and location. Since they are constituted recursively, compatibility between socio-economic structure and practice necessitates that one changes with the other; or one is excluded from the other. That is, if practice is incompatible with a socio-economic structure, then the practice will have to change (and vice versa), or the socio-economic structure will exclude that form of practice (and, again, vice versa). Hence, the UK approach to shareholder practice can only successfully operate in other socio-economic contexts if those contexts are broadly equivalent. Similarity in terms of context requires the rules and resources that underpin the reproduction of institutionalised practices to be equally comparable. Yet this is unlikely. For example, rules vary across situational contexts as they come from and apply to different levels of activity (e.g., statutes, common law, European and international regimes); they require different types of information to be gathered, dealt with and administered; and they can range from being intensive to shallow, tacit to discursive, informal to formalised, and in the extent to which they are weakly or strongly sanctioned. Comparability of resources as a determinant of similarity of context is equally improbable. For example, shareholders vary in size and this will affect their resource profile and thus their ability to act. Likewise, this will likely shape their views on issues to do with shareholder activities and indeed on how proactive they should be on shareholder issues. Linked to this, since minority shareholders are a differentiated group, often competing with one another for shareholder funds, it makes sense for them to protect their competitive advantage by having resources that are difficult to copy. We can even go as far as to say that shareholders can be equated to firms and are competitively distinct owing to their being unequal in their ability to acquire and utilise resources (Dierickx and Cool, 1989; Peteraf, 1993). This affects the tone of the strategy-making processes and hence the preferences of the shareholder. It corresponds with the view that shareholders, as with firms, have bounded rationalities and cultures and that these guide their decision-making (Prahalad and Bettis, 1986; Park et al., 2014).

These bounded rationalities and cultures can also be self-sustaining. A straightforward explanation for persistence of approach is that we tend to stick to, and build on, what has worked in the past. This can be attributed to reinforcement-expectancy learning (Cyert and March, 1963; Prahalad and Bettis, 1986), the efficiency of maintaining proven competences over developing new ones (Levitt and March, 1988), performance exceeding aspirations (Lant and Montgomery, 1987; Greve, 1998) and the difficulty of changing organisational structures (Hannan and Freeman, 1989). Audia, Locke and Smith (2000) also found that firms (and we would argue shareholders) would seek to continue to pursue the strategies that had provided previous success, even when pursuit of a different strategy, owing to changes in the external environment, would have proven more beneficial. This is consistent with the idea that history is important, where the conditions that give rise to self-reinforcing feedback (to help maintain existing structures) are attributed to the historically embedded nature of cognitive selections, to sunk costs making it difficult to switch to alternatives, to complex interrelatedness (e.g., social, institutional and technical) and to increasing returns when using a common method (David, 1985, 1987; Arthur, 1989).

Following the ideas developed by Douglass North (1990, 1993, 2005), we can say that an institutional environment affects how resources are allocated to shareholder actions and how their use by shareholders reinforces that practice. In broad terms, shareholders apply and help create the rules of the game, which are derived from and help create the shareholders' institutional setting, with the rules being both informal (e.g., norms, routines, political processes) and formal (e.g., incentives, authority). As indicated, these informal and formal factors vary across different settings and, in doing so, support different forms of stability by virtue of the shared meanings and conceptions of social life they engender (Geertz, 1973; Meyer and Scott, 1983; D'Andrade, 1984; Granovetter, 1985; Hofstede, 1991; Scott, 2013). Also, being self-constituting, these different meaning systems affect how organisational knowledge is acquired – and, by inference, how organisational knowledge shapes the ongoing development of social networks and social capital (Granovetter, 1985; Putnam, 2000; Woolcock, 2001).

These different regularities of behaviour, particularly when there is uncertainty owing to the complexity of modern economic systems, have the effect of producing 'selective alertness' to information, which prompts particular actions even when they are non-profit-maximising (Heiner, 1983; Greif, 1997), depending on the values of the company, which may or may not concern profit maximisation. Likewise, North (1990) posits that path dependence will be linked with selective alertness as this is the mechanism that provides resistance to path-altering change. This suggests that, while it may be quite easy to change formal rules in organisations, it will be much more difficult to alter informal rules (Zenger et al., 2002).

On the basis of what has been said, that shareholders will differ for the reasons described and that those differences are intrinsic to their rule-following practices, we need to ask the following question: what is it about regulation and governance that enables those mechanisms to accommodate those differences? To understand the answer, we must first look at the requirements that a regulation or governance framework demands of a shareholder for compliance to occur. We call these demands the conditions of regulation.

6.4 CONDITIONS OF REGULATION

All forms of regulation and governance place a set of demands on their regulated entities; for compliance to occur, those demands must be met by those being regulated. These conditions of regulation are *knowledge*, *acceptance* and *resource*. Since these are constituent features of regulation, being embedded into the actual functioning of a regulation, it is necessarily true that they must be responded to, in terms of being complied with, by the regulatee. If these conditions are absent in the shareholder, either in part or in full, then there will be a regulation deficit and an accompanying degree of failure to deliver the intended outcomes. This is why, if we consider our earlier analysis, we posit that shareholders' differences (e.g., their features, capacities, institutional settings and interactions with the markets and social contexts in which they operate) produce different endowments of knowledge, acceptance and resource. Likewise, it is why we would anticipate that shareholder regulation would inevitably underperform when it requires a specific level of knowledge, acceptance and resource. Specifically, when shareholder regulation requires a level of knowledge to understand what is required by it, when it requires acceptance of what is being requested by it and when it requires a level of resource to deliver on what is being asked, we would venture that these requirements will vary across shareholders and that levels of compliance will vary.

Looking at this more closely, the knowledge condition necessitates that there is an understanding that the law exists and what its requirements are. The acceptance condition pertains to a willingness to meet the requirements of a regulation, where acceptance to comply can be 'voluntary', 'chosen', 'desired', 'preferred', as well as being 'forced' through appropriate enforcement actions or pressurised through appropriate social pressure or norms. The resource condition is the capacity to meet the requirements of the regulation such that the shareholder has the capability to acquire the relevant regulatory knowledge and implement what is required. Importantly, the level of shortfall in one or more of the three conditions of regulation will determine the level of non-compliance by shareholders. Indeed, we can envisage at least three scenarios of shareholder practice:

1. There is universal understanding of shareholder regulation (i.e., knowledge condition), all shareholders are willing to comply with the requirements of shareholder regulation (i.e., acceptance condition) and shareholder regulation accommodates all shareholder capacities to comply (i.e., resource condition).

2. Shareholder understanding of shareholder regulation is patchy (i.e., knowledge condition), willingness to comply with shareholder regulation varies (i.e., acceptance condition) and shareholder regulation does not accommodate different shareholder capacities to comply (i.e., resource condition).
3. Shareholder understanding of shareholder regulation is implicit, with shareholders adhering to the spirit rather than the letter of shareholder regulation (i.e., knowledge condition), there is widespread willingness to comply with the spirit of shareholder regulation (i.e., acceptance condition) and shareholder regulation accommodates shareholder capacities to comply (i.e., resource condition).

Looking at the first two scenarios, we have shown that they result from the interaction of four factors (Williamson and Lynch-Wood, 2021). These are the aforementioned *conditions of regulation*, which operate in conjunction with their equivalent knowledge, acceptance and resource within shareholders, which we will term the *conditions within shareholders*. The third interaction is with the rule following *predicate of regulation*, which pertains to whether the regulation is based on values rule-following, utility rule-following or obedience rule-following. Finally, these *predicates of regulation* work in conjunction with the rule-following *predicate of the shareholder*, which is where the rule-following behaviour of the shareholder is based on values, utility or obedience. Each of the four factors can exist to differing degrees at the same time, and they eventually play out to determine the effectiveness of shareholder regulation.

The effect of these four factors on levels of compliance is evident when shareholder regulation is pitched at a level where the *conditions of regulation* are matched by the *conditions within shareholders*. That is, the knowledge, acceptance and resource conditions demanded by the regulation are matched by the knowledge, acceptance and resource conditions existing within firms. When that is the case, it must also be true that the *predicate of regulation* is matched by the *predicate of the shareholder*. This means that when a regulation is predicated on values rule-following, which would be the case with self-regulation, on the basis that self-regulation presupposes voluntary motives, it would then be reciprocated by the shareholder since the shareholder is likewise driven by voluntary motives. The same would apply if the regulation were predicated on utility (i.e., economic instruments) or obedience (i.e., command-and-control instruments). Overall, we can say that full compliance is achieved when the four factors are aligned; zero compliance is achieved when the four factors are completely unaligned.

Looking at this more closely, as you increase the requirements of regulation by increasing the knowledge, acceptance and resource conditions of a regulation (i.e., *conditions of regulation*), you duly increase the pressure on firms by requiring that they are matched in their equivalent *conditions within firms*. This also applies to the rule-following *predicate of regulation* and the rule-following *predicate of the shareholder*, in that as you increase the focus on a predicate of regulation, such as obedience, you likewise increase the reliance on the obedience predicate in shareholders. And this is where the problem of reciprocity becomes extenuated since the increase in the *conditions of regulation* and the *predicate of regulation* necessitates a widespread increase in those factors in shareholders, which is extremely unlikely because of the differences that are part of the population of shareholders.

When we look at the third scenario, when shareholder understanding of shareholder regulation is implicit, such that shareholders adhere to the spirit rather than the letter of the law, we refer to the distinction between 'law in books' and 'law in action' (Pound, 1910; also see Halpérin 2012). Indeed, the work of Macaulay (1963), who argued that formal mechanisms like the private law of contracts cannot, on their own, replace trust in business relationships, would provide that parties co-operate (or fail to co-operate), either implicitly or explicitly, in the 'shadow' of the law. Therefore, what matters in this situation is what is done rather than what is prescribed to be done (Gilson, 2001). It is why, in economic exchange, for example, we can infer that informal governance mechanisms are likely to be as important as formal governance mechanisms (Granovetter, 1985; Zenger et al., 2002; Dalton and Dalton, 2011). Macneil (1978, 1980) makes a similar point by positing a relational model, premised on repeated interactions: that is, you can only understand a contract when you appreciate that it is one of many influences on a commercial relationship and, likewise, that those influences shape how the contract is interpreted by the parties involved. In short, social interactions affect information costs, opportunism and the enforcement of agreements, such that regulation on its own is incapable of explaining the governance of exchange as it is premised on specific, point-in-time and person-neutral transactions and relies on the courts to resolve conflicts. A noteworthy example of commercial relationships being the result of different influences and being pluralistic in form is provided by Francis Snyder (1999). Through an analysis of economic globalisation, in the form of the governance arrangements in the international commodity chain in toys, he shows the arrangement to be situationally specific and strategically determined and that it accrues from the interplay of 'structural' and 'relational' factors. The structural aspect involves a variety of institutions, norms and procedures, and these can be located at sites that can include states, international organisations, trade associations and so on. Alongside this, the relations among those sites are affected by their levels of autonomy, their interconnectedness in systems of multilevel governance, and by how much they co-operate or compete with each other and so on. Together, they constitute the global legal playing field for international commodity chain in toys and, in doing so, they provide both 'the rules of the game . . . and the game itself, including the players' (Snyder, 1999, p. 343).

From a *conditions of regulation* point of view, being implicitly compliant (or implicitly non-compliant) is fully explainable. Specifically, operating within the spirit or the shadow of the law is subject to the same *conditions of regulation* factors as previously mentioned (i.e., *conditions of regulation*, *conditions within shareholders*, *predicate of regulation*, *predicate of the shareholder*). Hence, for the third scenario that was detailed earlier, compliance with regulation may be implicit, such that, for example, knowledge of the regulation may be partially known, there is acceptance of the intent of the regulation and there are resources to comply with the regulation. In other words, the third scenario is the same as the first scenario but different in the form of the delivery. The same would be true for the second scenario, when the knowledge is partially known, when there is no acceptance to comply with the intent of the regulation and when resources are not made available for compliance. We should also add that this applies no matter the form of the regulatory intervention, no matter whether it is a strictly defined regulation or a soft form of governance. For instance, in the above-mentioned work of Snyder (1999), the rules of the game for the international commodity chain in toys are the result of how the *conditions of regulation* play out in states, international organisations, trade associations and so on, which are in turn a feature of levels of autonomy and interconnectedness and so forth. The *conditions of regulation* are therefore operating at both the micro and the macro level, with the end result being the rules of the game for that particular case as well as levels of compliance with those rules.

In a similar manner, when it is claimed that there is a convergence of practice in areas such as corporate governance, it reflects, if it is true, a convergence of different *conditions of regulation* practices. It should also be noted that this can also work in the opposite direction, in that we can have a convergence of rules and regulations (by different states and institutions) and a divergence of practice. Put simply, a specification of a regulation, with its attendant *conditions of regulation*, is of little worth if the *conditions within shareholders* (or the group being regulated) is at odds with what is required by the regulation. This would explain, we would argue, why there has been a convergence of regulations in shareholder protection while shareholder protection, in terms of enforcement of that protection, has not kept pace with that protection (Katelouzou and Siems, 2015). Similar findings exist in the areas of bribery and corruption (Batory, 2012), family law in Morocco (Eisenberg, 2011) and federal court systems (Church, 1985; Lynch and Omori, 2014). These examples show, in their different ways, what we would expect to happen when behaviours differ, when the conditions within shareholders (and other groups) are at odds with law in books, even when the convergence of regulation might suggest otherwise.

Overall, the important point is that there has to be a correspondence of knowledge, acceptance and resource (i.e., within both the *conditions of regulation* and the *conditions within shareholders*), as well as a correspondence of values, utility and obedience (i.e., within both the *predicate of regulation* and the *predicate of the shareholder*) for compliance to occur. To simplify this further, we shall, as we have done in the above discussion, call these the conditions of regulation; as we will now show, they hold the key to how shareholder regulation can be better configured to improve compliance.

6.5 IMPROVING SHAREHOLDER REGULATION

To improve compliance with shareholder regulation we must first draw the distinction between minimum compliance and beyond compliance behaviour. Minimum compliance is when the threshold for compliance has been satisfied, while beyond compliance behaviour, as the name suggests, is when minimum compliance is exceeded. Both are a consequence of the structure of regulation, since the structure of regulation determines the form and outcome of the compliance interaction. This can be represented by the compliance line shown in Figure 6.1.

The compliance line portrays the interaction of a regulation with the *conditions of regulation* and the *conditions within shareholders*. For shareholder regulation, as depicted by the angled line in Figure 6.1, the *conditions of regulation* at position 'A' are less demanding than at position 'B'. Closer inspection reveals that at compliance position 'A' the *conditions of regulation* are more easily satisfied by shareholders. This means that the knowledge condition of the regulation is understood by the majority of shareholders, that there is widespread acceptance of the regulation and that most shareholders have the resources to comply. In comparison, at compliance position 'B', the regulation has a more demanding *conditions of regulation* requirement, such that there is a significant body of knowledge that has to be acquired and understood, the hurdle that the regulation sets is accepted and they have the necessary resources to comply. As a consequence, the number of shareholders that have the capacity to comply with the *conditions of regulation* at compliance position 'B' is much less compared to compliance position 'A'. This presents a significant challenge for shareholder regulation, and indeed for regulation in general, because the form of the regulation has to be very different at compliance positions 'A' and 'B'.

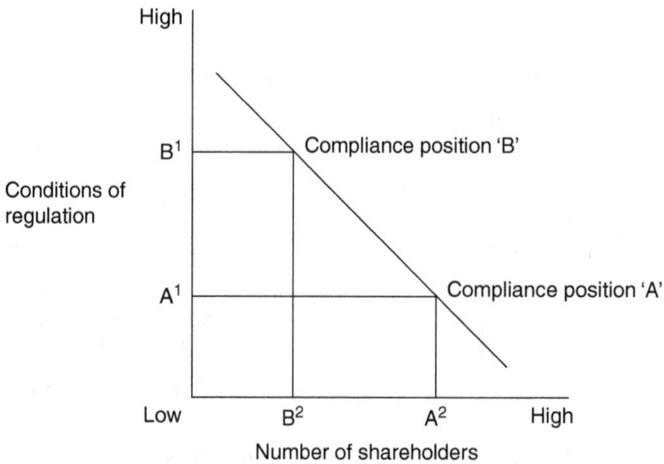

FIGURE 6.1 The compliance line
Source: Adapted from Williamson and Lynch-Wood, 2021.

At compliance position 'A', to have a lower *conditions of regulation* requirement, the knowledge requirement must be easily understood. This requires that the knowledge is seen as applicable to as many shareholders as possible, by being less targeted in terms of its technical specification and, hence, by necessitating less knowledge on the part of the shareholder. To meet this requirement, the regulation must be as open-ended as possible, less prescribed in its requirements. A principles-based approach such as the UK Corporate Governance Code would therefore fit this requirement. At compliance position 'B', the UK Corporate Governance code would be unfit for purpose. This is because compliance position 'B' requires a higher degree of specificity; having a higher degree of specificity demands a higher degree of certainty that the threshold at compliance position 'B' has been satisfied. Indeed, there is no point in having a high degree of specificity in a regulation if securing compliance is not important. It is why a nuclear facility has a highly prescribed and technical set of regulations and why, by comparison, a local convenience store has a much less onerous set of legal requirements.

The dilemma for shareholder regulation is therefore one between a widespread level of compliance where the *conditions of regulation* requirements are quite minimal, and where compliance with the regulatory threshold is quite variable owing to the less specific nature of the *conditions of regulation*, compared to a less widespread level of compliance where the *conditions of regulation* are high and, accordingly, where the certainty of compliance can be more easily measured. This is why the 'prudent person' rule and the UK Stewardship Code are widely welcomed as forms of regulation, as they accommodate the variability of the shareholder population. Likewise, it is why the opposite is true and why there is an absence of more stringent regulatory requirements. It represents a trade-off between: flexibility (i.e., low *conditions of regulation* providing flexibility of response; high *conditions of regulation* curtailing the flexibility of response) and certainty (i.e., low *conditions of regulation* providing little certainty on compliance; high *conditions of regulation* providing greater certainty on compliance). Calls for increased regulatory oversight therefore fail to recognise the consequences of any proposed actions. To be sure, you can increase the regulatory oversight, but this will be a cost. If the increase in regulatory oversight focusses on the stringency of the regulation, then the cost is fewer shareholders being able to comply.

Alternatively, if the increase in regulatory oversight focusses on a greater range of regulatory instruments rather than on their stringency, then the *conditions of regulation* problem only materialises in a different way. Having a mix of regulations, as advocated by many people and institutions (Gunningham and Grabosky, 1998; Howlett and Rayner, 2004; Van Gossum et al., 2010; European Commission, 2015), is premised on the weaknesses of one regulation being compensated by another, and yet this still increases the collective burden of the conditions of regulation on the regulatee. Thus, when there are three regulations rather than a single regulation, there are two additional conditions of regulation requirements.

For some shareholders the additional knowledge, acceptance and resource conditions may be beyond their capacity, while for others the challenge will be met relatively easily. When they are beyond their capacity, the regulations may then clash with one another, where, for example, the resource needed to comply with one regulation undermines the ability to comply with another. It is equally the case that the rule-following predicates of regulation can clash. If the rule following *predicate of regulation* is based on utility, through the use of an economic instrument, and the rule-following *predicate of the shareholder* is focussed on values, by being a voluntary code, then we can expect that compliance with utility will take second place to compliance with values.

Given these constraints, what then is the way forward? Is there a viable way, one that embraces a range of situations, events, entities, as well as pluralities of practice, into a regulatory strategy? The answer is a cautious yes if we adopt a *minmax* methodology (Williamson and Lynch-Wood, 2021). It requires that the regulatory strategy incorporates a minimum general requirement, which is set as low as possible by having the *conditions of regulation* set as low possible, as this enables the maximum number of shareholders to satisfy the *conditions of regulation* (i.e., the *conditions within shareholders* match the *conditions of regulation*). The minimum requirement must also be as specific as possible if we wish this to provide a level of certainty on compliance. Yet, by making the minimum requirement specific, we know that we likewise make the *conditions of regulation* specific, which excludes shareholders. This is precisely why the *conditions of regulation* must be set as low as they possibly can. However, since this is the lowest possible threshold, it may achieve very little, which is why the minimum requirement for achieving meaningful change still needs to be set to a level that does produce change, and thus why the setting of a meaningful minimum requirement will always exclude some shareholders. For example, you do not override the rule-following *predicate of the shareholder* when it is based on utility by setting it to be based on values, even when the values-based minimum requirement is set at a low level. The setting of the minimum requirement is therefore needed if we are to maximise compliance, but it must not be so low that it has no effect, and we should expect to see that some shareholders will fail to comply. When set at an optimal level, we would expect the minimum requirement to provide the 'rules of the game' for most shareholders, enabling those rules to be contextualised and embedded, and indeed contested, in a multiplicity of sites.

What about shareholders who have the capacity to do more than comply with the minimum requirement? You can increase the magnitude of the minimum requirement, but this will exclude more shareholders. On that basis, we would posit that, since the minimum requirement seeks to maximise compliance, it is imperative that there should be an accompanying regulatory mechanism that is designed to incentivise above minimum requirement compliance, for those shareholders with the capacity. Moreover, this needs to be an incentive that applies to shareholders, no matter whether they can perform only slightly better than the minimum requirement or much better than the minimum requirement (i.e., it must provide a continuous incentive). Combining this with the minimum requirement, and the compliance consequences that follow from the positions chosen, we can envisage the three compliance positions shown in Figure 6.2.

The first compliance consequence of the minimum requirement level chosen is that some shareholders will be non-compliant. They do not have the necessary *conditions of regulation* to comply (i.e., the *conditions within shareholder* are insufficient to meet the *conditions of regulation*). The second compliance consequence is that most shareholders will meet the minimum compliance level. If we were to increase the height of the minimum compliance level, we would exclude more shareholders. If we were to lower the position of the minimum compliance level, we would incorporate more shareholders (i.e., there is an optimal match between the *conditions within shareholders* and the *conditions of regulation*). Therefore, the position of the minimum requirement level has to be based on the number of shareholders you want to achieve compliance relative to the constraints imposed by the *conditions of regulation*. The third compliance consequence is that shareholders will respond to a beyond compliance incentive relative to the *conditions within shareholders*. That is, the shareholders will seek to respond to an incentive that is within their reach, such that fewer shareholders will be able to respond to a higher level of incentive while many more shareholders will be able to respond to a lower-level incentive (i.e., the *conditions of regulation* of the incentive have to match the *conditions within shareholders* for beyond compliance to occur at that particular

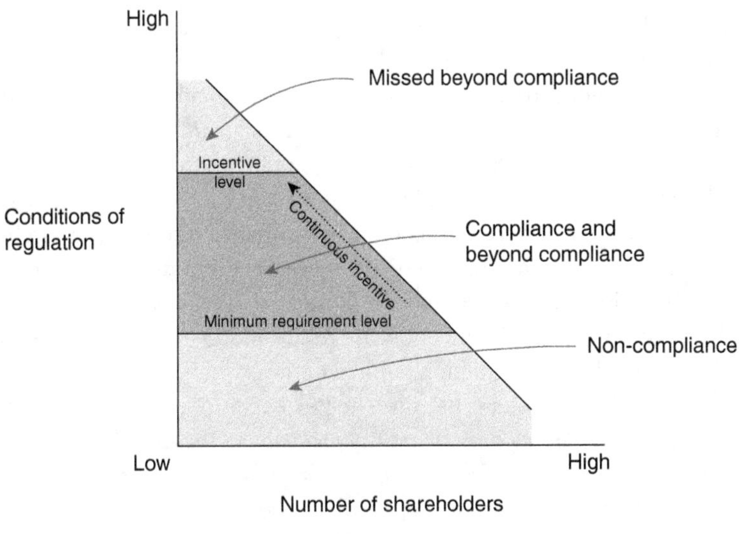

FIGURE 6.2 Compliance consequences of having a minimum requirement and a beyond minimum requirement structure

point). The fourth compliance consequence is missed beyond compliance as a consequence of the *conditions of regulation* being below the *conditions within shareholders*. It represents what could have been achieved if the incentive level had been set at a higher level.

Once the minimum requirement and the beyond compliance incentive have been decided upon, it is possible to support the *conditions within shareholders* to improve compliance. For example, you support the knowledge condition by providing the required knowledge to the shareholder. This may be through expert support, online materials, simplification of technical terms and so forth. The acceptance condition can be affected by increasing the severity of the sanction, or by name and shaming and so forth. Regulators can support the resource condition by providing low-interest loans and reduced taxes. Yet there are limits to the support that can be provided and, indeed, to the support that will be accepted by the shareholder. Support can therefore only ameliorate the consequences of the levels chosen for the minimum requirement and the incentive; it cannot overcome them.

6.6 CONCLUSIONS

The structural impediments to what regulation can achieve have been briefly outlined. It is evident that it is folly to believe that it is possible to fully control shareholder behaviour by regulation. Regulation, in fact, involves a series of trade-offs. You can have a very high threshold for shareholder regulation, a very ambitious baseline for what shareholders can do, and this will exclude many shareholders from meeting that baseline. If you have it too low you will achieve very little, even though many shareholders will comply. Likewise, you can have very detailed and specific regulations, but, since this places extra demands on the *conditions within shareholders*, you can expect that this will exclude many shareholders. Alternatively, you can have very open-ended and general regulations, providing great flexibility for shareholders by being easily aligned to the *conditions within firms*. However, this level of generality also enables the requirements of the regulation to be interpreted and acted upon in numerable ways, to the extent that there is very little regulatory control. Similarly, we can have an incentive to facilitate a response by shareholders; in the absence of a minimum requirement, however, there is no control over what shareholders will do, or over those shareholders who fail to respond. Combining the minimum requirement with an incentive therefore addresses some of the structural problems that shareholder regulation will encounter.

We say 'some' of the problems because the task becomes more complex when we factor in the *predicates of regulation* and the *predicate of the shareholder*. There can be a minimum requirement of the *predicate of regulation* based on obedience and a minimum requirement of the *predicate of the shareholder* based on utility, such that the *predicate of regulation* has no bearing on the compliance behaviour for a shareholder who is driven by utility. In that scenario, the minimum requirement has no relevance. Likewise, we can have an incentive based on utility with a shareholder driven by obedience, with the shareholder thus failing to respond to the incentive. Other incompatibilities are also possible, and they too would illustrate the limits of what regulation can achieve.

That said, the minmax methodology is the best approach for regulating shareholders. It necessitates a minimum requirement based on a clear line in the sand. This is needed because it has to be understood by most shareholders, which in turn demands that it should be kept as simple as possible. It must also be enforceable, and this demands a clearly defined rule, which implies that the minimum requirement should be focussed on obedience. The incentive can be based on utility and/or values, and should reward behaviour (e.g., financially, motivationally) in a continuous way to a point where the reward exceeds the benefit gained.

Looking at shareholder regulation in the UK, it was shown to involve a complex system of requirements that involve law, codes and reporting. It is a mature system, having developed over many years, and is frequently held up as a model of 'good' governance. Yet it continues to increase in complexity, with issues around shareholder rights, executive pay, risk-taking and so forth, providing the raw material for the provision of additional, and often more intricate, regulatory mechanisms. This increase in regulatory complexity illustrates the problem encountered with an approach that draws upon mixes of regulation, in that the *conditions of regulation* will differ for each of the regulations in the mix. Thus, the resource condition for one regulation can be competing against the resource condition of another regulation, potentially undermining the ability of the shareholder to respond optimally to both regulations. The same would be true for the knowledge and acceptance conditions, as well as for the *predicates of regulation*. It is therefore imperative that we simplify shareholder regulation wherever possible and that, in doing so, we move away from the idea that open-textured rules, when those are built around minimally acceptable normative behaviour based on the presumption of a commonly held view on what constitutes legitimate (i.e., good) governance behaviour, are appropriate for the minimum requirement. In fact, the opposite is true: we need the incentive to be open-textured so that it applies to as many shareholders as possible.

The minmax approach to shareholder regulation therefore requires a simplification of the structure of regulation. At its core, it should have the minimum requirement coupled with an incentive for beyond minimum requirement responses. The minimum requirement would apply to all shareholders and could necessitate, for example, a mandatory requirement to vote at AGMs. Building on this hypothetical example, companies could be required to notify all shareholders of dates, voting mechanisms, the agenda of the meeting and so forth, to reduce the burden on the shareholder. There could also be a reverse incentive built into the requirement to vote to cover the penalty aspect of non-compliance; for instance, a shareholder would automatically receive a tax relief if they were to vote, but they would lose if they failed to vote. The incentive would likely apply only to institutional investors and other large shareholders and could be based on the Stewardship Code, with tax relief for actions that are commensurate with the range of interventions they have engaged in. It is up to parties more qualified than ourselves to devise the mechanism that would work best, but what is important is that they focus on the logic of the minmax structure. What has to be avoided is the ad hoc accumulation of regulations, each of which is well-meaning but, when joined collectively with the others, undermines the efficiency and effectiveness of regulatory design.

NOTES

* David Williamson is a Professor Emeritus at Staffordshire University and an Honorary Senior Research Fellow at the School of Law, University of Manchester. David has a long-standing interest in how firms are regulated, mainly in the environmental, social responsibility and corporate governance areas. His early research focussed on the regulation of smaller firms and this has, over time, migrated to questions relating to the structure of regulation itself. Having published more than forty publications in these areas, including, with Gary Lynch-Wood, *The Structure of Regulation: Explaining Why Regulation Succeeds and Fails* (Edward Elgar, 2021), he is now focussing on the jurisprudential implications of his work.

1. Companies Act 2006, s. 310.
2. Ibid., s. 423.
3. Ibid., s. 336.
4. For example, the Pensions Act 1995.
5. For example, on the website.
6. For example, the Association of British Insurers, the Pensions and Lifetime Saving Association, and Pension Investment Research Consultants.
7. That is, their stake is high relative to that of other shareholders.

REFERENCES

Alrayes, S. A. (2019). Shareholder empowerment, steps forward and steps back: comparative analysis of the US and UK regulations. *Journal of Financial Regulations and Compliance*, 27(2), 169–96.

Arthur, W. B. (1989). Competing technologies, increasing returns, and lock-in by historical events. *Economic Journal*, 99(394), 116–31.

Audia, P. G., Locke, E. A. and Smith, K. G. (2000). The paradox of success: an archival and a laboratory study of strategic persistence following radical environmental change. *Academy of Management Journal*, 43(5), 837–53.

Australian Securities Exchange Corporate Governance Council. (2014). *Corporate Governance Principle and Recommendations*. www.asx.com.au/regulation/corporate-governance-council.htm.

Bainbridge, S. M. (1993). In defence of the shareholder maximisation norm: a reply to Professor Green. *Washington and Lee Law Review*, **50**(4), 1423–47.

Bargh, J. A., Chaiken, S., Govender, R. and Pratto, F. (1992). The generality of the automatic attitude activation effect. *Journal of Personality and Social Psychology*, **62**(6), 893–912.

Batory, A. (2012). Why do anti-corruption laws fail in Central Eastern Europe? A target compliance perspective. *Regulation and Governance*, **6**(2), 66–82.

Bebchuk, L. A. (2005). The case for increasing shareholder power. *Harvard Law Review*, **18**(3), 833–914.

Bebchuk, L. A. (2006). Letting shareholders set the rules. *Harvard Law Review*, **119**(6), 1784–1813.

Bebchuk, L. A. (2007). The myth of the shareholder franchise. *Virginia Law Review*, **93**(3), 675–732.

Blair, M. M. (1995). *Ownership and Control: Rethinking Corporate Governance for the Twenty-First Century*. Washington, DC: The Brookings Institution.

Bourdieu, P. (1980). *The Logic of Practice*. Stanford, CA: Stanford University Press.

Bourdieu, P. (1984). *Distinction: A Social Critique of the Judgement of Taste*. Cambridge, MA: Harvard University Press.

Church, T. W. (1985). Examining local legal culture. *Law& Social Inquiry*, **10**(3), 449–510.

Coffee, J. C. (2008). Financial crises 101: what can we learn from scandals and meltdowns – from Enron to subprime? In R. P. Austin, eds., *The Credit Crunch and the Law*. Sydney: Ross Parsons Centre of Commercial, Corporate and Taxation Law, University of Sydney, pp. 37–56.

Cyert, R. M. and March, J. G. (1963). *A Behavioral Theory of the Firm*. Englewood Cliffs, NJ: Prentice-Hall.

Dalton, D. R. and Dalton, C. M. (2011). Integration of micro and macro studies in governance research: CEO duality, board composition, and financial performance. *Journal of Management*, **37**(2), 404–11.

D'Andrade, R. G. (1984). Cultural meaning systems. In R. A. Shweder and R.A. Le Vine, eds., *Culture Theory: Essays on Mind, Self and Emotion*. Cambridge: Cambridge University Press, pp. 88–119.

David, P. A. (1985). Clio and the economics of QWERTY. *American Economic Review*, **75**(2), 332–7.

David, P. A. (1987). Some new standards for the economics of standardization in the information age. In P. Dasgupta and P. Stoneman, eds., *Economic Policy and Technological Performance*. Cambridge: Cambridge University Press, pp. 206–39.

Davies, G., Mulley, G. and Bardell, M. (2019). United Kingdom. In F. J. Aquila, ed., *The Shareholder Rights and Activism Review*, 4th ed. The Law Reviews. London: Law Business Research, pp. 146–61.

Della Croce, R. (2014). Are institutional investors the answer for long-term development financing? In Organisation for Economic Co-operation and Development. (OECD), *Development Co-operation Report 2014: Mobilising Resources for Sustainable Development*, ch. 6, pp. 79–89. http://dx.doi.org/10.1787/dcr-2014-en.

Dierickx, I. and Cool, K. (1989). Asset stock accumulation and sustainability of competitive advantage. *Management Science*, **35**(12), 1504–11.

Donaldson, T. and Preston, L. E. (1995). The stakeholder theory of the corporation: concepts, evidence and implications. *Academy of Management Review*, **20**(1), 65–91.

Eisenberg, A. M. (2011). Law on the books vs. law in action: under-enforcement of Morocco's reformed 2004 family law, the Moudawana. *Cornell International Law Journal*, **44**, 693–728.

European Commission. (2015). *Commission Staff Working Document: Better Regulation Guidelines*. Strasbourg, 19.5.2015 SWD(2015) 111 final. https://eur-lex.europa.eu/legal-content/EN/TXT/PDF/?uri=CELEX:52015SC0111&from=EN.

Fairfax, L. A. (2011). *Shareholder Democracy: A Primer of Shareholder Activism and Participation*. Durham, NC: Carolina Academic Press.

Fama, E. F. and Jensen, M. C. (1983).Separation of ownership and control. *Journal of Law and Economics*, **26**(2), 301–25.

Filatchev, I. and Dotsenko, O. (2015). Shareholder activism in the UK: types of activists, forms of activism, and their impact on a target's performance. *Journal of Management & Governance*, **19**, 5–24.

Financial Conduct Authority (FCA). (2020). *FCA Handbook: Listing Rules*. www.handbook.fca.org.uk/handbook/LR.pdf.

Financial Reporting Council (FRC). (2012). *The UK Stewardship Code*. www.frc.org.uk/Our-Work/Publications/Corporate-Governance/UK-Stewardship-Code-September-2012.pdf.

Financial Reporting Council (FRC). (2016). *The UK Corporate Governance Code*. www.frc.org.uk/getattachment/ca7e94c4-b9a9-49e2-a824-ad76a322873c/UK-Corporate-Governance-Code-April-2016.pdf.

Freeman, E. and Reed, D. (1983). Stockholders and stakeholders: a new perspective on corporate governance. *California Management Review*, **25**(3), 88–106.

Geertz, C. (1973). *The Interpretation of Cultures*. New York: Basic Books.

Gilson, R. J. (2001). Globalizing corporate governance: convergence of form or function. *American Journal of Comparative Law*, **49**(2), 329–57.

Goodpaster, K. (1991). Business ethics and stakeholder analysis. *Business Ethics Quarterly*, 1 (1), 53–73.

Granovetter, M. (1985). Economic action and social structure: the problem of embeddedness. *American Journal of Sociology*, **91**(3), 481–510.

Greenwald, A. and Banaji, M. (1995). Implicit social cognition: attitudes, self-esteem, and stereotypes. *Psychological Review*, **102**(1), 4–27.

Greif, A. (1997). On the interrelations and economic implications of economic, social, political, and normative factors: reflections from two late medieval societies. In J. N. Drobak and J. V. C. Nye, eds., *The Frontiers of the New Institutional Economics*. San Diego, CA: Academic Press, pp. 57–94.

Greve, H. (1998). Performance, aspirations, and risky organizational change. *Administrative Science Quarterly*, **43**(1), 58–86.

Gunningham, N. and Grabosky, P. (1998). *Smart Regulation: Designing Environmental Policy*. Oxford: Oxford University Press.

Halpérin, J. (2012). Law in books and law in action: the problem of legal change. *Maine Law Review*, **64**(1), 46–76.

Hannan, M. T. and Freeman, J. H. (1989). *Organizational Ecology*. Cambridge, MA: Harvard University Press.

Heiner, R. A. (1983). The origin of predictable behavior. *American Economic Review*, **73**(4), 560–95.

Hill, J. G. (2010). The rising tension between shareholder and director power in the common law world. *Corporate Governance: An International Review*, **18**(4), 344–59.

Hofstede, G. (1991). *Culture and Organizations: Software of the Mind*. New York: McGraw-Hill.

Holland, J. (1999). The regulation of price-sensitive information. In G. Morgan and L. Engwell, eds., *Regulation and Organizations: International Perspectives*. London: Routledge, pp. 123–44.

Howlett, M. and Rayner, J. (2004). (Not so) 'smart regulation'? Canadian shelfish aquaculture policy and the evolution of instrument choice for industrial development. *Marine Policy*, **28**(2), 171–84.

Jensen, M. C. and Meckling, W. C. (1976). Theory of the firm: managerial behavior, agency costs, and ownership structure. *Journal of Financial Economics*, **3**(4), 305–60.

Katelouzou, D. and Siems, M. (2015). Disappearing paradigm in shareholder protection: Leximetric evidence for 30 countries, 1990–2013. *Journal of Corporate Law Studies*, **15**(1), 127–60.

Keay, A. R. (2007). Tackling the issue of the corporate objective: an analysis of the United Kingdom's 'enlightened shareholder value approach'. *Sydney Law Review*, **29**(4), 577–612.

Lant, T. K. and Montgomery, D. (1987). Learning from strategic success and failure. *Journal of Business Research*, **15**(6), 503–17.

Levitt, B. and March, J. (1988). Organizational learning. *Annual Review of Sociology*, **44**, 319–40.

Lynch, M. and Omori, M. (2014). Legal change and sentencing norms in the wake of Booker: the impact of time and place on drug trafficking cases in Federal Court. *Law & Society Review*, **48**(2), 411–45.

Macaulay, S. (1963). Non-contractual relations in business: a preliminary study. *American Sociological Review*, **28**(1), 55–67.

Macneil, I. R. (1978). Contracts: adjustment of long-term economic relations under classical, neoclassical, and relational contract law. *Northwestern University Law Review*, **72**(6), 854–905.

Macneil, I. R. (1980). *The New Social Contract: An Inquiry into Modern Contractual Relations*. New Haven, CT: Yale University Press.

Meyer, J. W. and Scott, W. R. (1983). *Organizational Environments: Ritual and Rationality*. Beverley Hills, CA: Sage.

Monks, R. A. G. (2013). *Citizen Disunited: Passive Investors, Drone CEOs, and the Corporate Capture of the American Dream*. Billerica, MA: Miniver Press.

North, D. C. (1990). *Institutions, Institutional Change and Economic Performance*. Cambridge: Cambridge University Press.

North, D. C. (1993). What do we mean by rationality? *Public Choice*, **77**(1), 159–62.

North, D. C. (2005). *Understanding the Process of Economic Change*. Princeton, NJ: Princeton University Press.

Organisation for Economic Co-operation and Development (OECD). (2015). *G20/OECD Principles of Corporate Governance*. www.oecd.org/daf/ca/Corporate-Governance-Principles-ENG.pdf.

Park, Y. K., Song, J. H., Yoon, S. W. and Kim, J. (2014). Learning organization and innovative behavior: the mediating effect of work engagement. *European Journal of Training and Development*, **38**(1/2), 75–94.

Parkinson, J. (2003). Models of the company and the employment relationship. *British Journal of Industrial Relations*, **41**(3), 481–509.

Peteraf, M. A. (1993). The cornerstones of competitive advantage: a resource-based view. *Strategic Management Journal*, **14**(3), 179–91.

Pound, R. (1910). Law in books and law in action. *American Law Review*, **44**, 12–36.

Prahalad, C. K. and Bettis, R. A. (1986). The dominant logic: a new linkage between diversity and performance. *Strategic Management Journal*, **7**(6), 485–501.

Putnam, R. (2000). *Bowling Alone: The Collapse and Revival of American Community*. New York: Simon & Schuster.

Roe, M. (2001). The shareholder wealth maximization norm and industrial organisation. *University of Pennsylvania Law Review*, **149**(6), 2063–81.
Ross, S. A. (1973). The economic theory of agency: the principal's problem. *American Economic Review*, **63**(2), 134–9.
Scott, W. (2013). *Institutions and Organizations: Ideas, Interests, and Identities*, 4th ed. Thousand Oaks, CA: Sage.
Shaw, B. and Post, F. R. (1993). A moral basis for corporate philanthropy. *Journal of Business Ethics*, **12**(10), 745–51.
Snyder, F. (1999). Governing economic globalisation: global legal pluralism and European law. *European Law Journal*, **5**(4), 334–74.
Subramanian, R. (2017). Shareholder spring and social activism: a study of 2013–2015 proxy filings. *Corporate Governance*, **17**(3), 560–73.
Van Gossum, P., Arts, B. and Verheven, K. (2010). From 'smart regulation' to 'regulatory arrangements'. *Policy Sciences*, **43**(3), 245–61.
Williamson, D. and Lynch-Wood, G. (2021). *The Structure of Regulation: Explaining Why Regulation Succeeds and Fails*. Elgar Studies in Law and Regulation. Cheltenham, UK: Edward Elgar.
Woolcock, M. (2001). The place of social capital in understanding social and economic outcomes. *Isuma Canadian Journal of Policy Research*, **2**(1), 11–17.
Zenger, T., Lazzarini, S. G. and Poppo, L. (2002). Informal and formal organization in new institutional economics. In P. Ingram and B. Silverman, eds., *The New Institutionalism in Strategic Management*. Vol. 19, Advances in Strategic Management. Oxford: Elsevier Science, pp. 277–306.

7

SMEs: An Untapped Platform for Sustainable CSR Penetration and Practice in Developing and Emerging Markets

Franklin N. Ngwu

7.1 INTRODUCTION

While the debates and studies on corporate social responsibility (CSR) have been on the increase, the focus has somewhat been on both developed economies and multinational corporations (MNCs) as compared to developing and emerging markets (DEMs) and small and medium-scale enterprises (SMEs) (see Amaeshi et al., 2016; Jamali and Karam, 2018). Arguably, this can be attributed to three factors. First is that, in the society–business relationship, big businesses such as MNCs are perceived as being more prepared and suitable for tackling social problems or demands on businesses on issues such as job creation, ESG, pollution and other negative externalities of business activities. The second one builds on the first by stating that SMEs are perceived as being too lean or poor in resources to be able to intervene or help with social problems, as the MNCs do. Third is that SMEs should neither be seen to be socially irresponsible nor unduly concentrate on addressing social problems (see Ladzani and Seeletse, 2012). However, if the interest is to advance awareness and practice of CSR across firms to achieve wider social impacts, particularly in DEMs, a rethink is pertinent. There is no doubt that MNCs have the resources and can have significant impacts on host communities; the challenge is to do with their internal implementation weaknesses, their number and reach in DEMs and their limited understanding of the development needs and peculiarities of DEMs.

In contribution-to-growth measures such as gross domestic product (GDP) and job creation, SMEs contribute more than MNCs. The functioning of most economies is mainly dependent on the activities of SMEs, with immense socio-economic and environmental benefits. Thus, SMEs account for more than 90 per cent of businesses globally and contribute about 60 per cent of jobs (Raynard and Forstater, 2002; Fox, 2004; Jamali et al., 2009). In Europe, 99 per cent of the firms are SMEs and they contribute about 80 per cent of the jobs. It is the same in Africa, Latin America and Asia (see Aruwa, 2004; Amaeshi et al., 2016). With such huge and higher contributions than MNCs, the question is who really should lead the crusade for more CSR in DEMs, SMEs or MNCs? Appreciating some of these factors, therefore, brings us to question the emphasis on MNCs and the view that SMEs might lack the structure, understanding and capacity to undertake CSR activities (see Baumann-Pauly et al., 2013; Amaeshi et al., 2016). Debatably, SMEs, in their formation, structure, ownership, vision and operations, are different from MNCs and seem to be more naturally aligned to the meaning and practice of CSR than MNCs. This is related to the embeddedness of SMEs in the social-cultural fabric of society, which places them at a vantage position of having better insight into the development peculiarities of DEM societies (see Azmat and Samaratunge, 2009; Knudsen, 2013; Aragon et al., 2016).

This chapter, therefore, aims to show that SMEs remain a limitedly explored platform for increased awareness and practice of CSR in DEMs, despite, even in comparison with MNCs, SMEs having a better understanding of the development challenges of DEMs and arguably more potential to have a higher impact. The chapter will proceed as follows: Section 7.2 will rethink the meaning of CSR with emphasis on DEMs and SMEs, while Section 7.3 will examine the institutional conditions that make firms behave in a socially responsible manner. Section 7.4 will compare CSR between MNCs and SMEs and Section 7.5 will show that SMEs are more suited for wider CSR activities and impacts in DEMs. Section 7.6 will examine how SMEs' CSR engagement and activities can be expanded and enhanced through support from other stakeholders, especially the government. Section 7.7 will conclude.

7.2 WHAT IS CSR IN DEMS?

A key question in the examination of CSR is what it really means. When we say that a firm's behaviours or activities are socially responsible, what does it entail? Given the wide perspectives through which CSR is understood (see Okoye, 2009), its meaning and implications are varied and can be both objective and subjective. For instance, it can be perceived as a firm's ability to pay a reasonable wage to its employees relative to their productivity and local cost of living and guided by international standards and organisations such as the International Labour Organization (ILO). According to Campbell (2012), for a firm to be adjudged as behaving in a socially responsible way, two conditions need to be fulfilled. While the first condition is that the firm will not intentionally act in ways that may be harmful to its stakeholders such as employees, customers, investors, suppliers and host communities, the second is that when it inadvertently, through actions or inactions, causes harm, the firm should be eagerly disposed to rectify or robustly ameliorate the harm when noticed or notified of. Expanding on this means that CSR can be described as conduct of firms with regard to employees' remunerations, benefits, workplace safety; customers in terms of quality of products and services, sincerity in advertising, pricing and reports; its relationships with suppliers on issues such as adhering to the sanctity of contracts and even informal agreements; its amenability to regulations and laws such as transparent tax compliance; and, then, its commitment and genuine desire for a better environment and community growth and development (see Rowley and Berman, 2000, Azmat and Samaratunge, 2009; Campbell, 2012; Aragon et al., 2016).

As a thriving area of study, CSR attracts wide understanding and meaning across DEMs and has both similarities to and differences from the CSR of developed markets. Irrespective of the environment, there is a general understanding that there is a link between business and society and, as such, businesses are expected to behave in certain ways which include helping in solving societal problems (Idemudia, 2009). With such an understanding, the expected contributions of businesses in solving societal problems are open to all businesses, irrespective of size (Fox, 2004; Worthington et al., 2006). While in developed markets the emphasis is on the firm and its actions and inactions in organisational stakeholder management, in DEMs it seems a bit deeper and more culturally embedded. There is an inherent interest in the intricate business–society relations with an emphasis on the normative factors that underlie and sustain the relationships. In essence, business–society interaction is approached and understood more from an inclination to the societal norms and values, and the responsibility of the firm in the social contract (Jamali and Karam, 2018). Therefore, CSR is understood and practised from a position of deep embeddedness in the cultural and religious values of society and focussed more on local communities (Visser, 2008; Jamali et al., 2009). In an African context, firms are expected to participate in and support efforts to address local social problems and needs (Frynas, 2005).

Nevertheless, CSR definitions and understandings from developed markets are also used and applied in the examination of CSR in DEMs.A few examples can be identified. First is McWilliams and Siegel's (2001) definition of CSR as firms' pursuit of social good far above what is required, based on either the firm's interests or legal obligations. In this definition, the firm's commitment to social good is driven not really by economic and legal considerations but more by an innate interest of the firm in the creation of a more sustainable society. While related to Carrol's (1999) pyramid model, the definition somewhat places CSR as dictated not mainly by economic and legal considerations, to which Carrol allocates more importance. By situating economic and legal requirements at the base of the pyramid, Carrol (1999) seems to attach more importance to economic and legal demands as compared to ethical and philanthropic inclinations that can be argued to be more in tune with McWilliams and Siegel (2001) (see also Nejati and Ghasemi, 2012; Jamali and Karam, 2018).

Another CSR perspective observable in both developed markets and DEMs is the 'business case' for CSR (Porter and Kramer, 2006), which somewhat reconciles the identified difference between Carrol (1999) and McWilliams and Siegel (2001). It emphasises not only that CSR and business performance are positively related but that a firm's profitability and business opportunities can also be improved through the firm's involvement in the socio-economic needs of society (CSR). Outside CSR definitions that are common to both developed markets and DEMs, the peculiarities of DEMs and the observed CSR practices and understandings all seem to have shaped or are shaping a set of definitions that can be described as DEMs-oriented. First is that CSR is seen as something beyond the firm; it is complex, with decisions reached through the engagement of stakeholders within and outside the firm. Second is that CSR should be understood and practised as a contextual issue, with practices or specific CSR activities varied and dictated by the peculiarities of the society and firm in question (Idemudia, 2008; Lund-Thomsen and Nadvi, 2010a; Muthuri and Gilbert, 2011). With this perspective, firms are perceived as having a duty of care and protection of society from both internal consequences of their activities and external forces of the market (Vachani and Smith 2004; Husted and Allen, 2006).

Related to the duty of care perspective is the view of CSR as normative and part of the socio-cultural and economic expectations or requirements in business–society relationships. In this vein, the firm is part of society and is thus expected to advance the sustainable growth of the society through activities that are in line with or moderated by the norms and values of the society. Therefore, CSR is relative to the environment in question and socio-culturally embedded (Idemudia, 2008; Matten and Moon, 2008; Gugler and Shi, 2009; Huemer, 2010). It can also be perceived as an aspect of the interactions and relationships in a normatively oriented society. With societies and their inherent norms and values varied, understanding CSR in DEMs requires a good appreciation of contextual differences, peculiarities and the many stakeholders with varied historical, socio-political and geopolitical dispositions (Jamali and Karam, 2018). This relates to institutional theory, which helps us understand the factors that influence or dictate how organisational choices are made and executed. Institutions provide the structure and incentives through which social relations and transactions are sustained. They can be formal or informal and include rules and laws, values and norms of society that help to reduce or eliminate uncertainties and inherent costs in human relations and transactions. They are the structures through which incentives are prescribed in all human engagements – political, economic and other social relations. Through the incentives provided by the institutions, organisations emerge or are created to pursue their goals within the standard constraints of economic theory. Organisations include economic, political, social, educational bodies such as firms, universities, churches, trade unions and even individuals or groups of individuals such as ethnic groups (see North, 1990). Also, an important concept within the institutional theory discourse is institutional 'isomorphism', which describes the homogeneity of organisations in a field. The framework, as developed by DiMaggio and Powell (1983), brought different mechanisms through which isomorphism occurs in the form of coercive, mimetic and normative isomorphism. Institutional isomorphism relates to the idea that organisational structure, rather than emanating from the rules of efficiency in the marketplace, occurs through the institutional constraints imposed by the state and the professions such that any effort to achieve rationality with uncertainty and constraint results in homogeneity of structure (DiMaggio and Powell, 1983).

In addition to institutional theory, variations of CSR in DEMs arguably might be related to the different theories through which CSR in DEMs has been examined; these include relational governance theory (Xun, 2013); transaction cost economics (Bhanji and Oxley, 2013); capitalism theory (Amaeshi and Amao, 2009); political theory (Castello and Galang, 2014); Sen's capability approach (Ansari et al., 2012); slack resource theory (Julian and Ofori-Dankwa, 2013); grounded theory (Newenham-Kahindi, 2011); and critical postcolonial theory (Khan and Lund-Thomsen, 2011). While these theories have been used based on their respective merits in relation to the context and disposition of the study, a key question is the understanding of the institutional factors that dictate or enhance a firm's CSR engagement and activities.

7.3 INSTITUTIONAL DETERMINANTS OF A FIRM'S CSR

In examining the institutional conditions that influence firms to act responsibly or irresponsibly, Campbell (2012) offers eight propositions. The first is that firms will more likely act in a socially responsible manner when their financial performance is strong. In situations where the business environment is inhibiting and unsustainable, financial performance is less guaranteed; the possibility of pursuing socially responsible decisions and activities will be less likely. The second proposition straddles situations of high to low competition and monopoly with less possibility of socially responsible behaviour in the two extremes. In situations of high competition, on the one hand, the main interest will be on how to survive and not really on pursuing socially responsible behaviours. On the other hand, in situations ranging from very low competition to monopoly, the outcome is similar, but the determinants of the outcome are different. In this case, there is no demand or pressure for the monopolist, for instance, to act in a socially responsible manner and so there will be limited socially responsible firms in such contexts. Based on this scenario, it means that socially responsible firms will be more in an environment of moderate competition.

Focussing more on institutional conditions, the third proposition is that a higher possibility of socially responsible behaviours of firms can be achieved in an environment of properly co-ordinated and enforced government regulation. The result is even better when the formulations and procedures for enforcement of the policies and regulations are consensually reached through robust engagement and dialogue with the relevant stakeholders. Fourth, firms' inclination to behave in a socially responsible manner will be more in an environment with well-established and active self-regulation mechanisms, especially when it is supported with government regulatory and enforcement frameworks. Fifth, in addition to self-regulation, firms will be more disposed to act in a socially responsible way in situations with active private, independent organisations such as non-governmental organisations (NGOs), social movement organisations, institutional investors and the media, all of which are positioned to observe, complain about and influence firms' actions and inactions. From a normative perspective, the sixth proposition is that firms behave in a more socially responsible way in societies or environments with institutionalised normative demands. This is, for instance, where there are publications and other avenues such as business schools and other educational institutions emphasising the importance of firms behaving and acting in a socially responsible way and they (the firms) are supported and encouraged to participate and learn.

Seventh, in environments where associations such as trade unions are active and organised, and promote socially responsible behaviours, firms are more likely to act accordingly. Related to the seventh proposition is the eighth, which states that expectations of socially responsible behaviour from firms will be higher in societies with institutionalised mechanisms for collaboration and dialogue with relevant stakeholders such as unions, employees, investors, communities and others. With insights from the above eight institutional factors, it might be pertinent to re-examine CSR in DEMs vis-à-vis MNCs and SMEs.

7.4 CSR IN DEMS: MNCS OR SMES?

In addition to the dimensions of what constitutes socially responsible behaviour of firms, its changing or transitory feature should also be noted. What is perceived as a commendable socially responsible behaviour today might be perceived as out of place in some years in the future. For instance, while reducing the working period from fourteen to ten hours was considered a responsible behaviour during the Industrial Revolution, anything beyond eight hours might presently be considered not responsible unless with overtime wages and other incentives (Campbell, 2012). This relates to what is described as stages of CSR. In managing both external and internal stakeholder pressures, a firm's approach changes over time, which indicates the beginning of a new development stage (Maon et al., 2010). As identified by Zadek's (2004) organisational learning model, firms generally transit and progress through five stages to reach full implementation of CSR. These stages are *denial*, *compliance*, *managerial*, *strategic* and *civil*. Using Zadek's (2004) framework, Baumann-Pauly et al. (2013) developed an assessment framework that can be used for both MNCs and SMEs.

While the *denial stage* relates to when companies are ignorant or refuse to acknowledge their responsibility for the social and environmental consequences of their business activities, the *compliance stage* describes the point at which firms are just interested in obeying stipulated rules and regulations. In the *managerial stage*, firms begin to exhibit more appreciation and understanding of social and environmental issues as well as their responsibility beyond legal demands. As the name suggests, the *strategic stage* is when firms accept and pursue CSR issues from a more strategic disposition, in the belief that their competitive advantage will be advanced through their CSR engagements. This will be noticed in the strategic ways that firms approach issues such as human rights, labour laws and practices such as workplace safety and environmental factors. The last segment, the *civil stage*, is where firms, without any form of regulation or private benefits, are sincerely interested in pursuing and practising CSR activities and even active in advocating CSR practices through collaborations with other stakeholders.

As noted earlier, MNCs seem to enjoy more attention and are somewhat perceived as being more prepared and disposed to engage in CSR activities than SMEs (see McWilliams and Siegel, 2001; Campbell, 2007). Enhancing such a perception is the lack of agreement from the few studies on CSR in SMEs on whether SMEs can be adjudged as more organised and skilled in carrying out CSR activities than MNCs (see Lepoutre and Heene, 2006). However, a few studies, such as Baumann-Pauly et al. (2013), maintain that the perception that MNCs are more advanced in implementing CSR activities seems flawed as there is no evidence to support that SMEs are less prepared in implementing CSR. The perception of MNCs' superior advancement and better preparedness has more to do with their higher media engagement and reporting demands than their actual engagement in CSR activities. In comparison, while SMEs are inherently not inclined to such high-profile media engagement and reporting requirements, they are significantly matured and more forward-thinking in pursuing CSR-oriented activities connected to core organisational issues and operations such as employee engagement (see Ram et al., 2001; Baumann-Pauly et al., 2013). Moreover, a major flaw in the perception of MNCs as more disposed to being involved in CSR activities might be the inappropriate use of standards peculiar to MNCs in assessing SMEs. For instance, while it is expected that the CSR activities of MNCs should be documented and reported as part of their governance and regulatory requirements, it is not so with SMEs. As CSR is perceived and practised from an intrinsic cultural inclination, there might not be a requirement for proper documentation and reporting.

Dimensioning CSR into bands such as 'Commitment to CSR; Internal Structures and Procedures; and External Collaboration', Baumann-Pauly et al. (2013) demonstrate the differences in focus between MNCs and SMEs, for a better understanding and assessment of the issues. A key factor is the need to appreciate the formal organisational orientation and approach of MNCs in comparison to the informal culture and implied approach of SMEs. In commitments to CSR, MNCs should be assessed using measurements such as the extent to which CSR issues and demands are included in the strategic plans and policies of the firm. This will be further demonstrated through apparent and unquestionable support and leadership for CSR activities from the management and board and co-ordination of CSR activities through specified units and employees (see Baumann, 2009).

For SMEs, the commitment to CSR should start with issues such as the level of the SME's awareness, particularly the owner-manager's, of what CSR entails. Good criteria to use are the ten principles of the UN Global Compact, which focus on issues such as human rights, labour norms, environmental responsibility and anti-corruption. A second aspect of checking the commitment to CSR might be the extent of the owner-manager's disposition towards the above issues in both their involvement and their engagement with external parties for the pursuit of identified CSR activities.

For the second dimension, internal structures and procedures, a firm can be assessed through measures that show the extent of incorporation of CSR in the practical activities and operations of the firm. In MNCs, this relates to well-organised efforts to promote CSR issues and demands through training and motivations across the organisation, with elements such as complaints channels, performance evaluation and reporting procedures used to imbibe CSR culture (Baumann, 2009). In SMEs, this can be deduced through the embedded, informalised culture and operations of the firm. With the informal approach to CSR and other issues, participation of employees is pursued through a somewhat relaxed and familiar approach, and disclosure and reporting of CSR activities to third parties are normally done as and when required (Wickert, 2011a).

The third dimension, external collaboration, relates to partnership and interaction with other CSR interested parties such as NGOs. For MNCs, it will entail the active involvement in and contribution to concerted CSR activities such as the UN Global Compact, in addition to encouraging partnerships with external stakeholders such as NGOs and other firms (Baumann, 2009). In SMEs, it relates to the extent of collaboration with other SMEs and suppliers for collective CSR activities and also membership in CSR-oriented groups such as industry associations (Wickert, 2011a).

Using the above three dimensions – commitment, internal structures and procedures, and external collaboration – in their examination of MNCs and SMEs, Baumann-Pauly et al. (2013) observed interesting differences. First, while most MNCs are highly committed to CSR, there is a gap between the professed commitment and the actual CSR policies and procedures. This is also the case with internal integration, which can be described as uneven, with effective integration of CSR across firm activities and operations lacking or weak, especially on issues such as the existence of grievance procedures. On the contrary, MNCs were observed to have robust reporting systems and procedures, but their interaction and engagement with external stakeholders lack a systematic approach (see also Baumann-Pauly et al., 2012). Moreover, as voluntary CSR communication helps to reduce the cost of equity capital of listed firms, MNCs seem to effectively engage in enhancing their image through external communication, which expectedly will take significant parts of their CSR budgets (see Baumann-Pauly et al., 2013; Reverte, 2012).

While not directly related, the perception of robust reporting systems of MNCs as compared to their weak stakeholders' engagement seems to be in line with the view that there is a negative relationship between firm size and properly organised communication of CSR activities (Gamerschlag et al., 2011). The observed variations in the performance of MNCs in the identified three dimensions indicate a challenge to the believability and success of MNCs' CSR execution efforts. First, with the lack of coherent implementation of CSR activities by MNCs, possible gaps between CSR talk and CSR walk (practices) will be more apparent. Second, MNCs' understanding of societal issues and CSR expectations will be impaired given their limited or lack of robust interaction with relevant stakeholders. Moreover, these challenges might likely widen given the differences between MNCs' publicly professed commitment to CSR activities and their actual poor engagement with stakeholders and unmethodical pursuit of CSR activities, which are more noticeably disappointing.

In comparison, while SMEs are observed to be effective in implementing CSR activities in essential business areas, they lack a proper reporting process. By extension, while they are low in CSR talk, they are high in CSR walk, with proper alignment to CSR of operations and decisions, with both formal and informal inclinations (see Murillo and Lozano, 2006). In the same vein, not only are SMEs observed to be characterised by robust engagement of stakeholders but their (SMEs') decisions and operations are impacted by insights from and interactions with stakeholders (see Wickert, 2011b). Drawing from this, it is maintained that while MNCs might be dominating CSR discussions and issues, SMEs seem to be higher in terms of CSR implementation and impacts. Using the relative cost of implementing CSR against that of reporting as a share of a firm's total costs, the differences in CSR between MNCs and SMEs can be better understood (Baumann-Pauly et al., 2013). In line with Downs's (1966) law of diminishing control, the better CSR implementation of SMEs can be attributed to their small size and consequently limited control and co-ordination costs as compared to MNCs with larger sizes and relatedly higher co-ordination costs and weak controls.

Similarly, while administrative and co-ordination costs might reduce in MNCs owing to economies of scale, the possibility of an increase owing to organisational complications and variations should be noted (see Blau, 1970). Examining the relationship between adaptation and co-ordination costs and the size of a firm, Camacho (1991) notes that firms with higher environmental differences such as MNCs (for instance, multiple locations) will expectedly have higher co-ordination and control costs. In comparison, SMEs are at an advantage as they are not as spread out as MNCs and consequently have lower co-ordination costs. Arguably, the gaps between SMEs and MNCs can be attributed to the differences in organisational costs of external reporting and those of embedding CSR in firms' cultures and operations. These differences lead to public relations and reporting gaps for SMEs and then an implementation gap for MNCs (Baumann-Pauly et al., 2013). To Kogut and Zander (1996), co-ordination and communication costs can be related to the level of perception of a firm as an identity-producing enterprise. The more a firm is regarded as such, the lower the identified costs. Given the smallness of SMEs, which guarantees and sustains regular employee interactions and an informal approach to rules and decisions, they (SMEs) have a higher level of identity and consequently lower co-ordination and implementation costs. With the identified CSR features of SMEs, the question is how they (SMEs) can be supported to achieve more awareness and practice of CSR in DEMs.

7.5 SMES AS CSR AGENTS IN DEMS

Interestingly, most SMEs are of the view that the social and environmental challenges of the society should attract their interest and action (Jenkins, 2006). Moreover, as most SMEs are managed by their founders and owners, it means that CSR decisions and activities are within the immediate purview of the highest authority in the firms (see Morsing and Perrini, 2009). However, with their sizes, nature, limited capital and business activities, most SMEs have neither well-planned CSR policies nor specific units or employees for CSR activities (see Spence, 2007; Sweeney, 2007).

In terms of what drives SMEs to engage in CSR activities, while many SMEs perceive and understand CSR as a process or system of giving back to society, they are motivated by different factors. Given their (SMEs') involvement and embeddedness in their respective societies, the interest of some SMEs in CSR activities is dictated and guided by their values, morals or religious beliefs. Others are driven by patriotic reasons, regulatory requirements or supply-chain demands (see Idemudia, 2011; Amaeshi et al., 2016). This is in line with Painter-Morland and Dobie's (2009) view that factors such as SME owners' ethical orientation, religion, educational background and exposition to international business standards influence SMEs' ethical understanding and practices. Given the importance attached to socio-cultural factors in DEMs, the CSR activities of SMEs can be better understood as evidence of institutional works in a socio-culturally embedded society (Amaeshi et al., 2016).

Delving more into a stakeholder perspective, it is argued that SMEs' immediate areas of interest in their CSR decisions and activities are normally their primary stakeholders, through things such as ensuring the welfare of their employees, and then the secondary ones such as other stakeholders. In addition to the employees, another primary stakeholder given special attention is the local community, possibly owing to the inherent deep relationship and embeddedness which manifests in the CSR (sometimes philanthropic) activities of SMEs (Lepoutre and Heene, 2006; Coppa and Sriramesh, 2013). According to Jamali et al. (2009), the CSR activities of some SMEs are sometimes dictated by the SMEs' involvement in a supply chain that demands compliance with certain conditions, whether informal requirements or part of the self-regulating rules of the network, in order to be part of the network and to sustain business relationships. Interestingly, while environmental issues occupy a prime position in the CSR list of MNCs, it is not the same with SMEs. In the same way, NGOs tend to address more of their demands to MNCs. This is likely owing to the fact that SMEs are not big brands that depend for success on their brand reputation and image (Coppa and Sriramesh, 2013; Demuijnck and Ngnodjom, 2013).

While most of the above-mentioned studies relate to CSR activities in DEMs, the similarities with the CSR behaviours and activities of SMEs in Europe are high (Azmat and Samaratunge, 2009; Demuijnck and Ngnodjom, 2013). Using Valente and Crane's (2010) public responsibility strategies and Crane et al.'s (2013) spaces of CSR in the workplace, marketplace, ecological environment and community, with a focus on Nigeria and Tanzania, it is argued that SMEs not only engage in CSR but do so in active ways in the workplace, the marketplace, the community and the ecological environment. Not only are their CSR activities beyond philanthropy, they can also be described as institutional works that solve or ameliorate institutional gaps in the society where these SMEs exist. Examples include providing staff training in general areas not directly connected to their work, making soft loans available to employees and providing solutions to societal problems such as supporting teachers with training and other needs (see Amaeshi et al., 2016). For CSR in workplaces, issues such as employee welfare, work–life balance, employee capacity building and equity/gender-related factors are common CSR practices of SMEs. For instance, most SMEs in Tanzania do not demand that their employees work more than 45 hours per week (Gamba, 2019). This is also the case with staff training, which seems to be widely practised across SMEs.

In SMEs, owner-managers most of the time engage in CSR not out of any regulation or pressure but through their willingness and choice (von Weltzien Hoivik and Melé, 2009). With the possibility that interest in engaging in CSR derives more from an innate inclination, it seems that such exists more in SMEs than in MNCs. Also enhancing the CSR engagement of SMEs is the possible lower pressure they face from their investors, which might provide room for utilisation of more resources for CSR activities (Quinn, 1997). While such presentation of SMEs' CSR activities as dependent on the understanding and dispositions of the owner-managers is valid, it seems to belittle the impacts of institutional factors on the firms' CSR decisions and activities. Moreover, the firms' decisions and activities are perceived as outputs of complex interactions of managerial, organisational and institutional dispositions (Jamali et al., 2015). While there is no doubt as to the agency powers of the SME owner-managers in making CSR decisions, it is also important to note that institutional contexts and factors can contribute to restraining or enhancing such powers (Crouch, 2005; Lawrence and Suddaby, 2006).

7.6 ENHANCING SMES' CSR CAPABILITY AND ENGAGEMENT

Arguably, given their dominance of most economies and their inherent inclination to CSR, SMEs remain a limitedly untapped platform for CSR expansion and growth. Pursuing CSR growth and impact in DEMs can therefore be achieved through deliberate efforts to address the conditions that enhance SMEs' responsible behaviours. Drawing from Campbell's (2018) eight propositions, explained in Section 7.3, the first strategy must create an appropriate business environment for SMEs to thrive and achieve sustainable financial performance and growth. Using the World Bank governance indicators, a starting point will be improving the key regulatory indicators such as the rule of law, regulatory quality and government effectiveness across the DEMs (see Kaufmann and Kray, 2020). As these variables in combination can be described as a reflection of the state of the regulatory environment, addressing the regulatory challenges in DEMs will directly or indirectly improve SMEs' operating environment and relatedly their financial performance. With a moderately competitive market most likely to support more responsible SME behaviour, the focus should be on addressing the factors that inhibit the emergence of competitive market environments in most DEMs. This might relate to excessive taxation and labour laws, tough operating procedures that constrain ease of doing business and competition laws that inhibit or restrain competition.

In the 2020 World Bank Ease of Doing Business Report, of the 190 countries surveyed, the last 50 countries are all DEMs. Examining the report further reveals that a key factor that might require significant reform is the regulatory framework and by extension the legal system of most DEMs (see World Bank, 2020). It is a kind of double jeopardy for SMEs. On the regulatory framework, there are challenges of multiple regulatory agencies and, as such, multiple fees and taxes, unclear and outdated regulations, corruption on the part of regulatory agencies, unwarranted barriers to entry and other factors. With the negative impacts of these challenges on the financial performance of SMEs, most that might not survive the formal regulatory environment will expectedly either exit the market or operate within the informal segment of the economy to avoid formal regulatory attention.

Moreover, as most SMEs are informal and operate within their normative societies, their preferred legal system is normally the informal one, which in most DEMs is different from the formal one used in the formal regulation of SMEs' activities. With their preference for informal laws enhanced by their embeddedness in the social fabric (norms and values) of their respective societies, their understanding, acceptance, internalisation and willingness to comply are a lot higher than they would be with formal laws, which most of the time are foreign and adopted (see Menski, 2006). There is therefore a gap or challenge in the demand for and use of formal laws on the part of SMEs in DEMs, which directly or indirectly affects their formal CSR engagement and activities. Recalling Campbell's (2012) counsel that more socially responsible behaviour of firms can be achieved in an environment of properly co-ordinated and enforced regulations that are consensually agreed with relevant stakeholders, the need for legal reform in DEMs is further strengthened. In examining the factors that enhance the effectiveness of a law, Cooter (2000) points out that it depends on the extent to which the law is understood, accepted, internalised and complied with and that these four factors are easier and better achieved when the law is aligned with the informal norms and values of society.

As noted earlier, it is not that SMEs are not involved in CSR activities; they are, but limitedly so within their respective normative societies. Moreover, as their involvement in CSR activities is more of a voluntary and intrinsic inclination, the focus or challenge, therefore, is on how to enhance and expand their CSR awareness and activities. With rules and regulations (laws) a central factor for business activities, the focus in the advocated legal reform is on two fronts. The first is on how to address some of the identified challenges such as tax, multiple regulations and barriers to entry within the confines of a formal regulatory framework. The second will focus on how to create a better synergy between the informal laws that SMEs are comfortable and better aligned with and the formal laws that are used in the formal regulation and supervision of SMEs, including their CSR activities.

Related to the legal reform is the need to devise strategies to encourage and support the formation and association of SMEs to enhance self-regulation. Given the SMEs' preference for informal laws as compared to formal laws, the required association can be stimulated by allowing SMEs to relate and possibly self-regulate using informal laws (norms and values) within societies and regions of common or similar informal laws. Arguably, this will help in creating the initial atmosphere for more voluntary participation of SMEs in CSR discussion and activities and expectedly move most SMEs more to the civil stage of CSR engagement and development (see Zadek, 2004). Moreover, as the associations develop, an opportunity for wider interaction and consultation with other stakeholders through which the government can deduce and craft better and more amenable CSR rules and regulations will emerge. As noted by Campbell (2013), firms behave in a more socially responsible way in an environment with active self-regulation that is reinforced with inclusively formulated government policies and regulations.

To achieve a wider impact and engender even higher CSR awareness and participation across the national and regional economies, the same inclusive approach might need to be extended to other sectors and associations such as NGOs, social movement organisations, institutional investors and the media. This is important given that they are all interconnected and part of the CSR ecosystem. Through their interactions, observations and feedback, not only will the CSR awareness and activities of SMEs be advanced but the socially responsible behaviour of all the stakeholders will be positively impacted. As institutionalisation of CSR importance across SMEs is critical for their sustainable CSR engagement and practice, deliberate efforts to achieve institutionalisation through educational institutions, such as primary, secondary and tertiary institutions, and other platforms of learning such as religious institutions, as well as regular publication and dissemination of CSR issues, might be pertinent. This will help in developing a critical mass of citizens that are properly acculturated in CSR issues, having been exposed to and trained on the importance of CSR from their formative years through primary to tertiary education. As the students graduate and secure employment or start their businesses, not only will they be very familiar with CSR issues but they will be more disposed to act in socially responsible ways in both private and corporate engagements.

Effectively sustaining these initiatives will require co-ordination using a well-developed regulatory or supervisory framework. What this suggests is that the government's task in ensuring the sustainable development and growth of CSR in DEMs cannot be overemphasised. In addition, as CSR demands differ based on the peculiarities of the society in question, it means that there might not a one-size-fits-all approach. Rather, what might be more effective is to agree on the CSR issues that are generally similar across the DEMs, and then to produce better guidelines as to what responsible behaviours in DEMs entail. With such guidelines, the CSR regulatory framework of the respective DEMs can be better formulated by the government through collaboration with other stakeholders.

7.7 CONCLUSION

While there is no doubt as to the size of MNCs and their possible CSR impact in the DEMs, the challenge is in their real impact as compared to SMEs. In line with the name, SMEs are smaller than MNCs, but their orientation, structure, ownership and activities seem to suggest that their CSR interest, engagement and impact might be higher and more inclined to the development needs of the DEMs than those of MNCs. As CSR implies that a firm's actions and inactions are for the sustainable growth of society, the inherent localisation of SMEs within their immediate societies places them at a vantage point when it comes to better understanding the peculiarities of DEMs and therefore makes it possible that they can have higher impact. The perceived greater involvement of MNCs as compared to SMEs can be attributed to higher reporting of CSR activities by MNCs as compared to SMEs. While MNCs can be described as higher in 'CSR talk' and lower in 'CSR walk', SMEs are lower in 'CSR talk' and higher in 'CSR walk'. Using dimensions such as 'Commitment to CSR; Internal Structures and Procedures; and External Collaborations' (Baumann-Pauly et al., 2013), SMEs in comparison with MNCs seem to be more intrinsically committed to CSR, exhibit an embedded integration of CSR in their structures and procedures, and engage in a normatively inclusive and sustainable way with relevant stakeholders in their CSR decisions and activities. With such features, SMEs can arguably be classified as being mainly in the civil stage of CSR development, requiring little or no regulation to behave in a socially responsible way.

What is required, therefore, is the sustained creation and expansion of business environments that encourage and enhance responsible behaviour and the inclinations of SMEs in the DEMs. Drawing from Campbell (2012), these factors include rules and regulation to enthrone fair competition and sustainable financial performance of SMEs, legal reform to create synergy between the informal laws (norms and values) preferred by SMEs and the formal laws (mainly adopted) used in the regulation of SMEs' activities, with higher preference attached to informal laws. Also required are efforts to promote collaboration and self-regulation among SMEs through which their individual and collective CSR understanding, engagement and activities will improve and expand. With the creation of such a collaborative environment for SMEs, the task for the government should be to support and sustain SMEs in their CSR engagement and development. This will require the formulation and enforcement of rules and regulations inclusively agreed with SMEs groups and other stakeholders. Efforts also need to be made to support the growth of related organisations such as NGOs, civil society organisations, social movements, institutional investors and the media, to shape and influence responsible practices by SMEs. This will also be the case with educational institutions such as business schools and trade unions, which should be incorporated to support CSR development through training and publications to emphasise the importance and benefits of SMEs' involvement in and pursuit of CSR activities.

REFERENCES

Amaeshi, K. and Amao, O. O. (2009). Corporate social responsibility in transnational spaces: exploring influences of varieties of capitalism on expressions of corporate codes of conduct in Nigeria. *Journal of Business Ethics*, 86, 225–39.

Amaeshi, K., Adegbite, E., Ogbechie, C., Idemudia, U., Seny Kan, K. A., Isa, M. and Anakwue, O. (2016). Corporate social responsibilities in SME: a shift from philanthropy to institutional works? *Journal of Business Ethics*. doi10.1007/s10551-015–2633–1.

Ansari, S., Munir, K. and Gregg, T. (2012). Impact at the 'bottom of the pyramid': the role of social capital in capability development and community empowerment. *Journal of Management Studies*, 49, 813–42.

Aragon, C., Narvaiza L. and Altuna M. (2016). Why and how does social responsibility differ among SMEs? A social capital systematic approach. *Journal of Business Ethics*, 138, 365–84.

Aruwa, S. A. S. (2004). Financing options for small and medium scale enterprises in Nigeria. *Nigerian Journal of Accounting Research*, 1(2). http://ssrn.com/abstract=1401583.

Azmat, F. and Samaratunge, R. (2009). Responsible entrepreneurship in developing countries: understanding the realities and complexities. *Journal of Business Ethics*, 90(3), 437–52.

Baumann, D. (2009). *Global Rules, Private Actors: The Role of the Multinational Corporation in Global Governance*. Doctoral dissertation. Zurich: University of Zurich.

Baumann-Pauly, D., Wickert, C., Spence, L. J. and Scherer, A. G. (2013). Organizing corporate social responsibility in small and large firms: size matters. *Journal of Business Ethics*, 115(4), 693–705.

Baumann-Pauly, D., Scherer, A. and Palazzo, G. (2012). *Navigating through paradoxical stakeholder expectations: organizational implications of managing corporate legitimacy in complex environments*. Zurich: University of Zurich. Institute of Business Administration. UZH Business Working Paper No. 321.

Bhanji, Z. and Oxley, J. E. (2013). Overcoming the dual liability of foreignness and privateness in international corporate citizenship partnerships. *Journal of International Business Studies*, **44**, 290–311.

Blau, P. (1970). Formal theory of differentiation in organizations. *American Sociological Review*, **35**(2), 201–18.

Camacho, A. (1991). Adaptation cost, coordination cost and optimal firm size. *Journal of Economic Behavior & Organization*, **15**, 137–49.

Campbell, B. (2012). Corporate social responsibility and development in Africa: redefining the roles and responsibilities of public and private actors in the mining sector. *Resources Policy*, **37**, 138–43.

Campbell, J. L. (2007). Why would corporations behave in socially responsible ways? An institutional theory of corporate social responsibility. *Academy of Management Review*, **32** (3), 946–67.

Campbell, J. L. (2018). Reflections on the 2017 Decade Award: corporate social responsibility and the financial crisis. *Academy of Management Review*, **43**(4), 1–11.

Carrol, A. B. (1999). Corporate social responsibility: evolution of a definitional construct. *Business and Society*, 38, 268–95.

Castello, I. and Galang, R. M. N. (2014). Looking for new forms of legitimacy in Asia. *Business & Society*, **53**, 187–225.

Cooter, R. D. (2000), Three effects of social norms on law: expression, deterrence, and internalization. *Oregon Law Review*, **79**(1), 1–22.

Coppa, M. and Sriramesh, K. (2013). Corporate social responsibility among SMEs in Italy. *Public Relations Review*, **39**(1), 30–9.

Crane, A., Matten, D. and Spence, L. J. (2013). *Corporate Social Responsibility: Readings and Cases in a Global Context*, 2nd ed. London: Routledge.

Crouch, C. (2005). *Capital Diversity and Change: Recombinant Governance and Institutional Entrepreneurs*. Oxford: Oxford University Press.

Demuijnck, G. and Ngnodjom, H. (2013). Responsibility and informal CSR in formal Cameroonian SMEs. *Journal of Business Ethics*, **112**(4), 653–65.

DiMaggio, P. J. and Powell, W. (1983). The iron cage revisited: institutional isomorphism and collective rationality in organizational fields. *American Sociological Review*, **48**, 147–60.

Downs, A. (1966). *Bureaucratic Structure and Decision Making*. Santa Monica, CA: Rand.

Fox, T. (2004). Corporate social responsibility and development: in quest of an agenda. *Development*, **47**(3), 29–36.

Frynas, J. G. (2005). The false development promise of CSR: evidence from multinational oil companies. *International Affairs*, 81(3), 581–98.

Gamba, F. J. (2019). SME development policies of Tanzania and Rwanda: comparability of policy presentation on focus, significance, challenges and participation. *Journal of Development and Communication Studies*, 6(1). www.ajol.info/index.php/jdcs/article/view/183519.

Gamerschlag, R., Möller, K. and Verbeeten, F. (2011). Determinants of voluntary CSR disclosure: empirical evidence from Germany. *Review of Managerial Science*, **5**, 233–62.

Gugler, P. and Shi, J. Y. J. (2009). Corporate social responsibility for developing country multinational corporations: lost war in pertaining global competitiveness? *Journal of Business Ethics*, 87, 3–24.

Huemer, L. (2010). Corporate social responsibility and multinational corporation identity: Norwegian strategies in the Chilean aquaculture industry. *Journal of Business Ethics*, **91**, 265–77.

Husted, B. W. and Allen, D. B. (2006). Corporate social responsibility in the multinational enterprise: strategic and institutional approaches. *Journal of International Business Studies*, **37**, 838–49.

Idemudia, U. (2008). Conceptualising the CSR and development debate. *Journal of Corporate Citizenship*, **29**, 91–110.

Idemudia, U. (2009). Oil extraction and poverty reduction in the Niger Delta: a critical examination of partnership initiatives. *Journal of Business Ethics*, **90**(1), 91–116.

Idemudia, U. (2011). Corporate social responsibility and developing countries: moving the critical CSR research agenda in Africa forward. *Progress in Development Studies*, **11**, 1–18.

Jamali, D. and Karam, C. (2018). Corporate social responsibility in developing countries as an emerging field of study. *International Journal of Management Reviews*, **20**(1), 32–61.

Jamali, D., Lund-Thomsen, P. and Jeppesen, S. (2015). SMEs and CSR in developing countries. *Business & Society*. doi:10.1177/0007650315571258.

Jamali, D., Zanhour, M. and Keshishian, T. (2009). Peculiar strengths and relational attributes of SMEs in the context of CSR. *Journal of Business Ethics*, **87**, 355–77.

Jenkins, H. (2006). Small business champions for corporate social responsibility. *Journal of Business Ethics*, **67**(3), 241–56.

Julian, S. D. and Ofori-Dankwa, J. C. (2013). Financial resource availability and corporate social responsibility expenditures in a sub-Saharan economy: the institutional difference hypothesis. *Strategic Management Journal*, **34**, 1314–30.

Kaufmann, D. and Kray, A. (2020). *Worldwide Governance Indicators*. Washington, DC: World Bank.

Khan, F. R. and Lund-Thomsen, P. (2011). CSR as imperialism: towards a phenomenological approach to CSR in the developing world. *Journal of Change Management*, **11**, 73–90.

Knudsen, J. S. (2013). The growth of private regulation of labour standards in global supply chains: mission impossible for Western small- and medium-sized firms? *Journal of Business Ethics*, **117**(2), 387–98.

Kogut, B. and Zander, U. (1996). What firms do? Coordination, identity, and learning. *Organization Science*, **7**(5), 502–19.

Ladzani, M. W. and Seeletse, S. M. (2012). Business social responsibility: how are SMEs doing in Gauteng, South Africa? *Social Responsibility Journal*, 8(1), 87–99.

Lawrence, T. B. and Suddaby, R. (2006). Institutions and institutional work. In S. R. Clegg, C. Hardy, T. Lawrence and W. R. Nord, eds., *The Sage Handbook of Organization Studies*, 2nd ed. London: Sage, pp. 215–54.

Lepoutre, J. and Heene, A. (2006). Investigating the impact of firm size on small business social responsibility: a critical review. *Journal of Business Ethics*, **67**(3), 257–73.

Lund-Thomsen, P. and Nadvi, K. (2010). Clusters, chains and compliance: corporate social responsibility and governance in football manufacturing in South Asia. *Journal of Business Ethics*, **93**, 201–22.

Maon, F., Lindgreen, A. and Swaen, V. (2010). Organizational stages and cultural phases: critical review and a consolidative model of CSR development. *International Journal of Management Reviews*, **12**, 20–38.

Matten, D. and Moon, J. (2008). Implicit and explicit CSR: a conceptual framework for a comparative understanding of corporate social responsibility. *Academy of Management Review*, **33**(2), 404–24.

McWilliams, A. and Siegel, D. (2001). Corporate social responsibility: a theory of the firm perspective. *Academy of Management Review*, **26**, 117–27.
Menski, W. (2006). *Comparative Law in a Global Context: The Legal Systems of Asia and Africa*. Cambridge: Cambridge University Press.
Morsing, M. and Perrini, F. (2009). CSR in SMEs: do SMEs matter for the CSR agenda? *Business Ethics: A European Review*, 18(1), 1–6.
Murillo, D. and Lozano, J. (2006). CSR and SMEs: an approach to CSR in their own words. *Journal of Business Ethics*, 67, 227–40.
Muthuri, J. N. and Gilbert, V. (2011). An institutional analysis of corporate social responsibility in Kenya. *Journal of Business Ethics*, 98, 467–83.
Nejati, M. and Ghasemi, S. (2012). Corporate social responsibility in Iran from the perspective of employees. *Social Responsibility Journal*, 8, 578–88.
Newenham-Kahindi, A. M. (2011). A global mining corporation and local communities in the Lake Victoria zone: the case of Barrick Gold multinational in Tanzania. *Journal of Business Ethics*, 99, 253–82.
North, D. (1990). *Institutions, Institutional Change and Economic Performance*. Cambridge: Cambridge University Press.
Okoye, A. (2009). Theorising corporate social responsibility as an essentially contested concept: is a definition necessary. *Journal of Business Ethics*, 89(4), 613–27.
Painter-Morland, M. and Dobie, K. (2009). Ethics and sustainability within SMEs in Sub-Saharan Africa: enabling, constraining and contaminating relationships. *African Journal of Business Ethics*, **14**(2), 7–19.
Porter, M. E. and Kramer, M. R. (2006). Strategy and society: the link between competitive advantage and corporate social responsibility. *Harvard Business Review*, **84**, 78–92.
Quinn, J. (1997). Personal ethics and business ethics: the ethical attitudes of owner-managers of small business. *Journal of Business Ethics*, 16, 119–27.
Ram, M., Edwards, P., Gilman, M. and Arrowsmith, J. (2001). The dynamics of informality: employment relations in small firms and the effects of regulatory change. *Work, Employment & Society*, **15**, 845–61.
Raynard, P. and Forstater, M. (2002). *Corporate Social Responsibility: Implications for Small and Medium Enterprises in Developing Countries*. Vienna: United Nations Industrial Development Organization (UNIDO) and the World Summit on Sustainable Development.
Reverte, C. (2012). The impact of better corporate social responsibility disclosure on the cost of equity capital. *Corporate Social Responsibility and Environmental Management*, 19, 253–72.
Rowley, T. and Berman, S. (2000). A brand-new brand of corporate social performance. *Business and Society*, **39**, 397–418.
Spence, L. J. (2007). CSR and small business in a European policy context: the five 'C's of CSR and small business research agenda. *Business and Society Review*, **112**(4), 533–52.
Sweeney, L. (2007). Corporate social responsibility in Ireland: barriers and opportunities experienced by SMEs when undertaking CSR. *Corporate Governance*, 7(4), 516–23.
Vachani, S. and Smith, C. N. (2004). Socially responsible pricing: lessons from the pricing of AIDS drugs in developing countries. *California Management Review*, **47**, 117–44.
Valente, M. and Crane, A. (2010). Public responsibility and private enterprise in developing countries. *California Management Review*, **52**(3), 52–78.
Visser, W. (2008). Corporate social responsibility in developing countries. In A. Crane, A. McWilliams, D. Matten, J. Moon and D. Siegel, eds., *The Oxford Handbook of Corporate Social Responsibility*. Oxford: Oxford University Press, pp. 473–503.

Von Weltzien Hoivik, H. and Melé, D. (2009). Can an SME become a global corporate citizen? Evidence from a case study. *Journal of Business Ethics*, 88, 551–63.

Wickert, C. (2011a). Organizing political corporate social responsibility in small- and medium-sized enterprises: a conceptual framework. Paper presented at the Academy of Management Annual Meeting 2011, San Antonio, TX (USA).

Wickert, C. (2011b). *Small- and medium-sized enterprises as private actors in global governance – evidence from a case study among Swiss SMEs in the textile industry*. IBW Working Paper Series: 121. Zurich: University of Zurich.

World Bank (2020). *Doing Business 2020: Comparing Business Regulation in 190 Economies.* Washington, DC: World Bank.

Worthington, I., Ram, M. and Jones, T. (2006). Exploring corporate social responsibility in the UK Asian small business community. *Journal of Business Ethics*, 67(2), 201–17.

Xun, J. (2013). Corporate social responsibility in China: a preferential stakeholder model and effects. *Business Strategy and the Environment*, **22**, 471–83.

Zadek, S. (2004). The path to corporate social responsibility. *Harvard Business Review*, **82**, 125–32.

PART III

Stimulating Private Regulation of Corporate Social Responsibility

8

Shareholders, Institutional Investors and Socially Responsible Investment

Franklin N. Ngwu

8.1 INTRODUCTION

Central to the survival and growth of any firm is the way the interest of shareholders is managed. It is the reason the origin of corporate governance can be traced to managing the differences between shareholders and managers, generally described as an agency problem. Arguably, the reason for such importance attached to shareholders is owing to their contribution of capital that qualifies them as shareholders or 'owners' of the business. Relating this to corporate social responsibility (CSR) throws up many questions. As the principal reason why an individual or entity contributes capital to a business is mainly for a good return on investment (ROI), the first interesting question is why such individual or entity will be interested in CSR. With CSR perceived as efforts of a firm beyond what is technically required for its profitability and growth, the pursuit of CSR should therefore not be the focus of a firm. This is in line with Milton Friedman's perspective that the focus of a firm is to generate profit and pay dividends to shareholders in line with their expectations for a good ROI (Friedman, 1970). Moreover, as CSR involves cost and other efforts, shareholders can perceive it as a deviation or distraction from the core business of the firm.

However, from both institutional and stakeholders' perspectives, a different disposition to shareholders' interest in CSR emerges, with the view that the main focus of a firm should be beyond the interests of only shareholders. As the firm operates within an environment occupied by different stakeholders, considering the interest of other stakeholders in addition to that of the shareholders might not be a misplaced approach. It might even be that the interests of the shareholders and other stakeholders are so interwoven and contextually embedded that pursuing the wider stakeholders' interests might be directly or indirectly related to the interest of shareholders (profit maximisation and ROI). If this is the case and particularly about CSR, the question is how can shareholders contribute to the awareness and practice of CSR in developing and emerging markets (DEMs)? This might require a rethinking of their investment options, including an inclination towards more socially responsible investment (SRI). Extending it further, it might be that supporting or pursuing CSR activities (SRI) is positively related to shareholders' interests. From such a premise, the question is how can shareholders contribute to the awareness and practice of CSR through SRI in DEMs.

The aim of this chapter is therefore to examine and understand the powers and responsibilities, procedures and opportunities available that can be used by different kinds of investor, particularly institutional investors, in promoting the long-term financial success of the company through SRI as part of their CSR strategy. It will explore how capital providers, including ordinary shareholders, institutional investors and socially responsible investors, can provide the stimulus for improved social standards and performance through legal and extralegal means such as contracts, shareholder resolutions, election into and removal from office, and naming and shaming.

The chapter will proceed as follows: Section 8.2 will rethink and provide a good understanding of the meaning and origin of SRI. Section 8.3 will examine why shareholders (institutional investors) are interested in CSR (SRI) and how they use their roles and powers to pursue SRI. Drawing from that, Section 8.4 will explore the similarities in the powers of shareholders with those of other capital providers (banks) and how they can be used to promote SRI. Section 8.5 will identify other factors that might have contributed or can contribute to the growth of SRI and Section 8.6 will look at lessons for DEMs. Section 8.7 will conclude.

8.2 UNDERSTANDING SRI: MEANING AND ORIGIN

To understand the meaning and origin of SRI, it might be important to recall the meaning of CSR and why firms/shareholders are interested in it. Broadly, CSR relates to the consideration of demands and expectations on environmental and social factors such as pollution, energy, consumption, labour conditions, human rights and interests of other stakeholders in a firm's activities and operations (Sjöström and Welford, 2009). According to Carroll (1991), total CSR is made up of four types: economic, legal, ethical and philanthropic. This classification enhances our comprehension of SRI and the increasing importance attached to it by institutional investors. But what is SRI? Related to the definition of CSR, SRI can be described as investments that are guided by a disposition towards incorporating or integrating the financial objective of investors with other commitments such as social justice, sustainable economic development, inclusive society, safe and healthy environment, equity and fairness (see Haigh and Hazelton, 2004).

It is a kind of investment that investors decide to make not by marginalising their financial expectations but by integrating them with other ethical, environmental and social considerations. Also known as ethical investing, responsible investing, green investing, impact investing or sustainable investing, it is not completely different from normal or conventional investing, particularly in terms of the relevance of profitability and the financial performance of a firm. The main difference is in the importance attached to social, ethical and environmental factors and the need to integrate them with the financial aspect in firms' decisions and management (see Domini and Kinder, 1984; Lowry, 1993). For investors, SRI involves making a moral choice about different firms and their values, with the aim of bringing about positive changes for both firms and society (Judd, 1990).

With the above insights and to provide a more comprehensive definition, the Forum for Sustainable and Responsible Investment (SIF, www.ussif.org) describes SRI as an investment method that considers and integrates environmental, social and governance (ESG) factors in investment decisions to achieve both positive long-term competitive financial returns and social impact. It is an investment procedure that aims to invest in firms that comply with or practise agreed standards of CSR. As will be further explained, the increasing interest in CSR (SRI) can be attributed to many factors such as the summits in Kyoto in 1997, Johannesburg in 2002, Copenhagen in 2009 and Durban in 2011, rating agencies, sustained campaigns from non-governmental organisations (NGOs), shareholder activism and media coverage. In 2006, the UN launched the global principles of responsible investment with the view that as finance can be regarded as the engine of economic growth and development, evidence from business decisions and activities does not show sufficient consideration of social and environmental factors (Ballestero et al., 2015).

The ten principles focussed on issues of human rights, labour, environment and anti-corruption. While Principles 7, 8 and 9 emphasised the need for proper consideration of the environment, other principles focussed on the importance of social and governance issues which, when combined, relate to ESG factors that businesses should consider in their investment and management decisions (see Ballestero et al., 2015; UN Global Compact, 2021). Expectedly, as the principles are from the UN, acceptance and adoption by both financial and non-financial organisations have been exponential. In adopting the principles, firms, including institutional investors, are expected not only to commit to their engagements with fund recipients but also to ensure that their investment decisions and performance expectations are not contrary to the wider stakeholders' and societal interests. With support from the UN and other organisations such as NGOs, religious organisations and pension funds, the growth of SRI was inevitable.

With regard to the origin of SRI, there are different perspectives but with somewhat consensus that it can be traced to the ethical financial inclination of religious institutions. In the Middle Ages, for instance, the Catholic Church banned loans with interest and, relying on the order of the Council of Nicea I (325 BC), the clergy were prohibited from receiving interest on their investments. After its practice for more than a century, its application was extended to all Catholics. Later in the eighth century, lending with usurious interest was banned by Emperor Charlemagne and punishable in case of non-adherence. This approach to lending continued to the fourteenth century when Pope Clement V further cancelled and invalidated any law supporting usurious loans (see Clavero, 1985; Ballestero et al., 2015). Moreover, not only did the Catholic Church frown at usurious interests and loans but it can also be described as a vanguard in the practice of ethical and responsible behaviour. In Latin America and other parts of the world, the Catholic Church has been a significant supporter of and investor in public health, education and other public interest activities. Not only does it invest, but a significant flow of financial support is also normally maintained for hospitals, nursing homes and schools (Ballestero et al., 2015).

While ethical and responsible investments took place in different parts of the world, starting with the practices of religious organisations, it can also be argued that the Vietnam War (1954–75) was a turning point in the proper awareness, recognition and practice of SRI. With an uncontrolled arms race, unwarranted loss of lives and negative environmental and human consequences, widespread protests took place across the United States with calls for and subsequent divestment from weapons and military electronics firms (see Marlin, 1986; Ballestero et al., 2015). Arguably, the high awareness and sensitisation of the negative consequences of the Vietnamese War created a change in investment approach and behaviour. Not only did divestment from arms-related firms take place, but other investment initiatives such as the creation of the Pax World Fund in 1971 by the Methodist Church and the UN General Assembly 1980 Resolution against South African apartheid all also enhanced the awareness, acceptance and practice of SRI (Marlin, 1986).

In addition to the Catholic Church, other religious organisations also promoted and practised investments that can be said to be SRI inclined. In most Anglo-Saxon countries, members of the Quakers (Religious Society of Friends) were counselled to imbibe certain criteria that promote peace, brotherhood and solidarity in their investment pursuits (Bjornsgaard, 2011). Also starting from the seventeenth and eighteenth centuries in Italy, Spain and other countries, lenders developed social elements or purposes in their lending activities and products. Described as solidarity financial activities, treasury bills, deposits and pawnshops or pawn broking were pursued with a social inclination. For instance, pawnbroking was linked to charity promotion – enhancing people's savings, interest-free loans to poor segments of society and pursuit of minimum levels of social welfare (Boto, 2009; Ballestero et al., 2015). The first ethical investment fund in Europe is said to be the Ansvar Aktiefond Sverige founded by the Swedish Church in 1965.

The growth of SRI continued in different parts of the world until the 1990s, which can be described as a period of exponential growth. Many indices such as the Domini 400 Social in 1990, the Citizens Index in 1994, the Dow Jones Sustainability Index (DJSI) World Indices, the Impax ET 500 in 1999, the Dow Jones Global Sustainability Index in 1999l the FTSE4Good Indices in 2001 and the FTSE4Good IBEX in 2008 were launched. In 1997, the UN Global Reporting Initiative was also launched, which led to the creation of other SRI forums. These include the Forum for Sustainable and Responsible Investment in the United States

(US SIF) and Europe's version (Eurosif) (see Cañal-Fernández and Caso, 2013). The practice of SRI by a firm can therefore be deduced as part of the CSR demands for proper consideration of the ethical, philanthropic, social and environmental impacts of its business decisions and actions (Kurtz, 2008). It has interesting that it has steadily grown, even during the last financial crisis of 2007–10 when it maintained continuous growth while other types of professionally managed investment did not record any significant growth (Social Investment Forum Foundation, 2011). It is even believed that for every professionally managed ten-dollar investment, about a dollar is invested with conditions that fall within the broad definition of SRI (Kurtz, 2008; Oh et al., 2013; Ballestero et al., 2015).

In reviewing the development and growth of SRI across the globe, it is evident that while the overall orientation of SRI in ethical and responsible investment is common, the specific approach and focus seem to be in line with national or regional cultural and socio-economic peculiarities and needs. For instance, in Anglo-Saxon and Nordic countries, good attention and importance are attached to environmental factors and ecology. There is also an acceptance of human beings as the centre of economic activity with good values attached to education, medicine and alternative therapies. For the Mediterranean countries, the emphasis is more on values of solidarity and the creation of inclusive society through activities that enhance inclusion of marginalised sections or groups of the society. Interestingly, the preferences of both the Anglo-Saxon and the Mediterranean countries are also observed in other countries such as France, Belgium and Austria, in addition to issues of labour and union rights (Ballestero et al., 2015). In examining the SRI markets in different regions and economies, what is evident is that cultural and historical peculiarities are still important and relevant. Using key factors such as growth, investment strategies, asset allocation and type of investment (institutional or retail) reveals wide variations across markets and economies (see Eurosif, 2012).

8.3 SRI, INSTITUTIONAL INVESTORS AND THEIR INVESTMENT STRATEGIES

With the understanding of what SRI entails, another interesting issue requiring further examination is the significant role ascribed to institutional investors in the promotion and practice of SRI. This can be attributed to the powers and influence of institutional investors, which they can use to pursue specific interests in two main ways. First is through more active engagement and involvement in the decision-making process of the firm. The second is a possible decision to only invest in businesses that consider CSR a core factor in business decisions and operations. Interestingly, with institutional investors increasingly becoming the majority shareholders (owners) of many businesses, their responsibility in promoting responsible management and governance of businesses is becoming more apparent. Not only are they supposed to protect the interests of other shareholders but they are also expected to ensure the alignment of other stakeholders' interests with those of the shareholders for the overall sustainable performance and growth of the firm (see Sparkes and Cowton, 2004; Ullah and Jamali, 2010).

With the increasing growth in CSR (SRI) awareness and practice, a likely deduction as to the interest of firms in SRI will be that it might be attributed to pressures and actions of shareholders such as institutional investors. While the pressures or influence of institutional investors might be an important factor, there are other factors related to the natures and types of social investor. Using a taxonomy of social investors, Kinder (2005) identifies three types – value-based investors, value-seeking investors and value-enhancing investors.

As the name indicates, value-based investors are influenced by their beliefs and moral standards. This might be related to their religious or ethical inclinations, which influence their interest to include non-financial factors such as environment, human rights, equity, gender and corporate governance in their investment decisions and partnerships. Most religious organisations involved in SRI are within this category (see Sparkes and Cowton, 2004; Ullah and Jamali, 2010). A further affirmation of the social and responsible orientation of value-based investment is that most of the funds and even the accrued interests are sometimes utilised to alleviate the socio-economic problems of the underprivileged or other needs of poor countries (Oh et al., 2013). Focussing on the religious inclination of Islamic financial institutions (IFIs), Ullah and Jamali (2010) maintain that there is a natural affinity between IFIs and CSR as IFIs are guided by the same ethical values as CSR, which they are required to follow, as compared to the voluntary requirements of other financial institutions.

Value-seeking investors leverage ESG and other related factors to improve portfolio performance. To support this position, while 89 per cent of more than 100 academic studies indicate that firms with good practice of ESG show better market performance, about 85 per cent of the studies further reveal that the firms with higher ESG rankings also outperform in accounting-based measures (Fulton et al., 2012).

The third group, value-enhancing investors, utilise shareholder participation and engagement to enhance their investments. Emphasis is normally placed on the good conduct and behaviour of their firms and executives on issues such as corporate governance, ethics, sustainability, community and stakeholders' engagement. With their powers, investors can engage and influence a firm's behaviour through strategies such as voting on crucial issues, initiating and sustaining dialogue, filing shareholder decisions and, most importantly, investing or divesting from a firm (Oh et al., 2013).

With a focus on value-seeking and value-enhancing investors, it can be argued that their increasing interest in CSR is driven more by how the performance, brand, growth or what can be termed the sustainable growth and performance of the firm is better achieved through CSR (SRI). This is in line with the view of Petersen and

Vredenburg (2009) that the interest of investors in CSR might not be driven so much by morals as by how CSR enhances the economic value of the firm. The exponential growth of SRI and even the increasing interest of shareholders (institutional investors) and the role of financial institutions in promoting it can therefore be attributed to some inherent special features of SRI. While the first is the embedded ability of SRI to influence investment decisions and the conduct of firms, the second is that while SRI might achieve the same financial performance in terms of ROI as other normal investments in the short run, SRI seems to outperform conventional investments in the long run (Oh et al., 2013). This is believed to be related to the superior advantage that accrues to firms that are significantly focussed and involved in SRI. With investment in SRI funds, retail investors will reap long-term profits expected and inherent in sustainability-oriented products (Haigh and Hazelton, 2004). An extensive study by Fulton et al. (2012) maintains that investments with a significant CSR inclination exhibit a positive correlation with good corporate performance and ROI equivalent to other conventional investments. This also relates to the increasing importance and linkage of corporate governance to the corporate performance of firms, and this interestingly includes ESG and other SRI issues.

From the discussion so far, it is evident that shareholders (particularly institutional investors) can, through the stock market, influence or shape the behaviour of firms in a certain direction such as towards more CSR practices, including SRI. Not only can they influence the cost of capital to a firm, but they can also deploy their powers (voices and actions) to shape and move firms to more socially responsible behaviours, including investment. With huge resources under the control of fund managers, they pursue two main goals through SRI. First is the demand for more SRI with the perceived better performance of SRI funds as compared to non-SRI funds mainly in the long run. The second relates to demands for corporate change through SRI-related practices.

8.3.1 *SRI Investment Strategies of Institutional Investors*

On investment strategies, there are about four main types: negative screening, positive screening, community investment and shareholder activism. In line with the name, negative screening is an SRI investment process in which firms whose products and services are perceived as having negative impacts on individuals, communities or the environment are avoided. On the contrary, positive screening is the strategy in which firms perceived to be having positive impacts or complying with ESG principles are patronised and invested in. For instance, a firm that is perceived to have good employer–employee relationships, to practice good environmental policies, to offer products and services that are considered unharmful to individuals and society, to respect human rights and to have an overall good corporate governance framework will be preferred and invested in as compared with firms that have negative attributes (Ballestero et al., 2015).

The third strategy, community investment, relates to the direct channelling of investments to communities and individuals classified as underserved and poor. It might entail the provision of financial services to the 'bottom of the pyramid' of the society and support for small businesses with subsidised credits or affordable housing, childcare, education and health care for the poor of the society. Of the different strategies, the fourth one, shareholder activism, has gained prominence, especially with shareholders. It is generally a process in which shareholders engage with companies on ESG issues that the shareholders consider are important to attend to. The engagement is normally through filing and co-filing shareholder resolutions on issues such as ESG and wider corporate governance. In consideration that shareholders can exercise their powers, their demands for more ESG compliance, for instance, are expectedly treated with attention by management. In situations where an amicable resolution cannot be achieved, the demands will be escalated as an issue for wider consideration and voting by all the shareholders of a firm. With increasing collaboration with other stakeholders such as NGOs and the media, shareholders have used their powers of filing resolutions to shape the policies and actions of firms with the aim not only of creating more responsible firms but also of achieving enhanced long-term shareholder value and sustainable financial performance (see SIF, 2011; Ballestero et al., 2015).

With screening perceived as the most common strategy used for SRI, while Heard (1978) maintains that socially responsible investors are motivated to ensure that firms act in line with their moral obligation to protect and not negatively affect society, Rudd (1981) contends that SRI seems to pursue activities with the potential to produce positive externalities for society in rejection of those with negative externalities. To Bruyn (1987), SRI is focussed on the selection of 'clean' products and the rejection of unclean products and activities such as alcohol, tobacco, pornography, gambling, weapons and military products.

8.3.2 *Role of Institutional Investors in Promoting SRI*

To better understand the role(s) of institutional investors in promoting SRI, a recap of the goals of two fund managers will be helpful. While Hunter Hall Investment Management states that its 'objective ... is to increase the wealth of investors by substantially outperforming the MCSI [Morgan Stanley Capital International] World Accumulation Net Return Index', another fund manager, Challenger International, maintains that its approach to effecting corporate change is focussed on 'identifying the most socially responsive companies in each industry and (may) encourage their competitors to improve on their standards' (see Haigh and Hazelton, 2004).

The influence of SRI on the decisions and behaviours of firms is therefore normally through shareholders, particularly institutional investors that can deploy their powers to effect a change in the decisions (including the investment ones) of firms. These include powers to pursue shareholder resolutions during annual general meetings, class-action lawsuits, media campaigns, specific demands and negotiations with the board and management of firms, and of course divestment and reinvestment in firms in line with their SRI interests (see Deutsche Bank Group, 2012; Oh et al., 2013).

In a study that examined the shareholder proposals of S&P 1500 companies from 1997–2009, it was discovered that institutional investors, after submitting about 2,392 proposals, withdrew about 810 (about 33.9 per cent) before meetings, which suggests a resolution of the withdrawn proposals before the annual general meetings (Bauer et al., 2012; Oh et al., 2013). In comparison, while the number of proposals submitted by individual investors (4,824) and by unions (2,275) is higher than that from institutional investors, the power and the impact of institutional investors on firms in promoting SRI, for instance, can be deduced from the withdrawal rate. While that of individual investors was just 4 per cent, that from co-ordinated activism was 27.7 per cent and 34.6 per cent from unions. The results from this study further affirm the importance and influence of shareholder activism, particularly that of institutional investors (Bauer et al., 2012; Oh et al., 2013).

To further affirm the power and role of institutional investors in influencing a change in firms, it was noted that in a space of three years from 2008 to 2010, more than 200 organisations such as public funds, labour funds, religious investors and foundations, as well as other investment firms, submitted or jointly submitted shareholder resolutions. In 2003 also, while religious organisations filed 129 resolutions, the SRI fund submitted about 56 resolutions with American and Canadian companies (see Oh et al., 2013). With collective control of more than USD 1.5 trillion of assets under management as of 2009, institutional investors' interest in issues such as SRI can be ignored only at huge cost to the firms in question. This is in line with Mitchell et al.'s (1997) view that corporate executives normally attend to shareholders' expectations and demands owing to the consequences of contrary actions, which might be detrimental to the market performance of the firm and, by extension, the remuneration of the executives.

According to Ethical Corporation (2008), Howard Pearce, then head of the UK Environmental Agency pension fund, worth about GBP 1.5 billion, discontinued the services of State Street and Capital International as his equity managers owing to poor performance and failure to sign up to the UN Principles for Responsible Investment, which demand the inclusion of ESG factors in investment decisions. Pearce maintained that inclusion of such factors, which relate to risks such as climate change, produces better outcomes for firms and is in line with managerial fiduciary duties. Arguably, the decision by Pearce demonstrates the importance of CSR/SRI and how shareholders (institutional investors) can influence both the CSR behaviour and the financial performance of firms (Sparkes and Cowton, 2004; Oh et al., 2013). In addition, since USD 1.5 billion is a substantial investment to lose, Pearce's decision to discontinue the services of the two financial institutions will expectedly influence the continued usage of the two institutions not only by other institutional investors but also by the wider users or consumers of financial services. This shows that while the direct impacts of ESG factors on the business activities of some firms such as financial institutions might even be small, the indirect impact through shareholder activism and institutional investors might be huge and even higher than the direct impacts. As seen here, it can even be from secondary or third-party firms (Oh et al., 2013).

There is, however, a limitation to the powers and actions of fund managers and institutional investors. First is that their funds are not limitless and second are the market peculiarities of most economies. For instance, while corporate governance understanding and practice are weak, particularly in DEMs, CSR/SRI are technically non-financial factors and, as such, there is a limited motivation to dutifully observe and report on non-financial performance in addition to the dispersed nature of stocks ownership (Oh et al., 2013). Rethinking these identified constraints reveals a responsibility on the part of banks and venture capitalists and their capability to make firms think and act in a more sustainable or socially responsible way. Hence, the role of banks in promulgating the need for firms to be more socially responsible is discussed in the following section.

8.4 ROLE OF BANKS IN PROMOTING SRI

Given their intermediation functions of providing external finance for businesses, they (banks) somewhat have powers like institutional investors (fund managers) to make firms act sustainably and responsibly. It is even in their interest to do so. As bank shareholders also expect good ROI, it is then in the interest of the banks for their borrowers to perform well through responsible investment and to act in ways that will directly or indirectly lead to better performance of the banks and then a better ROI and better satisfaction of bank shareholders (investors). It therefore means that, just as shareholders' powers can be used to shape and influence business decisions, other sources of finance such as private capital and bank credits are also important factors (see Scholtens, 2006). Interestingly, this special feature of the financial institutions (ability to give credit) provides an important difference between the financial sector and other sectors, particularly in CSR expectations and practice. While financial institutions can both do right and invest right, firms in other sectors have one option: they can only do right. Such special features and advantages of the financial sector further indicate that it has a crucial role in advancing SRI as compared to firms in other sectors (Oh et al., 2013).

In assessing the banking sector, it is believed that, while there are limited SRI standards and shareholder activism, there is an increasing appreciation and integration of environmental and social factors in their strategic decision processes, but a trust deficit exists among the banking sector stakeholders that needs to be addressed (SAM, 2012a). There are, however, some banks that can be considered role models in the practice and pursuit of SRI principles. Awarded the DJSI global leader in the banking sector, Australia & New Zealand Banking Group Ltd (ANZ), founded in 1835 and offering different kinds of banking services and products to more than 8 million customers in thirty-two countries, is arguably a role model in SRI. In assessing its SRI inclination and practice, it is stated that 'ANZ sustainable business practices, exceptional risk and crisis management procedures, and its strong focus on sustainable investment products have earned it the leading position in the banking subsector. In addition to using comprehensive social and environmental screening tools for its credit assessment process, it is actively engaged in the financing of renewable energy and emission trading' (see SAM, 2012a, p. 1).

Expanding the assessment to the wider financial sector, other important factors in CSR practice include globalisation, stakeholder pressure, climate change and having properly educated employees, which is considered the most important resource for effective CSR practice (SAM, 2012b; Oh et al., 2013). As many banks and other financial services institutions are increasingly becoming aware of and integrating CSR (SRI) in their business decisions and operations, a key question is how they do it in terms of the strategies they apply. Insights from some banks that can be regarded as role models will be helpful.

8.4.1 *Strategies for SRI and Shareholder Activism in the Banking Sector*

UBS, a multinational financial services institution founded through a merger between the Union Bank of Switzerland and the Swiss Bank Corporation, has about 64,000 employees with operations in 50 countries and pursues CSR through a focus on 5 key areas: 1) governance and strategy/responsible banking; 2) engagement and voting rights; 3) corporate responsibility in operations, including in-house environmental management, responsible supply chain management and health/safety/accessibility; 4) employees; and 5) community investments. Using a top-down approach, both the formulation and the execution of its CSR strategy are led by the board and senior management (Oh et al., 2013). In affirming UBS's CSR orientation, then Group Chief Risk Officer Philip Lofts stated: 'We conduct our business in a sustainable way and pay heed to human rights . . . By including environmental and social considerations in our strategic thinking, risk management, and control framework, and in products and services we offer our clients, we gain and retain business, enhance our reputation and position ourselves for future growth' (cited in Oh et al., 2013, pp. 8–9).

In 2011, a cross-divisional, values-based and sustainable initiative that supports clients to invest in line with their personal beliefs and values was launched. It enabled UBS to help clients and to be perceived as not only interested in financial returns but also interested in encouraging and supporting clients in the direction of responsible investment. Partnering with experts in environmental and social responsibility, UBS developed new procedures to identify and select possible business partners, vendors and customers with regard to environmental risk. In a demonstration of further commitment to SRI, UBS aligns with the UK Financial Reporting Council Stewardship Code published in 2010, which focusses on how to create and sustain better stakeholder management, particularly between institutional investors and the firm's management team, to enhance sustainable long-term returns for shareholders and the wider good governance of firms (Financial Reporting Council of Nigeria, 2013). To help embed better governance and CSR across firms it has interests in, UBS in 2011 voted on about 50, 000 different resolutions during more than 4,600 company meetings.

Another interesting aspect of UBS's support for SRI is the way it communicates with firms involved in the SRIs under UBS's management. With an effective team of analysts and portfolio managers that regularly communicates on ESG matters, it maintains a proactive approach by not only providing firms with ESG trends and information but working with firms with ESG issues on how best to resolve them. As part of its wider CSR practice, UBS also maintains an active community engagement and participation through both direct cash donations and other activities such as employee volunteering, matched-giving schemes and disaster relief interventions. It also partners with educational institutions, cultural organisations and other community associations. As a demonstration of its commitment to CSR, the SRI invested assets as a percentage of total assets under UBS's management increased from 1.2 per cent in 2009 to 11 per cent in 2011 (UBS, 2012; Oh et al., 2013).

Another interesting bank that can be described as a role model in CSR and SRI is the Co-operative Banking Group (CBG), UK. It is a subsidiary of the Co-operative Group that has more than 600 million members. Providing mainly insurance/banking products and services through more than 14,000 employees, CBG pursues and practices CSR focussing on six areas. These include UK communities, international development and human rights, animal welfare, diet and health, responsible finance, and social inclusion. With a focus on responsible finance and its relevance to sustainable development, CBG boasts a variety of products and services aimed at enhancing sustainable development. In addition to products and services for renewable energy, energy efficiency and the co-operative, other areas include charity, and social enterprise sectors (Oh et al., 2013). Developing from a culture of integration and co-operative community, CBG is guided by a set of values that includes uprightness, transparency, oneness and inclination to social responsibility and these values have characterised its ESG practices (CBI, 2005).

In a bid to recover from the reputation crisis that the UK banking industry suffered in the late 1980s, CBG relied on its co-operative origin and legacy to relaunch the brand. Promoting co-operative values as modern and appropriate, a limited but reasonable number of its customers, driven mainly by ethical values, rejoined. This provided a great insight that propelled the formulation of CBG's Ethical Policy to guide investments. First published in 1992, the policy committed to investing clients' funds in firms with no or limited damage to the environment. This was followed in

1996 by CBG's Ecological Mission Statement, which emphasised the minimum ecological level for maintaining a sustainable society, in 1997 with the bank's partnership approach and in 2021 with its sustainability report, both of which emphasised CBG's appreciation for and inclination to provide stakeholder value through a socially responsible and ecologically sustainable approach (see Oh et al., 2013; Co-operative Banking Group, 2021).

To further demonstrate its commitment to ethics and responsible investment, CBG's core business activities normally go through transparent and independent examination and review. In 2011, a total of 437 financial opportunities, which is an increase from the 408 available in 2010, were reviewed by the bank's Ethical Policy Unit. Citing conflicts with CBG's Ethical Policy, about 35 (8 per cent) of the 437 opportunities were rejected. In addition, customers with a turnover of about GBP 1.4 million are normally examined and reviewed for ethical compliance and all recommendations to the Ethical Policy Unit are further reviewed by an independent third party (Co-operative Banking Group, 2012).

While CBG might be perceived as being strict in ESG and related matters, the approach has also been beneficial and worthwhile. In 2003, while about 17 per cent of CBG's profit can be traced to customers that are primarily driven by CBG's ethical stance to products and services, about 30 per cent of the profits can be linked to customers who consider ethics an important factor. From 2008, when many financial institutions noted reduced business activities from the voluntary sector, CBG's own exponentially increased. In 2011, about 42 per cent of its total corporate and business banking liabilities came from deposits of about GBP 2.88 billion from social co-operative and environmentally oriented businesses with community and charitable deposits increasing by GBP 127 million and deposits from public services jumped by GBP 220 million. In appreciation and recognition of CBG's ethical and responsible commitment, both the Financial Times and the International Finance Corporation selected the bank as the most sustainable in 2010 and 2011 (Co-operative Banking Group, 2012).

8.5 OTHER FACILITATORS OF SRI GROWTH

While there is no doubt that institutional investors and banks are very important in the growth of SRI, as will be further explained, there are other factors that can be identified as facilitators of SRI growth.

1. The increasing growth of pension funds, the huge pool of funds that they control and their encouraging interest in CSR (SRI) can be said to be a very important factor in the growth of SRI across both developed and developing/ emerging economies. In the United States, for instance, the largest group of institutional SRI investors are pension funds. They are also the group with the highest number of submitted shareholder resolutions. In the UK also, the

biggest pension funds have more than 60 per cent of their invested funds classified as SRI (see Oxford Business Knowledge (OBK), 2007; European Commission, 2019). This can arguably be attributed to the long-term investment interests of the funds and the factor of regulation. In many countries, there is a regulatory demand on pension funds to follow an SRI approach or to invest a significant level of their funds in SRI. As part of the regulatory requirement, they are meant to disclose their level of SRI compliance in their reports (see Clark and Hebb, 2004; Sjöström and Welford, 2009).

2. A second important supportive factor for SRI growth is the availability and effective functioning of NGOs focussed on the financial sector. With the availability of such NGOs, there can be both direct and indirect advocacy and pressure on fund managers, banks and other relevant institutions to adopt an SRI approach in their management and investment decisions. The presence of NGOs can also serve as a fulcrum of partnership with other stakeholders to push SRI values across the economy. While, in some instances, NGOs have partnered with shareholders to file shareholder resolutions, they have also invested in businesses and as such act as shareholders, including through exercising their shareholder rights (Sjöström, 2007; Sjöström and Welford, 2009).
3. The presence of influential and investment-inclined religious groups has also been noted as one of the important facilitators of SRI. As indicated earlier, the origin of SRI as an investment approach can be attributed to earlier activities of religious organisations such as the Catholic and Methodist Churches. It is even maintained that SRI was more of an investment of religious groups until 1960 when the stock market emerged as a good platform for more SRI awareness and practice (see Sparkes, 2002). With such historical insights, the current efforts for more SRI awareness and practice can be better approached (Sjöström and Welford, 2009).
4. Another important facilitator of SRI across many economies is corporate governance in line with its allocation of roles, responsibilities and expected relationships to the different stakeholders of the business such as shareholders, boards, senior management and other employees, host communities, government and the business itself. With shareholders consisting of more majority and minority shareholders with their rights properly stated in codes of corporate governance, it means that even minority shareholders can file resolutions for SRI-related issues provided they have held a specified number of shares over a certain period. Generally referred to as shareholder activism, minority shareholders have been very active in filing resolutions in both developed and developing economies and as such are major drivers of shareholder activism (see Eurosif, 2006; SIF, 2006; Sjöström and Welford, 2009).
5. Related to the role of corporate governance in promoting SRI is the inherent interest of the corporate sector in CSR and thus in increased SRI. With

transparency, accountability and disclosure as key elements of corporate governance and CSR, having interesting CSR practices is perceived as being beneficial to the firm, particularly as a factor to attract investors and to get the firm branded and perceived as being in tune with both investors and societal expectations. Disclosure and reporting, therefore, provide a good opportunity for shareholders and the firm to pursue SRI as it is expected and appropriate to do. In situations where there is no or limited CSR activity, shareholders and even the business will be concerned with the negative consequences for the business of such disclosure (see Eurosif, 2004; Sjöström and Welford, 2009). While there might be other factors that enhance SRI, it is important to appreciate the interconnectedness of the factors and how they can individually or jointly enhance the practice and growth of SRI. For instance, an active NGO in the financial sector can collaborate with minority shareholders to campaign and pressure a firm to follow a certain direction and pursue an investment perceived as SRI compliant. An NGO can also, following scrutiny of a firm's reports, put pressure on a pension fund to reconsider its investment in a particular firm or to invest in a new firm based on the disclosed information that might be considered SRI inclined (Sjöström and Welford, 2009).

8.6 LESSONS FOR DEMS

With these insights and given the fact that SRI awareness and practice is still emerging in many countries, particularly in developing and emerging economies, a key question is whether there are lessons that can be learnt from economies with more advanced SRI practices and experience for the benefit of DEMs. First, SRI is an investment that benefits all stakeholders. In comparison, the ROIs for SRI in the medium to long term might be higher than normal investments lacking SRI components such as ESG considerations. With ESG components, for instance, SRI benefits not only the investors but other stakeholders, including the unborn generation and society in general. Given such wide, long-term and sustainable benefits, it is arguably therefore the most appropriate investment approach to adopt and practise.

Second, for wide awareness, adoption and effective practice, SRI requires good collaboration and shared responsibility. Recalling the origin of SRI in religious organisations and their inclusive approach, which contributed to the growth and success of SRI in the early years, suggests that effective adoption and practice of SRI in DEMs might be better achieved through such a collaborative approach. It will involve key stakeholders such as religious organisations, institutional investors, banks and other financial institutions, rating agencies, governments, NGOs and others. For instance, with the high religiosity and the continued importance attached to religious organisations in DEMs, it might be the appropriate platform of campaign and advocacy for wider adoption and practice of SRI.

Interestingly, as most of the other stakeholders all belong to and partake in the activities of religious organisations, the awareness and early bonding required for easier acceptance, adoption and practice of SRI can be provided by religious organisations. With such initial advocacy and awareness, other stakeholders such as institutional investors, banks, NGOs and even the government can now further engage in the promotion of SRI across DEMs. As indicated earlier, the demand for more CSR (SRI) in some instances can be started by minority shareholders who then collaborate with NGOs to give it the publicity and attention needed to ensure wider adoption and implementation. In the same vein, as institutional investors are important in the implementation of SRI practices, their limited development in DEMs as compared to the more developed economies can be improved through partnerships with religious organisations and other stakeholders. With the inherent orientation of religious organisations to both ethical activities and an inclusive governance approach, synergy between institutional investors and religious organisations can be achieved, with the institutional investors providing the expertise required to manage the investments while the religious organisations provide the capital and membership needed.

Third, as SRI is part of CSR and given the positive sustainable development impacts of CSR, particularly for DEMs, it is in the interest of the public sector (government) to promote awareness and practice of SRI. It is a win–win situation for the public sector. Recalling the sustainable development tasks expected of governments and the limited resources at their disposal, especially in DEMs, suggests that any partnership or support that will contribute to the achievement of the Sustainable Development Goals (SDGs) will be welcomed. Interestingly, that is what SRI is all about. For instance, ESG demands that firms include ESG factors in their business and investment decisions and in so doing the sustainable development tasks and challenges of the government will be complemented and tackled.

It is therefore in the government's interest to promote awareness and practice of SRI. The question is how it should be approached. This will depend on the socio-economic peculiarities of the society in question and the level of SRI development. However, irrespective of the peculiarities and the level of SRI development, what is central and most important is the visible commitment of the government in promoting SRI awareness and practice. A starting point will be for the government to lead by example through effective and visible incorporation of SRI components (for instance, ESG) in its government activities and investment decisions. With the government seen and perceived as truly practising and supporting SRI practices, the conviction and involvement of the private sector and other stakeholders will be more achievable.

Fourth, in addition to the need for the government to be leading in SRI advocacy and practice, there are also instruments that the government can use to further motivate and embed SRI development and practice. As explained in Chapter 3 of this book, these include informational instruments, fiscal-economic instruments, legal instruments (mandating and soft laws), partnering and hybrid instruments (Steurer, 2013). Using informational instruments, the government can raise awareness of the benefits of SRI and the need for its adoption by both public and private sectors. By highlighting, disseminating and practising how SRI contributes to inclusive and sustainable development, the government will be sending strong signals to the private sector on the need to follow the SRI direction as the unwritten but accepted norm of the government and society. When combined with fiscal-economic and legal instruments such as tax incentives, rebates, involvement in government committees, grants and licensing, the seriousness of the government in pursuit and support of SRI will be more apparent to private sector organisations. With such incentives granted to firms with visible evidence of SRI practice and compliance, even firms reluctant to accept and practise SRI will be both internally and externally influenced by their stakeholders to join the SRI crusade. Moreover, given the powers of a government, the incentives can be further legitimised through official backing with effective legislation. With such legislation, the government can even go further to embed SRI awareness and practice through a combination of the instruments in a hybrid and partnership approach.

8.7 CONCLUSION

While the importance and benefits of SRI are arguably not in doubt, the challenge remains how to increase awareness and practice, particularly across DEMs. Two options rooted in partnerships seem plausible. The first option, described as private sector–led, relates to how key stakeholders in private sector organisations such as shareholders (institutional investors) contribute to and shape firms towards SRI. Being the shareholders of firms, what are the roles and strategies that can be used by institutional investors and others to advance SRI awareness and practice? With SRI noted to achieve a higher ROI in the long run as compared to non-SRIs, it means that the pursuit of SRI by institutional investors can be argued to be in their self-interest. If this is the case, what is then required is the effective deployment of their (institutional investors') powers and opportunities in engaging with the management and boards of firms to achieve higher SRI awareness and practice. These powers include the ability to vote in meetings, submit demands, collaborate with other stakeholders and even influence the recruitment of senior managers who are committed to SRI.

In addition to shareholders, other stakeholders with significant influence to enhance SRI awareness and practice are the financial institutions, especially the banks. The intermediation functions they (banks) perform provide them with an advantage of engagement and influence that can be used to advance awareness and practice of SRI. In the provision of banking services, the banks can use a combination of approaches such as persuasion, advisory, compliance (in terms of compliance with SRI requirements to get bank services such as loans) and partnership to embed SRI practices not only in the bank but across business organisations and individuals who are bank customers.

While the important roles of key stakeholders such as shareholders (institutional investors) and banks in the growth of SRI are noted, other factors have contributed. These include the existence of religious organisations with deep SRI inclination, and the growth of pension funds and NGOs interested in SRI issues. Other important factors are increasing growth and practice of corporate governance and CSR. While these factors have contributed to the growth of SRI, their impacts have been felt more in developed economies. The challenge is how to achieve the same success and growth in DEMs. Given the peculiarities of DEMs, good awareness and practice of SRI might require the involvement of the government to provide the required support and co-ordination for the growth of SRI. This can be achieved using different instruments such as informational, fiscal-economic, partnering, legal and hybrid instruments depending on the purpose and locality.

REFERENCES

Ballestero, E., Pérez-Gladish, B. and García-Bernabeu, A. (2015). The ethical financial question and the MCDM framework. In E. Ballestero, B. Pérez-Gladish and A. García-Bernabeu, eds., *Socially Responsibility Investment: A Multi-criteria Decision Making Approach. International Series in Operation Research and Management Sciences.* Cham: Springer International Publishing Switzerland, pp. 3–22.

Bauer, R., Moers, F. and Viehs, M. (2012). *The determinants of withdrawn shareholder proposals.* Working paper. https://web.archive.org/web/20120317070403id_/http://www.fma.org:80/Atlanta/Papers/Determinants_of_withdrawn_shareholder_proposals_FMA.pdf.

Bjornsgaard. (2011). Religious society of Friends (Quakers). *The Encyclopedia of Christian Civilization.* Malden, UK: Wiley-Blackwell.

Boto, M. J. (2009). *Las competencias de la Comunidad Europea en materia social.* Cizur Menor: Thomson-Aranzadi.

Bruyn, S. T. (1987). *The Field of Social Investment.* New York: Cambridge University Press.

Cañal-Fernández, V. and Caso, C. (2013). *Caracterización de los Inversores Españoles: la Influencia de la Inversión Socialmente Responsable (Spanish Investors' Characterization: The Influence of Socially Responsible Investment).* Revista Española de Financiación y Contabilidad (REFC). http://ssrn.com/abstract=2252932.

Carroll, A. B. (1991). The pyramid of corporate social responsibility: towards the morals management of organizational stakeholders. *Business Horizon*, **34**(4), 39–45.

CBI. (2005). Co-operative Financial Services, CBI – CSR Case Study Series, Article 13, May 2005.

Clark, G. and Hebb, T. (2004). Pension fund corporate engagement: the fifth stage of capitalism. *Relations Industrielles/Industrial Relations*, **59**(1), 142–71.

Clavero, S. B. (1985). *Usura: del uso económico de la religión en la historia.* Madrid: Tecnos.

Co-operative Banking Group. (2012). *Building the Compelling Co-operative Alternative: Financial Statements 2011.* Manchester: Co-operative Bank. www.co-operativebank.co.uk/assets/pdf/bank/investorrelations/financialresults/bank-financial-statement-2011.pdf.

Co-operative Banking Group. (2021). *Our Values and Ethics in Action: Sustainability Report 2021*. Manchester: Co-operative Bank. www.co-operativebank.co.uk/assets/pdf/bank/investorrelations/2021-sustainability-report.pdf.

Deutsche Bank Group. (2012). *Deutsche Bank Annual Report 2012*. https://annualreport.deutsche-bank.com/2012/ar/servicepages/downloads.html.

Domini, A. L. and Kinder, P. D. (1984). *Ethical Investing: How to Make Profitable Investments Without Sacrificing Your Principles*. Reading, MA: Addison-Wesley.

Ethical Corporation. (2008). *Ethical Leaders of 2008*. 1 December. www.ethicalcorp.com/communications-reporting/ethical-leaders-2008.

European Commission. (2019). *Study on the Drivers of Investments in Equity by Insurers and Pension Funds*. https://ec.europa.eu/info/sites/default/files/business_economy_euro/growth_and_investment/documents/191216-insurers-pension-funds-investments-in-equity_en_5.pdf.

Eurosif. (2004). *Pension Programme SRI Toolkit 2004–2005*. Paris: Eurosif.

Eurosif. (2006). *European SRI Study 2006*. Paris: Eurosif.

Eurosif. (2012). *European SRI Study 2012*. Paris: Eurosif.

Financial Reporting Council of Nigeria. (2013). *Annual Report 2013*. www.financialreportingcouncil.gov.ng/board-activities/annual-report–2013/.

Friedman, M. (1970). The social responsibility of business is to enhance its profits. *New York Times*, **32**(13), 122–6. Previously published in M. Friedman (1962) *Capitalism and Freedom*. Chicago, IL: University of Chicago Press.

Fulton, M., Kahn, B. and Sharples, C. (2012). Sustainable investing: establishing long-term value and performance. *Journal of Banking and Finance*, 1–72. https://papers.ssrn.com/sol3/papers.cfm?abstract_id=2222740.

Haigh, M. and Hazelton, J. (2004). Financial markets: a tool for social responsibility? *Journal of Business Ethics*, **52**(1), 59–71.

Heard, J. (1978). Investor responsibility: an idea whose time has come? *Journal of Portfolio Management*, **4**(3), 12–14.

Judd, E. (1990). *Investing with a Social Conscience*. New York: Pharos Books.

Kinder, P. (2005). *Socially Responsible Investing: An Evolving Concept in a Changing World*. Boston, MA: KLD Research & Analytics.

Kurtz, L. (2008). Socially responsible investment and shareholder activism. In A. Crane, A. McWilliams, D. Matten, J. Moon and D. S. Siegel, eds., *The Oxford Handbook of Corporate Social Responsibility*. Oxford: Oxford University Press, pp. 249–80.

Lowry, R. P. (1993). *Good Money: A Guide to Profitable Social Investing in the '90s*. New York: W.W. Norton & Company.

Marlin, A. (1986). Social investing: potent force for political change. *Business and Society Review*, **57**, 96–100.

Mitchell, R., Agle, B. and Wood, D. J. (1997). Toward a theory of stakeholder identification and salience: defining the principle of who and what really counts. *American Management Review*, **22**(4), 853–86.

Oh, O., Agrawal, M. and Rao, H. R. (2013). Community of intelligence and social media services: a rumor theoretic analysis of tweets during social crises. *MIS Quarterly*, **37**(2), 407–26.

Oh, C. H., Park, J.-H. and Ghauri, P. N. (2013). Doing right, investing right: socially responsible investing and shareholder activism in the financial sector. *Business Horizons*, **1074**. www.academia.edu/24357978/Doing_right_investing_right_Socially_responsible_investing_and_shareholder_activism_in_the_financial_sector.

Oxford Business Knowledge (OBK). (2007). Recent trends and regulatory implications of socially responsible investment for pension funds. In Organisation for Economic Co-operation and

Development (OECD), *The OECD Guidelines for Multinational Enterprises and the Financial Sector*. www.oecd.org/corporate/mne/38550550.pdf.
Petersen, H. L. and Vredenburg, H. (2009). Morals or economics? Institutional investor preferences for corporate social responsibility. *Journal of Business Ethics*, 90(1), 1–14.
Rudd, A. (1981). Social responsibility and portfolio performance. *California Management Review*, 23(4), 55–61.
SAM. (2012a). Australia & New Zealand Banking Group Ltd. Supersector Leader Report.
SAM. (2012b). Itausa – Investimentos Itau SA. Supersector Leader Report.
Scholtens, B. (2006). Finance as a driver of corporate social responsibility. *Journal of Business Ethics*, 68(1), 19–33.
Sjöström, E. (2007). Translating ideologically based concerns: how civil society organisations use the financial market to protect human rights. *International Journal of Environment and Sustainable Development*, 6(2), 157–73.
Sjöström, E. and Welford, R. (2009). Facilitators and impediments for socially responsible investment: a study of Hong Kong. *Corporate Social Responsibility and Environmental Management*, 16, 278–88.
Social Investment Forum Foundation (SIF). (2011). *2010 Report on Socially Responsible Investing Trends in the United States*. www.ussif.org/store_product.asp?prodid=10.
Sparkes, R. (2002). *Socially Responsible Investment: A Global Revolution*. London: Wiley.
Sparkes, R. and Cowton, C. J. (2004). The maturing of socially responsible investment: a review of the developing link with corporate social responsibility. *Journal of Business Ethics*, 52(1), 45–57.
Steurer, R. (2013). Disentangling governance: a synoptic view of regulation by government, business and civil society. *Policy Science*, 46, 387–410.
UBS.(2012). *Annual Report: Our Performance in 2012*. www.annualreports.com/HostedData/AnnualReportArchive/u/NYSE_UBS_2012.pdf.
Ullah, S. and Jamali, D. (2010). Institutional investors and corporate social responsibility: the role of Islamic financial institutions. *International Review of Business Research Papers*, 6, 619–30.
United Nations Global Compact. (2021). *UN Global Compact Strategy 2021–2023*. New York: United Nations.

9

Professional Advisory Services and CSR Responsibilisation, Accountability and Transparency

Onyeka K. Osuji

[M]ost business reporting on sustainability and much business representative activity around sustainability actually have little, if anything to do with sustainability.

(Gray, 2010, p. 48)

[A] failure ... to speak might be regarded as morally questionable [but] that is different from ... a legal duty to speak.[1]

9.1 INTRODUCTION

This chapter underlines the role of professional advisory services such as accounting and auditing firms, management consultancies, rating agencies, external company secretaries, and public relations, advertising and marketing firms and suggests that they should be made responsible and accountable within a legal and regulatory framework for corporate social responsibility (CSR). The chapter draws theoretical insights from 'enforced self-regulation' (Ayres and Braithwaite, 1992, pp. 101–12) as well as institutional theory (Hoffman, 1999; Scott, 2001, 2008; Hodgson, 2006) to propose innovative ways in which professional advisory services can be made to reflect CSR responsibility, accountability and transparency. The proposition is based on the critical role that professional advisory services play in the corporate governance of companies, particularly large corporations (Kraakman, 1986; Cheffins, 1997; Coffee, 2006; Smith and Walter, 2006, pp. 242–6; Singh, 2013; McNulty and Stewart, 2015). As discussed in detail in Chapter 5 of this book, CSR is an integral part of modern corporate governance owing to its importance to firms, stakeholders and society.

The role of CSR in corporate governance is implicit from the definitions of CSR such as 'a firm's voluntary actions to mitigate and remedy social and environmental consequences of its operation' (Fransen, 2013, p. 13) and 'the responsibility of enterprises for their impacts on society' (Commission of the European Communities (CEC), 2011). The preamble to the OECD guidelines on corporate governance likewise recognises that 'factors such as business ethics and corporate awareness of environmental and societal interests of the communities in which they operate can also have an impact on the reputation and long-term success of a company' (Organisation for Economic Co-operation and Development (OECD), 1999, p. 142). This suggests that firms that pay little attention to wider society issues in their corporate governance structures and procedures are unlikely to consider the long-term financial consequences of their activities. As a corollary, professional advisers play critical roles in promoting or discouraging CSR in their business activities and relationships (see generally Idowu and Filho, 2009). In addition to their own business and corporate governance procedures, firms also use professional CSR advisory services and this is likely to have an influence on how client firms approach CSR and address matters within its purview. Rinaldi (2019, p. 2) consequently emphasised 'the role of accounting in affecting social and environmental outcomes'. The role of professional advisory services is also buttressed by the emerging association of CSR performance to credit ratings (Scalet and Kelly, 2009; Attig et al., 2013) and investment covenants (Shi and Sun, 2015).

A recent illustration of the role and impact of professional advisory services in corporate social responsiveness and attitude to public interest matters is the US opioid crisis. As Deputy Attorney-General Jeffery Rosen observed, '[t]he abuse and diversion of prescription opioids has contributed to a national tragedy of addiction and deaths, in addition to those caused by illicit street opioids' (United States Department of Justice, 2020). Consulting firm McKinsey reached financial settlements of USD 573 million, USD 23 million and USD 45 million with the US states (BBC, 2021; Forsythe and Bogdanich, 2021) for being 'the driving force behind many of the aggressive sales tactics used by US opioid manufacturers' (Dyer, 2021). In its court complaint, the state of Massachusetts noted that it acted against McKinsey 'for the consulting services it provided to opioid companies in connection with designing the companies' marketing plans and programs that helped cause and contributed to the opioid crisis'.[2] The consent judgment acknowledged the public interest dimensions of that enforcement action.[3] It is noteworthy that enforcement action against the consulting firm was thought necessary notwithstanding that the US Department of Justice had earlier entered into a settlement with a major opioid manufacturer, Purdue, which included billions of dollars of criminal and civil penalties and precipitated the company's liquidation. Individual shareholders of Purdue from the Sackler family also agreed to pay USD 225 million in civil penalties to the department (US Department of Justice, 2020).

Accordingly, the chapter demonstrates that significant regulatory vacuums may exist if professional advisory services that can influence the activities of other business organisations are excluded from the legal infrastructure surrounding CSR. While Chapter 5 of this book focusses on 'company management' as insiders, it is increasingly clear that 'outsiders' like professional advisers play a vital role in corporate governance as emphasised in the Principles for Service Providers in the

UK Stewardship Code 2020 (Financial Reporting Council (FRC), 2020, pp. 26–9). Professional advisers arguably assist in ensuring 'the efficient use of resources and equally to require accountability for the stewardship of those resources [with the aim of aligning] as nearly as possible the interests of individuals, corporations and societies', which is a mission of corporate governance as emphasised by Sir Adrian Cadbury in a foreword to *Global Corporate Governance Forum* (World Bank, 2003). This perhaps explains the prominent references to auditing in Articles 19(a)(5), 20(3) and 29(5) of Directive 2013/34/EU[4] as amended by Article 1 of Directive 2014/95/EU on non-financial and diversity information.[5]

Nonetheless, several corporate failures, including the collapse of some large corporations, are partly attributed to corporate governance weaknesses (Cheffins, 1997, p. 612; Smith and Walter, 2006, pp. 242–6) that heighten concerns about the role of professional advisers like auditors (Kraakman, 1986; Coffee, 2006; Singh, 2013). Major auditing firms have been embroiled in scandals across jurisdictions owing to lack of an independent and professional approach to their services, among other factors, prompting calls for reassessing the accountability of auditors (Coffee, 2019). Auditing is a key professional advisory service that features prominently in major corporate scandals and failures as exemplified by the cases of HBOS (United Kingdom House of Commons, 2016) and Carillion (United Kingdom House of Commons, 2018) in the UK. Other high-profile cases in the USA (e.g., Enron), the UK (e.g., Robert Maxwell's Maxwell Communications and Mirror Group Newspapers) and Italy (e.g., Parmalat) (Smith and Walter, 2006, pp. 248–51) illustrate linkages between professional advisory services and corporate governance failures in client firms. The case of *Secretary of State* v. *Weston*,[6] concerning an accounting firm's collusion in the clients' evasion of statutory requirements, demonstrates the impact of professional advisers on corporate governance. A number of regulatory interventions, including the US Sarbanes-Oxley Act 2002, also underscore difficulties arising from inadequate corporate governance and professional advisers' roles.

There is therefore an increasing awareness that reforms for improving corporate governance should include professional advisory services. For example, two UK parliamentary committees investigating the collapse of the BHS Group and the resultant pensions deficit scandal observed that professional advisers, like auditors, appeared unconcerned by reputational risks in associating with particular clients and even engaged in 'group-think' triggered simply by reliance on each other's presence (UK House of Commons, 2016, p. 25 [64]). Furthermore, the recent case of *Rihan* v. *Ernst & Young Global Ltd*[7] highlights how auditors motivated by commercial considerations can condone and participate in hiding unethical and illegal conduct of their clients.

While there are concerns about the roles of professional advisory services in corporate governance and CSR, the issues can be traced to the adequacy of the regulatory infrastructure involving public agencies and self-regulation. For example, the UK parliamentary committees (UK House of Commons, 2016,

p. 20 [49]) noted that '[i]t is essential that [a regulator] has the powers, resources, leadership and professional acumen to act decisively'. The committees also criticised the regulator (the Pensions Regulator) for being 'reactive' and 'slow moving' in 'a fast moving and uncertain environment' (UK House of Commons, 2016, p. 21 [49]).

Owing to the linkages between corporate governance and CSR, it is therefore imperative to design and implement a system of CSR responsibility and accountability for professional advisory services. Using auditing as a case study, this chapter shows that such a system can encourage a proactive CSR approach by professional advisers (auditors and audit firms) by ensuring real consequences for their business and reputation if responsibility is shirked. Auditing is a notable case study because the number and the persistence of corporate scandals challenge the effectiveness of auditing regulation even in jurisdictions with strong traditions of professional self-regulation. Owing to differences in perception of the role of auditing, there may exist an 'audit expectation gap' (Mock et al., 2013) in reference to 'what the auditor's report is *intended* to communicate or the *level of assurance* being provided by the report' (Gray et al., 2011). For instance, unlike auditors, stakeholders such as non-professional investors are more likely to use auditors' reports as a tool for assessing fraud risks (Asare and Wright, 2012).

Moreover, there is a market for CSR assurance services in several jurisdictions provided principally by accounting firms and rating agencies to accompany social reports (Scalet and Kelly, 2009; Junior et al., 2014; Casey and Grenier, 2015; Chapple and Mui, 2015; Cohen and Simnett, 2015; Stuart et al., 2020). Following a rapid increase in CSR reporting by businesses (KPMG, 2015, 2017), accounting professionals have adapted financial auditing terms and mechanisms (O' Dwyer, 2011; O' Dwyer et al., 2011; Andon et al., 2014, 2015) to the emergent but equally exponentially growing field of CSR assurance (Canning et al., 2019). While the credibility of CSR reports can be linked to the availability of assurance services (Fuhrmann et al., 2017; Du and Wu, 2019), the resultant social audits raise different regulatory challenges (Rahim and Idowu, 2015), including the responsibility and liability of external auditors (Chapple and Mui, 2015).

This leads to a number of questions relating to the effectiveness of regulatory schemes. How can the public interest in CSR be protected in professional advisory services provided to client firms? Who is obliged to report cases of malfeasance contrary to the public interest? To whom should professional advisers owe accountability? What are viable methods of monitoring and enforcement for the promotion of the public interest? What are the comparability criteria and opportunities for CSR-related peer review? What is the role of collective responsibility of professional advisers in promoting CSR? The last question relates to the role and viability of 'clubs' within the club theoretic model (Osuji, 2019) which, combined with other theories, underlines the need for a more effective approach to regulating professional advisory services.

Focussing on auditing, which has seen an exponential growth in CSR assurance services in several jurisdictions (Casey and Grenier, 2015), this chapter therefore makes the original argument that transparency, responsibility and accountability provisions under an enforced self-regulatory scheme of stringent voluntary clubs that reflects a more inclusive, accountable and limited stakeholder approach to CSR may be imperative for professional advisory services. Transparency, responsibility and accountability provisions can encourage professional advisers such as auditors to use the instrumentality of their voluntary clubs to proactively develop, adopt and demonstrate the professional curiosity they need to perform their stewardship and investor and creditor functions. These independent but interrelated provisions (see Figure 9.1) are justified by the public interest dimensions of auditing and other professional advisory services in addition to their private governance elements,

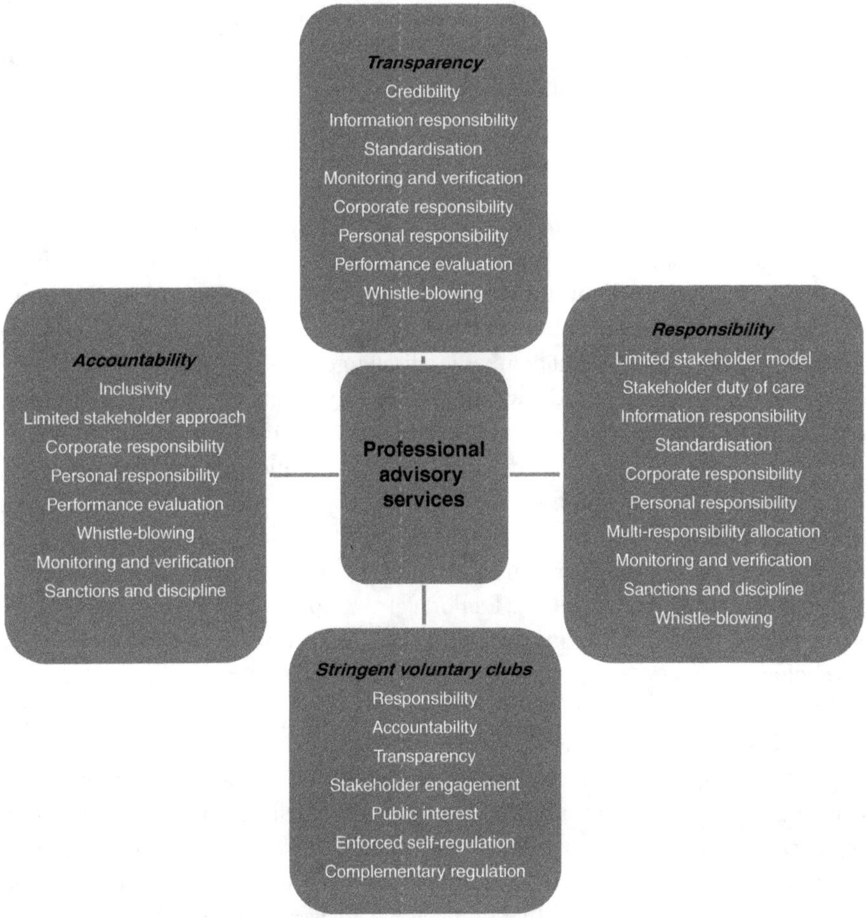

FIGURE 9.1 CSR responsibilisation of professional advisory services

which require legal and professional rules and processes to be strengthened for the promotion of CSR.

The rest of this chapter is structured as follows. Focussing on auditing, the chapter examines the corporate governance roles of professional advisory services and how these are connected to the promotion of CSR by professional advisers and their clients. The aim is to show that the focal stewardship and investor and creditor functions of professional advisory advisers underline the need for addressing stakeholder and public interest issues that may arise. The chapter then proposes creative ways for promoting responsibility, accountability and transparency in CSR through the adoption of an inclusive and limited stakeholder approach by professional advisory services. These uncommon suggestions include linking credibility to responsibility and provisions for information responsibility, stakeholder duty of care, standardisation, stakeholder-centred reasonableness test, monitoring, performance evaluation, personal and corporate responsibility, apportionment of responsibility and whistleblowing. Furthermore, an enforced self-regulatory scheme is proposed for professional advisory services under stringent voluntary clubs that promote and enforce CSR responsibility, accountability and transparency.

9.2 PROFESSIONAL ADVISORY SERVICES AND CSR

As shown in Section 9.1, the role of professional advisory services is clear from an exploration of linkages to corporate governance and CSR with their own business and their influence on client firms. As a starting point, if corporate governance can be described as 'the system of checks and balances, both internal and external to companies, which ensures that companies discharge their accountability to all their stakeholders and act in a socially responsible way in all areas of their business activity' (Solomon, 2007, p. 14) or as 'the determination of the broad uses to which organisational resources will be deployed and the resolution of conflicts among the myriad participants in organisations' (Daily et al., 2003, p. 371), it would be clear that professional advisory services play important direct and indirect roles in corporate governance. This is particularly in relation to promoting and evaluating transparency (Lowenstein, 1996, pp. 1361–2; La Porta et al., 2002), which should be a key goal of corporate governance mechanisms for protecting investors and other stakeholders.

First, it is possible for professional advisory services to be directly and actively involved in directing the affairs of clients to the extent of being regarded as part of the corporate management team. Accounting, for example, is not all about giving advice to clients. Modern accounting functions can also include reporting, regulatory, investigatory and administrative roles, while there is also the likelihood of the roles becoming 'extensive and intrusive' (Powell and Stewart, 2007, pp. 1215–16). The courts have therefore indicated that professional advisers, whatever the designation, may in fact be part of the management structure of companies just like the formally appointed directors. As the English Court of Appeal, for instance, pointed out, the provision of advice may also bring a person classed as a 'shadow director' into situations where the person exerts real influence over a company's affairs.[8] In *Re Tasbain (No. 3)*,[9] an accountant employed as a consultant was held to come within the definition of shadow director of a company in financial difficulties. The court's decision was influenced by the fact that the accountant's actions went beyond the provision of advice. Another court held on the facts of a case that a 'management consultant' had acted as a director of a company.[10] The principle was similarly applied to a bank[11] under the amended, but previously applicable, provisions of section 251(3) of the Companies Act 2006 that a company could be a shadow director of another non-subsidiary company.

Second, professional advisory services such as auditing are among indirect mechanisms for ensuring efficient resources management and accountability, particularly owing to their assurance role in promoting transparency. As noted by the UK government, transparency is 'an essential element of good corporate governance [that] gives investors and others a means to hold companies to account', while accountability 'creates a level playing field' for investment activities that benefit society (Department for Business, Innovation and Skills (DBIS), 2014, p. 4). Giving credence to the assurance role of professional advisers in corporate governance is the fact that investors and other users of auditors' reports regard them as important tools for assessing management, investment and strategic goals (Asare and Wright, 2012). If properly undertaken, auditing, for example, may help to expose bad and irresponsible corporate governance practices and therefore constitutes a vital component of effective financial and non-financial disclosure.

Third, the corporate governance–CSR linkage has made it particularly pertinent for narrative statements of CSR policies and activities that have impact on firms' financial performance. Investors, for instance, are interested in corporate governance and CSR matters in addition to financial performance (Cohen et al., 2011, 2015; Brown-Liburd et al., 2018) and are potentially influenced by auditors' reports and statements in making decisions (Elliott et al., 2020). While non-financial measures like employee, store, factory and patent numbers are components of the financial reporting process (Brazel and Lail, 2019; Brazel and Schmidt, 2019), narrative reporting can also reflect the broader social context of business (Guthrie and Parker, 2014; Sinkovics et al., 2016). There is evidence of increasing adoption of different forms of qualitative and quantitative narrative reporting by firms (de Villiers et al., 2014; Kiliç and Kuzey, 2018). This type of reporting is recognised by the *G20/OECD Principles of Corporate Governance* (OECD, 2015, pp. 38–9).

Furthermore, reports of professional advisers assist in providing a more complete picture of the affairs of businesses, including non-financial information. For example, if auditing's traditional role is to provide a method for the verification of firms' financial processes and documentation, then its facilitation of management appraisal and investor/creditor information can be equally significant for non-financial reporting. The role of accounting in auditing non-financial information has consequently been receiving attention over the years (Abou-El-Sood, 2008; Bennington, 2008). The European Commission (CEC, 1994) acknowledged accounting's role in measuring environmental objectives and performance even as far back as 1993. Likewise, accountants have for some time been looking into technical issues of non-financial accounting and auditing (Zadek et al., 2003; The Economist, 2004, pp. 13–14) and have, for example, established the Institute of Social and Ethical Accountability to promote social reporting (Gray et al., 1997). As early as 1993, a UK accountancy body issued some guidelines for reporting environmental objectives, performance and expenditure measurement (Institute of Chartered Accountants in England and Wales (ICAEW), 1993).

It is also increasingly clear that there are no insurmountable conceptual and practical obstacles to measuring CSR performance (Turker, 2009) while it is now evident that at least some aspects of CSR-based non-financial information are measurable (Abou-El-Sood, 2008; Bennington, 2008). Businesses may rely on assurance, ratings and certification services providers in making CSR-related and other transactional decisions. The emergence, growing influence and popularity of socially responsible investment (Renneboog et al., 2008; Landier and Nair, 2009; Scholtens and Sievaänen, 2013; Capelle-Blancard and Monjon, 2014; Peifer, 2014; Scholtens, 2014; Trinks and Scholtens, 2017) is a good example (see Chapter 8 of this book). The socially responsible investment industry is even supported by fund managers, analysts, rating agencies, research organisations and ethical indices in stock exchanges (Parkinson, 2006, p. 13).

CSR-related reporting facilitated by professional advisory services is therefore an integral component of transparency in corporate governance. As Hargovan (2009, p. 1016) stated, '[an] effective disclosure system will often be a significant inhibition on questionable corporate conduct. Knowledge that such conduct will be quickly exposed to the glare of publicity ... makes it less likely to occur in the first place.' In its assurance role in relation to the accuracy of financial reports, for instance, auditing aims to protect firms from errors or wrongdoing, especially by directors, and assist shareholders to play indirect roles in managing firms' affairs.[12] The *G20/OECD Principles of Corporate Governance* (OECD, 2015, pp. 42–3), for example, recommend that '[a]n annual audit should be conducted by an independent, competent and qualified, auditor in accordance with high-quality auditing standards in order to provide an external and objective assurance to the board and shareholders that the financial statements fairly represent the financial position and performance of the company in all material respects'. This is an acknowledgement of the core assurance role that auditing plays in corporate governance, especially against the backdrop of the regulation of relevant relationships. In this regard, corporate governance involves 'a set of relationships between a company's management, its board, its shareholders and other stakeholders' (OECD, 2015, p. 9).

Likewise, another indirect role of professional advisory services relates to stakeholder engagement and management. Businesses of various kinds and sizes are increasingly exposed to litigation and extralegal actions by stakeholders with respect to their CSR commitments, actions and performance and, as such, may need to have recourse to professional advisers to ensure good standing with stakeholders. In addition to the emergence of specific CSR consultancies, some professional advisers provide CSR services within their larger portfolio of services. The stakeholder and qualitative approach of CSR reporting (Villiers, 2006, pp. 253–6) is therefore arguably applicable to assurance and consultancy services that professional advisers provide to clients.

Nonetheless, the stakeholder elements may at best receive symbolic acknowledgement if professional advisers such as accountants and auditors are motivated by economic objectives that conflict with the social or public interest objectives in CSR. This is particularly possible if there are no provisions for CSR transparency or for the responsibilisation and accountability of professional advisers. To this extent, the next part of this chapter looks at different ways a legal and regulatory infrastructure for CSR could encompass professional advisory services for a more balanced and effective approach to regulation.

9.3 ACCOMMODATING PROFESSIONAL ADVISORY SERVICES IN CSR REGULATION AND GOVERNANCE

The linkages between CSR and corporate governance suggest that the latter can be a starting point for reconsideration of the position of professional advisory services. The shareholder primacy approach of the Anglo-American corporate governance model (see Chapter 5 of this book) does not enable transparency, stakeholder responsibilisation and accountability of corporate participants, including professional advisers. Accordingly, the UK Cadbury Committee (Committee on the Financial Aspects of Corporate Governance, 1992: [2.5]) stated that '[t]he shareholders' role in governance is to appoint the directors and the auditors and to satisfy themselves that an appropriate governance structure is in place'. This statement implies that auditing is one of the mechanisms for evaluating the performance and effectiveness of the board of directors and it therefore ought to provide useful information for shareholders' decisions and involvement in corporate governance. The statement also reflects the application of the shareholder-centred corporate governance model to auditing as exemplified by the auditor appointment provisions in sections 485–91 of the UK Companies Act 2006. The *G20/OECD Principles of Corporate Governance* (OECD, 2015, pp. 42–4) equally appear to reflect the shareholder-centred model in suggesting that auditor accountability should be owed to shareholders.

Despite this, the central tenets of the shareholder primacy model, responsibility and accountability of professional advisers to shareholders are far-fetched. *Caparo* v. *Dickman*[13] is illustrative. The case confirms that auditors are accountable to the company as a distinct entity and, consequently, shareholders have no right of action against auditors for negligent reports. Only the company that has a direct contractual relationship with the auditors can act through its appropriate organ, usually the board of directors.[14] The board of directors can choose to act however it wishes so long as it is a matter within its powers under the corporate constitution. The position of the law does not change even if shareholders (and other stakeholders) have suffered financial and other losses from the reports of professional advisers insofar as no contractual relationship exists between them and the professional advisers have not taken steps to assume tortious responsibility. The UK Supreme Court reiterated this legal position in the more recent case of *Steel* v. *NRAM Limited*[15] (solicitor and lender to solicitor's clients).

Clearly, there is room for enhancing the transparency, responsibility and accountability processes for professional advisers if experiences such as the US opioid crisis are anything to go by. When professional advisory services such as auditing fail to live up to public interest expectations, the results can be devastating for investors, market participants, employees and even society. For example, audit failure has been linked to corporate scandals such as Enron and WorldCom (Benston and Hartgraves, 2002; Quick et al., 2008; Shapiro and Matson, 2008) and the 2007–8 global financial crisis (Sikka, 2009). The scandals occurred even though applicable standards and principles appeared reasonably clear and, in addition to investigation, verification, inspection and other powers, the auditors had been empowered to request documents. In Enron's case, the auditors failed to disclose instances of misconduct by the firm's management (Rachagan and Kuppusamy, 2013, p. 368). Furthermore, in a case that triggered sanctions from the Financial Reporting Council (FRC), the professional services firm PwC admitted that it did not 'exercise appropriate scepticism or gather sufficient evidence for the audit' (Compliance and Risk, 2017, p. 20).

These audit failures could be attributed to a clash between self-centred commercial interest and public or stakeholder interest (Gendron and Spira, 2009; Mueller et al., 2011) which the auditors appeared to resolve in favour of the former. The desire to attract and sustain other audit and non-audit businesses from clients may be prioritised (Velte and Freidank, 2015) notwithstanding that the accounting profession carrying out the auditing function is supposed to acknowledge the public interest (Carter and Spence, 2014). In other words, the stakeholder model, which is an alternative to the shareholder primacy approach, played no role in the decision-making processes of the professional advisory services firms. Owing to the resultant auditing scandals, there have been calls for expanding auditors' accountability to include investors (Coffee, 2019) which is an implicit nod to a form of stakeholder approach.

It is, however, interesting that the stakeholder model seems to have received support from a section of the accounting profession despite its lack of recognition in the UK company law, for example (Villiers, 2006, pp. 98–103), and the profession's apparent conservatism (García Lara et al., 2009). As early as 1975, the UK accounting body supported calls for wider accountability and reporting to interests beyond shareholders (Accounting Standards Steering Committee (ASSC), 1975), although the relevant authorities rejected the proposal (Tricker, 2009, pp. 12, 229). The Hampel Committee (1998) equally rejected the stakeholder approach.

Nevertheless, the general principle of the common law is that there are no private rights unless such rights are expressly stipulated in statutes that create or impose legal duties even if the statutes are for the protection of a certain category of persons.[16] Since the law normally can provide for the functions and content of professional advisory services such as auditing,[17] it can equally extend the scope of responsibility and accountability to include stakeholders. The proposition here is for a limited stakeholder approach to the role of professional advisory services in CSR.

A limited stakeholder model can provide a guide for the identification and classification of recipients of reports of professional advisers such as auditors. Auditors' direct accountability to shareholders, for example, can help, especially since auditors' reports are really an evaluation of directors' decisions and performance. Thus, the opportunity in section 415 of Nigeria's Companies and Allied Matters Act 2020 for shareholder action when the directors fail to bring negligence claims against auditors is a step in that direction, although its scope is restricted to audited financial statements. The section allows a shareholder to institute proceedings against auditors for negligence for losses or damage to the company after the expiration of a thirty-day notice to the directors. The availability and risk of investor (shareholder and lender) litigation against auditors can lead to improved audit quality and enhance the transparency of the overall financial reporting process (Ball, 2001). For example, in cases of bribery of foreign public officials, there is a significant improvement in audit quality in jurisdictions with extensive reporting requirements and where stakeholder litigation and sanctions risk also exist for auditors (Khalil et al., 2015).

As discussed in Chapter 5 of this book, a stakeholder approach is easier to undertake in respect of reporting obligations, which would include those of professional advisers. A stakeholder approach is possible regarding the reports of auditors and other professional advisers despite the difficulty of reconciling different stakeholder interests in corporate decisions and actions. Moreover, since the stakeholder model provides the theoretical underpinning for CSR and sustainability reporting by companies (Bhattacharya et al., 2009; Prado-Lorenzo et al., 2009), consistency and clarity are possible grounds for recognising a similar approach for related assurance services. The proposed limited stakeholder approach to professional advisory services can be manifested in a number of ways as detailed in the rest of this section (Sections 9.3.1–9.3.8).

9.3.1 *Linking Credibility and Responsibility*

Following acknowledgement of the public interest or stakeholder dimensions of professional advisory services as discussed earlier in the chapter, there is therefore the need for appropriate responsibilisation of practitioners along the lines of a more inclusive approach to their professional duties. Responsibility in this regard can be defined as 'a capacity to engage in reasoned decision making' or 'liability for the consequences of one's action' (Dubbink and Smith, 2011, p. 239). This could, for instance, suggest that training and professional development and evaluation programmes are explicitly designed and implemented to reflect the proposed inclusive approach. In effect, responsibility for inclusivity can be linked to the credibility of relevant individuals and organisations. The credibility of professional advisory services largely correlates to the qualification and competence of professional advisers such as auditors as well as the effectiveness of the processes and procedures.

9.3.2 *Information Responsibility and Stakeholder Duty of Care*

Responsibilisation is arguably constrained if there are no consequences for CSR information created or facilitated by professional advisers for their clients, including when stakeholders are reasonably expected to have access to such information. Questions arise particularly when third parties rely on reports issued by professional advisers.[18] This suggests the need for a stakeholder duty of care on professional advisory services providers arising from CSR information responsibility. There are, however, four main obstacles in English law for information responsibility of professional advisers.

First, the courts differentiate between 'information' and 'advice' in relation to professional advisers' assumption of responsibility and liability for negligence.[19] Traditionally, the common law adopts a narrow approach by requiring evidence of assumption of responsibility in providing information.[20] In *BPE Solicitors* v. *Hughes-Holland*,[21] the Supreme Court stated that, unlike information provision where accuracy is the only requirement, an adviser has 'a duty to protect his client (so far as due care can do it) against the full range of risks associated with a potential transaction, [*sic*] the client will not have retained responsibility for any of them'. Second, it is clear from *BPE Solicitors* v. *Hughes-Holland* and cases such as *Steel* v. *NRAM Limited*[22] that duty can only be owed to clients of professional advisers with whom they have a contractual relationship. The supply of information by professional advisers, or its availability, to stakeholders is apparently not a consideration. Third, there is no general liability for even financial statements except when there is an assumption of duty of care by professional advisers.[23]

The fourth obstacle is company law's constraints on professional advisers' responsibility. While company law does not appear to recognise a general exclusion of liability of professional advisers such as auditors, as illustrated by section 532 of the UK Companies Act 2006, there are provisions that seem to provide a generous protective screen. For instance, section 152(8) of the UK Financial Services and Markets Act 2000 excludes professional advisers' liability for statements in documents for a securities issue or offer. Section 251(2) of the Companies Act 2006 excludes provision of professional advice from liability if it is given by a 'shadow director'. Likewise, in Australia, 'advice given by the person in the proper performance of functions attaching to the person's professional capacity'[24] is outside the concept of shadow director and the consequences it entails. These provisions raise concerns since there may be 'a thin line between giving advice and authorising the contents' (Turnbull, 2000, p. 36) of corporate statements.

There may be good reasons, including the need to avoid opening a floodgate and liability to an indeterminate number of persons, for excluding responsibility for information provided to clients and accessible to stakeholders. This, however, does not take into consideration the twin components of responsibility as discussed in Section 9.3.1. When responsibility is imposed, it does not automatically mean that the consequences of its exercise will be determined by the persons sought to be protected by that responsibility. In other words, responsibility towards stakeholders does not need to translate to a right of action for those stakeholders. The consequences can be determined by public agencies or voluntary clubs of professional advisers, as discussed in Section 9.4. This may be particularly crucial when professional advisers actively participate in the CSR processes and in critical decisions of clients, as the McKinsey case discussed in Section 9.1 suggests. If CSR disclosures are, for instance, false or misleading, there are good reasons for treating actively involved professional advisers in a similar way to the client's directors and officers.

9.3.3 *Standardisation*

Another method for promoting inclusivity responsibility in professional advisory services is through standardisation. While professional bodies such as accounting bodies play crucial roles in the standardisation of financial and non-financial measures, indicators and risk measurement of environmental risks (International Accounting Standards Board (IASB), 2007, [144], [147]), this, at best, seems to reflect the 'capacity' aspect of responsibility without addressing its 'consequences', as highlighted in Dubbink and Smith's (2011, p. 239) definition. Even then, the range of matters for consideration in decision-making can be made more inclusive and context-specific for the regulating jurisdiction.

Standardisation can lead to 'greater consistency in reporting' by firms (IASB, 2007, [149]) and may include limiting the flexibility of professional advisory services to promote the public interest. Accounting principles, for example, can be defective when multiple principles apply to similar situations and can potentially yield different results. In a more inclusive approach, accounting firms may then need to follow specific policies and standards that provide a more complete estimate of the client's financial and non-financial position. This type of standardisation can be useful for improving audit quality by reducing opportunism and preventing information manipulation and misleading reporting (Ball, 2001; Guedhami and Pittman, 2006; Lennox and Pittman, 2010). In relation to assurance services for narrative reporting, for example, standardisation can promote consistency in issues such as 'qualitative characteristics [of] understandability, relevance, supportability, balance and comparability' (IASB, 2007, [38], [40], [58–95], [A19–A25]).

9.3.4 *Stakeholder-Centred Reasonableness Test*

A plausible element of responsibilisation of professional advisory services is a stakeholder-centred reasonableness test for assessing the decisions and (in)actions of professional advisers. The stakeholder-centred reasonableness test can be part of the standardisation process in the regulatory scheme. In English law, however, the negligence liability of professional advisers is determined by the *Bolam* test, which excludes the possibility of negligence by professional advisers who acted in accordance with how a significant body of reasonable professionals would have acted, notwithstanding that some other professionals might have taken a different approach.[25] By prioritising the dominant professional view and allowing the possibility of even disregarding alternative and more reasonable minority positions in the same industry, there is little room for a stakeholder-centred approach within the *Bolam* test.

In contrast, the UK Supreme Court noted in *Montgomery* v. *Lanarkshire Health Board* that the *Bolam* test can open up the possibility of 'the sanctioning of differences in practice which are attributable not to divergent schools of thought in medical science, but merely to divergent attitudes among doctors as to the degree of respect owed to their patients'.[26] The court therefore held that the test of a doctor's duty to disclose medical information is whether 'a reasonable person in the patient's position would be likely to attach significance to the risk, or the doctor is or should reasonably be aware that the particular patient would be likely to attach significance to it'.[27] This patient-centred approach is more in line with the stakeholder-centred approach, which stresses the need for professional advisory services to reflect an inclusive approach.

9.3.5 *Monitoring Responsibility*

As already indicated, an essential element of responsibility is provisions for 'consequences' (Dubbink and Smith, 2011, p. 239) of decisions and actions. It is therefore important to provide for monitoring of how responsibility is exercised by professional advisers within the two distinct definitional elements. To reflect the consequences dimension of responsibility, monitoring assessments need to be accompanied by sanctions and disciplinary ramifications for irresponsible acts to ensure transparency. This has, for example, been found to be useful in tackling business bribery of public officials (Guedhami and Pittman, 2006, 2011).

Monitoring can occur at the individual and organisational levels of professional advisory services quality to promote responsibility for stakeholder and public interests. It can be carried out at regular intervals and may also be triggered by stakeholder concerns and complaints. For example, the UK's independent FRC conducts annual audit quality assessment of firms, although, in principle, individual professional advisers can also be monitored.

Monitoring enables evaluation of the performance of professional advisory services providers, including referencing appropriate stakeholder and public interests subsumed under CSR. Otherwise, there may be a mismatch between the changing roles and perceptions of professional advisory services providers and their performance evaluation. Auditing is an example (Soh and Martinov-Bennie, 2011). Moreover, monitoring can facilitate the comparability of professional advisory services firms and encourage intra-sector competition for the benefit of clients and stakeholders. Market competition between professional advisers provides the advantage of cost-effective access to services for clients (Humphrey, 2011) in addition to enabling improved service quality measured according to defined criteria.

9.3.6 *Personal Responsibility*

Personal responsibility is essential for responsibilisation of professional advisers, especially senior officers of professional services firms, for consideration of stakeholder and public interests at individual and organisational levels. This is about combining firm responsibility with individual responsibility for an inclusive approach to professional advisory services. Insights from tone-at-the-top studies (Lail et al., 2015; Patelli and Pedrini, 2015; Fischer and Friedman, 2019) suggest that it is helpful to ensure that senior management officers of professional advisory services firms exercise responsibility and are liable for irresponsibility. Arguably illustrative is *Secretary of State* v. *Weston*[28] where the trigger for disqualification proceedings included the actions of a defendant who, as the director of an accounting firm, facilitated the client companies' false reporting and non-compliance with statutory requirements.

Concerns about personal irresponsibility emerged around how the UK independent regulator FRC had repeatedly imposed financial penalties on PwC, a prominent professional services firm, for accounting and auditing misconduct (Compliance and Risk, 2017). A retired partner with PwC was also fined, which suggested that the partner was solely responsible for the misconduct. There were, however, no penalties for individual senior management, despite the fact that the firm was sanctioned three times for serious infractions between 2012 and 2017. Similarly, in the case of the public relations firm Bell Pottinger, discussed in detail in Section 9.4, the industry body, the Public Relations and Communications Association, found that 'senior management should have known that the campaign was at risk of causing offence [and in] such circumstances, BP ought to have exercised extreme care and should have closely scrutinised the creation of content for the campaign' (Johnston, 2017, n.p.). Nonetheless, the industry body penalised only the firm, thereby raising questions regarding the culpability of the senior officers. To ward off persistent concerns, the firm dismissed or suspended four employees, while the chief executive officer resigned.

An unhelpful regulatory vacuum for professional advisory services is therefore created if no provisions exist for personal responsibility. Even when a firm fails because of sanctions imposed on it, its senior management officers can potentially move on to other jobs, allowing a cycle of individual irresponsibility to exist. On the other hand, personal responsibility can make senior management officers develop and exhibit an attitude of professional curiosity and oversight which, even if triggered by self-interest, can advance organisational interest and public interest in good-quality professional advisory services.

9.3.7 *Allocation of Stakeholder Responsibility*

CSR responsibilisation of professional advisory services arguably includes, firstly, the recognition that failures in promoting the stakeholder and public interests as demonstrated in the corporate scandals considered already are often attributable to both actors in client companies and professional advisers. Secondly, there should be provisions for allocating responsibility to actors to whom the causative factors can be traced. The idea of apportioning responsibility and liability when contribution to culpability can be traced to two or more parties is well established in tort law.[29] A stakeholder approach is necessary for these twin components of responsibility allocation since the shareholder primacy model largely adopted in the Anglo-American company law and corporate governance system provides little room for protecting stakeholder and public interests.

There are four implications of the shareholder primacy model that are particularly relevant here. First, there is no issue with the relationship between the client company and professional advisers employed under a contract as the terms are normally stipulated under the contract. Professional advisers may also be tortiously liable to the other contracting parties for breaches of duty of care.[30] In other words, the cause of action can be framed either as contract or as tort. Even where parties other than the company are involved, the contract will still govern the relationship. Second, when a company contracts with third parties, such as professional advisory services providers, the counterparties owe their duties to the company as a distinct entity, as clarified in *Caparo* v. *Dickman*.[31] The rules of privity of contract will also normally exclude contractual duties by professional advisory services providers to stakeholders. The professional services providers can be tortiously liable to clients such as companies[32] or to stakeholders[33] in negligence only if they have specifically assumed a duty of care to them. Third, if a company suffers losses owing to a third party's failure in carrying out the third party's duties properly, only the company represented by its duly authorised corporate organ, usually the board of directors, can enforce the company's rights. If the authorised corporate organ fails to act, even shareholders are not permitted to represent the company except in the limited grounds of derivative claims and, therefore, section 415 of Nigeria's Companies and Allied Act 2020, mentioned in Section 9.3, is an emergent outlier. The fourth implication is that the company can recover from professional advisers only for the losses it has suffered[34] and cannot recover for losses suffered by stakeholders and other third parties.[35]

9.3.8 *Whistle-Blowing*

As discussed already, professional advisers can be confronted by the public interest versus commercial self-interest clash. This is epitomised by the recent case of *Rihan* v. *Ernst & Young Global Ltd*[36] where the court held that a firm of auditors failed in its duty of care towards a former partner who was forced to resign from its employment after disclosing a client's illegal and unethical practices.

Solutions advanced by the law (Gendron and Spira, 2009; Samsonova-Taddei and Siddiqui, 2016) and in accounting professional codes (Neil et al., 2005; Clements et al., 2009) for resolving the commercial versus public interest conflict largely stress the need for the independence, integrity and ethical duties of professional advisers. Nevertheless, as explored in Chapter 10 of this book, the very existence and persistence of the conflict can be attributed to relational and solidarity signals in professional advisory services that may give priority to commercial interest when it clashes with the public interest. These signals in turn create personal and situational factors that can discourage whistle-blowing (Vadera, 2009; Keil et al., 2010; Cassematis and Wortley, 2013; Trongmateerut and Sweeney, 2013; Cho and Song, 2015; Culiberg and Mihelič, 2017, pp. 794–6).

To overcome those whistle-blowing-impeding signals, it may be useful to establish procedures that recognise and protect professional advisers as stakeholders and whistle-blowers. While internal whistle-blowing procedures may be helpful, their effectiveness in promoting the public interest is doubtful (Pittroff, 2014). The US Sarbanes-Oxley Act 2002, for example, mandated public companies to establish formal and anonymous internal procedures, but this requirement has had, at best, a modest impact (Baker, 2008).

A whistle-blowing framework is therefore proposed to reflect the stakeholder approach with a twofold stakeholder role for professional advisory services. Professional advisers, firstly, may be a whistle-blowing reference channel for public-interest-motivated persons within and outside their clients. Secondly, they may act as whistle-blowers when the situation demands. This is where voluntary clubs for professional advisory services (see Section 9.4) can play crucial roles.

Voluntary clubs can be a whistle-blowing channel for professional advisers and stakeholders and an appellate style system can be established for disclosures to industry and government regulators in defined serious cases. It may even be useful to legally require whistle-blowing in certain circumstances to emphasise professional advisers' individual responsibility and encourage a culture of whistle-blowing within sectors of professional advisory services. The quotation from the case of *Hamilton* v. *Allied Domecq Plc*[37] at the beginning of this chapter suggests that legal responsibility for disclosure via whistle-blowing can encourage professional curiosity among professional advisers for the protection of the public interest.

To further strengthen the CSR-related responsibilisation of professional advisers, it may be recognised as public interest disclosure along the lines of statutes such as the UK Public Interest Disclosure Act 1998. While it seems to focus on employees, the principle can be extended to protect professional advisers acting in the public interest in making CSR-related disclosures. It can be an offence for anyone within and outside the professional advisory services firms and their clients to disclose the identity of CSR whistle-blowers or to cause them to suffer any detriment.

9.4 VOLUNTARY CLUBS FOR PROFESSIONAL ADVISORY SERVICES

Apart from demonstrating different ways in which the responsibility, accountability and transparency of professional advisory services can be promoted in a CSR regulatory scheme, issues revealed in the preceding discussions include, firstly, an 'expectation gap' between professional advisory services and stakeholders, suggesting the need for a forum for articulating stakeholder and public interests encompassed in CSR. Secondly, the forum may assist in dispelling far-fetched assumptions and guiding individuals and organisations in different professional advisory services sectors on concrete steps for meeting contextually realistic CSR expectations. As such, it may be easier to determine what is reasonable for specific sectors in different areas of CSR.

The club theory (see Osuji, 2019) suggests that voluntary clubs can provide a balanced and efficient medium for protecting the respective interests of stakeholders and professional advisers. Sector clubs of professional advisory services can provide opportunities for engaging stakeholders (see Deegan and Blomquist, 2006), for instance, in determining content and quality that in turn will enhance the credibility and comparability of CSR reports provided or facilitated by professional advisers. A club approach can help to assist closing the 'expectation gap' between public and private stakeholders, on the one hand, and professional advisory services, on the other. In the case of auditing, for example, an auditors' club working with stakeholders can determine the nature and presentation of 'key/critical audit matters' (Sirois et al., 2018) and provide a framework for social audit, which currently seems fluid (Morimoto et al., 2005; Zu, 2013). Lamberton (2000, p. 602) equally suggested that '[d]ue to the complexity of the task of measuring performance towards sustainable development, accountants need to form multidisciplinary teams together with professionals from the environmental and social disciplines, with the goal of evolving and interpreting the information set that provides relevant measures of sustainable development'. Such clubs can constitute 'advice networks'

(Bruynseels and Cardinaels, 2014) for professional advisers and other market participants which, in contrast to friendships and other social networks, may not hamper their independence and the quality of their work and reports.

It is arguable that the professional accounting bodies such as the Association of Chartered Certified Accountants (ACCA) and the Institute of Chartered Accountants in England and Wales (ICAEW) already appear to provide self-regulation for the stewardship and investor and creditor functions of some professional advisory services, including auditing. International and national accounting bodies (Villiers, 2006, pp. 42–50) perform guidance, standardisation and legitimacy, valuation and measurement, verification, evaluation and auditing, and internationalisation and harmonisation roles and organisations such as the Institute of Professional Auditors seem to serve as voluntary clubs for promoting international best standards. These professional bodies can arguably address the twin components of responsibility in relation to audit quality. They can provide membership qualification and competence criteria, including rigorous series of pre-qualification education and examinations, professional training, certified post-qualification experience in auditing principles and applications, and self-policing tools such as codes of ethics, complaints and grievance mechanisms, and disciplinary processes.

Nonetheless, the professional bodies' corporate governance role appears limited, particularly in addressing stakeholder and public interest expectations in CSR. For instance, the post-event idea of 'professional scepticism' (Payne and Ramsay, 2005; Kim and Trotman, 2014; Quadackers et al., 2014) is largely favoured by professional bodies in contrast to the 'professional curiosity' approach to risk assessment. The backward-looking nature of 'professional scepticism' prompted the UK Parliament's Treasury Committee to propose that accounting professional bodies should 'consider what further assurance auditors should give shareholders in respect of the risk management processes of a company' (United Kingdom House of Commons, 2008, 115 [299]). This suggests that, apart from generally adopting a reactive approach, the effectiveness of self-regulatory systems may be affected by professional advisers' constricted responsibility and accountability base.

Furthermore, there have been calls for increased monitoring and enforcement roles for those professional bodies (Romero, 2010). These suggest some difficulties with the professional bodies' self-regulatory regimes that may not be 'enforced' in the sense that their membership may not be an automatic legal requirement for undertaking professional advisory services in some jurisdictions. The self-regulatory schemes of the professional bodies are not necessarily 'enforced self-regulation' in the conceptual framework provided by Ayres and Braithwaite (1992, pp. 101–12), particularly with regard to the availability and application of administrative and other public enforcement mechanisms for such schemes. When they are unattached to public enforcement mechanisms, the schemes are likely to reflect a pure self-regulation model that does not necessarily reflect a stakeholder approach or promote inclusivity and wider accountability.

A professional self-regulatory body is therefore not necessarily a stringent club in terms of responsibility and accountability and may not be backed by public enforcement. The existence of voluntary clubs does not automatically translate to legal rights and commensurate obligations. As the Supreme Court of Canada recently noted in *Ethiopian Orthodox Tewahedo Church* v. *Aga*,[38] 'legal rights which can ground jurisdiction include private rights – rights in property, contract, tort or unjust enrichment – and statutory causes of action'. In other words, the law can facilitate the transformation of self-regulatory schemes to 'enforced stringent clubs' that protect and promote the interests of wider society in professional advisory services through provisions for legal rights and obligations.

It is also noteworthy that 'free riding' (Tashman and Rivera, 2010) in purely voluntary CSR initiatives can lessen their impact. The difficulties are illustrated by the dilemma the International Accounting Standards Board (IASB) faced with regard to its management commentary proposal. In relation to the operating and financial review (OFR) statement the implementation of which the UK later aborted in 2005, the IASB noted widespread disparities in the adoption of and compliance levels with the OFR requirements as well as defaults by 'a significant proportion' of large firms. The IASB consequently indicated its preference for a standard instead of a non-mandatory guidance (IASB, 2005, [212–14]).

To complement formal regulations in areas where industry practice traditionally influences legal policy and serves as a regulatory and accountability mechanism, an enforced self-regulatory system under the auspices of professional advisers' voluntary clubs needs to be 'stringent' with enforceable rules, standards and sanctions that reference international best practices. The issue of 'overprescription' (Moore, 2008) of legal rules can be addressed through stringent voluntary clubs for a more informed regulatory approach. For instance, the accounting profession's significant influence in financial reporting and tax law (Green, 1995; Macdonald, 2002) includes the law's acceptance of 'generally accepted principles of accounting' for determining business profit.[39] The law, however, provides overarching objectives for financial reporting and taxation and is not bound by accounting practice.[40] An example is the direction for a 'true and fair' view of firms' financial position under section 464 of the UK Companies Act 2006. As the court observed in *Lloyd Cheyham* v. *Littlejohn*,[41] accounting principles can provide only 'very strong evidence as to what is the proper standard which should be adopted'. Stringent voluntary clubs can therefore provide supervised and detailed implementation of overarching legal standards for CSR within fields of professional advisory services. This may reflect a principles-based (Black et al., 2007) approach to regulation.

Arguably, a recent example of the complementary regulatory mechanism could be the sanctions imposed on Bell Pottinger by the Public Relations and Communications Association, a UK public relations industry body with more than 20,000 members. The association found a member multinational firm, Bell

Pottinger, guilty of running a 'hateful and divisive campaign to divide South Africa along the lines of race' contrary to the industry code of conduct (BBC, 2017a, 2017b, 2017c). The social media campaign on behalf of a company representing an influential and politically connected family triggered a complaint to the association by South Africa's main opposition party. Bell Pottinger, which lost customers' accounts in different countries, apologised for the offensive campaign, terminated its underlying contract, and commissioned a law firm to review its management and governance procedures. The association later expelled Bell Pottinger for five years, making its survival 'highly questionable' (Johnston, 2017, n.p.). The Bell Pottinger case might seem a reactive example, but it involved a proactive system of rule design, implementation and enforcement in the public interest. A voluntary club of professional advisers should similarly be able to formulate, implement and enforce standards that recognise and protect different areas of CSR.

9.5 CONCLUSION

This chapter proceeded on the basis of the crucial roles of professional advisory services such as accounting and auditing firms, management consultancies, rating agencies, external company secretaries, and public relations, advertising and marketing firms in their clients' corporate governance and CSR activities and approaches. As such, institutional theory would suggest the need for integrating professional advisory services in CSR regulatory arrangements. Since, like other social actors, the behaviour of professional advisers and their clients may be determined by 'a structure in their organisations, institutions, and relationships which makes events clearly interpretable and predictable' (Hofsted, 1994, p. 116), the effectiveness of the regulatory scheme for CSR requires acknowledgement of the linkages to professional advisory services.

Accordingly, this chapter demonstrates that responsibility, accountability and transparency are critical independent and interrelated elements for promoting CSR in professional advisory services. Using auditing as a case study, it shows how professional advisory services can undertake stewardship and investor and creditor functions with regard to the stakeholder and public interest in CSR, which the 2008 global financial crisis and several corporate scandals attest. Since there is inadequate room for the shareholder primacy corporate governance model in reframing professional advisory services for CSR, a limited stakeholder approach is primarily proposed to balance private and public interests.

The proposition favours 'enforced self-regulation' (Ayres and Braithwaite, 1992, pp. 101–12) for professional advisory services in relation to CSR to provide opportunities for establishing, promoting and strengthening CSR responsibility, accountability and transparency through a more inclusive and stakeholder approach to professional advisory services. Creative proposals in the chapter for advancing CSR responsibility, accountability and transparency include attaching responsibility to the credibility of professional advisory services and the information and statements they supply; providing for stakeholder duty of care, standardisation and a stakeholder-centred reasonableness test; and facilitating monitoring of the exercise of responsibility, performance evaluation, personal and corporate responsibility, apportionment of responsibility and whistle-blowing. Stringent voluntary clubs of professional advisers can assist in promoting CSR responsibility, accountability and transparency and provide room for stakeholder engagement in an efficient manner while playing a complementary regulatory role in advancing overarching public interest standards in formal regulations. An enforced self-regulatory scheme by stringent voluntary clubs could improve standardisation and promote personal and organisational responsibility, as well as encouraging transparency and accountability by firms and individuals.

The proposals in this chapter reflect the private governance role of professional advisory services and their stakeholder and public interest dimensions. Professional curiosity for CSR is imperative and this can be facilitated by effective and proactive self-regulatory schemes propped up by law. The more 'enforced' and 'stringent' the voluntary clubs are, the more likely it is that they might protect and promote stakeholder and public interest in professional advisory services.

NOTES

1. *Hamilton* v. *Allied Domecq Plc* [2007] UKHL 33 [20].
2. *Commonwealth of Massachusetts* v. *McKinsey & Company, Inc. United States* (complaint), 4 February 2021 [9]. www.mass.gov/doc/massachusetts-mckinsey-complaint/download.
3. *Commonwealth* v. *McKinsey & Company, Inc. United States* (Suffolk Superior Court), [1].
4. Directive 2013/34/EU of the European Parliament and of the Council of 26 June 2013 on the annual financial statements, consolidated financial statements and related reports of certain types of undertakings, amending Directive 2006/43/EC of the European Parliament and of the Council and repealing Council Directives 78/660/EEC and 83/349/EEC, *OJ L* 182, 29.6.2013, 19.
5. Directive 2014/95/EU of the European Parliament and of the Council of 22 October 2014 amending Directive 2013/34/EU as regards disclosure of non-financial and diversity information by certain large undertakings and groups *Official Journal of the European Union* L/330/1, 15.11.2014.
6. *The Secretary of State for Business, Innovation and Skills* v. *Weston* [2014] EWHC 2933 (Ch).
7. *Rihan* v. *Ernst & Young Global Ltd and others* [2020] EWHC 901 (QB).
8. *Secretary of State for Trade and Industry* v. *Deverell* [2001] Ch 340.
9. *Re Tasbain (No. 3)* [1992] BCC 358.

10. *R* v. *Campbell* (1984) 78 Cr. App R 95.
11. *Re a Company No. 005009 of 1987* [1988] 4 BCC 424.
12. *Caparo Industries Plc* v. *Dickman* [1990] 2 AC 605 at 630 (Lord Oliver).
13. [1990] 1 All ER 568.
14. See *Gramophone and Typewriter Ltd* v. *Stanley* [1908] 2 KB 89; *Quin & Axtens Ltd* v. *Salmon* [1909] AC 442; *Shaw & Sons Ltd* v. *Shaw* [1935] 2 KB 113; *Howard Smith Ltd* v. *Ampol Petroleum Ltd* [1974] AC 821.
15. [2018] UKSC 13.
16. *Poole Borough Council* v. *GN & Anor* [2019] UKSC 25; *Campbell* v. *Gordon* [2016] UKSC 38; *McDonald* v. *National Grid Electricity Transmission Plc* [2014] 53; *Baker* v. *Quantum Clothing Group Ltd* [2011] UKSC 17.
17. *Pacific Acceptance Corporation Ltd* v. *Forsyth* (1970) 92 WN (NSW) 29, 51 (Moffitt J).
18. See e.g. *Smith* v. *Eric S. Bush* [1990] 1 AC 831.
19. *BPE Solicitors* v. *Hughes-Holland* [2017] UKSC 21 [39]; *Halsall* v. *Champion Consulting Ltd* [2017] EWHC 1079 (QB); *Various Claimants* v. *Giambrone & Law (a firm) & Ors* [2015] EWHC 1946 (QB).
20. Contrast *Williams and Glyn's Bank Ltd* v. *Barnes* [1981] Com LR 205 and *Verity and Spindler* v. *Lloyds Bank plc* [1995] CLC 1557.
21. [2017] UKSC 21 [41].
22. [2018] UKSC 13.
23. *Caparo* v. *Dickman*. Cf. *Henderson* v. *Merrett Syndicates Ltd* [1995] 2 AC 145; *Electra Private Equity Partners* v. *KPMG Peat Marwick* [2001] 1 BCLC 589.
24. Corporations Act 2001 (Commonwealth) (Australia) s. 9.
25. *Halsall* v. *Champion Consulting Ltd* [2017] EWHC 1079 (QB).
26. *Montgomery* v. *Lanarkshire Health Board* [2015] UKSC 11 [84].
27. *Montgomery* v. *Lanarkshire Health Board* [2015] UKSC 11 [87].
28. *The Secretary of State for Business, Innovation and Skills* v. *Weston* [2014] EWHC 2933 (Ch).
29. See *Fish & Fish Ltd* v. *Sea Shepherd UK* [2015] UKSC 10; *Jackson* v. *Murray* [2015] UKSC 5; *Williams* v. *The Bermuda Hospitals Board (Bermuda)* [2016] AC 888; *International Energy Group Ltd* v. *Zurich Insurance Plc UK* [2015] UKSC 33; *Barker* v. *Corus (UK) plc* [2006] UKHL 20; *Durham* v. *BAI (Run Off) Ltd* [2012] UKSC 14.
30. *Henderson* v. *Merrett Syndicates Ltd (No. 1)* [1995] 2 AC 145.
31. [1990] 1 All ER 568.
32. *BPE Solicitors v. Hughes-Holland* [2017] UKSC 21.
33. *Steel* v. *NRAM Limited* [2018] UKSC 13; *Robinson* v. *Chief Constable of West Yorkshire Police* [2018] UKSC 4.
34. *Tiuta International Ltd (In Liquidation)* v. *De Villiers Chartered Surveyors Ltd* [UKSC] 77.
35. *Swynson Ltd* v. *Lowick Rose LLP* [2017] UKSC 32.

36. *Rihan* v. *Ernst & Young Global Ltd and others* [2020] EWHC 901 (QB).
37. [2007] UKHL 33 [20].
38. *Ethiopian Orthodox Tewahedo Church of Canada St. Mary Cathedral* v. *Aga*, 2021 SCC 22 (Rowe J).
39. *Gallagher* v. *Jones (Inspector of Taxes)*, *Threfall* v. *Jones* [1993] STC 537 (Court of Appeal); *Johnston* v. *Britannia Airways Ltd* [1994] STC 763; *Herbert Smith* v. *Honour* [1999] STC 173; *Odeon Associated Theatres Ltd* v. *Jones* [1973] Ch 288, 48 TC 257.
40. See *Heather* v. *PE Consulting Group* [1973] 1 All ER 843 (Lord Denning).
41. [1987] BCLC 303 at 313 (Woolf J).

REFERENCES

Abou-El-Sood, H. (2008). The usefulness of accounting information, economic variables, and corporate governance measures to predict corporate failure. *Journal of Applied Business Research*, **24**(4), 1–9.

Accounting Standards Steering Committee (ASSC). (1975). *The Corporate Report: A Discussion Paper*. London: Accounting Standards Steering Committee.

Andon, P., Free, C. and O'Dwyer, B. (2015). Annexing new audit spaces: challenges and adaptions. *Accounting, Auditing & Accountability Journal*, **28**(8), 1400–30.

Andon, P., Free, C. and Sivabalan, P. (2014). The legitimacy of new assurance providers: making the cap fit. *Accounting, Organizations and Society*, **39**(2), 75–96.

Asare, S. K. and Wright, A. M. (2012). Investors', auditors', and lenders' understanding of the message conveyed by the standard audit report on the financial statements. *Accounting Horizons*, **26**(2), 193–217.

Attig, N., El Ghoul, S., Guedhami, O. and Suh, J. (2013). Corporate social responsibility and credit ratings. *Journal of Business Ethics*, **117**(4), 679–94.

Ayres, I. and Braithwaite, J. (1992). *Responsive Regulation: Transcending the Deregulation Debate*. New York/Oxford: Oxford University Press.

Baker, N. (2008). See no evil, hear no evil: effective whistleblower programs encourage employees who witness company wrongdoing to speak out rather than look the other way. *Internal Auditor*, **65**, 38–43.

Ball, R. (2001). Infrastructure requirements for an economically efficient system of public financial reporting and disclosure. In R. E. Litan and R. J. Herring, eds., *Brookings-Wharton Papers on Financial Services: 2001*. Washington, DC: Brookings Institution Press, pp. 127–69.

BBC. (2017a). Bell Pottinger row: PR boss sorry for S Africa campaign. 7 July [online]. www.bbc.co.uk/news/business–41142478.

BBC. (2017b). Bell Pottinger found in breach of code for South African campaign. 24 August [online]. www.bbc.co.uk/news/business–41036967.

BBC. (2017c). PR firm failed in 'race hate' campaign. 4 September [online]. www.bbc.co.uk/news/business-4114588.

BBC. (2021). McKinsey agrees $573 m opioid settlement in US. 4 February [online]. www.bbc.co.uk/news/business–55939224.

Bennington, L. (2008). Book review: managing corporate social responsibility in action: talking, doing and measuring. *International Journal of Innovation and Sustainable Development*, **3**(3/4), 366–8.

Benston, G. J. and Hartgraves, A. L. (2002). Enron: what happened and what we can learn from it. *Journal of Accounting and Public Policy*, **21**(2), 105–27.

Bhattacharya, C. B., Korschun, D. and Sen, S. (2009). Strengthening stakeholder–company relationships through mutually beneficial corporate social responsibility initiatives. *Journal of Business Ethics*, **85**(2), 257–72.

Black, J., Hopper, M. and Band, C. (2007). Making a success of principles-based regulation. *Law and Financial Markets Review*, **1**(3), 191–206.

Brazel, J. F. and Lail, B. E. (2019). How the interplay between financial and nonfinancial measures affects management forecasting behaviour. *Journal of Management Accounting Research*, **31**(3), 41–63.

Brazel, J. F. and Schmidt, J. J. (2019). Do auditors and audit committees lower fraud risk by constraining inconsistencies between financial and nonfinancial measures? *Auditing: A Journal of Practice & Theory*, **38**(1), 103–22.

Brown-Liburd, H., Cohen, J. and Zamora, V. L. (2018). CSR disclosure items used as fairness heuristics in the investment decision. *Journal of Business Ethics*, **152**(1), 275–89.

Bruynseels, L. and Cardinaels, E. (2014). The audit committee: management watchdog or personal friend of the CEO? *Accounting Review*, **89**(1), 113–45.

Canning, M., O'Dwyer, B. and Georgakopoulos, G. (2019). Processes of auditability in sustainability assurance – the case of materiality construction. *Accounting and Business Research*, **49**(1), 1–27.

Capelle-Blancard, G. and Monjon, S. (2014). The performance of socially responsible funds: does the screening process matter? *European Financial Management*, **20**(3), 494–520.

Carter, C. and Spence, C. (2014). Being a successful professional: an exploration of who makes partner in the Big Four. *Contemporary Accounting Research*, **31**(4), 949–81.

Casey, R. J. and Grenier, J. H. (2015). Understanding and contributing to the enigma of corporate social responsibility (CSR) assurance in the United States. *Auditing*, **34**(1), 97–130.

Cassematis, P. G. and Wortley, R. (2013). Prediction of whistleblowing or non-reporting observation: the role of personal and situational factors. *Journal of Business Ethics*, **117**(3), 615–34.

Chapple, L. E. and Mui, G. Y. (2015). Social audit failure: legal liability of external auditors. In M. M. Rahin and S. O. Idowu, eds., *Social Audit Regulation – Development, Challenges and Opportunities*. Heidelberg/Dordrecht: Springer, pp. 281–300.

Cheffins, B. R. (1997). *Company Law: Theory, Structure and Operation*. Oxford: Clarendon Press.

Cho, Y. K. and Song, H. J. (2015). Determinants of whistleblowing within government agencies. *Public Personnel Management*, **44**(4), 450–72.

Clements, C., Neil, J. D. and Stovall, O. S. (2009). An analysis of International Accounting Codes of Conduct. *Journal of Business Ethics*, **87**(1), 173–83.

Coffee, J. (2006). *Gatekeepers: The Role of the Professions in Corporate Governance*. Oxford: Oxford University Press.

Coffee, J. C. (2019). Why do auditors fail? What might work? What won't? *Accounting and Business Research*, **49**(5), 540–61.

Cohen, J. R. and Simnett, R. (2015). CSR and assurance services: a research agenda. *Auditing: A Journal of Practice & Theory*, **34**(1), 59–74.

Cohen, J. R., Holder-Webb, L. and Zamora, V. L. (2015). Nonfinancial information preferences of professional investors. *Behavioural Research in Accounting*, **27**(2), 127–53.

Cohen, J., Webb, L., Nath, L. and Wood, D. (2011). Retail investors' perception of the decision usefulness of economic performance, governance, and corporate social responsibility disclosures. *Behavioural Research in Accounting*, **23**(1), 109–29.

Commission of the European Communities (CEC). (1994). *Directions for the EU on Environmental Indicators and Green National Accounting: The Integration of Environmental and Economic Information Systems*. COM(94) 670 final. Brussels: European Commission.

Commission of the European Communities (CEC). (2011). *Communication from the Commission to the European Parliament, the Council, the European Economic and Social Committee and the Committee of the Regions. A Renewed EU Strategy 2011–14 for Corporate Social Responsibility*, COM(2011) 881 final. Brussels: European Commission.

Committee on the Financial Aspects of Corporate Governance (Cadbury Committee). (1992). *Report of the Committee on the Financial Aspects of Corporate Governance*. London: Committee on the Financial Aspects of Corporate Governance and Gee and Co. Ltd.

Compliance and Risk (2017). FRC fines PwC £5 m for audit misconduct. *Compliance and Risk*, 6(3), 19–20.

Culiberg, B. and Mihelič, K. K. (2017). The evolution of whistleblowing studies: a critical review and research agenda. *Journal of Business Ethics*, **146**, 787–803.

Daily, C., Dalton, D. and Cannella Jr, A. (2003). Corporate governance: decades of dialogue and data. *Academy of Management Review*, **28**(3), 371–82.

de Villiers, C., Rinaldi, L. and Unerman, J. (2014). Integrated reporting: insights, gaps and agendas for future research. *Accounting, Auditing & Accountability Journal*, **27**(7), 1042–67.

Deegan, C. and Blomquist, C. (2006). Stakeholder influence on corporate reporting: an exploration of the interaction between WWF-Australia and the Australian minerals industry. *Accounting, Organizations and Society*, **31**(4–5), 343–72.

Department for Business, Innovation and Skills (DBIS). (2014). *Transparency and Trust: Enhancing the Transparency of UK Company Ownership and Increasing Trust in UK Business*. Government Response April 2014. London: DBIS.

Du, K. and Wu, S. (2019). Does external assurance enhance the credibility of CSR reports? Evidence from CSR-related misconduct events in Taiwan. *Auditing: A Journal of Practice & Theory*, **38**(4), 101–30.

Dubbink, W. and Smith, J. (2011). A political account of corporate moral responsibility. *Ethical Theory and Moral Practice*, **14**(2), 223–46.

Dyer, O. (2021). McKinsey agrees to pay $574 m to US states to settle opioid claims. *BMJ*, 373: n360. www.bmj.com/content/372/bmj.n360.full.

Economist. (2004). Corporate storytelling. *The Economist*, 6 November, 13–14.

Elliott, W. B., Fanning, K. and Peecher, M. E. (2020). Do investors value higher financial reporting quality, and can expanded audit reports unlock this value? *Accounting Review*, **95** (2), 141–65.

Financial Reporting Council (FRC). (2020). *The UK Stewardship Code 2020*. London: Financial Reporting Council.

Fischer, D. and Friedman, H. H. (2019). Tone-at-the-top lessons from Abrahamic justice. *Journal of Business Ethics*, **156**, 209–25.

Forsythe, M. and Bogdanich, W. (2021). McKinsey settles for nearly $600 million over role in opioid crisis. *NY Times*, 3 February. www.nytimes.com/2021/02/03/business/mckinsey-opioids-settlement.html.

Fransen, L. (2013). The embeddedness of responsible business practice: exploring the interaction between national-institutional environments and corporate social responsibility. *Journal of Business Ethics*, **115**, 213–27.

Fuhrmann, S., Ott, C., Looks, E. and Guenther, T. W. (2017). The contents of assurance statements for sustainability reports and information asymmetry. *Accounting and Business Research*, **47**(4), 369–400.

García Lara, J. M., García Osma, B. and Penalva, F. (2009). Accounting conservatism and corporate governance. *Review of Accounting Studies*, **14**(1), 161–201.

Gendron, Y. and Spira, L. (2009). What went wrong? The downfall of Arthur Andersen and the construction of controllability boundaries surrounding financial auditing. *Contemporary Accounting Research*, **26**, 987–1027.

Gray, R. (2010). Is accounting for sustainability actually accounting for sustainability . . . and how would we know? An exploration of narratives of organisations and the planet. *Accounting, Organizations and Society*, **35**(1), 47–62.

Gray, R., Dey, C., Owen, D., Evans, R. and Zadek, S. (1997). Struggling with the praxis of social accounting: stakeholders, accountability, audits and procedures. *Accounting, Auditing and Accountability Journal*, **10**(3), 325–64.

Gray, G. L., Turner, J. L., Coram, P. J. and Mock, T. T. (2011). Perceptions and misperceptions regarding the unqualified auditor's report by financial statement preparers, users, and auditors. *Accounting Horizons*, **25**(4), 659–84.

Green, S. (1995). Accounting standards and tax law: complexity, dynamism and divergence. *British Tax Review*, **5**, 445–52.

Guedhami, O. and Pittman, J. A. (2006). Ownership concentration in privatized firms: the role of disclosure standards, auditor choice, and auditing infrastructure. *Journal of Accounting Research*, **44**, 889–929.

Guedhami, O. and Pittman, J. A. (2011). The choice between private and public capital markets: the importance of disclosure standards and auditor discipline to countries divesting state owned enterprises. *Journal of Accounting and Public Policy*, **30**, 395–430.

Guthrie, J. and Parker, L. D. (2014). The global accounting academic: what counts! *Accounting, Auditing & Accountability Journal*, **27**(1), 2–4.

Hampel Committee. (1998). *Report on Corporate Governance*. London: Gee.

Hargovan, A. (2009). Australian Securities and Investments Commission v MacDonald [No 11]: corporate governance lessons from James Hardie. *Melbourne University Law Review*, **33**, 984–1021.

Hodgson, G. (2006). What are institutions? *Journal of Economic Issues*, **40**, 1–25.

Hoffman, A. J. (1999). Institutional evolution and change: environmentalism and the U.S. chemical industry. *Academy of Management Journal*, **42**(4), 351–71.

Hofsted, G. (1994). *Cultures and Organizations*. London: HarperCollins.

Humphrey, C. (2011). Regulating audit beyond the crisis: a critical discussion of the EU Green Paper. *European Accounting Review*, **20**(3), 431–57.

Idowu, S. and Filho, W. L. (2009). *Professionals' Perspectives of Corporate Social Responsibility*. Berlin/Heidelberg: Springer-Verlag.

Institute of Chartered Accountants in England and Wales (ICAEW). (1993). *Business, Accountancy, and the Environment: A Policy and Research Agenda*. London: ICAEW.

International Accounting Standards Board (IASB). (2005). *Discussion Paper. Management Commentary*. London: IASB.

International Accounting Standards Board (IASB). (2007). *Information for Observers: Agenda Proposal (Agenda Paper 5D)*. London: IASB.

Johnston, C. (2017). Bell Pottinger expelled from trade body for South African campaign. 4 September [online]. www.bbc.co.uk/news/business–41151361.

Junior, R. M., Best, P. J. and Cotter, J. (2014). Sustainability reporting and assurance: a historical analysis on a world-wide phenomenon. *Journal of Business Ethics*, **120** (1), 1–11.

Keil, M., Tiwana, A., Sainsbury, R. and Sneha, S. (2010). Toward a theory of whistleblowing intentions: a benefit-to-cost differential perspective. *Decision Sciences*, **41**, 787–812.

Khalil, S., Saffar, W. and Trabelsi, S. (2015). Disclosure standards, auditing infrastructure, and bribery mitigation. *Journal of Business Ethics*, **132**, 379–99.

Kiliç, M. and Kuzey, C. (2018). Determinants of forward-looking disclosures in integrated reporting. *Managerial Auditing Journal*, **33**(1), 115–44.

Kim, S. and Trotman, K. T. (2014). The comparative effect of process and outcome accountability in enhancing professional scepticism. *Accounting and Finance*, **55**(4), 1015–40.

KPMG, 2015. *Currents of Change: The KPMG Survey of Corporate Responsibility Reporting 2015*. Amsterdam: KPMG International.

KPMG, 2017. *KPMG Survey of Corporate Responsibility Reporting 2017*. Amsterdam: KPMG International.

Kraakman, R. (1986). Gatekeepers: the anatomy of a third-party enforcement strategy. *Journal of Law Economics and Organization*, **2**, 53–104.

Lail, B., MacGregor, J., Stuebs, M. and Thomasson, T. (2015). The influence of regulatory approach on tone at the top. *Journal of Business Ethics*, **126**, 25–37.

Lamberton, G. (2000). Accounting for sustainable development – a case study of city farm. *Critical Perspectives on Accounting*, **11**(5), 583–605.

Landier, A. and Nair, V. B. (2009). *Investing for Change: Profit from Responsible Investment*. New York: Oxford University Press.

La Porta, R., Lopez-de-Silanes, F., Shleifer, A. and Vishny, R. (2002). Investor protection and corporate valuation. *Journal of Finance*, **62**(3), 1147–70.

Lennox, C. and Pittman, J. (2010). Auditing the auditors: evidence on the recent reforms to the external monitoring of audit firms. *Journal of Accounting and Economics*, **49**, 84–103.

Lowenstein, L. (1996). Financial transparency and corporate governance: you manage what you measure. *Columbia Law Review*, **96**(5), 1335–62.

Macdonald, G. (2002). *The Taxation of Business Income: Aligning Taxable Income with Accounting Income*. Tax Law Review Committee (TLRC) Discussion Paper No. 1. London: TLRC and Institute of Fiscal Studies. https://ifs.org.uk/comms/dp2.pdf.

McNulty, T. and Stewart, A. (2015). Developing the governance space: a study of the role and potential of the company secretary in and around the board of directors. *Organisational Studies*, **36**(4), 513–35.

Mock, T. T., Bédard, J., Coram, P. J., Davis, S. M., Espahbodi, R. and Warne, R. C. (2013). The audit reporting model: current research synthesis and implications. *Auditing: A Journal of Practice & Theory*, **32**(1), 323–51.

Moore, M. (2008). Averting the overprescription of UK corporate governance norms. *Journal of Securities Law Regulation and Compliance*, **2**(1), 71–87.

Morimoto, R., Ash, J. and Hope, C. (2005). Corporate social responsibility audit: from theory to practice. *Journal of Business Ethics*, **62**, 315–25.

Mueller, F., Carter, C. and Ross-Smith, A. (2011). Making sense of career in a Big Four accounting firm. *Current Sociology*, **59**(4), 551–67.

Neil, J. D., Stovall, O. S. and Jinkerson, D. L. (2005). A critical analysis of the accounting industry's voluntary code of conduct. *Journal of Business Ethics*, **59**(1–2), 101–8.

O' Dwyer, B. (2011). The case of sustainability assurance: constructing a new assurance service. *Contemporary Accounting Research*, **28**(4), 1230–66.

O' Dwyer, B., Owen, D. and Unerman, J. (2011). Seeking legitimacy for new assurance forms: the case of assurance on sustainability reporting. *Accounting, Organizations and Society*, **36**(1), 31–52.

Organisation for Economic Cooperation and Development (OECD) Directorate for Financial, Fiscal and Enterprise Affairs (Ad Hoc Task Force on Corporate Governance). (1999). *OECD Principles of Corporate Governance*. Geneva: OECD. www.oecd.org/officialdocuments/publicdisplaydocumentpdf/?cote=C/MIN(99)6&docLanguage=En.

Organisation for Economic Cooperation and Development (OECD). (2015). *G20/OECD Principles of Corporate Governance*, Paris: OECD Publishing. www.oecd-ilibrary.org/docserver/9789264236882-en.pdf?expires=1648926477&id=id&accname=guest&checksum=54DE5EABF52ECE285C544268798F227C.

Osuji, O. K. (2019). Club theory and performance evaluation. In F. Ngwu, O. Osuji, C. Ogbechie and D. Williamson, eds., *Enhancing Board Effectiveness – Institutional, Regulatory and Functional Perspectives for Developing and Emerging Markets*. New York: Routledge, pp. 151–83.

Parkinson, J. (2006). Corporate governance and the regulation of business behaviour. In S. MacLeod (ed.), *Global Governance and the Quest for Justice. Volume II: Corporate Governance*. Oxford: Hart, pp. 1–26.

Patelli, L. and Pedrini, M. (2015). Is tone at the top associated with financial reporting aggressiveness? *Journal of Business Ethics*, **126**, 3–19.

Payne, E. A. and Ramsay, R. J. (2005). Fraud risk assessments and auditors' professional scepticism. *Managerial Auditing Journal*, **20**(3), 321–30.

Peifer, J. L. (2014). Fund loyalty among socially responsible investors: the importance of the economic and ethical domains. *Journal of Business Ethics*, **121**, 635–49.

Pittroff, E. (2014). Whistle-blowing systems and legitimacy theory: a study of the motivation to implement whistle-blowing systems in German organisations. *Journal of Business Ethics*, **124**, 399–412.

Powell, J. L. and Stewart, R. (2007). Accountants and auditors. In *Jackson & Powell on Professional Liability*, 6th ed., J. Powell, R. Stewart and the Hon. Mr Justice Jackson, eds. London: Sweet & Maxwell.

Prado-Lorenzo, J. M., Gallego-Alvarez, I. and Garcia-Sanchez, I. M. (2009). Stakeholder engagement and corporate social responsibility reporting: the ownership structure effect. *Corporate Social Responsibility and Environmental Management*, **16**(2), 94–107.

Quadackers, L., Groot, T. and Wright, A. (2014). Auditors' professional scepticism: neutrality versus presumptive doubt. *Contemporary Accounting Research*, **31**(3), 639–57.

Quick, R., Turley, S. and Willekens, M. (2008). *Auditing, Trust and Governance: Developing Regulation in Europe*. New York: Routledge.

Rachagan, S. and Kuppusamy, K. (2013). Encouraging whistle blowing to improve corporate governance? A Malaysian initiative. *Journal of Business Ethics*, **115**, 367–82.

Rahim, M. M. and Idowu, S. O. (2015). *Social Audit Regulation: Development, Challenges and Opportunities*. Heidelberg/Dordrecht: Springer.

Renneboog, L., Ter Horst, J. and Zhang, C. (2008). Socially responsible investments: institutional aspects, performance, and investor behaviour. *Journal of Banking and Finance*, **32**(9), 1723–42.

Rinaldi, L. (2019). Accounting for sustainability governance: the enabling role of social and environmental accountability research. *Social and Environmental Accountability Journal*, **39**(1), 1–22.

Romero, S. (2010). Auditor independence: third party hiring and paying auditors. *Euromed Journal of Business*, **5**(3), 298–314.

Samsonova-Taddei, A. and Siddiqui, J. (2016). Regulation and the promotion of audit ethics: analysis of the content of the EU's Policy. *Journal of Business Ethics*, **139**, 183–95.

Scalet, S. and Kelly, T. F. (2009). CSR rating agencies: what is their global impact? *Journal of Business Ethics*, **94**(1), 69–88.

Scholtens, B. (2014). Indicators of responsible investing. *Ecological Indicators*, **36**(1), 382–5.

Scholtens, B. and Sievaänen, R. (2013). Drivers of socially responsible investing: a case study of four Nordic countries. *Journal of Business Ethics*, **115**(3), 605–16.

Scott, W. (2001). *Institutions and Organizations*. Thousand Oaks, CA: Sage.
Scott, W. (2008). Approaching adulthood: the maturing of institutional theory. *Theory and Society*, **37**(5), 427–42.
Shapiro, B. and Matson, D. (2008). Strategies of resistance to internal control regulation. *Accounting, Organizations and Society*, **33**(2/3), 199–228.
Shi, G. and Sun, J. (2015). Corporate bond covenants and social responsibility investment. *Journal of Business Ethics*, **131**, 285–303.
Sikka, P. (2009). Financial crisis and the silence of the auditors. *Accounting, Organizations and Society*, **34**(6–7), 868–73.
Singh, D. (2013). Role of external auditors in bank supervision: a supervisory gatekeeper. *International Lawyer*, **47**(1), 65–98.
Sinkovics, N., Hoque, S. F. and Sinkovics, R. R. (2016). Rana plaza collapse aftermath: are CSR compliance and auditing pressures effective? *Accounting, Auditing & Accountability Journal*, **29**(4), 617–49.
Sirois, L., Bédard,J. and Bera, P. (2018). The informational value of key audit matters in the auditor's report: evidence from an eye-tracking study. *Accounting Horizons*, **32**(2), 141–62.
Smith, R. C. and Walter, I. (2006). *Governing the Modern Corporation: Capital Markets, Corporate Control and Economic Performance*. New York: Oxford University Press.
Soh, D. S. B. and Martinov-Bennie, N. (2011). The internal audit functions: perceptions of audit roles, effectiveness and performance. *Managerial Auditing Journal*, **26**(7), 605–22.
Solomon, J. (2007). *Corporate Governance and Accountability*. Hoboken, NJ: John Wiley & Sons.
Stuart, A. C., Bedard, J. C. and Clark, C. E. (2020). Corporate social responsibility disclosures and investor judgments in difficult times: the role of ethical culture and assurance. *Journal of Business Ethics*. https://doi.org/10.1007/s10551-020-04454-z
Tashman, P. and Rivera, J. (2010). Are members of business for social responsibility more socially responsible? *Policy Studies Journal*, **38**(3), 487–514.
Tricker, B. (2009). *Corporate Governance: Principles, Policies, and Practices*. Oxford: Oxford University Press.
Trinks, P. J. and Scholtens, B. (2017). The opportunity cost of negative screening in socially responsible investing. *Journal of Business Ethics*, **140**, 193–208.
Trongmateerut, P. and Sweeney, J. T. (2013). The influence of subjective norms on whistle-blowing: a cross-cultural investigation. *Journal of Business Ethics*, **112**(3), 437–51.
Turker, D. (2009). Measuring corporate social responsibility: a scale development study. *Journal of Business Ethics*, **85**(4), 411–27.
Turnbull, S. (2000). The statutory framework. In M. Button and K. Hatchley, eds., *A Practitioner's Guide to the Financial Services Authority Listing Rules 2000/2001 Edition*. Old Woking: City & Financial Publishing, pp. 15–37.
United Kingdom House of Commons, Business, Energy and Industrial Strategy and Work and Pensions Committees. (2018). *Carillion: Second Joint Report from the Business, Energy and Industrial Strategy and Work and Pensions Committees of Session 2017–19; Tenth Report of the Business, Energy and Industrial Strategy Committee of Session 2017–19; Twelfth Report of the Work and Pensions Committee of Session 2017–19*. London: House of Commons.
United Kingdom House of Commons, Treasury Committee. (2008). *The Run on the Rock. Fifth Report of Session 2007-08 Vol. 1*. London: The Stationery Office.
United Kingdom House of Commons, Work and Pensions and Business, Innovation and Skills Committees. (2016). *BHS. First report of the Work and Pensions Committee and*

Fourth Report of the Business, Innovation and Skills Committee of Session 2016–17. London: House of Commons.

United States Department of Justice, Office of Public Affairs. (2020). Justice Department announces global resolution of criminal and civil investigations with opioid manufacturer Purdue Pharma and civil settlement with members of the Sackler Family. 21 October. www.justice.gov/opa/pr/justice-department-announces-global-resolution-criminal-and-civil-investigations-opioid.

Vadera, A. K., Aguilera, R. V. and Caza, B. B. (2009). Making sense of whistle-blowing's antecedents. *Business Ethics Quarterly*, 19(4), 553–86.

Velte, P. and Freidank, C. (2015). The link between in- and external rotation of the auditor and the quality of financial accounting and external audit. *European Journal of Law and Economics* 40(3), 225–46.

Villiers, C. (2006). *Corporate Reporting and Company Law*. Cambridge: Cambridge University Press.

World Bank. (2003). *Global Corporate Governance Forum*. Washington, DC: World Bank.

Zadek, S., Pruzan, P. and Evans, R. (2003). How to do it. In S. Zadek, R. Evans and P. Pruzan, eds., *Building Corporate Accountability: Emerging Practices in Social and Ethical Accounting, Auditing and Reporting*. Abingdon, UK: Earthscan, pp. 35–49.

Zu, L. (2013). Social auditing. In S. O. Idowu, N. Capaldi, L. Zu and A. Das Gupta, eds., *Encyclopaedia of Corporate Social Responsibility*. Heidelberg: Springer, pp. 2179–88.

10

Inventive Interventionist Regulation of Transnational Business, Sport, Cultural and Entertainment Organisations

Onyeka K. Osuji

10.1 INTRODUCTION

This chapter aims to investigate the potential and the limitations of a regulated form of corporate social responsibility (CSR) for transnational business, sport, cultural and entertainment organisations. Contemporary discussions of the notion of CSR reveal a degree of flexibility and adaptability to different national and transnational contexts. While multinational enterprises (MNEs) and other commercial organisations are originally the focus of CSR, the discourse has extended to transnational business, sport, cultural and entertainment organisations. The world's football governing body, Fédération International de Football Association (FIFA), for example, once acknowledged its obligation 'that goes beyond the game and [that it] aspires to setting an example for international organisations in sustainability and corporate social responsibility' (Wilson, 2014, n.p.). Supporting the application of CSR principles to transnational non-governmental organisations (NGOs) was Danuta Sacher, chief executive of the Swiss-based NGO Terre des Hommes, who argued: 'Just as garment retailers bear responsibility for the production conditions of their suppliers, this must also apply to FIFA and the whole of its "commercial product" – the World Cup tournament' (Wilson, 2014, n.p.).

There are varied reasons for the growing prominence of such organisations in CSR debates and adaptation of CSR discourse to them. First is the realisation that resolution of some issues of global concern requires the involvement of individuals and organisations, including dominant private actors in national and international affairs. Sustainable development is an example, as is evident from the Sustainable Development Goals 2015 and the Paris Agreement of the United Nations Framework Convention on Climate Change 2015. Second, context-specific CSR issues have been raised against transnational NGOs in addition to governance of their supply and purchasing chains. Examples include the International Chamber of Commerce (ICC), which referred to 'the economic and social benefits of diversity, while undertaking efforts to improve cultural and gender balances to benefit our own services and operations' (International Chamber of Commerce (ICC), 2020a, n.p.) and transnational beauty pageant organisations such as the Miss World Organization, the Miss Universe Organization, the International Culture Association and the Miss Earth Foundation confronted by questions of feminism, human rights, racism, gender identity, equality, corporate sponsorships and host countries' profile at various times. Third is an emergent recognition of transnational NGOs' governance roles within and outside those organisations. The ICC (2020b), for example, acknowledged its representation of business interests and collaboration with multilateral institutions such as the United Nations (UN), the World Trade Organization, the World Intellectual Property Organization, the Economic and Social Council, the International Telecommunication Union and G20 and participation in global governance forums such as the World Summit on Sustainable Development, the UN Framework Convention on Climate Change, the Conference on Financing for Development and the World Summit on the Information Society. Fourth is the fact that the self-regulatory systems operated by transnational non-governmental business, sport, cultural and entertainment organisations provide almost no room for interventions by national laws and institutions, while international regulation is ordinarily non-existent owing to the peculiar nature of international law and multilateral institutions. There is also the question of the effectiveness of transnational self-regulatory arrangements in advancing CSR.

There are opportunities for regulating transnational non-governmental business, sport, cultural and entertainment organisations through the instrumentality of CSR. Using sport organisations as a case study, this chapter proposes CSR as a potentially efficient and effective inventive interventionist regulatory method (Osuji, 2015). The choice of sport organisations is owing to the unprecedented challenges they pose to national legal orders and the modest attempts that have been made to regulate them. Linked to the organisations are CSR concerns such as corruption (Osuji, 2019), with national and transnational implications. The chapter therefore makes a number of original and innovative contributions to CSR, transnational governance and regulation. First, it demonstrates how an indirect regulatory approach through CSR can overcome obstacles faced by national regulation of transnational non-governmental business, sport, cultural and entertainment organisations and fill regulatory gaps in international law and national law. Often regarded as voluntary regulation, the potential of the increasingly popular concept of CSR as a tool for public regulation and co-regulation is slowly gaining recognition (Osuji, 2015; Osuji and Obibuaku, 2016). Second, a regulated form of CSR can promote substantive outcomes, multi-stakeholder empowerment and effective disclosure by transnational non-governmental business, sport, cultural and entertainment organisations. Third, CSR can address relational and solidarity signals that aggravate regulatory challenges such as transactional secrecy, organisational loyalty, information asymmetry, whistle-blowing and availability of evidence. Another contribution is therefore challenging existing orthodoxies on CSR and national and transnational regulation by exploring the complex ways in which a regulated CSR can facilitate self-regulation and co-regulation in transnational non-governmental business, sport, cultural and entertainment organisations and also enable national governments to play indirect regulatory roles that are not objectionable in the international legal order.

The chapter continues as follows. Focussing on athletics and football, it outlines CSR-related governance issues in sport governing bodies before examining the regulatory structure of transnational sport organisations in relation to the ability to resolve CSR issues. The chapter further investigates the role and components of an inventive interventionist approach to CSR for regulating transnational NGOs. Analysis is then undertaken of the role of inventive interventionism in addressing relational and solidarity signals that present significant problems in regulating transnational NGOs and their associates.

10.2 TRANSNATIONAL SPORT GOVERNANCE AND CSR

Sport governance is largely through private systems co-ordinated by the International Olympic Committee (IOC) and international federations outside formal international and national legal orders. While the governance structures have facilitated several successes, recent corruption, money laundering, drug-related cheating, poor labour standards, weak corporate governance, irresponsible environmental practices, supply chain irresponsibility and other scandals have heightened questions about the regulation of sport and sport organisations.

Doping, for example, is a prominent global issue and casts shadows on the credibility of individuals, states, sport events and sport governing bodies. Scandals and allegations of state-sponsored doping and doping test irregularities have persisted, despite efforts from different quarters to promote clean sport. An exemplar case is the four-year ban from sporting competitions that the World Anti-Doping Agency (WADA) imposed on the Russian Federation in December 2019 (WADA, 2019). WADA also suspended Moscow's anti-doping laboratory (WADA, 2020a) and requested the Court of Arbitration for Sport to resolve its non-compliance dispute with Russia's Anti-Doping Agency (WADA, 2020b, 2020c). Prior to these decisions, WADA's Independent Observers Report into the 2016 Rio Olympic Games catalogued several doping test irregularities, while the Robert McLaren Independent Person WADA Investigation into Sochi Allegations reports of July 2016 and December 2016 established corruption-doping linkages (WADA, 2016a, 2016b, 2016c). A 2014 German television documentary similarly alleged systematic doping and widespread doping-related corruption in Russian athletics, including payments by athletes to officials and inaction on the part of the Russian Athletics Federation and the International Association of Athletics Federations (IAAF) (BBC, 2014). Lamine Diack, IAAF's past president, was undergoing trial in France for corruption and money laundering (Roan, 2020) related to money allegedly received to cover up cheating and defer doping-related sanctions against Russia. In November 2015, French prosecutors, in response to information provided by WADA, announced that Mr Diack was under criminal investigation (BBC, 2015a). In January 2016, the Richard Pound-led WADA Independent Commission found that 'corruption was embedded in [IAAF and] cannot be ignored or dismissed as attributable to the odd renegade acting on his own' (WADA, 2016a). In its November 2015 Part I report, the Independent Commission underlined 'the apparent unwillingness of IAAF to acknowledge' the problem of widespread doping in Russian athletics (WADA, 2015).

Similarly, corruption in football governance has been widely reported (see Blake and Calvert, 2015; Bean, 2016; Esposito, 2016; Conn, 2017; Sugden and Tomlinson, 2017; Mersiades, 2018; Gill et al., 2019). In May 2015, the Swiss police, at the US Justice Department's request, raided a Zurich hotel and arrested seven top FIFA officials for corruption and money laundering (BBC, 2015b). The US Justice Department alleged the existence of 'rampant, systemic, and deep-rooted' corruption in FIFA and indicted fourteen FIFA officials for racketeering, fraud and money laundering[1] relating to millions of dollars over a twenty-year period (BBC, 2015c, 2015d). The corruption scandal and its officials' arrest resulted in the 'FIFA brand becoming synonymous with allegations of bribery, corruption and money laundering at the very highest levels' (Allan-Jones and Loxton, 2015).

Among other regional football governing bodies, the Confederation of African Football (CAF) has also been in the news for weak corporate governance. A recent audit by Pricewaterhouse Coopers (PwC) reported that CAF's 'unreliable and not trustworthy' accounting processes included several 'unusual' large payments with 'little or no supporting documentation' (Edwards, 2020). In relation to labour standards, the auditors indicated that the 'understaffed' CAF workers were 'overworked' and 'generally demotivated'. Other issues reported included missing financial data, questionable selection of suppliers and 'highly suspicious' transactions with commercial parties. Although CAF is based in Cairo, Egypt, and serves African countries, no government commented on the audit report that FIFA commissioned and intended to be confidential.

The accounts of governance of the IAAF (now called World Athletics), FIFA and CAF illustrate some of the key inter-linking issues for global sports and sporting organisations including corruption, doping, weak corporate governance and poor labour practices. Other documented issues such as human rights, poverty, sexual exploitation, human trafficking, and children, family and community rights, match-fixing, sustainable financing and money laundering (see Suurballe, 2008; Brackenridge et al., 2013; Reider-Gordon, 2014; Wilson, 2014; Transparency International, 2016)[2] have also led to the erosion of trust in the organisations' ability to manage sport in privately arranged governance systems. Since 'with no apparent legal oversight such regimes of global governance have appeared accountable to no one but their own internal procedure' (Foster, 2012), concerns about the effectiveness of self-regulation are aggravated by the almost non-existent regulation of sport organisations at the international and national levels. Nationally, sport regulation faces obstacles such as the sport organisations' relative power over many states and inter-state competitiveness. The extraterritorial global reach of sport activities hinders attempts by some governments to directly regulate sport and sport organisations; such attempts are often viewed with suspicion and even outright hostility by those organisations, sport officials and other states. Sport is therefore arguably governed by a self-regulatory system that provides almost no room for interventions by national laws and institutions that might be 'perceived as posing a threat to the autonomy of sporting institutions' (Casini, 2011, p. 27). However, as Jens Sejer Andersen, a director of Play the Game, an NGO for promoting ethical values in sport, noted:

> We have seen and documented so many instances of corruption, democratic deficiencies and sporting swindles, which can neither be solved by sports organizations' own ethical committees – which in reality function as bottles for delicate questions – nor by the Court of Arbitration for Sport (CAS) or the International Olympic Committee. There are too many opportunities for corruption and cheating in international sport. (Suurballe, 2008)

In addition to regulatory competence and legitimacy concerns are the issues of how to regulate and ensure the viability of a collective approach to regulation in cases such as sport where individuals share relational and solidarity signals. For example, while the WADA-imposed global ban on Russia applied to both sport federations and individual athletes (WADA, 2019), the IOC demurred a blanket ban on Russian athletes from the Rio 2016 Olympics and left the decision to individual transnational sport federations. The IOC insistence that it had 'balanced on the one hand, the desire and need for collective responsibility versus the right to individual justice of every individual athlete' (BBC, 2016) was controversial and widely condemned, including by WADA. The IAAF (World Athletics) was the only federation to ban Russian athletes from the 2016 Olympics, while some individual federations allegedly faced enormous pressure from Russian authorities to adopt different approaches. In contrast, the International Paralympics Committee imposed a blanket ban on Russian athletics from the 2016 Paralympic Games.

Clearly, CSR issues exist in transnational sport governance and need resolution. Since the problems persist despite increased and more widespread awareness of the importance of good governance and CSR, the next part of the chapter considers if there are linkages between the transnational sport organisations' regulatory structure and inadequate resolution of CSR issues.

10.3 TRANSNATIONAL SPORT REGULATORY STRUCTURE

Sport's global regulatory structure is projected in the concept of specialised 'sports law', although this has been described as 'a label for permanent self-regulation by international federations' (Siekmann, 2011, p. 6) that 'acts as a cloak for continued self-regulation for international sports federations [to prevent] intervention by sovereign actors' (Foster, 2003, p. 1). Globally, sport's regulatory structure is based on privately designed and implemented arrangements with the IOC and international federations at the apex, with implications for both international law and national law.

Internationally, sport is not regulated by multilateral institutions owing to a number of factors, including lack of provision for transnational NGOs in international law. Despite suggestions that non-state entities 'may[,] to a limited extent, be directly subject to rights and duties under international law' (Alford, 2011, p. 234), states are the subjects of classical international law[3] to the exclusion of entities such as MNEs, international sport federations and other transnational NGOs. Secondly, while the transnational reach of sport activities and international sport federations makes it difficult to attach them to specific countries, a state's regulatory, administrative and judicial jurisdiction is normally limited to matters and persons within its territory.[4] Thirdly, a multilateral treaty for sport regulation, including the establishment of a supranational authority, is theoretically possible, but its practicality is far-fetched since states have not demonstrated the willingness and ability to even take the initial steps towards such a regulatory infrastructure. This is partly because states' political capacity is a product of interstate relations involving regulators and non-state actors to be regulated (Börzel et al., 2010; Koutalakis et al., 2010), and even international co-ordination for discussing governance issues of transnational NGOs is not evident.

Another factor is the relative power of transnational NGOs such as FIFA, which is more economically and politically powerful than most countries (Blake, 2015). The more powerful that non-state actors like such organisations are, the more unlikely it is that regulation is going to emanate from multilateral activity. The corollary is that, in practice, only the more powerful countries can attempt to exercise a form of extraterritorial jurisdiction extending over those organisations. Examples can be drawn from the US and UK laws prohibiting bribery of foreign public officials (Witten et al., 2008–9, pp. 691–5; Darrough, 2010; Osuji, 2011). Nevertheless, the legitimacy of using the national law of powerful states to control global sport bodies is not uncontroversial, with concerns expressed, for instance, about overreaching extraterritorial jurisdiction and 'new legal imperialism' following the US criminal investigation, indictment and arrest of FIFA officials (Sopel, 2015).

The position in national legal systems is not very different from international law and multilateral practice. As Duval (2013, p. 827) observed, sport is a 'world apart, self-regulated by its own rules, and through its own political processes: a private society that sets its own guiding principles in apparent isolation of national legal systems'. The implications of the recognition, application and enforcement of sports law in regulating sport and sport governing bodies in both international law and national law can be seen in Figure 10.1, which shows that sport's global regulatory structure has at least six components.

The first element is the emergence of a body of privately formulated sport rules with features distinct from international law and national law. Using the label of

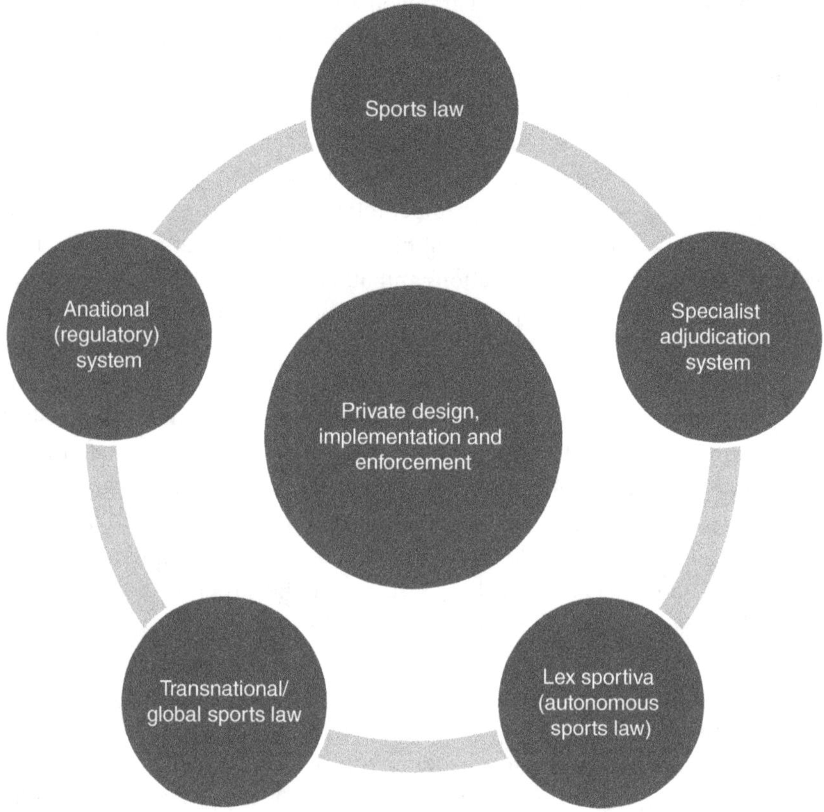

FIGURE 10.1 Sport regulation and enforcement

'sports law' is therefore not simply about 'how law in general interacts with the activity known as sport' but refers to 'an increasing body of law, which is specific to sport' (Opie, 2007, pp. 89–90). The Court of Arbitration for Sport (CAS) has similarly acknowledged the emergence of sports law, specifically noting that 'sports law has developed and consolidated along the years, particularly through the arbitral settlement of disputes, a set of unwritten legal principles'.[5]

The second element is the development and operation of an adjudication scheme that is separate from formal national and international judicial institutions through a system of tribunals with CAS as the ultimate authority. Generally, these tribunals are not answerable to any national or multilateral institution and their independent status has facilitated the development of rules and procedures that are widely accepted within the sport sector. Among other advantages of the uniquely designed rules and procedures are 'specialist tribunals … to utilise more easily a sports-sympathetic approach to the disputes coming before them' (James, 2013, p. 6). Consequently, CAS is now recognised as having evolved as 'a forum for the world's athletes and sports federations to resolve disputes through a single, independent, and accomplished sports adjudication body that is capable of consistently applying the rules of different sport organizations' (McLaren, 2000, p. 381).

The third component of sports law flows from the independent status of its adjudication institutions – this time from the executive and legislative branches of the organisations. The attempt to mirror separation of powers and judicial independence in modern constitutional democracies has enhanced the status of sports law before national and multilateral authorities. As the *Gundel* (1993)[6] case exemplifies, some questioned the independent status of CAS when it was originally set up by the IOC, but by 2003 the Swiss Federal Tribunal had upheld its independence and acknowledged that it was no more 'the vassal of the IOC'.[7]

The recognition of 'an autonomous law of sport' (Duval, 2013, p. 842) that projects sports law as a distinct 'legal discipline in its own right' (Opie, 2007, p. 90) is the fourth factor. Nonetheless, the distinctiveness and autonomy of sports law as a legal discipline is a subject of scholarly debates (Duval, 2013, p. 842). On the one hand, the narrow view that integrates sports law and the decisions of CAS (Nafziger, 2004, p. 3) is based on the argument that CAS formulates a 'unique body of law known as lex sportiva' and therefore sports law 'is limited to its original definition as a body of rules and principles derived from awards made by [CAS]' (Nafziger, 2010, pp. 3–4). The alternative and more dominant view, however, does not see a strong tie between sports law and decisions of CAS (de Oliveira, 2017) and, for instance, recognises custom as a source of sports law. Thus, Mitten (2010, p. 289) described sports law as 'an emerging body of international law with some similarities to lex mercatoria', while Kolev (2008, p. 57) argued that 'sports law is highly potential to become a world law similar to mercantile law'; CAS appears to have adopted this broader view in declaring sports law 'a sort of lex mercatoria for sports'.[8] Likewise, the European Court of Justice, which normally upholds sport customs, has apparently accepted the broader position in *Jyri Lehtonen*.[9]

The fifth aspect is the global application of a body of sports law, hence the recognition of sports law as a transnational law. The status and implications of sports law as transnational law are clearer if the meaning of the latter concept is explored. For a start, transnational law is defined variously as 'the study of legal phenomena, including law making processes, rules, and legal institutions, that affect or have the power to affect behaviours beyond a single state border' (Menkel-Meadow, 2011, p. 1), 'all law that has cross-border effect' (Hathaway, 2005, p. 473) and 'all law, which regulates actions or events that transcend national frontiers' (Jessup, 1956, p. 2). The corollary is the emergence of the notion of 'global sports law' described as 'a transnational autonomous legal order created by the global private institutions that govern international sport' (Foster, 2003, 2; Siekmann, 2012, 1–33) to underscore the transnational reach of sport's private regulatory structure.

The autonomous and transnational nature of sports law leads on to the final aspect of its regulatory structure, which is its autonomy from national regulatory and judicial authorities in a way that is similar to the status of transnational commercial law. Owing to the fact that 'lex mercatoria, the transnational law of economic transactions, is the most successful example of global law without a state' (Teubner, 1997, p. 23), by analogy, sports law is 'an anational legal system' (Kolev, 2008, p. 57) and 'global law without a state' (Foster, 2003, p. 2) that provides for its independence and leaves little room for national law intervention in sport-related matters (Foster, 2003, p. 1; Mitten, 2009, p. 9). Some have therefore concluded that global sports law 'implies a claim of immunity from national law' (Foster, 2003, p. 2) and 'de facto immunity of sports law from state court interference' (Hess and Kaps, 2015).

National courts largely respect sports law's autonomy and immunity from national law. The English courts, which normally enforce and refrain from tampering with decisions of sport tribunals,[10] exemplify this attitude. In *Flaherty v. National Greyhound Racing Club*, for instance, Baker LJ emphasised that 'it is not in the interest of sport … for the courts to seek to double guess regulating bodies … Sports regulating bodies ordinarily have unrivalled and practical knowledge of the particular sport that they are required to regulate.'[11] Along a similar path is the UK government with one-time sports minister Hugh Robertson believing 'very strongly that sport, not government, should run sport' (BBC, 2011). In 2011, the government confirmed 'that there is a legitimate role for the national governing body, working hand in hand with competition organisers, to ensure that appropriate and consistent checks and balances are in place to protect the overall financial integrity of the national game and its long-term viability' (BBC, 2011).

Clearly, prescriptive regulations from sources such as national governments and multilateral institutions that are external to transnational non-governmental business, sport, cultural and entertainment organisations may have legitimacy and other issues to contend with owing to the entrenched private governance systems. Moreover, studies have shown that prescriptive regulations can have limited effectiveness in different national (Lozano et al., 2008; Ho, 2013, pp. 375–6) and international (Zerk, 2006, pp. 69–72; Abbott and Snidal, 2009) contexts, leading to an emergent recognition of alternative regulatory strategies for CSR (Osuji, 2015). In the specific context of transnational non-governmental sport organisations, the chapter has already shown a lack of oversight from international law and national law. Owing to the necessity of exploring alternative regulatory strategies that balance the needs for autonomy and responsibility while enabling national law to fill regulatory vacuums in a more legitimate way, the next part considers CSR as an inventive interventionist regulation tool.

10.4 TRANSNATIONAL NGOS, CSR AND INVENTIVE INTERVENTIONISM

Inventive interventionism, which acknowledges regulatory roles for stakeholders, including those outside a state's territorial jurisdiction, can be utilised as a regulatory strategy for transnational non-governmental governance of business, sport, cultural and entertainment organisations. Being an 'analytical approach [that] proceeds on the assumption that CSR is both a product of the regulatory system and a phenomenon of business and can provide processes for the transmission and transplantation of domestic and international norms to businesses' (Osuji, 2015), inventive interventionism is a functional model for applying a global multi-stakeholder and multidimensional view of CSR at national and transnational spaces to resolve public governance challenges through enforceable substantive and procedural requirements such as regulatory outcomes, stakeholder empowerment, effective social disclosure and CSR-specific regulatory, administrative and independent bodies (Osuji, 2015).

An initial step in undertaking an inventive interventionist approach is apprehension of different elements in CSR and the need to resolve potential conflicts between them in advancing regulatory goals. In this regard, CSR can be, firstly, seen as 'a set of related mechanisms for aligning corporate behaviour with wider social and environmental goals, in which managerial, financial and regulatory aspects are combined in a mutually reinforcing way [as] a mechanism for stimulating organisational change' (Deakin and Hobbs, 2007, pp. 69–71). Secondly, inventive interventionism captures the need for the law to prop up CSR to achieve regulatory goals. The backdrop is the law's role in directing and ensuring the achievement of desired outcomes, including ethical orientations. The law's essential nature helps since '[b]eing lawful is not a choice we make or reject simply on our own [and y]ou can volunteer to avoid acting ethically, or to avoid even thinking about the topic' (Preston, 2010, pp. 259–60). This enables multidimensional, multi-stakeholder-oriented legal interventions that can operate, and have effect, at national, global or transnational levels. In other words, inventive interventionism promotes appropriate legal arrangements to support CSR and places it in an institutional capacity framework for effective exercise of legal powers of public and independent agencies and enforcement of stakeholder rights. It is context-specific and, as such, possible components of an inventive interventionist approach to regulating sport as exemplar transnational NGOs are outlined in Figure 10.2.

10.4.1 *CSR Definition in the Context of Transnational Non-governmental Governance*

The first component of inventive interventionism in transnational nongovernmental governance is a context-specific definition of CSR which requires, for example, specifying sport as a core CSR matter. A definition is necessary since it clarifies language which in turn helps regulators, regulatees and other persons in shaping their perceptions, assumptions, attitudes and behaviour (Baden and Harwood, 2013, pp. 621–4). Second, the legal definition needs to highlight the ethical fundamentals of CSR to prevent recourse to economic language and business case analysis that can

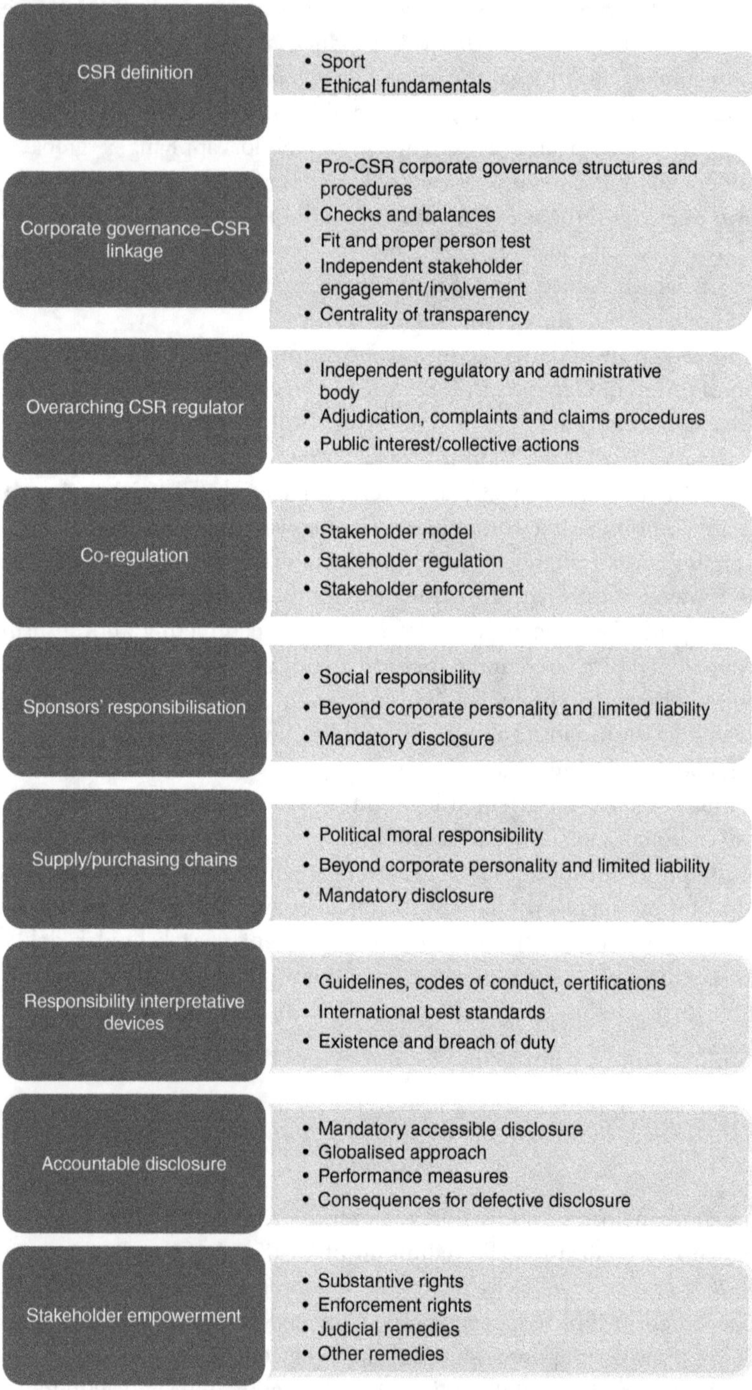

FIGURE 10.2 Inventive interventionist regulation of transnational non-governmental governance

promote thoughts, assumptions, principles and strategies that hinder the adoption and pursuit of desired ethical practices (Poruthiyil, 2013). This is particularly important in addressing doping, corruption, money laundering and other practices that require ethical reorientations.

These two steps are possible owing to CSR's flexible and contextualist nature, which allows jurisdictions to adopt suitable definitions for specific issues and goals (Osuji and Obibuaku, 2016). The adaptability of CSR to 'political, economic, and cultural context' (Ho, 2013, p. 388) is evident in national jurisdictions such as India where a statutory definition of CSR in the Companies Act 2013 has a lot to do with the country's socio-economic circumstances and needs. Schedule VII of the Companies Act 2013, for instance, delimits CSR to include 'eradicating extreme hunger and poverty' and 'contributing to the Prime Minister's National Relief Fund or any other fund set up by the Central Government or the State Government for socio-economic development and relief' to underscore the country's understanding of CSR and what its mission should include. While India is a national context-specific provision, a similar approach to transnational NGOs is both possible and useful owing to the peculiar issues these organisations present or are confronted with. The law can, for example, specify aspects of sport and sport governance as CSR matters and deploy CSR to address the challenges that the sector faces.

10.4.2 *Corporate Governance–CSR Linkage*

Partly owing to the governance issues that transnational NGOs are sometimes confronted with, an inventive interventionist approach identifies and emphasises corporate governance–CSR linkages in its regulatory schemes. The Richard Pound-led WADA Independent Commission, for example, reported that a former IAAF president, Lamine Diack, was 'responsible for organising and enabling the conspiracy and corruption that took place in the IAAF' and establishing 'an informal illegitimate governance structure' (WADA, 2016d). Recognition that the relationship between corporate governance and CSR is imperative for the existence, survival and welfare of corporations and other organisations, on the one hand, and society, on the other, also necessitates the explicit statement of their linkages. If CSR is supposed to advance societal good beyond the organisations undertaking it, then it requires appropriate governance structures, processes and procedures within those organisations. This is implicit from the description of CSR as

> a way of doing business whereby enterprises try to find a state of equilibrium between the need to achieve financial and developmental objectives and the social and environmental impact of their activities. It is a mode corporations use to achieve commercial success in ways that also honour the ethical, legal, as well as

> environmental and other societal expectations. It considers a corporation not just a self-centred profit-making entity, but also an integral part of the economy, society and environment. (Li, 2006, p. 346)

The CSR–corporate governance linkage is also reflected implicitly in the widely cited statement of Sir Adrian Cadbury in a foreword to *Corporate Governance: A Framework for Implementation* (Iskander and Chamlou, 2000). Cadbury explained that the concept of corporate governance 'is concerned with holding the balance between economic and social goals and between individual and communal goals. The corporate governance framework is there to encourage the efficient use of resources and equally to require accountability for their management and stewardship. The aim is to align as nearly as possible the interests of individuals, corporations and societies' (Iskander and Chamlou, 2000, p. vi). Arguably, social irresponsibility can be evidence of weak corporate governance with consequences for corporate reputation and performance. As the *OECD Guidelines for Multinational Enterprises*, for instance, confirmed, 'factors such as business ethics and corporate awareness of environmental and societal interests of the communities in which they operate can also have an impact on the reputation and long-term success of a company' (Organisation for Economic Co-operation and Development (OECD), 2011, p. 142).

Inventive interventionism therefore promotes CSR engagement through properly designed and implemented internal corporate governance structures and procedures (Harjoto and Jo, 2011) in transnational NGOs. To ensure that sport-specific CSR is promoted, this may include having adequate checks and balance of power arrangements, fit and proper persons tests, independent stakeholder engagement, and stakeholder involvement in governance structures, decision-making and consultations. These suggestions promote transparency as a guiding principle and 'an essential element of good corporate governance [that] gives investors and others a means to hold companies to account' (Department for Business and Innovation (DBIS), 2014, p. 4).

10.4.3 *Overarching CSR Regulator*

The substance of inventive interventionism includes the establishment of an independent regulatory and administrative body and efficient adjudication process for CSR (Osuji, 2015). The transnational nature of NGOs may not be an impediment to setting up a national CSR oversight body as analogy can be drawn from the existence of national agencies dealing with trans-border matters such as human trafficking and human rights in the digital media. A public or independent body can formulate, issue and adopt standards, guidelines and CSR-related public procurement policies. It can establish monitoring, inspection and verification procedures, and impose sanctions in collaboration with public agencies and private organisations. The body's remit can include adjudication processes such as complaints and claims procedures, public interest and collective actions by public agencies, public interest groups and private persons, and award of injunctive orders, damages, apology and other remedies. National legal systems can employ these tools for activities and persons operating within their territorial boundaries, even if they are equally transnational.

10.4.4 *Co-regulation*

Owing to the prominence of voluntariness in the emergence and operation of CSR, inventive interventionism is designed to ensure effective co-regulation among public agencies, NGOs and stakeholders. Regulatory collaboration as a component of an inventive interventionist approach to regulating transnational NGOs can be justified on several grounds. The first is the realisation that stakeholder involvement is essential for a 'shared ethical approach' (Hodges, 2016, p. 3) in regulating fields in which those organisations function and where ethical values are necessary. The foundation of an activity such as sport can be undermined if unethical practices can prevail. Second, the understanding that 'compliant behaviour cannot be guaranteed by regulation alone and that ethical culture in business is an essential component that should be promoted and not undermined' (Hodges, 2016, p. 3) is gaining traction. Sport, for instance, can be successful with integrity in its governance systems and competitions, but when trust is undermined, the consequences for stakeholders can be far-reaching.

As a corollary, the third factor is 'that regulatory and other systems need to be designed to provide evidence of business commitment to ethical behaviour, on which trust can be based' (Hodges, 2016, p. 3). In fields such as sport, stakeholder collaboration is essential to upholding ethical commitments. The fourth justification for co-regulation arises from the fact that a number of developments, including globalisation, have opened up both national and transnational regulatory spaces to a variety of actors. Since the recent decades, it is increasingly accepted that '[t]he era in which nations rule the world is over [since] three groups have joined nations as important global players: transnational corporations, international organizations, and special interest groups' (Morss, 1991, p. 55), which suggests the need for integrating the governance role of transnational NGOs within an inventive interventionist regulatory framework.

10.4.5 *Sponsors' Responsibilisation*

Inventive interventionism includes recognising external sponsors of transnational NGOs as a key co-regulation stakeholder group. External sponsors, which are often corporate entities such as MNEs with ties to national jurisdictions as home or host states, are vital to the activities of transitional non-governmental business, sport, cultural and entertainment organisations. For instance, FIFA earns billions of dollars from direct sponsorships, broadcasting, marketing and licensing rights (Sargeant, 2015), but its recent corruption scandal and the arrests it occasioned 'left sponsors with an inevitable dilemma: should they wait and hope it will blow over, cut and run, or try to influence change?' (Allan-Jones and Loxton, 2015).

An inventive interventionist approach will encourage sponsoring firms and organisations to appreciate that CSR 'involves the exercise of social responsibility in how profits are made' (McBarnet, 2007) and not merely philanthropy or marketing. Rather, sponsors need to act on the basis that CSR is a leverage-based responsibility that 'arises from an organisation's ability to influence the actions of other actors through its relationships, regardless of whether the impacts of those other actors' actions can be traced to the organizations' (Wood, 2012, p. 64). This type of responsibilisation is, for example, implicit from the stipulation in the United Nations Global Compact 2004 (Berliner and Prakash, 2012) that firms need 'to work against corruption in all its forms' (Principle 10). Wilks (2013, p. 197) similarly observed that 'the CSR phenomenon illustrates, and provides evidence for corporate political power'.

How external sponsors of transnational NGOs can be made to exercise responsibilities as 'most powerful citizens' obtaining 'all the benefits of citizenship' (Kercher, 2007, p. 3) is the question. Inventive interventionism will prod sponsors to be proactive co-regulators by linking firms closely to transnational NGOs such as sporting governing bodies, their officials and persons or organisations they do business or partner with. To establish this linkage, it is important to acknowledge that legal boundaries of responsibility cannot hinder CSR-related obligations. While concepts such as corporate personality and limited liability[12] can insulate firms from other persons' activities (Easterbrook and Fischel, 1991; Foster, 2008), CSR is not constrained by, and can require moral responsibility beyond, such limitations of legal responsibility. This element, which is evinced by the Australian James Hardie cases[13] triggered essentially by a parent company's acknowledgement of responsibility for its two subsidiaries' asbestos-related liabilities (Livas, 2004; Mahne, 2004; Nolan, 2004), justifies sponsors' social responsibility in sport matters.

Disclosure requirements are another method of establishing sponsors' linkage to transnational NGOs. Again, this is not impeded by corporate personality and limited liability, as the James Hardie cases also show. In promising to set up a trust fund for its subsidiaries' liabilities, the parent company attempted to 'deflect attention from a controversial issue which might otherwise attract undesirable publicity' (Hargovan, 2009, p. 988) and 'influence the market'.[14] An inventive interventionist approach can therefore mandate disclosures by external sponsors that can include their association with transnational NGOs, their officials and other stakeholders and how proactive they are in promoting ethical values. This will directly link the sponsors' corporate reputation to other organisations and persons they associate with. Inventive interventionism-based disclosure requirements will provide a clear path for corporate decision-making, as otherwise the dilemma is 'what can sponsors do to avoid their own brands being tarnished by association or, better still, how can sponsors use it as an opportunity to highlight the best of their own brand values?' (Allan-Jones and Loxton, 2015).

10.4.6 *Supply/Purchasing Chain Responsibility*

An inventive interventionist approach can include responsibilisation of the supply and purchasing chains of transnational NGOs, which have attracted publicity recently, particularly in relation to human rights and labour standards. For example, following concerns about the living and working conditions of the mostly migrant workers working on stadiums and other construction projects across Qatar in preparation for the 2022 World Cup, the host government commissioned a law firm to conduct investigations (Stephenson, 2015). Russia's preparation for the 2018 World Cup also attracted similar concerns (Luhn, 2017).

Like the case of external sponsors, using inventive interventionism to impose responsibility on, and for, supply and purchasing chains reflects political moral responsibility that is now arguably recognised in CSR. An example is *Kasky* v. *Nike*[15] where 'sweatshop' allegations about South East Asian factories prompted Nike to issue defensive public statements (Mokhiber and Weissman, 1999; Scherer and Smid, 2000; Kazer and Williams, 2005). Even though it was not legally responsible for the factories' activities, Nike needed to react to reputation-damaging criticisms of its perceived failure to exercise political moral responsibility over completely independent legal entities mostly based abroad. The law can require this type of responsibility through disclosure requirements, as exemplified by emergent transparency provisions against modern slavery such as the UK Modern Slavery Act 2015, which ensures that '[o]rganisations have a legal duty to drive out poor practices in their business and a moral duty to influence and incentivise continuous improvements in supply chains' (Syder, 2016, p. 22).

10.4.7 *Responsibility Interpretative Devices*

Since CSR-related obligations potentially have different dimensions, including divergence from usual legal boundaries of responsibilities, provisions for CSR responsibilities should be clear to stakeholders. Inventive interventionism therefore supports the use of guidelines, codes of conduct and certification schemes to promote CSR and provide 'an efficient fluid interpretative device' for regulators and stakeholders (Osuji, 2015). It may help to reference the existence, elements and breach of legal duties in those interpretative devices and ensure that stakeholders, including transnational NGOs, their officials, sponsors and supply and purchasing chains, acknowledge and apply industry and international best standards. Such explicit references are 'not without significance'[16] as a Netherlands court confirmed in relation to commitments to the *OECD Principles of Corporate Governance* (OECD, 1999).

Interpretative devices can be designed, issued and monitored by public, independent or third-party agencies in accordance with industry and international best standards. For example, anti-corruption, financial clarity, accounting and auditing provisions can reference initiatives such as ISO 37001, the Global Reporting Initiative's G3 Guidelines 2006, the FTSE4Good Index, Countering Bribery Criteria 1997 and the ICC's Rules of Conduct on Bribery 1999. Compliance with principles, guidelines and standards indicated in interpretative devices can, for instance, be used to determine public procurement and participation in public–private partnerships.

10.4.8 *Accountable Disclosure*

Disclosure obligations are another component of inventive interventionism that can be applied to a CSR regulatory scheme for transnational NGOs. As suggested earlier, disclosure requirements may be imposed on, for example, external sponsors and the supply and purchasing chains of transnational NGOs. Mandatory disclosure is a middle ground approach to regulation that may appear less 'contentious' (Ferran, 2003, p. 497) and more legitimate, including in relation to transnational governance matters. It can support suitable industry due diligence schemes such as the apparel industry's factory/supplier disclosure scheme (Doorey, 2011) owing to disclosure's deterrent role against socially irresponsible practices through its link to reputation (Osuji, 2012).

Since CSR-related disclosure 'is primarily driven by a desire for accountability' (Bouten et al., 2011, p. 189), inventive interventionism supports mandatory and accountable disclosure on a globalised basis unconstrained by territorial boundaries (Osuji, 2015) and to be based on credible, objective and assessable performance measures with legal consequences for defective disclosure (Osuji, 2012). Disclosures need to be visible to stakeholders and interest groups in accessible forms and through mass participation outlets to facilitate a communicative role since stakeholders need to be able to catch sight of relevant policies and activities to associate firms and organisations with social responsibility and responsiveness.

10.4.9 *Stakeholder Empowerment*

Stakeholder empowerment is a concomitant to co-regulation, dimensions of responsibilisation and disclosure obligations and, to this extent, inventive interventionism promotes a range of substantive and enforcement rights such as verification of disclosures, administrative complaints, protective statutory torts, judicial redress and remedies for stakeholders potentially exercisable against organisations and individuals tasked with responsibilities under a CSR regulatory framework (Osuji, 2015). Judicial remedy is particularly important owing to the potential regulatory role of litigation and private remedies in controlling the behaviour (Funk, 2011) of organisations and persons charged with responsibilities. It also assists in promoting corrective and distributive justice among stakeholders as envisaged by a regulatory scheme.

In the absence of stakeholder empowerment, disclosure and other CSR regulatory tools may be inadequate for promoting desired goals and encouraging appropriate conduct from responsibilised organisations and persons. For example, *Kasky* v. *Nike*, discussed in Section 10.4.6, was brought under Californian unfair competition and false advertising legislation that allowed private claims. Although it was ultimately settled out of court, the case compelled Nike to improve labour standards in its supply chains and the quality of its social reporting (Nike, 2004; Muchlinski, 2009; Yandle et al., 2011). Another lesson from *Kasky* v. *Nike* is possible polarity between CSR-related claims and actual practices arising when 'organisations create symbolic structures as visible efforts [that] do not guarantee substantive change' (Edelman et al., 1991, p. 75). While some attribute legal ambiguity as a causative factor for symbolic compliance (Edelman et al., 1991), the nature of interpersonal relationships and interactions within and outside organisations can provide institutional settings for organisational and individual attitudes to rules. Hence, the chapter next considers the need for addressing relational and solidarity signals in transnational NGOs.

10.5 INVENTIVE INTERVENTIONISM AND RELATIONAL AND SOLIDARITY SIGNALS IN TRANSNATIONAL NGOS

While shared bonds in transnational NGOs can include national, ethnic and geographical origins, family and friendship, several cases show that informal relational and solidarity signals from those bonds can generate judgements and encumber the establishment of an organisational culture that promotes compliance with formal and ethical rules. For example, the Report of WADA Independent Observers into the 2016 Rio Olympic Games catalogued an array of irregularities in doping tests with secrecy, loyalty and solidarity-related issues occluding the identification of 'factors that influence the use of doping substances and methods' and those for fostering 'future prevention and doping control' and 'ethical behaviour in sport' (WADA, 2016a).

The experience of Yulia Stepanova (née Rusanova), whose whistle-blowing led to the blanket ban of Russian track and field athletes from the 2016 Rio Olympics, is another example. In an implied response to solidarity signals from her Russian nationality, Ms Stepanova insisted: 'I don't consider myself a traitor, I didn't reveal any scientific secrets [and] I simply revealed the shameful truth, which our country doesn't want to confront, and the only reason I told the truth about it all, was to try and put a stop to it' (Ash, 2016, n.p.). In other words, solidarity signals prevented Russian nationals from reporting or discouraging doping to protect the country's reputation. Some Chinese athletes allegedly follow a similar nationalist ideology that impedes rule compliance and fairness in sport competitions. In this regard, a Chinese studies expert explained:

> For a long time, no individualism has existed in Chinese society. Everyone belongs to the state and has to obey to the nation. The interests of nation and the state always come first when social members make their decisions. This ideology is also reflected in sport. To guarantee the final success of the games, the team manager has the right to decide which player is going to play and win for next matches ... [The athletes'] job is to win medals and serve the nation. Emotionally, the sports teams are their second homes and they have to listen to their coaches, managers, who play the roles like their parents. (Suurballe, 2008, n.p.)

FIFA is the fourth example owing to the perception that its dominant corporate governance system is one of a 'football family' and 'solidarity-based' patronage system of exchange of favours (Jorge, 2014, p. 13). Therefore, FIFA's corporate governance system is indicative of neo-patrimonialism occurring when

> the chief executive [of an organisation] maintains authority through personal patronage, rather than through ideology or law ... [R]elationships of loyalty and dependence pervade a formal political and administrative system and leaders occupy bureaucratic offices less to perform public service than to acquire personal wealth and status. The distinction between private and public interests is purposely blurred .... [P]ersonal relationships ... constitute the foundation and superstructure of political institutions. (Bratton and van de Walle, 1994, pp. 458–9)

Possible explanations are varied for these relational and solidarity signals, with adverse consequences for rules and regulatory standards. First, from institutional theory is the institutional role of informal signals in line with the definition of institutions as 'formal and informal procedures, routines, norms and conventions embedded in the organizational structure of the polity or political economy' (Hall and Taylor, 1996, p. 940). This suggests the existence of informal signals in social relationships that can be interpreted by social actors to influence and control the behaviour of others, even when it would be contrary to rules and regulatory standards. For example, in relation to corruption as 'the misuse of public office, public resources or public responsibility for private – personal or group – gain' (Szeftel, 2000, p. 427), the consequences of informal signals have shown that 'corruption is universally disapproved yet universally present' (Hess and Dunfee, 2000, p. 595).

Another explanation from actor–network theory and organisational studies relates to interpersonal relationships and interactions. Actor–network theory confirms that society is a complex and fluid diversified collection of relationships and alliances with consequences for behaviour and regulation (Latour, 2005). Organisational studies similarly show that a social cocoon for overt or covert 'normalisation' of corruption can arise through the mechanisms of rationalisation, socialisation and institutionalisation (Ashforth and Anand, 2003; Pinto et al., 2008; Spicer, 2009; Campbell and Göritz, 2014).

The third explanation is from the concept of group polarisation, which suggests that shared bonds can affect individuals even to the extent of exhibiting 'extreme' behaviours. Group polarisation theory is that '[w]hen people find themselves in groups of like-minded types, they are especially likely to move to extremes. And when such groups include authorities who tell group members what to do, or put them into certain social roles, very bad things can happen' (Sustein, 2009, p. 2). Of particular relevance to transnational NGOs where shared bonds abound is the fact that 'polarisation is all the greater and all the most likely when people are attached by bonds of affection, commonality or solidarity' (Levmore and Nussbaum, 2011, p. 2).

The final explanation is that, in interpreting social interactions, informal signals may reference personal and collective attributes mainly through attitude and motivation (Dijksterhuis and Aarts, 2010) that link rule compliance to perceptions of regulatory environments. As 'a relatively enduring organisation of beliefs, feelings, and behavioural tendencies towards socially significant objects, groups, events or symbols' (Hogg and Vaughan, 2005, p. 150), attitude can determine how individual actors interact with others and interpret rules. Similarly, motivation ensures that solidarity relationships based on shared norms, trust, identity and objectives can exist in horizontal interactions, even in regulated environments (Etienne, 2013). An actor's motivation can lead to postures that reflect the actor's commitment to formal rules, or resistance to, disengagement from or game-playing with those rules, owing to the fact that motivational postures are

> sets of beliefs and attitudes that sum up how individuals feel about and wish to position themselves in relation to another social entity . . . Postures are subjective – they bind together the cognitive, emotional and behavioural components of attitude. They provide the narrative within which the authority's message is given meaning. They have coherence for the self and are socially acceptable to significant others. (Braithwaite, 2009, p. 20)

Likewise, Selznick (2002, p. 101) explained that 'an "organisational culture" [is] a framework within which the main goals of the enterprise are pursued' and has both formal and informal determinants. While awareness of the normative and substantive importance of informality in governance is consequently increasing (see Christiansen and Neuhold, 2012), subjugating informal relational and solidarity signals in transnational NGOs is pertinent since they can hinder the institution and implementation of CSR. These signals are salient considerations in establishing and sustaining an auspicious organisational culture for 'a corporate conscience' which 'is created when values that transcend narrow self-interest are built into the practice and structure of the enterprise' (Selznick, 2002, p. 101). Inventive interventionism therefore advocates setting up of structures and procedures to enable universal ethical standards to prevail over conflicting informal relational and solidarity signals in organisations. This requires the need to proactively monitor, prevent, detect, report and deal with issues arising from relational and solidarity signals and their effects on individual behaviour and organisational culture and practices.

One possible method for tackling informal signals in transnational NGOs is individual and collective responsibilisation that recognises relational and solidarity groups as informal institutions. This will also enhance individual and organisational co-regulation and regulatory engagement capability within groups. In this regard, regulators will need to create primary rules that are predicated on individual and collective responsibilities for rule compliance through monitoring, detection, evidence and reporting and may then compel individuals and groups to establish secondary rules on peer interactions, as well as attitude to and compliance with primary rules.

This sort of participant regulation once occurred in the UK A level examinations when the regulator, AQA, on its website, instructed candidates to report cases of cheating (defined as unfair advantage) to a teacher upon being aware of the circumstances. In one incident, a member of a WhatsApp revision chat group, who sat a sociology examination earlier owing to a timetable clash, posted three out of its four questions on the morning of the day the examination was ordinarily scheduled. Later, AQA disqualified some members of the WhatsApp group who failed to notify teachers as instructed (Rosney, 2016). The WhatsApp chat group was regarded as an 'informal institution' providing both challenges to and opportunities for regulation, including co-regulation by its participants. The challenges would include secrecy and disguise that hinder the primary regulator's ability to monitor rule compliance, investigate and detect breaches, and locate evidence or proof of unfair advantage. Opportunities, however, existed for co-regulation through responsibilisation of chat group members for monitoring, detecting, reporting and providing evidence of cheating. Transnational non-governmental governance arguably provides similar opportunities that can be utilised for regulatory purposes owing to the key stakeholders' relationships and interactions.

A second method of overcoming conflicting relational and solidarity signals in transnational NGOs is through provisions that enable and protect whistle-blowing. The backdrop is that '[t]he debate on morality whistleblowing centres on the conflict between the duty of loyalty to the firm or organizations in which one works and the liberty to speak out against wrongdoing' (Lindblom, 2007, p. 415). The case of Russian athlete Ms Stepanova typifies the need for whistle-blowing provisions and protecting whistle-blowers. Prior to submitting secret recordings of fellow athletes, officials and doctors to a German filmmaker for a documentary broadcast in 2014, Ms Stepanova wrote a ten-page confession which WADA ignored. WADA also failed to act on several letters by Vitaly, Ms Stepanova's husband and an employee of Russia's anti-doping agency (Rusada). Ms Stepanova, her husband and her son now live in a secret location in the United States (Ash, 2016, n.p.).

The case demonstrates the need for provisions to encourage whistle-blowing and to establish proper channels for raising concerns, providing confidentiality of sources, facilitating appropriate responses and enabling post-whistle-blowing protection. Nonetheless, self-designed and implemented whistle-blowing procedures have been found to be largely ineffective instruments for promoting ethical values and societal good within organisations (Pittroff, 2014). Some studies suggest that internal procedures can present actors with moral dilemmas that obstruct disclosures of corrupt, unethical and unlawful practices (Lindblom, 2007; Knoll and van Dick, 2013; Paeth, 2013; Andrade, 2015; Hoffman and Schwartz, 2015), making some independent oversight necessary. An inventive interventionist approach consequently requires the establishment of truly independent, externally guaranteed and effective whistle-blowing structures and procedures for transnational NGOs and stakeholders. In the case of sport organisations, for example, stakeholders may include athletes, officials, employees, sponsors, and supply and purchasing chains.

10.6 CONCLUSIONS

This chapter builds on inventive interventionism (Osuji, 2015) to propose a regulated CSR model for transnational non-governmental business, sport, cultural and entertainment organisations to tackle the exponentially increasing ethical and governance issues in some organisations which existing private and self-regulatory systems appear unsuited for. Owing to institutional and governance voids in international law; lack of supranational authority, political incapacity and legitimacy; and legal imperialism concerns about prescriptive national regulations, a CSR-based inventive interventionist model seems a more uncontentious and viable alternative regulation for transnational NGOs. Inventive interventionism provides room for co-regulation between public and private actors through limited government intervention, proactive stakeholder involvement and reasonable levels of non-governmental autonomy and self-regulation. Its indirect approach can facilitate the achievement of regulatory goals in an efficient and effective manner.

Focusing on sport, the chapter provides original suggestions for effective application of inventive interventionism by national authorities over organisations and activities with transnational flavour. It proposes enforceable substantive and procedural components of inventive interventionist regulation that include context-specific CSR definition, explicit provisions for corporate governance–CSR linkages, an overarching CSR regulatory body, recognition of, and provisions for, responsibilisation and co-regulation to be exercised particularly by external sponsors and the supply and purchasing chains of transnational NGOs, formulation of interpretative devices such as guidelines, codes of conduct and certification schemes, accountable disclosure by responsibilised organisations and individuals, and stakeholder empowerment through enforcement rights and remedies.

By drawing on inventive interventionism, the chapter offers novel solutions to the problem of conflicting demands and goals arising from informal relational and solidarity signals, which can impede rule compliance and the effectiveness of regulatory schemes for transnational NGOs. Proceeding on the basis that these signals are informal institutions that provide governance challenges and opportunities, the chapter uniquely proposes individual and collective responsibilisation that facilitates co-regulation and regulation engagement by stakeholders within groups. It also underlines the need for provision of independent and externally guaranteed whistle-blowing procedures as well as protection of whistle-blowers. This is to ensure that formal structures and rules are accompanied by appropriate attitudes to secure real, and not merely symbolic, compliance.

The chapter therefore contributes fresh insights to CSR, corporate governance and transnational regulation, particularly in relation to NGOs. It makes the case for inventive interventionism to facilitate the application of ethical standards in such organisations through appropriate rule design, implementation, structures and procedures. The unique sets of proposals for an inventive interventionist approach to transnational non-governmental business, sport, cultural and entertainment organisations provide a viable outlet for using CSR to fill regulatory vacuums existing in international law and national legal systems.

NOTES

1. *Olo*, 15 CR 0252 (RJD) (RML) of 20 May 2015. www.justice.gov/opa/file/450211/download.
2. See also Resolution of the Council and of the Representatives of the Governments of the Member States, meeting within the Council, of 21 May 2014 on the European Union Work Plan for Sport (2014–2017) (2014/C 183/03).
3. *Anglo-Iranian Oil Company Case (UK* v. *Iran)* (1952) ICJ 93.
4. *British Property in Spanish Morocco (Spain* v. *The United Kingdom)*, 1925, 2, UNRIAA, 636, 641–2 (Judge Huber); *Trail Smelter Case*, 1941, 2, UNRIAA, [1165].
5. *AEK Athens and SK Slavia Prague* v. *UEFA*, CAS 98/200 Award of 1999, Digest of CAS Awards II, 1998–2000.
6. *Gundel* v. *Fed. Equestre Int'l*, CAS 92/63, Award of 1993, Digest of CAS Awards I 1986–98.
7. *A & B* v. *IOC and FIS* 4P.267/2002; 4P.268/2002; 4P.269/2002, Award of 2003, 3 Digest of CAS Awards 2004, 674–95.
8. *AEK Athens and SK Slavia Prague* v. *UEFA*, CAS 98/200 Award of 1999, Digest of CAS Awards II, 1998–2000.
9. *Jyri Lehtonen and others* v. *Fédération Royale Belge des Sociétés de basketball ASBL* [2000] Case C-176/96.
10. See *Flaherty* v. *National Greyhound Racing Club* [2005] EWCA Civ 1117; *Stretford* v. *The Football Association* [2006] EWHC 479 (Ch).

11. *Flaherty* v. *National Greyhound Racing Club* [2005] EWCA Civ 1117 [19–20] (Baker LJ).
12. *Salomon* v. *Salomon & Co.* [1897] AC 22; *Williams* v. *Natural Life Health Foods* [1998] 1 WLR 830, 835 (Lord Steyn).
13. *Australian Securities & Investments Commission* v. *Hellicar & Ors* [2012] HCA17; *Shafron* v. *Australian Securities & Investments Commission* [2012] HCA 18.
14. *Australian Securities and Investments Commission* v. *Macdonald (No. 12)* (2009) 259 ALR 116, 133–4 (Gzell J).
15. 27 Cal. 4th 939, 946, 45 P.3d 243, 247, 119 Cal. Rptr 2d 296 (Cal. 2002).
16. *Batco Tobacco*, NJ 1980, 71 [6] (Court of Appeal of Amsterdam, 21 June 1979).

REFERENCES

Abbott, K. W. and Snidal, D. (2009). Strengthening international regulation through new governance: overcoming the orchestration deficit. *Vanderbilt Journal of Transnational Law*, **42**, 501–78.

Alford, R. P. (2011). Apportioning responsibility among joint tortfeasors for international law violations. *Pepperdine Law Review*, 38(2), 233–55.

Allan-Jones, A. and Loxton, K. (2015). Footballing lesson. 6 July. www.intellectualproperty magazine.com/trademark/footballing-lesson-110063.htm.

Andrade, J. A. (2015). Reconceptualising whistleblowing in a complex world. *Journal of Business Ethics*, **128**, 321–35.

Ash, L. (2016). 100 women 2016: Russian doping whistleblower gives rare interview. www .bbc.co.uk/news/world-europe–38253541.

Ashforth, B. E. and Anand, V. (2003). The normalization of corruption in organizations. *Research in Organizational Behaviour*, **25**, 1–52.

Baden, D. and Harwood, I. A. (2013). Terminology matters: a critical exploration of corporate social responsibility terms. *Journal of Business Ethics*, **116**, 615–27.

BBC (2011). Government tells English football: change or be changed. 12 October. www .bbc.co.uk/sport/0/football/15275218.

BBC (2014). Russian doping claims: 99% of athletes guilty, German TV alleges. 4 December. www.bbc.co.uk/sport/athletics/30324812.

BBC (2015a). Lamine Diack, ex-athletics chief investigated in corruption inquiry. 2 November. www.bbc.co.uk/sport/athletics/34721317.

BBC (2015b). FIFA corruption: Swiss banks 'reported possible money laundering'. 17 June. www.bbc.com/news/world-europe-33163918.

BBC (2015c). FIFA corruption crisis: key questions answered. 7 June. www.bbc.co.uk/news/ world-europe–3289706.

BBC (2015d). Chuck Blazer secretly co-operated with FIFA investigation from 2011. 16 June. www.bbc.co.uk/sport/0/football/33145539.

BBC (2016). Rio Olympics 2016: Russia not given blanket ban by IOC. 24 July. www.bbc.co.uk /sport/olympics/36878983.

Bean, B. W. (2016). An interim essay on FIFA's World Cup of corruption: the desperate need for international corporate governance standards at FIFA. *ILSA Journal of International and Comparative Law*, **22**(2), 367–92.

Berliner, D. and Prakash, A. (2012). From norms to programs: the United Nations global compact and global governance. *Regulation and Governance*, **6**, 149–66.
Blake, P. (2015). FIFA scandal: why the US is policing a global game. 27 May. www.bbc.co.uk/news/world-us-canada–32889845.
Blake, H. and Calvert, J. (2015). *The Ugly Game: The Corruption of FIFA and the Qatari Plot to Buy the World Cup*. New York: Scribner.
Börzel, T. A., Hofmann, T., Panke, D. and Sprungk, C. (2010). Obstinate and inefficient: why member states do not comply with European Law. *Comparative Political Studies*, **43**(11), 1363–90.
Bouten, L., Everaert, P., Van Liedekerke, L., De Moor, L. and Christiaens, J. (2011). Corporate social responsibility reporting: a comprehensive picture. *Accounting Forum*, **35**, 187–204.
Brackenridge, C. H., Palmer-Felgate, S., Rhind, D., Hills, L., Kay, T., Tiivas, A., Faulkner, L. and Lindsay, I. (2013). *Child Exploitation and the FIFA World Cup: A Review of Risks and Protective Interventions*. Uxbridge: Brunel University London & Oak Foundation.
Braithwaite, V. (2009). *Defiance in Taxation and Governance: Resisting and Dismissing Authority in a Democracy*. Cheltenham, UK: Edward Elgar.
Bratton, M. and van de Walle, N. (1994). Neo-patrimonial regimes and political transition in Africa. *World Politics*, **XLVI**, 453–89.
Campbell, J. and Göritz, A. S. (2014). Culture corrupts! A qualitative study of organizational culture in corrupt organizations. *Journal of Business Ethics*, **120**, 291–311.
Casini, L. (2011). The making of a lex sportiva by the Court of Arbitration for Sport. *German Law Journal*, **12**(5), 1317–40.
Christiansen, T. and Neuhold, C. (2012). *International Handbook on Informal Governance*. Cheltenham, UK: Edward Elgar.
Conn, D. (2017). *The Fall of the House of FIFA: The Multimillion-Dollar Corruption at the Heart of Global Soccer*. New York: Nation Books.
Darrough, M. N. (2010). The FCPA and the OECD convention: some lessons from the U.S. experience. *Journal of Business Ethics*, **93**, 255–76.
Deakin, S. and Hobbs, R. (2007). False dawn for CSR? Shifts in regulatory policy and the response of the corporate and financial sectors in Britain. *Corporate Governance*, **15**(1), 68–76.
de Oliveira, L. V. P. (2017). *Lex sportiva* as the contractual governing law. *The International Sports Law Journal*, **17**, 101–16.
Department for Business and Innovation (DBIS). (April 2014). *Transparency & Trust: Enhancing the Transparency of UK Company Ownership and Increasing Trust in UK Business. Government Response*. www.gov.uk/government/uploads/system/uploads/attachment_data/file/304297/bis-14-672-transparency-and-trust-consultation-response.pdf.
Dijksterhuis, A. and Aarts, H. (2010). Goals, attention, and (un)consciousness. *Annual Review of Psychology*, **61**, 467–90.
Doorey, D. J. (2011). The transparent supply chain: from resistance to implementation at Nike and Levi-Strauss. *Journal of Business Ethics*, **103**, 587–603.
Duval, A. (2013). Lex sportiva: a playground for transnational law. *European Law Journal*, **19** (6), 822.
Easterbrook, F. H. and Fischel, D. R. (1991). *The Economic Structure of Corporate Law*. Cambridge, MA: Harvard University Press.
Edelman, L., Petterson, S., Chambliss, E. and Erlanger, H. (1991). Legal ambiguity and the politics of compliance: affirmative action officers' dilemma. *Law & Policy*, **13**(1), 73–97.
Edwards, P. (2020). African football body CAF in disarray, audit reveals. 13 February. www.bbc.com/sport/africa/51478837.

Esposito, C. (2016). A red card for FIFA: corruption and scandal in the world's foremost sports association. *Richmond Journal of Global Law & Business*, **16**(1), 45–60.

Etienne, J. (2013). Ambiguity in relational signals in regulator–regulatee relationships. *Regulation & Governance*, 7(1), 30–47.

Ferran, E. (2003). The role of the shareholder in internal corporate governance: enabling shareholders to make better-informed decisions. *European Business Organization Law Review*, 4(4), 491–516.

Foster, K. (2003). Is there a global sports law? *Entertainment and Sports Law Journal*, **2**(1), 1–18.

Foster, K. (2012). Global administrative law: the next step for global sports law? *Sport and the Law Journal*, **19**(1), 45–51.

Foster, N. (2008). Personal civil liability of company officers for workplace torts. *Torts Law Journal*, **16**, 20–68.

Funk, W. (2011). Regulation by litigation: not so bad? *Regulation and Governance*, **5**, 275–85.

Gill, S., Adelus, E. and de Abreu Duarte, F. (2019). Whose game? FIFA, corruption and the challenge of global governance. *European Journal of International Law*, **30**(3), 1041–66.

Hall, P. A. and Taylor, R. C. R. (1996). Political science and the three new institutionalisms. *Political Studies*, **44**, 936–57.

Hargovan, A. (2009). Australian Securities and Investments Commission v MacDonald [No 11]: corporate governance lessons from James Hardie. *Melbourne University Law Review*, **33**, 984–1021.

Harjoto, M. A. and Jo, H. (2011). Corporate governance and CSR nexus. *Journal of Business Ethics*, **101**(1), 45–67.

Hathaway, O. A. (2005). Between power and principle: an integrated theory of international law. *University of Chicago Law Review*, **72**(2), 469–536.

Hess, B. and Kaps, F. (2015). Claudia Pechstein and SV Wilhelmshaven: two German higher regional courts challenge the Court of Arbitration for Sport. Conflict of Laws.net: News and Views in Private International Law. http://conflictoflaws.net/2015/pechstein-and-sv-wilhelmshaven-two-german-higherregional-courts-challenge-the-independence-of-the-court-of-arbitration-for-sport/.

Hess, D. and Dunfee, T. W. (2000). Fighting corruption: a principled approach. *Cornell International Law Journal*, **33**(3), 593–626.

Ho, V. H. (2013). Beyond regulation: a comparative look at state-centric corporate social responsibility and the law in China. *Vanderbilt Journal of Transnational Law*, **46**, 375–442.

Hodges, C. (2016). *Ethical Business Regulation: Understanding the Evidence*. London: Department for Business Innovation & Skills, Better Regulation Delivery Office.

Hoffman, W. M. and Schwartz, M. S. (2015). The morality of whistleblowing: a commentary on Richard T. De George. *Journal of Business Ethics*, **127**, 771–81.

Hogg, M. and Vaughan, G. (2005). *Social Psychology*, 4th ed. Hoboken, NJ: Prentice-Hall.

International Chamber of Commerce (ICC). (2020a). Diversity. https://iccwbo.org/global-issues-trends/diversity/.

International Chamber of Commerce (ICC). (2020b). Global governance. https://iccwbo.org/global-issues-trends/global-governance/.

Iskander, M. R. and Chamlou, N. (2000). *Corporate Governance: A Framework for Implementation Overview*. Washington, DC: International Bank for Reconstruction and Development/World Bank.

James, M. (2013). *Sports Law*, 2nd ed. London: Palgrave Macmillan.

Jessup, P. (1956). *Transnational Law*. New Haven, CT: Yale University Press.

Jorge, G. (2014). Fixing FIFA: the experience of the independence governance committee. *Southwestern Journal of International Law*, **XXI**(1), 9–26.

Kazer, A. K. and Williams, C. A. (2005). The future of social reporting is on the line – Nike v Kasky could undermine the ability to require accurate reporting. www.business-ethics.com/nikevkasky.htm.

Kercher, K. (2007). Corporate social responsibility: impact of globalisation and international business. *Corporate Governance E-Journal*, 4(12), 1–12.

Knoll, M. and van Dick, R. (2013). Do I hear the whistle . . . ? A first attempt to measure four forms of employee silence and their correlates. *Journal of Business Ethics*, **113**, 349–62.

Kolev, B. (2008). Lex sportiva and lex mercatoria. *The International Sports Law Journal*, 1(2), 57–62.

Koutalakis, C., Buzogany, A. and Börzel, T. A. (2010). When soft regulation is not enough: the integrated pollution prevention and control directive of the European Union. *Regulation and Governance*, **4**, 329–44.

Latour, B. (2005). *Re-assembling the Social: An Introduction to Actor-Network Theory*. Oxford: Oxford University Press.

Levmore, S. and Nussbaum, M. C. (2011). *The Offensive Internet: Speech, Privacy, and Reputation*. Cambridge, MA: Harvard University Press.

Li, H. H. (2006). Finding sustainable profitability: the U.S. financial services industry's pursuit of corporate social responsibility. *Corporate Governance Law Review*, **2**(3), 343–73.

Lindblom, L. (2007). Dissolving the moral dilemma of whistleblowing. *Journal of Business Ethics*, **76**, 413–26.

Livas, K. (2004). AMWU battle against James Hardie goes global. www.imfmetal.org/index.cfm?c=9357&l=2.

Lozano, J. M., Albareda, L. and Ysa, T. (2008). *Governments and Corporate Social Responsibility: Public Policies Beyond Regulation and Voluntary Compliance*. London: Palgrave Macmillan.

Luhn, A. (2017). 'Like prisoners of war': North Korean labour behind Russia 2018 World Cup. www.theguardian.com/football/2017/jun/04/like-prisoners-of-war-north-korean-labour-russia-world-cup-st-petersburg-stadium-zenit-arena.

Mahne, C. (2004). Building giant caught in asbestos row. http://news.bbc.co.uk/1/hi/business/4058007.stm.

McBarnet, D. (2007). Corporate social responsibility beyond law, through law, for law. In D. McBarnet, A. Voiculescu and T. Campbell, eds., *The New Corporate Accountability: Corporate Social Responsibility and the Law*. Cambridge: Cambridge University Press, pp. 9–58.

McLaren, R. H. (2000). The Court of Arbitration for Sport: an independent arena for the world's sports disputes. *Valparaiso University Law Review*, **35**(2), 379–405.

Menkel-Meadow, C. (2011). Why and how to study transnational law. *UC Irvine Law Review*, **1** (1), 97–129.

Mersiades, B. (2018). *Whatever It Takes: The Inside Story of the FIFA Way*. Cheyenne, WY: Powderhouse.

Mitten, M. (2009). Judicial review of Olympic and international sport arbitration awards: trends and observations. *Pepperdine Dispute Resolution Law Journal*, **10**(1), 51–67.

Mitten, M. (2010). Sports law: implications for the development of international, comparative, and national law and global dispute resolution. *Tulane Law Review*, **85**(2), 269.

Mokhiber, R. and Weissman, R. (1999). *Corporate Predators: The Hunt for Mega-profits and the Attack on Democracy*. Monroe, ME: Common Courage.

Morss, E. R. (1991). The new global players: how they compete and collaborate. *World Development*, **19**(1), 55–64.

Muchlinksi, P. (2009). The provision of private law remedies against multinational enterprises: a comparative law perspective. *Journal of Comparative Law*, 4(2), 148–70.
Nafziger, J. A. R. (2004). Lex sportiva. *The International Sports Law Journal*, 4(1–2), 3–4.
Nafziger, J. A. R. (2010). The principle of fairness in the lex sportiva of CAS awards and beyond. *The International Sports Law Journal*, 10(3–4), 3–9.
Nike. (2004). 2004 corporate social responsibility report. www.nike.com/nikebiz/nikebiz.jhtml?page=29.
Nolan, J. (2004). Brought to account: the business of honour in the boardroom. www.smh.com.au/articles/2004/07/22/1090464797690.html?oneclick=true.
Opie, H. (2007). Sports associations and their legal environment. In S. Gardner, M. James, J. O'Leary and R. Welch, eds., *Sports Law*. London: Cavendish, pp. 89–90.
Organisation for Economic Co-operation and Development (OECD). (2011). *OECD Guidelines for Multinational Enterprises: Recommendations for Responsible Business in a Global Context*. Paris: OECD.
Organisation for Economic Co-operation and Development (OECD) Directorate for Financial, Fiscal and Enterprise Affairs (Ad Hoc Task Force on Corporate Governance). (1999). *OECD Principles of Corporate Governance*. Paris: OECD.
Osuji, O. (2011). Fluidity of regulation–CSR nexus: the multinational corporate corruption example. *Journal of Business Ethics*, **103**, 31–57.
Osuji, O. (2012). Corporate social responsibility: fairness and promise as the fundaments for juridification of social disclosures. *Contemporary Issues in Law*, **12**(1), 46–76.
Osuji, O. (2015). Corporate social responsibility, juridification and globalization: 'inventive interventionism' for a 'paradox'. *International Journal of Law in Context*, **11**, 265–98.
Osuji, O. K. (2019). Tackling corruption through corporate social responsibility. In J. Seabrook, ed., *Corruption, Law and Society: Explorations in the Law and Beyond*. Abingdon, UK: Routledge, pp. 101–32.
Osuji, O. and Obibuaku, U. (2016). Rights and corporate social responsibility: competing or complementary approaches to poverty reduction and socioeconomic rights? *Journal of Business Ethics*, **136**(2), 329–47.
Paeth, S. R. (2013). The responsibility to lie and the obligation to report: Bonhoeffer's 'What does it mean to tell the truth?' and the ethics of whistleblowing. *Journal of Business Ethics*, **112**, 559–66.
Pinto, J., Leana, C. and Pil, F. K. (2008). Corrupt organizations or organizations of corrupt individuals? Two types of organization-level corruption. *Academy of Management Review*, **33**(3), 685–709.
Pittroff, E. (2014). Whistle-blowing systems and legitimacy theory: a study of the motivation to implement whistle-blowing systems in German organizations. *Journal of Business Ethics*, **124**, 399–412.
Poruthiyil, P. V. (2013). Weaning business ethics from strategic economism: the development ethics perspective. *Journal of Business Ethics*, **116**, 735–49.
Preston, I. L. (2010). Interaction of law and ethics in matters of advertisers' responsibility for protecting consumers. *Journal of Consumers Affairs*, **44**(1), 259–64.
Reider-Gordon, M. (2014). Money laundering, corruption and the World Cup in the wake of Brazil 2014. *Southwestern Journal of International Law*, **21**(1), 98–123.
Roan, D. (2020). Lamine Diack: former athletics chief's trial set to start in Paris. 13 January. www.bbc.com/sport/athletics/51082302.
Rosney, D. (2016). A-level student feels victimised for 'cheating' but exam board stands by decision. 28 July. www.bbc.co.uk/newsbeat/article/36916351/a-level-student-feels-victimised-for-cheating-but-exam-board-stands-by-decision.

Sargeant, P. (2015). How FIFA makes and spends its money. 29 May. www.bbc.co.uk/news/world-europe–32923882.

Scherer, A. G. and Smid, M. (2000). The downward spiral and the U.S. model business principles: why MNEs should take responsibility for improvement of world-wide social and environmental conditions. *Management International Review*, 40(4), 351.

Selznick, P. (2002). *The Communitarian Persuasion*. Washington, DC: Woodrow Wilson Centre Press.

Siekmann, R. C. R. (2011). What is sports law? lex sportiva and lex ludica: a reassessment of content and terminology. *The International Sports Law Journal*, 11(3–4), 3–13.

Siekmann, R. C. R. (2012). *Introduction to International and European Sports Law: Capita Selecta*. The Hague: TMC Asser Press.

Sopel, J. (2015). FIFA scandal: is the long arm of US law now overreaching? 4 June. www.bbc.co.uk/news/world-us-canada–33011847.

Spicer, A. (2009). The normalization of corrupt business practices: implications for integrative social contracts theory (ISCT). *Journal of Business Ethics*, 88(4), 833–40.

Stephenson, W. (2015). Have 1,200 World Cup workers really died in Qatar? 6 June. www.bbc.co.uk/news/magazine–33019838.

Sugden, J. and Tomlinson, A. (2017). *Football, Corruption and Lies: Revisiting 'Badfellas', the Book FIFA Tried to Ban*. New York: Routledge.

Sustein, C. R. (2009). *Going to Extremes: How Like Minds Unite and Divide*. Oxford: Oxford University Press.

Suurballe, M. (2008). Players take up the fight against match-fixing in badminton. 21 July. www.playthegame.org/news/news-articles/2008/players-take-up-the-fight-against-match-fixing-in-badminton/.

Syder, C. (2016). The Modern Slavery Act 2015: what businesses need to know. *The Commercial Litigation Journal*, **65**, 22–4.

Szeftel, M. (2000). Clientalism, corruption and catastrophe. *Review of African Political Economy*, **27**(85), 427–41.

Teubner, G. (1997). Global bukowina: legal pluralism in the world society. In G. Teubner, ed., *Global Law Without a State*. Aldershot, UK: Dartmouth, pp. 3–28.

Transparency International. (2016). *Global Corruption Report: Sport*. Abingdon, UK: Routledge.

Wilks, S. (2013). *The Political Power of the Business Corporation*. Cheltenham, UK: Edward Elgar.

Wilson, B. (2014). FIFA World Cup hits the poorest hardest. 8 September. www.bbc.co.uk/news/business–28881952.

Witten, R. M., Parker, K. A., Holtmeier, J. and Koffer, T. J. (2008–9). Prescriptions for compliance with the Foreign Corrupt Practices Act: identifying bribery risks and implementing anti-bribery controls in pharmaceutical and life sciences companies. *Business Law*, **64**, 691–737.

Wood, S. (2012). The case for leverage-based corporate human rights responsibility. *Business Ethics Quarterly*, **22**(1), 63–98.

World Anti-Doping Agency (WADA). (2015). *The Independent Commission Report #1: Final Report*. 9 November. www.wada-ama.org/sites/default/files/resources/files/wada_independent_commission_report_1_en.pdf.

World Anti-Doping Agency (WADA). (2016a). Report of the independent observers at the 2016 Rio de Janeiro Summer Olympics. 27 October. www.wada-ama.org/en/resources/report-independent-observers-2016-rio-de-janeiro-summer-olympics.

World Anti-Doping Agency (WADA). (2016b). Richard H. McLaren independent person WADA investigation into Sochi allegations. 18 July. www.wada-ama.org/sites/default/files/resources/files/20160718_ip_report_newfinal.pdf.

World Anti-Doping Agency (WADA). (2016c). Richard H. McLaren independent person WADA investigation into Sochi allegations Part II. 9 December. www.wada-ama.org/sites/default/files/resources/files/mclaren_report_part_ii_2.pdf.

World Anti-Doping Agency (WADA). (2016d). *The Independent Commission Report #2*. 14 January, amended 27 January. www.wada-ama.org/sites/default/files/resources/files/wada_independent_commission_report_2_2016_en_rev.pdf.

World Anti-Doping Agency (WADA). (2019). WADA Executive Committee unanimously endorses four-year period of non-compliance for the Russian Anti-Doping Agency. www.wada-ama.org/en/media/news/2019-12/wada-executive-committee-unanimously-endorses-four-year-period-of-non-compliance.

World Anti-Doping Agency (WADA). (2020a). WADA provisionally suspends approved status of Moscow Laboratory. 22 January. www.wada-ama.org/en/media/news/2020-01/wada-provisionally-suspends-approved-status-of-moscow-laboratory.

World Anti-Doping Agency (WADA). (2020b). WADA files official request with the Court of Arbitration for Sport to resolve RUSADA dispute. 9 January. www.wada-ama.org/en/media/news/2020-01/wada-files-official-request-with-court-of-arbitration-for-sport-to-resolve-rusada.

World Anti-Doping Agency (WADA). (2020c). WADA asks for RUSADA dispute hearing to be held in public. 3 February. www.wada-ama.org/en/media/news/2020-02/wada-asks-for-rusada-dispute-hearing-to-be-held-in-public.

Yandle, B, Dorchak, A. and Morriss, A. P. (2011). Regulation by litigation. *Regulation and Governance*, 5, 241–9.

Zerk, J. A. (2006). *Multinationals and Corporate Social Responsibility: Limitations and Opportunities in International Law*. Cambridge: Cambridge University Press.

11

Postscript: Rendezvous of Regulation and Corporate Social Responsibility

Onyeka K. Osuji and Franklin N. Ngwu (with contributions from Gary Lynch-Wood)

When we first agreed to put together some commentaries on the theme of business and social responsibility from a multijurisdictional perspective, a number of difficult choices had to be made, given the available word limit. Could we explore the issue from the perspective of different sectors and industries? Are the challenges facing the mineral extraction industries comparable to those facing the retail sector? What are the challenges facing the agricultural sector, and do challenges affecting this sector differ from those, for example, facing the transportation sector or the energy sector? Would it be appropriate for us to explore the issues and challenges in terms of how they manifest across different national jurisdictions or continents? As the economic interactions of firms and nations have grown over past decades (e.g., through globalisation), so too have the concept and practices of corporate social responsibility (CSR) spread throughout different jurisdictions (see Davidson et al., 2018). Thus, it is pertinent to ask: are the problems facing South America similar to those of Africa or Asia? Do firms operating within these different parts of the world face similar or distinct challenges? Are the regulatory structures similar, and if not why? Is it even possible for an approach that is considered suitable in one jurisdiction to be simply lifted and transferred to another jurisdiction? What are the challenges and barriers, if any? What are the best practices in CSR policies across different jurisdictions? What are the worst?

In the end, we elected to provide an account of the different styles and objectives of regulation and governance, and how these different styles and objectives interact with, and attempt to foster, CSR and greater levels of corporate connectivity. Given the potential scale of this subject, we therefore opted to look across a range of issues that have varying degrees of overlap and connection. Thus, in trying to bring the work together, to a conclusion, it is in many respects perhaps far better to view this book not as a coherent argument that starts at the beginning, progresses through a body of arguments and ends with a neat conclusion but as a loose collection of stories around the themes of law, regulation, governance and CSR. It thus attempts to provide an account of the imaginative ways in which regulation and governance can and have been used to address CSR challenges across a range of national, supranational and organisational contexts.

Our account is therefore interesting since it shows the extent to which (policy) actions and activities around CSR have changed over the years, and in particular the ways in which polices, laws, regulations and governance activities are steadily becoming embedded into corporate social affairs and situations: regulation and governance, as it were, seem to be finding a way! In many ways, then, a transformation has been taking place: a marked shift from the view that dominated earlier CSR debates that such responsibility should be something done voluntarily. While it is possible to trace the origins of the social component in corporate behaviour to entities such as asylums, homes for the poor and the elderly, hospitals and orphanages, the modern era of CSR can be traced to the 1950s and 1960s (Agudelo et al., 2019). In fact, the term CSR is attributed to the work of Howard Bowen (1953) on *Social Responsibilities of the Businessman.* Bowen's work was important as he recognised the power of corporations and the impacts they had on wider society. Recognising this power and impact, Bowen talked of social responsibility as the 'obligations of businessmen to pursue those policies, to make those decisions, or to follow those lines of action which are desirable in terms of the objectives and values of our society' (Bowen, 1953, p. 6). It was in some ways a pioneering view. Moreover, it encapsulated the initial phase of CSR: a corporatist, market economy approach that was to be 'accomplished voluntarily and with minimal government direction' (Fredrick, 2018, p. 11).

The status of the corporation, and the notion of what it means to be a socially responsible corporation that practises responsible citizenship, has since undergone a significant shift (Chaffee, 2017). For example, in the 1960s and 1970s the growing protests over corporate actions as well as the rise of powerful interest groups and important social causes (e.g., equality) meant that corporations were expected to do more than distribute funds to charitable causes (Fredrick, 2018). An important development was the work of Carroll (1979, p. 499), who, in offering a comprehensive framework for understanding CSR, suggested that to 'fully address the entire range of obligations business has to society, it must embody the economic, legal, ethical, and discretionary categories of business performance'. In the 1980s and 1990s, CSR began to evolve as a concept, with the recognition that firms exist owing to public consent and they have an obligation to contribute to society's needs. The interests of corporations and the interests of society were seen as coming closer together, with a need for firms to be more responsive to all of their stakeholders, not just their primary stakeholders. Another significant development was Freeman's (1984) seminal work on strategic management and stakeholders, which advanced views around the importance of stakeholders and stakeholder management. Particularly since the 1990s, the CSR concept has become almost universally endorsed by a range of national bodies and international institutions, such as the United Nations, the World Bank and the Organisation for Economic Co-operation and Development (Moura-Leite and Padgett, 2011). What is more, on a growing scale, firms have incorporated social interests and wider stakeholder concern into their strategies and practices.

But, importantly, it took some time for issues of law, regulation and policy to take any type of firm foothold in discussions of CSR. Traditionally, issues to do with regulatory governance were not associated with the CSR literature. This literature was inclined to focus on more conventional and established business and management fields such as accounting and finance and corporate strategy (see Carroll and Shabana, 2010; Wartick and Cochran, 1985; Wood, 1991; Okoye, 2009, 2012). The idea that CSR was the domain of the state was regarded as antithetical to the fundamental voluntary and market-based notion of it (Panwar et al., 2018; Okoye, 2012; Dahlsrud, 2008); CSR was seen as something done voluntarily by firms, something willingly and freely given. That law and regulation should play a part was seen as contradictory. If an organisation desired to be truly responsible, it should act willingly, or independently of the commands of law and regulation. As the notion of CSR started to enter policy discourse, the emphasis on voluntarism and voluntary actions was clear. It was strongly reflected in European policy on CSR; a Green Paper described it as 'a concept whereby companies integrate social and environmental concerns in their business operations and in their interaction with their stakeholders on a voluntary basis' (European Commission, 2001). By now, CSR was seen as something that involved firms going beyond their legal obligations. It is a sentiment that was reflected in other European, national and international policy developments.

Many of the debates about whether regulation should have a role took place during the 1990s and 2000s. A series of entrenched positions were outlined. There were many who advocated for CSR to be a voluntary matter, particularly with arguments being made that (one-size-fits-all) regulatory solutions were inappropriate and that regulation would be counterproductive and stifle pioneering responses. It was argued that it would in any case be impossible to properly regulate the inherently complex and dynamic processes of CSR, where firms function within, and have to be responsive to, a plurality of social and economic contexts and institutional settings (e.g., a small firm trading in a local community will face different pressures from a well-known multinational corporation). It was also argued that regulation was unnecessary. After all, there exists a 'business case' for CSR and so firms would benefit from CSR initiatives since this would make them more appealing to a wider range of stakeholders and would potentially reduce corporate risk. On the other hand, it was argued that CSR, in the absence of state intervention, would never go far enough, and that additional laws and regulations were necessary to protect effectively the rights and interests of workers and citizens. While some firms might engage in social responsibility initiatives, the market incentive – or business case argument – would never be sufficient to incentivise the requisite levels of investment and activity from a sufficient number of firms.

From our perspective, we are now at a point where the debates that have taken place, over whether CSR should be voluntary or mandatory, seem somewhat outmoded. As our series of stories in this book have clearly shown, it is now naïve to talk of CSR in purely voluntary terms. The varying regulatory developments that have occurred in a number of jurisdictions oppose the pure market convention of voluntary CSR. Governments and organisations across a number of jurisdictions have developed rules, regulations and guidelines, for example in relation to social and environmental reporting or systems management. Increasingly, it can be seen not only that meeting regulatory standards is a necessary component of responsibility but, importantly, that some regulatory frameworks create a context that is more encouraging of CSR initiatives; that regulation and governance can foster, or provide an important outlet for, CSR.

As we have seen, the concepts of regulation and CSR have come together. They have found several areas of common ground, although there is still much to be explored. The important recognition that traditional modes of command-based law have their limits, that events and issues are difficult to control using substantial (command-and-control) rules and that there are issues around the enforcement of rules has steadily facilitated new modes – softer modes – of regulation that have come to complement the traditional mode of law. New forms and modes of regulation – such as proceduralised modes of regulation – have assisted in the facilitation of levels of connectivity between firms and wider society.

So, what is the future of CSR, given that the global social and economic challenges we face are far from over? One thing that seems inevitable is that new forms and modes of regulation will evolve as we learn more about social problems and about what does and does not work in particular contexts. There is an ongoing dissatisfaction with regulation and a constant drive to develop and implement new approaches, along with a strong likelihood that we will see similar developments with respect to a range of CSR issues, whether those are in relation to the responsibilities of directors, more sophisticated reporting initiatives or regulatory initiatives that can better regulate across value chains. It is likely that we will see stronger regulatory initiatives in relation to critical issues such as climate change and the protection of human rights.

From a regulatory perspective, the exploration of CSR is likely to be embedded in smart-mix or smart-regulation discourse. As we have seen on more than one occasion, the smart-mix approach has become an established response to the question of what appropriate policy design should look like. Given the importance of CSR, and the inherent weaknesses in voluntary approaches, more discussions and empirical data will be needed across a whole range of social and economic contexts, in order to help with the design of effective combinations of policy instruments that are tailored to particular goals and circumstances. It will be a challenging task to design a regulatory framework that maximises the benefits of regulation (social improvement) while minimising the negative impacts (economic harm). The journey will no doubt be a long one, but one of critical importance.

REFERENCES

Agudelo, M. A. L., Jóhannsdóttir, L. and Davídsdóttir, B. (2019). A literature review of the history and evolution of corporate social responsibility. *International Journal of Corporate Social Responsibility*, 4(1), 1–23.

Bowen, H. (1953). *Social Responsibilities of the Businessman*. Iowa City: University of Iowa Press.

Carroll, A. B. (1979). A three-dimensional conceptual model of corporate performance. *Academy of Management Review*, 4, 497–505.

Carroll, A. and Shabana, K. (2010). The business case for corporate social responsibility: a review of concepts, research and practice. *International Journal of Management Reviews*, 12(1), 85–105.

Chaffee, E.C. (2017). The origins of corporate social responsibility. *University of Cincinnati Law Review*, 85, 347–373.

Dahlsrud, A. (2008). How corporate social responsibility is defined: an analysis of 37 definitions. *Corporate Social Responsibility and Environmental Management*, 15(1), 1–13.

Davidson, D. K., Tanimoto, K., Jun, L. G., Taneja, S., Taneja, P. K. and Yin, J. (2018). Corporate social responsibility across Asia: a review of four countries. In J. Weber and D. M. Wasieleski, eds., *Corporate Social Responsibility*. Business and Society 360 Vol. 2. Bingley, UK: Emerald, pp. 73–132.

European Commission. (2001). *Promoting a European Framework for Corporate Social Responsibility (Green Paper)*. Luxembourg: Office for Official Publications of the European Communities.

Fredrick, W. (2018). Corporate social responsibility: from founders to millennials. In J. Weber and D. M. Wasieleski, eds., *Corporate Social Responsibility*. Business and Society 360 Vol. 2. Bingley, UK: Emerald, pp. 3–38.

Freeman, R. E. (1984). *Strategic Management: A Stakeholder Approach*. Boston, MA: Pitman.

Moura-Leite, R. and Padgett, R. (2011). Historical background of corporate social responsibility. *Social Responsibility Journal*, 7(4), 528–39.

Okoye, A. (2009). Theorising corporate social responsibility as an essentially contested concept: is a definition necessary? *Journal of Business Ethics*, 89(4), 613–27.

Okoye, A. (2012). Exploring the relationship between corporate social responsibility, law and development in an African context: should government be responsible for ensuring corporate responsibility? *International Journal of Law and Management*, 54(5), 364–78.

Panwar, R., Nawani, S. and Pandey, V. (2018). Legislated CSR: a brief introduction. In J. Weber and D. M. Wasieleski, eds., *Corporate Social Responsibility*. Business and Society 360 Vol. 2. Bingley, UK: Emerald, pp. 133–46.

Wartick, S. and Cochran, P. (1985). The evolution of the corporate social performance model. *Academy of Management Review*, 10(4), 758–69.

Wood, D. (1991). Corporate social performance revisited. *Academy of Management Review*, 16 (4), 691–718.

For EU product safety concerns, contact us at Calle de José Abascal, 56–1°,
28003 Madrid, Spain or eugpsr@cambridge.org.

www.ingramcontent.com/pod-product-compliance
Lightning Source LLC
LaVergne TN
LVHW011810200926
848484LV00005B/1138

* 9 7 8 1 1 0 8 4 7 0 0 2 5 *